GERMANY

GERMANY

A Short History

THIRD EDITION

Donald S. Detwiler

Southern Illinois University Press

CARBONDALE & EDWARDSVILLE

In memory of my

Göttingen mentor

PERCY ERNST SCHRAMM

1894–1971

Copyright © 1976, 1989, 1999 by the Board of Trustees,
Southern Illinois University
All rights reserved
Second Edition 1989
Third Edition 1999
Printed in the United States of America
Designed by Guy Fleming
02 01 00 99   4 3 2 1

Library of Congress Cataloging-in-Publication Data

Detwiler, Donald S.
Germany : a short history / Donald S. Detwiler. — 3rd ed.
    p.   cm.
Includes bibliographical references and index.
1. Germany—History. I. Title.
DD89.D4 1999
943—dc21   98-23290
ISBN 0-8093-2231-5 (pbk. : alk. paper)   CIP

The paper used in this publication meets the minimum
requirements of American National Standard for Information
Sciences—Permanence of Paper for Printed Library
Materials, ANSI Z39.48-1984. ∞

CONTENTS

LIST OF MAPS

PREFACE

A FULL GENERATION HAS PASSED since the end of the Second World War. Since 1970 a complex series of international and intra-German agreements has gone a long way toward defining the international status and reciprocal relations of the two German states and Berlin. Despite inevitable imperfections and inequities, this network of accords represents the tentative stabilization of central Europe and, as such, a milestone in German history. The purpose of this book is to look back and retrace Germany's path to this milestone. The four chapters of narrative are supplemented by a brief chronology, a selected bibliography, twelve maps, and an index. The first two chapters interpret the history of central Europe from antiquity through the eighteenth century, providing the background for the nineteenth and twentieth centuries, which are treated in the third and fourth chapters.

History is the seamless garment of the past. Political, social, economic, and intellectual history do not exist separately, but are interwoven in a fabric that includes them all. Scanning two thousand years of German history, I have followed the thread of political events, examining other strands only when they became politically predominant — as in the case of the religious reform movements that disrupted Germany in the eleventh century and again in the sixteenth. "Whatever else history may be," observed the Cambridge historian Geoffrey Elton not long ago, "it must at heart be a story, a story of the changing fortunes of men, and political history therefore comes first because, above all the forms of historical study, it wants to, even needs to, tell a story." *

* G. R. Elton, *Political History: Principles and Practice* (New York and London: Basic Books, 1970), p. 5.

For constructive criticism, I am indebted to Geoffrey Barraclough, Harold von Hofe, Georg G. Iggers, Arnold H. Price, and Norman Rich, who read the entire draft, and to Lewis W. Spitz, who read the section on the Reformation. Col. Eldon W. Downs, USAF, editor of *Air University Review,* afforded me the occasion to develop my interpretation, as reflected in the fourth chapter, of Hitler's diplomatic, economic, and military preparations for the Second World War by soliciting three review articles for the professional journal of the United States Air Force. Drawn by Daniel Irwin, the maps were hand-lettered by Ilse E. Detwiler, who prepared the index. Monty R. Baker and Louis A. Cretella helped with the bibliography. Further support was arranged through the Southern Illinois University Office of Research and Projects.

This book is dedicated to the memory of Percy Ernst Schramm, late Professor Emeritus of Medieval and Modern History at Göttingen University and Chancellor of the Order *Pour le Mérite* for the Sciences and the Arts, under whom I received my doctorate in Germany fourteen years ago. I have described his life and work elsewhere.* Relevant here is that although he was most widely known as an historian of the Middle Ages and the Second World War, the United States always interested, even fascinated him. He first came to America as a young professor on a visiting fellowship at Princeton in the early thirties. Over twenty years later, he returned for an extensive tour sponsored by the United States Department of State. He supported university exchange programs with America as well as the pursuit of American studies in Germany. Every other year he gave a popular series of lectures, one evening per week, on the history of the United States. If this volume orients American readers in the history of Germany as effectively as my late mentor's biennial public course introduced his Göttingen listeners to that of America, it will serve a cause he strongly supported: affording those without intimate first-hand knowl-

*The obituary in *Central European History* 4, no. 1 (March 1971): 90–93 is supplemented by the introduction to Percy E. Schramm, *Hitler: The Man and the Military Leader,* edited and translated by Donald S. Detwiler (Chicago: Quadrangle, 1971; now issued by Robert E. Krieger Publ. Co., Malabar, Florida), pp. 3–16.

PREFACE

edge of his country and its people a keener appreciation of the depth and complexity, the tragic dimensions, and the overall contours of German history. In this sense I hope that it may serve as a useful introduction and guide, leading to further interest in the German past and greater understanding of the present.

DONALD S. DETWILER

Carbondale, Illinois
July 1975

PREFACE TO THE SECOND EDITION

TWELVE YEARS HAVE PASSED since *Germany: A Short History* was first published. The gratifying interest in the book led to five printings of the first edition.

In this second edition, the final chapter and the chronology have been extended to provide coverage of developments since the mid-1970s, but the body of the main text remains unchanged. The bibliographical essay has been expanded to about twice its original length: current material on the recent past was added, new publications on earlier German history were cited, and a number of titles on German cultural history were included. Work on the bibliography, with the collaboration of Ilse E. Detwiler, was facilitated by just having completed a book-length annotated bibliography on West Germany.*

I wish to acknowledge the cooperation of Morris Library and the support of the Office of Research Development and Administration, both at Southern Illinois University.

Carbondale, Illinois   DONALD S. DETWILER
January 1988

*Donald S. Detwiler and Ilse E. Detwiler, *West Germany: The Federal Republic of Germany*, World Bibliographical Series, vol. 72 (Oxford and Santa Barbara, Calif.: Clio Press, 1987).

PREFACE TO THE THIRD EDITION

THE THIRD EDITION is an extension of the second to the present, tracing the most important strands in the dramatic but complex process whereby the collapse of the East German communist regime and the end of the Cold War led to German unification and the simultaneous transformation of the European Community into the European Union (a far more tightly integrated confederation than the Common Market).

The chronology has been extended to provide coverage of the great watershed of 1989–90 and its aftermath, and an addendum to the bibliographical essay considers a selection of the more accessible literature in English on recent German history.

Carbondale, Illinois   DONALD S. DETWILER
December 1997

GERMANY

1

Antiquity to 1250

G ERMAN HISTORY BEGAN at no specific place or date. Its origins cannot be traced exclusively to those Germanic tribes whose descendants later merged into the modern German people. The terms *German, Germanic, Teuton,* and *Teutonic* — though often used interchangeably — are by no means synonymous. Among the Germanic peoples were not only the East Franks and Alemanni, many of whom settled in what is now Germany, but also, for example, the Angles and Saxons who landed in England. Their language was an ancestor of modern English, no less a Germanic tongue than the Danish, Dutch, Norwegian, and Swedish spoken in other areas permanently settled by Germanic tribes.

The case of the Teutons was different; they did not settle where their descendants could establish themselves permanently as an identifiable group. But before migrating to oblivion, they left their mark in history: toward the end of the second century B.C., they and their allies, the Cimbri and the Ambrones, mounted so formidable an attack on the Romans that their very name became a byword for the barbarian menace from the north. Subsequent Germanic invaders were identified with them, so that the term *Teuton* came to be applied to the Germanic peoples in general and, in modern times, to the Germans in particular.

1 / ROMAN GERMANY

In 12 B.C., the Romans under Augustus set out to conquer Germania between the Rhine, the eastern border of Gallia (Gaul or modern France), and the Elbe, which with the Danube was to have provided the new natural boundary of the empire in northern and eastern Europe. Twenty years later the all-but-pacified province of Germania was lost in a sudden uprising that began in A.D. 9 with the ambush and annihilation of a Roman army in the Battle of Teutoburg Forest; of the Roman outposts east of the Rhine, only Aliso on the Lippe was not immediately overwhelmed. Augustus permitted no attempt to restore the province, but on succeeding him as emperor in A.D. 14, Tiberius did. However, the cumulative costs of the inconclusive campaigns of A.D. 14–16 convinced him to settle for a Rhine-Danube rather than an Elbe-Danube frontier. West of the Rhine the two border provinces of Germania Superior and Germania Inferior (upper and lower Germany) were established. From late in the first century until the barbarian invasions of the third, Germania Superior and the neighboring province of Raetia were extended northeastward to include the Agri Decumates, the Tithe Lands, a district bounded by the Rhine, the Danube, and the three-hundred-mile fortified Roman frontier between them, the *limes*.

There is also imprecision in the use of *Germanic* and *German*. The latter term has become closely associated with the modern conception of national identity that has arisen only within the past two centuries. Thus nineteenth-century French and German nationalists debated whether Charles the Great, the Germanic emperor crowned in Rome by the pope on Christmas Day of the year 800, was "really" French or German. Unconsciously projecting their own views back over a thousand years, they failed to perceive that the great Frankish monarch could not possibly have been assigned exclusively to either camp — and therefore could equally well be claimed as *Charlemagne* by the French and *Karl der Grosse* by the Germans.

As a geographical term, *Germany* has had different meanings at different times. Roman Germany, *Germania Romana,*

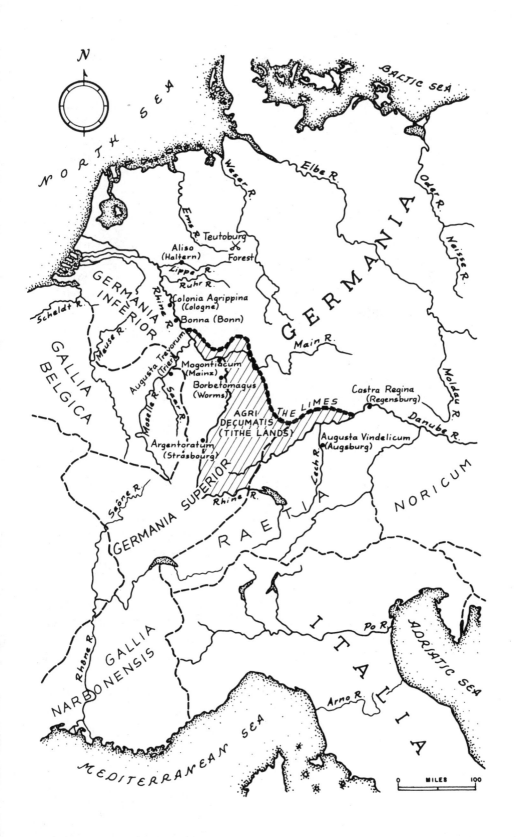

included much of the southern and western part of today's Federal Republic, the Low Countries south and west of the Rhine, northwestern Switzerland, and segments of northern and eastern France. Stretching eastward from the lower Rhine lay barbarian Germany, *Germania barbara,* a land the Romans tried to conquer. Between 12 B.C. and A.D. 16 they attempted to incorporate Germania from the Rhine to the Elbe into the empire as a great province adjoining Gaul, which comprised the greater part of what is known today as modern France.

Germania had initially been subdued by Drusus, the adopted son of Augustus (and father of the later emperor Claudius). When Drusus died in the field, the Roman command in Germania was assumed by his brother Tiberius, also adopted by Augustus and named crown prince. Tiberius had all but completed the conquest and consolidation of the new province when diverted by a dangerous uprising in what is today Austria and Yugoslavia. Germania was left under Quintilius Varus, who recently had been governor of Syria. A laconic report on his reputation there was given by Velleius Paterculus, a senior officer under Tiberius: Varus had gone to that "rich province poor and left the poor province rich." Theodor Mommsen, the Nobel laureate historian of Rome, characterized Varus as "a man of evilly acquired but princely wealth, and of princely arrogance but lazy in body, dull in mind, and without the slightest military ability or experience." *

His military incompetence was fatal, for under the Roman system of the time, the governor was also military commander in a province. Returning with the field army to winter quarters in the latter part of A.D. 9, Varus let himself be duped into making a detour off the military highway into the Teutoburg Forest of modern Westphalia. Native insurgents led by the Germanic prince Arminius, a Roman knight who had served as a Roman auxiliary commander, ambushed and annihilated the entire force of some twenty thousand, including Legions XVII, XVIII, and XIX (which were never reconstituted). Aside from a few individuals who managed to survive and escape, those

* Theodor Mommsen, *Römische Geschichte,* vol. 5, *Die Provinzen von Caesar bis Diocletian* (5th ed., Berlin: Weidmannsche Buchhandlung, 1904), p. 40.

who neither fell in combat nor followed Varus in taking their own lives were either enslaved, crucified, buried alive, or sacrificed to heathen gods in sanguinary rituals.

East of the Rhine, only the Roman bastion at Aliso was not immediately overwhelmed by the Germanic rising. A major base on the military road along the Lippe, probably not far from modern Haltern, the fortified camp at Aliso was commanded by Lucius Caedicius, a veteran primipile, a chief centurion who, though technically not commissioned, held a rank comparable at least to that of a senior warrant officer today. After failing to take the fort by storm, the natives next sought to lay siege to it, but were forced to withdraw from the immediate perimeter and to blockade it from a safer distance. Their bulky armor stood them in good stead in hand-to-hand combat with opponents using weapons such as their own, but left them grievously vulnerable to projectiles such as heavy javelins from the Roman ballista, which were used with deadly accuracy at close range and could have crushing impact even at distances of several hundred yards. Caedicius waited until supplies and hope of relief were gone, broke out on a dark night, and succeeded — despite heavy losses from repeated attacks — in leading his men, together with their wives and children, back to the safety of the Rhine, which the Germanic insurgents did not cross. When reinforcements arrived and Tiberius himself returned to the north, it was not to recover what had been lost, for the aging Augustus had decided against extending the frontier to the Elbe. With the eight legions under his command, the crown prince could have reconquered the land. But Rome did not rule by conquest alone; it was an empire of government. To pacify, assimilate, and govern Germania against the will of its intractable, unpredictable inhabitants would overextend the resources of Rome. Augustus therefore ordered that Germania east of the Rhine be abandoned.

When Tiberius succeeded his stepfather in A.D. 14, he reversed this decision. Germanicus, the son of his late brother Drusus and named after the latter's conquest, was determined to reverse the verdict of the Battle of the Teutoburg Forest. The new emperor, who had adopted Germanicus as heir and successor at the insistence of Augustus, loyally supported him in mounting three major campaigns into the hostile province. In A.D. 14 Germanicus led his legions deeply into the interior, laying waste Germanic villages and reestablishing Rome's military presence. During his second campaign, in the year A.D. 15, the Romans returned to the site of the disaster in the Teutoburg Forest six years earlier, where solemn rites for the fallen were finally conducted. But it was only in the third campaign, the following summer, that Germanicus succeeded in decisively defeating his Germanic adversaries. Arminius escaped wounded, but the eagle standards of two of the three annihilated legions were recovered. The honor of Roman arms had now been vindicated; yet Germania was still far from pacified. Roads and supply lines were inadequate and insecure. At the beginning of this third campaign, Germanicus had moved his great army of eighty thousand in a fleet of a thousand transports along the coast of the North Sea to the river Ems. Returning by the same route, the Romans suffered losses as heavy as from a disastrous battle when an autumn storm on the North Sea engulfed them, scattering battered ships and wreckage as far as the British coast. Undaunted by this new catastrophe, Germanicus insisted that only one more campaign was needed to rewin Germania. His uncle was impressed less by such optimism than by the cumulative costs of the war against an implacable foe. On succeeding Augustus, he had suppressed his misgivings and reversed imperial policy, steadfastly supporting the ambitious crown prince's struggle to reconquer the land whose name he bore. But in the three years since his accession, Tiberius had come to appreciate the limits of Roman power, the peril of its overextension, and the wisdom of his stepfather's decision. He recalled Germanicus to Rome, placated him with an extraordinarily lavish triumph, and ruled once and for all against any further attempts to restore the great province stretching eastward to the Elbe.

The Rhine and the Danube were to serve as the border of the empire for centuries, except where their upper reaches approach one another in the Alpine highlands of present-day southern Germany and northern Switzerland. There the headwaters of the two rivers form the two sides of a blunt triangle pointed, like a great spearhead, toward southern Gaul. Repeated Germanic incursions led the Romans to close the base of that triangle with a line of fortifications, the *limes,* extending over three hundred miles from the Rhine south of Bonn to the Danube southwest of Regensburg. This undertaking was begun toward the end of the first century by Domitian and essentially completed during the first half of the second century by Hadrian, who is also remembered for the great wall he erected from Solway Firth to the river Tyne, protecting Roman Britain from the unconquered Caledonians of Scotland.

Looking back, one might speculate what would have happened had all of Western and much of Central Germany been held by Rome. Reflection on what did not happen may be helpful in understanding what did happen. Had the imperial boundary been moved from Rhine to Elbe, and had Germany been governed by Rome as long as Gaul, the Germanic inhabitants of the entire region would have been drawn into the orbit of classical civilization. Their history and that of Western Christendom would necessarily have taken a different course. The modern Germanic languages, including English, would hardly have developed as we know them. Codified Roman law would at least partly have displaced the tradition-oriented approach still seen in the heritage of English common law, with its organic extension from precedent to precedent, as opposed to the imposition of allegedly rational prescriptive norms.

Most of all, the course of German history itself would have been profoundly affected had the Romans been able to establish themselves on the Elbe. The pattern of division between East and West that has persevered from the first century to the present would not have been established as it was. It began with the division between Roman and barbarian Germany. During the Middle Ages it was gradually transformed into a division between "old" Christian Germany in the South and West, and the more recently converted and colonized lands to the East. During the age of the Reformation and the Wars of Religion, these "younger" lands of the Northeast became the center of Protestantism, as opposed to the largely Roman Catholic South and West. The more violent religious animosity dividing Germany subsided by the nineteenth century, but only to be overlaid with a new polarization that was in some ways its secularized counterpart: an ideologically racist nationalism that celebrated the strength and purity of German culture, with its untainted roots reaching back to the Germanic peoples from the North and East (led by the great hero Arminius) — as opposed to the decadence and corruption of Latinized westward-oriented civilization proclaimed to be in its final stages of decline. Finally, it was the destruction of the Third Reich, which so diligently institutionalized many of the more brutal tenets of this sinister ideology, that led to the present division of Germany following the Second World War.

Could this sequence of division, polarization, and partition perhaps have been avoided if the Romans had only held and civilized Germany from the Rhine to the Elbe? That kind of question can no more be answered than the question of a chess player who, having lost his game on the fortieth move, asks what would have happened if he had played his tenth move differently. All one can say is that it would probably have been a different game.

In any case, although there are some who suggest that Rome could and should have assimilated and administered the lands between Rhine and Elbe, adding them to its vast realm from the North (and soon the Irish) Sea to the Euphrates, withdrawal to the Rhine and the subsequent division of Germany may well have been unavoidable. Augustus and Tiberius had good reasons for their prudence. After all, even restive Gaul had been conquered only a few decades earlier by Caesar; and it was a rebellion in the provinces of southeastern central Europe, still more recently subdued by Augustus, that had made the Romans so vulnerable to the uprising under Arminius in the first place. Historical maps showing the Roman Empire at the time of Augustus and his successor Tiberius may seem very impressive, but their clearly drawn lines showing fixed imperial frontiers rarely suggest how tenuous and how recent was the Romans' dominion or how costly its maintenance.

The fact that the Romans consolidated their frontier along the Rhine and the Danube, with the *limes* enclosing the corner of southwest Germany between the upper reaches of the two rivers, did not mean that the peoples living beyond the border were sealed off from the commercial and cultural life of the empire. On the contrary, many of the camps and bases established on or near the imperial frontier became trade centers that thrived on commerce across the border and developed in time into great cities — such as Cologne, Strasbourg, and Vienna — while the frontier itself, with its network of secure roads, served as a highway running like a seam between two worlds which gradually tended to merge.

The Germanic peoples who moved into the Roman Empire during the early centuries of the Christian era have often been identified with the later inhabitants of the medieval and modern German empires, but, as already noted, the modern Germans are descended from only certain Germanic tribes. Most medieval European states were Germanic in origin. Germanic ancestors may be claimed not only by the modern Germans, Scandinavians, and Danes, but also by the English, French, Italians, and Spaniards, in whose lands Germanic kingdoms gradually came to supplant the rule of Rome. From the welter of amorphous Germanic kingdoms of late antiquity and the early Middle Ages, one emerged that was to have particular importance in German history: the kingdom of the Franks.

❧ The Frankish Period
(Early Middle Ages)

First moving into the disintegrating Roman Empire in the latter half of the fifth century, the Franks gradually established a tenuous hegemony over much of Western Europe. On Christmas Day of the year 800, their greatest ruler, Charlemagne, was crowned emperor by the pope in Rome. His coronation has been described as the restoration of the empire in the West, but

2 / THE CAROLINGIAN EMPIRE

In 768 Charlemagne inherited the Kingdom of the Franks, which extended from central Germany to the Pyrenees. In the course of his long reign, which lasted until 814, he subdued Bavaria, conquered Lombardy and Saxony, consolidated the Breton and Spanish marches, established his authority in central Italy, and, on Christmas Day of the year 800, was crowned emperor by the pope in Rome, nominally restoring the Roman Empire in the West. In 812, by the Treaty of Aachen, the Byzantine emperor in Constantinople acknowledged Charlemagne's imperial dignity, while Charlemagne withdrew the claim he had exercised since 806 to the Byzantine holdings in the Adriatic, including the city of Venice. Also in 806 Charlemagne provided for the division of the empire among his three sons. Since only one of them, Louis the Pious, survived him, partition of the empire was postponed for a generation. In 843 two of Charlemagne's grandsons, Louis and Charles, allied themselves against their elder brother Lothair, who had succeeded Louis the Pious as emperor, and forced him to accept the Treaty of Verdun, by which he was denied imperial authority over Louis and Charles. Moreover, as shown on the inset, his dominions north of the Alps were limited to an indefensible corridor between what in time would become France and Germany.

the Carolingian Empire was radically different from the Roman. The great medieval synthesis of Christianized Graeco-Roman civilization with Germanic culture was already under way. The barbarian invaders had drastically diluted the still sophisticated culture of many of the lands they had conquered. Yet by the eighth century, they themselves had long since begun to assimilate its rudiments. Whatever they were able to learn, whatever they tried to imitate, they inevitably reshaped to fit their own cast of mind, values, and social and political heritage. Charles might claim imperial dignity in the West as the peer of his "brother" in Constantinople, but the Carolingian idea of monarchy had less in common with the late Roman and Byzantine tradition, not to mention the sophisticated concep-

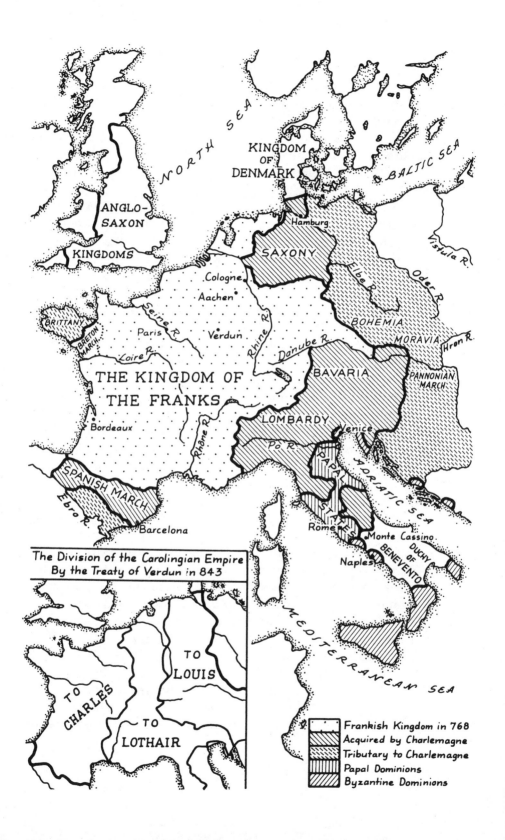

NORTH SEA

KINGDOM
OF
DENMARK

BALTIC SEA

ANGLO-
SAXON

KINGDOMS

Hamburg

SAXONY

Vistula R.

Cologne

Aachen

Elbe R.

Oder R.

BOHEMIA

MORAVIA

BRITTANY

BRETON
MARCH

Paris

Seine R.

Verdun

Rhine R.

Danube R.

Hron R.

THE KINGDOM OF
THE FRANKS

Loire R.

BAVARIA

PANNONIAN
MARCH

Bordeaux

Rhône R.

LOMBARDY

Venice

SPANISH MARCH

Po R.

PAPAL

ADRIATIC SEA

Ebro R.

STATES

Barcelona

Rome

Monte Cassino

DUCHY
OF
BENEVENTO

Naples

The Division of the Carolingian Empire
By the Treaty of Verdun in 843

TO
LOUIS

TO
CHARLES

TO
LOTHAIR

MEDITERRANEAN SEA

Frankish Kingdom in 768
Acquired by Charlemagne
Tributary to Charlemagne
Papal Dominions
Byzantine Dominions

tion of sovereignty in Roman law, than with Old Testament models of kingship and the tradition of leadership still preserved in Germanic tribal customs.

In the course of an almost fifty-year reign, Charlemagne extended his sway from Saxony, Bavaria, and Lombardy to the Spanish March between the Pyrenees and the Ebro. But unlike the Roman Empire, the Carolingian was an empire less of government than conquests — conquests never pacified and fused into a single state. It could hardly have been otherwise. The ancient Romans, even at their best, had only been partially successful in different areas, and many of the factors that contributed to the dissolution of the late empire in the West were far more pronounced in the early Middle Ages than in late antiquity — notably the political atomization accompanying economic disintegration, the decline of commerce, and the stagnation of urban life. Considering the circumstances, Charlemagne's failure to establish a strong central government is not striking, but rather the extent, however limited, to which he did succeed in consolidating his realm. Thus he continued the subjugation, begun by his predecessors, of the tribal dukes, supplanting them where possible by counts. Appointed by the king and governing in his name, these royal agents might expect to hold office for life, but their positions were not supposed to be hereditary, and they were subject to discipline and even dismissal by traveling inspectors — the *missi dominici,* "emissaries of the king," commonly a count and a bishop riding circuit as a team.

The relatively limited administrative centralization that Charlemagne achieved by such measures was made possible by his extraordinary personal authority, not by the institutional strength of his innovations, and still less by wide support for them based on general appreciation of their intrinsic necessity as means of maintaining the unity of the empire. It is possible that Charlemagne himself did not consider it indivisible: in accordance with Frankish custom, he formally decreed in 806 that on his death the realm should be divided between his sons Charles, Pippin, and Louis — none of whom was designated to receive the imperial title. But Charles and Pippin died before

Charlemagne, whom Louis the Pious succeeded as emperor in 814. Division was postponed only temporarily, however, for the reign of Louis was dominated by a bitter struggle, scarcely interrupted by his death in 840, over the partitioning of the empire. By the terms of the settlement reached by his three surviving sons in the Treaty of Verdun of 843, the western part of the Carolingian realm went to Charles the Bald, and the eastern part to Louis the German; between them, a hardly viable corridor from the North Sea to central Italy was assigned to the eldest brother, Lothair, who held the title of emperor, but was denied imperial authority over his brothers.

Only once was virtually all the Carolingian Empire reunited, and then only briefly — under Emperor Charles III, one of the younger sons of Charlemagne's grandson, Louis the German. Since the division of 843 at Verdun, the empire had been further fragmented. But Charles III, who had already become king of Swabia in 876, took over the kingdom of Italy from his dying brother Carloman in 879. In 881 the pope crowned him emperor, and in 882 he succeeded his ailing second oldest brother, Louis the Younger, who was king of Saxony, thereby uniting under his aegis all of the East Franks. In 884 he was also chosen king of the West Franks instead of his five-year-old cousin, Charles the Simple. The magnates of the moribund empire, east and west, had united behind him in the desperate hope that he might succeed in coordinating resistance to the barbarian incursions that seemed to become more terrible year by year. In shallow-draft boats, swiftly propelled by oar and sail, each capable of carrying two or three score fully armed warriors, whole fleets of Norsemen followed the rivers deeply into the interior, ravaging dozens of cities, including Bordeaux, Paris, and Hamburg. In the South, Saracen marauders established themselves on a number of Mediterranean islands and in bases on the mainland, from which they conducted extensive raids throughout present-day southern France and Italy, scourging the towns and countryside alike, kidnapping merchants and pilgrims, and pillaging not just smaller abbeys and churches, but Monte Cassino and even St. Peter's in Rome. From the East, the Magyars — superb horsemen from the

Asiatic steppes, linguistically related to the Turks and Finns —
swept not only through Saxony, Bavaria, and the Rhineland,
but also much of northern Italy and eastern France.

In his expeditions to Italy, Charles III failed to check the
Saracens. In the East, he also failed to move effectively. Against
the Norsemen, who had recently been checked in England by
Alfred the Great, he twice led great armies, but concluded both
campaigns by buying them off rather than risking open battle.
The test of arms he thereby avoided might possibly have been
more costly than appeasement, but his contemporaries, frus-
trated and alarmed by his growing lassitude, decided he was
unfit to rule and acted accordingly. Late in 887 the magnates
of the East Frankish kingdom solemnly deposed him. He acquiesced, retired, and died only two months later, not yet fifty.
Known only since the twelfth century as Charles the Fat, he
had increasingly been handicapped not by obesity, but apparently by an hereditary susceptibility to epilepsy or possibly
paralytic stroke — a similar condition to that which seems to
have prematurely claimed the lives of the two brothers from
whom he had inherited part of his realm, Carloman of Bavaria
and Louis of Saxony. On his fall, Charles was succeeded by his
nephew, Carloman's illegitimate son Arnulf of Carinthia, who
in 891 defeated the Norsemen in a battle on the Dyle near Lou-
vain in the Netherlands, virtually ending their incursions in
the Rhineland. In 896 Arnulf was crowned emperor by the
pope, but before he could firmly establish his authority in Italy,
he was lamed by a stroke and brought back to Germany, where
he swiftly declined, dying in 899, no older than his uncle had
been. He was succeeded by his six-year-old son, Louis the Child,
whose death in 911 ended the male line of the Carolingians in
the East. Rather than recognizing the dynastically legitimate
successor in the West, the East Frankish magnates elected from
their midst Duke Conrad of Franconia, the duchy regarded as
constituting the core of the old Frankish monarchy. Though
Conrad had been one of a small group of virtual co-regents
during the nominal reign of Louis the Child, he proved unable,
as king, to assert royal authority. The inroads of the Magyars
became increasingly audacious; the East Frankish monarchy

threatened to disintegrate altogether. Conrad's precarious reign was abruptly ended after little over seven years by mortal wounds that he suffered in a futile campaign against the recalcitrant duke of Bavaria. Convinced that his people, the Franks, had lost the mandate of fortune without which no king could rule, he designated, from his deathbed, his strongest antagonist as his successor, Duke Henry of Saxony.

❧ The Saxon and Salian Dynasties (919–1125)

In accordance with Conrad's final wish, the magnates of Franconia and Saxony gathered in April 919 in Fritzlar and hailed as king the able and energetic Henry the Fowler (so known because of his devotion to falconry). Conrad had been unable to bring together the East Frankish remnants of the Carolingian Empire, yet the continuing depredations of the Magyars, if nothing else, made strong, unified leadership vitally necessary. Under Henry the Fowler, the duchy of Saxony had become all but autonomous, while Conrad's attempt to subjugate Bavaria had literally cost him his life. By leaving his crown to the powerful Saxon recalcitrant, Conrad did perhaps the only thing possible to restore even the most tenuous unity among the East Franks. Far from recognizing Henry as king, Duke Arnulf of Bavaria initially challenged him as a pretender until 921, but then — assured prerogatives approaching autonomy — relinquished his own claim and accepted the Saxon. Duke Burchard of Swabia was won over, after a show of force, by somewhat less sweeping concessions, and, in 925, Henry was able to recover Lorraine. Initially part of the Middle Kingdom of Charlemagne's grandson, Emperor Lothair I (whose name is readily recognizable in the German form of its name, *Lothringen*), it had become part of the East Frankish kingdom. When the East Frankish Carolingians died out, it had come under the West Frankish line. With the prior understanding of the king of the West Franks, Henry first subdued Duke Giselbert of Lorraine and then sealed the bond of dynastic loyalty through nuptial diplomacy by giving him the hand of his daughter Gerberga in marriage.

In the history of Germany's emergence as a separate kingdom in the early tenth century, Conrad of Franconia clearly had been a transitional figure, but Henry I may well have been recognized, even in his own time, as king of what was apparently beginning to be called the *Regnum Teutonicorum,* the kingdom of the Germans. This phrase has repeatedly been cited by historians as the expression of an emerging sense of national identity, but its earliest authenticated use is open to question. Whether it was actually first used in 919, as claimed by some authorities, is less important than what it really meant at the time. One must guard against reading alien meaning into suggestive words and phrases found in records from a distant age. From the tenth century onward, there is documentation that demonstrates what in a very circumscribed sense may have been a sort of emerging national self-consciousness, as in the case of political polemics on behalf of a few emperors, or expressions of a self-awareness bordering on cultural nationalism on the part of certain German Renaissance humanists. But it would be a delusion to interpret this as evidence of nineteenth- and twentieth-century values, ideals, and ideologies. By retrospective projection, some very influential historians have managed to "discover" strong German nationalism and patriotism, and even widespread public perception of a need for German national unity — well before the end of the eighteenth century. What was important in the Middle Ages, however, and remained important down to modern times has been something quite different: a deeply rooted sense of identification with the land expressed in local and regional loyalties that tended to strengthen the allegiance of the people to their local lords and to those who stood over them at the regional level, territorial magnates or princes — many of whom repeatedly resisted subordination to the authority of the central monarchy. This was the pattern from the very beginning of the kingdom of Germany. Although several medieval emperors did succeed to a remarkable degree in asserting themselves over these regional potentates, the tension between the king (or emperor) and the greater nobility was never fully resolved. Even today, the regional particularism of the contemporary Federal Republic continues to echo what has always been one of the dominant themes of German history.

Unlike Conrad of Franconia, Henry of Saxony was able to pass the crown to his son as successor and is consequently considered to be the founder of the first distinctly German dynasty. Essentially his kingdom was limited to the lands of the East Frankish part of the old Carolingian Empire, which we can now refer to as Germany. He effectively defended his kingdom against the Magyars, defeating them in a major battle in 933. This did not permanently end their incursions, but his success greatly enhanced his personal authority, as well as that of the monarchy and his dynasty.

On his death in 936, his son and designated successor, Otto I, was crowned by the archbishop of Mainz at Aachen (in French, Aix-la-Chapelle), where he mounted the great stone throne of Charlemagne. In the course of his unusually long reign of almost forty years (936–73), he substantially increased the territorial scope and political sophistication of the realm under the Saxon dynasty. Otto the Great, as he came to be called even during his lifetime, tightened royal authority over the duchies and the church, permanently united Franconia with the crown, and put other lands in the hands of his family. He crushed the Hungarian Magyars in the decisive Battle of the Lechfeld near Augsburg and secured the Bavarian Eastern March, which later developed into Austria. To the northeast, meanwhile, in 955, the same year as his epoch-making victory over the Hungarians, he defeated the Slavs in what was to become Mecklenburg, Brandenburg, and Lusatia, carrying the eastern border of Germany roughly to the Oder River, the eastern border of the German Democratic Republic today. While his margraves (counts of the marches or frontiers) erected their network of fortresses and levied tribute from the native population, the church carried the faith, the tithe, and ecclesiastical administration loyal to the king into the chain of new eastern bishoprics founded and endowed by Otto with large grants of land — the most important being the diocese of Prague and the archdiocese of Magdeburg.

Having already claimed the title of king in northern Italy a decade earlier, Otto marched to Rome in 962, where he received the imperial crown. Once more substance was given, however tenuously, to the tradition of the Roman Empire in the West. By his coronation as emperor, Otto the Great reaffirmed the fateful dualism that characterized medieval German history and ultimately found expression in the term "Holy Roman Empire of the German Nation."

In our thinking today, Germany and the much larger medieval empire are considered to have been two very different things. During the Middle Ages the two concepts, although essentially distinct, tended to merge, the one fading off into the other. It came to be taken for granted that the king of Germany would become or at least aspire to become Holy Roman Emperor: it was simply part of his job description and long went unchallenged, no matter how unrealistic it actually was. That he was conducting his quest as the holder of a sacred office acting under a divine mandate was what counted.

Whatever else it may have been, the Holy Roman Empire was neither a truly universal monarchy, which it lacked the resources to become, nor a purely German state, which its rulers did not intend it to be. The first Holy Roman Emperor to take the title "king of Germany" *(Germaniae rex)* was Maximilian I (1493–1519), although the titles "king of the Germans" *(rex Germanorum)* or "king of the Teutons" *(rex Teutonicorum)* had often occurred earlier. The two titles invariably used from the eleventh to the sixteenth century, however, were "king of the Romans, always Augustus" *(Romanorum rex semper Augustus)* until the monarch was crowned by the pope in Rome, and thereafter, "emperor of the Romans, always Augustus" *(Romanorum Imperator semper Augustus)*. The point is that a German king, limited though his resources may have been, was committed even before his coronation in Rome to the ideal of the Roman Empire by his title: he might be merely king rather than emperor, but he was "always [i.e., from the very moment of his accession] Augustus" — holding the same exalted title that had been borne by the two senior emperors, each assisted by a junior partner designated as a "Caesar," under the administrative reorganization of the empire as a tetrarchy in 293 by Diocletian.

In the context of modern nationalism, it is understandable that the medieval emperors have been bitterly criticized for the unrealistic pretentions which led them to squander Germany's political, economic, and military resources in a vain struggle with the Roman Catholic Church for imperial dominion, rather than concentrating on the more modest but also more attainable goal of ruling their own country wisely and well. If only they had done this, it has been argued, Germany would have emerged at the end of the Middle Ages united as a modern state, as did France, Spain, and England, rather than remaining a fragmented mosaic of principalities until belatedly united by Bismarck in the second half of the nineteenth century. Although this historiographically dubious indictment — which has been propagated in countless variations during the past century and more — does justice to neither the church nor the empire, it is significant and instructive, for it illustrates the problem modern man faces when trying to understand medieval institutions and, more broadly, the problem a person of any era may face when trying to come to terms with the remote past.

The fundamental fallacy in this common German nationalist judgment concerning the medieval church and empire does not lie in the information on which it is based; the papal-imperial conflict gravely weakened the medieval German monarchy and thus contributed as much as any other single factor to the fragmentation of modern Germany. But the challenge here is not merely to find out what finally happened; it is also to understand how and why it came to pass. In practical terms, this can be seen in connection with one of the most fundamental problems that plagued medieval German monarchs right down to the beginning of the sixteenth century: the imperial coronation.

To become emperor, the German king had to go to Rome for his coronation by the pope. This was a tradition that held until

1508, when Maximilian I, with papal sanction, introduced the title "emperor elect" *(Imperator Electus),* which was assumed by all succeeding emperors except his immediate successor, Charles V (the last to be crowned by a pope, though not in Rome; the last crowned in Rome was Maximilian's predecessor, Frederick III). The pilgrimage to Rome undertaken by medieval German kings seeking the imperial crown generally involved nothing less than a military campaign across the Alps and then southward through northern and central Italy. It was costly and often hazardous; but successful assertion of imperial authority in Italy as well as in Germany was generally worthwhile and often vital. The tax revenues from Italian sources nominally due the emperors — and assiduously collected by many — were substantial. The German monarch who failed to conduct an active Italian policy not only forfeited much of this revenue, but also risked having his powerful south German vassals preempt the field. Since the dukes of Bavaria and Swabia controlled access to the Alpine passes, they were in a strategic position to establish such strong bases of power athwart the Alps that the titular ruler might never be able to assert his authority in much of southern Germany, let alone Italy. For several years during the last decade of the eleventh century, for example, Emperor Henry IV was trapped in Venetia: denied escape to the south or west by his enemies in Italy, his retreat route northward over the Alps was sealed by the enmity of Duke Welf of Bavaria.

Aside from geographical considerations, there was also the force of the Carolingian tradition and beyond it the idea of the Roman Empire. The *Imperium* had, after all, been renewed by Charlemagne, and the idea that the empire was a divinely ordained part of the natural order of things persisted in men's minds and long outlived the shadowy figures who followed the great Frankish leader. Then as now, the ideal of a peaceful world commonwealth appealed to many. In the twentieth century, idealists have sought its realization first in the League of Nations and, more recently, in the United Nations. Medieval man did not consider himself dependent upon such fragile constructions of human ingenuity; for him there was a divinely ordained universal order under the spiritual leadership of the pope and the secular rule of the emperor.

When we used the word *empire,* what comes to mind may be the British Empire, the Roman, or the Napoleonic, but in any case our idea of what the term means is apt to be conditioned by our knowledge of modern history and particularly of more recent examples, such as the Austrian, German, and Russian empires which fell during the First World War. The modern conception of empire is so different from the medieval, however, that virtually any modern analogy tends to be misleading. To begin with, the medieval idea of the empire permitted no plural. There was and there could be one empire only. This empire was not merely a super-monarchy greater than the rest, but rather the divinely ordained world commonwealth embracing all of Christendom. Considering the severe limitations of the medieval empire, it obviously would be disqualified for "empire-hood" if evaluated by the prevailing standards of the later nineteenth or early twentieth century. But such standards are totally irrelevant. Medieval man did not think in such terms. To understand how he did think, one must be prepared to see things as nearly as possible in his way, no matter how different this may be from ours. Perhaps we come closest, in terms of our modern frame of reference and vocabulary, to the most widely held conception of the empire in the Middle Ages by thinking of it as the equivalent of what we mean today by the term *Christendom.*

It may seem pretentious to many modern readers, and conceivably even blasphemous to some devout Christians, to be told medieval man should have almost unconsciously equated the empire with Christendom. But he did not look at things the modern way. He tried to look at them God's way. Inevitably there was a certain amount of pretentiousness and complacency, but again and again it was overshadowed or even displaced, especially in the case of several of the emperors themselves, by an almost oppressive awareness of their heavy responsibility to realize the Divine Will.

Beyond the borders of the empire, composed chiefly of Germany and northern Italy, the emperors had relatively few formal legal prerogatives. But their precedence in honor, spelled out by the formal titles "Head of Christendom" and "Protector of Palestine and the Catholic Faith," accounts for the role of Frederick Barbarossa, until his death, as the nominal leader of the Third Crusade. To cite another example, his grandson Frederick II illustrated a further theoretical prerogative of the emperor in the Golden Bull of Rimini (1226); in this imperial decree, the importance of which was attested by its being affixed with a seal *(bulla)* of gold, he granted the Teutonic Knights whatever territories they might conquer in their crusade to convert the heathen inhabitants of what in time became Prussia. The emperor could do this because he had nominal jurisdiction over all heathen lands not yet under a Christian prince. Finally, as head of Christendom, the emperor had the prerogative of calling a general council of the church, which Emperor Sigismund for all practical purposes did in 1414, convening the Council of Constance that ended the Great Schism which for almost four decades had divided the church in allegiance to rival claimants to the papacy.

The exalted view of the emperor as the first prince of Christendom, "the Temporal Head of the Faithful" (another of his official titles), was perhaps most eloquently formulated in Dante Alighieri's trenchant polemical essay entitled *De Monarchia* ("On Monarchy," or, freely rendered in an extended sense, "On Good Government"). Christ himself, Dante argued, willed to be born under circumstances determined by a decree of Emperor Augustus and to die by the authority of Roman law, under which he was judged by the procurator of Judaea, Pontius Pilate, in order to prove the legitimacy of the Roman Empire — demonstrating that the empire was sanctioned by God not merely as one state among others but rather as the government of all mankind. In Dante we see that the classical conception of the *Imperium Romanorum* as the temporal government of all mankind, dating back to the *Pax Romana* of antiquity, has been immeasurably expanded: the empire has been merged with the church as the Body of Christ for the eternal salvation of all mankind. A date for the merger can no more be cited than A.D. 476 can be defended as the date of the collapse of the Roman Empire. In the conventional sense it never "fell" at all. In the Latin West, as opposed to the Byzantine East, the institutions of imperial government broke down over a long period of time for many interacting reasons. But the church in the West survived and even flourished, and as it did, it not only assimilated a good deal of the institutional structure of the imperial government but also much of its authority.

With the nominal restoration of the empire in the West, first in the year 800 under Charlemagne and again over a century and a half later under Otto the Great, the church did not turn this authority back over to the state. This would have been unthinkable in the literal sense of the word, for the thought of it would have presupposed our modern conception of a rational division between church and state. What happened, rather, was that the pope performed the imperial coronation in a liturgical rite of consecration, and in the course of the ceremony, the emperor partook of the communion in both kinds, bread and wine, as a cleric rather than a layman, who would not have received the chalice. Today we involuntarily think of the world as divided into church, state, and society, each somehow a separate entity. Medieval man did not have our fragmented view of the world. To understand this — and unless we do, we cannot understand either the Holy Roman Empire or German history — we must realize that he had the idea — now commonly regarded as quaint by some, beautiful by others — that the world was part of God's creation as a whole, and what we almost absentmindedly differentiate as church, state, and society were all integral parts of Christendom. It is therefore historically inaccurate to represent the pope as head of the church and the emperor as head of the empire, as though church and empire were entirely discrete entities. We come closer to understanding the matter by thinking of the pope as the supreme pontiff of Christendom and the emperor as its supreme ruler, or, as Lord Bryce put it in his treatise on *The Holy Roman Empire* (in its day almost as famous as his classic work on *The American Commonwealth*), "the Viceroy of God." The various functions of emperor and pope might indeed differ, as those of head and heart, but they were part of one body, the Body of Christ: Christendom.

Once we think of Christendom in these terms, as an unfragmented world in which the spiritual and secular overlapped and even became virtually indistinguishable, we can see that interpenetration of ecclesiastical and imperial institutions was as inevitable as were the conflicts in authority and jurisdiction to which it led. Only during relatively brief periods, as during the reigns of Charlemagne, Otto the Great, and Henry III, did the emperors in the West approach, in their control of the Latin church, the degree of theocratic control exercised by their eastern counterparts over the Greek church. However, the functional dependence of the western emperors upon the church grew steadily as they sought to consolidate their rule, for they were dependent upon the church for the services of the sole widespread administrative bureaucracy in Christendom.

Considering the interpenetration and interdependence of church and state, a relationship so intimate that functional separation was impossible, it was only natural that one emperor after another became profoundly involved in ecclesiastical affairs, particularly when called upon for support by the popes or leaders of the powerful reform movement associated with the great Burgundian abbey of Cluny. One of the emperor's titles was "Defender and Advocate of the Christian Church," and time and time again his advocacy and defense of its integrity were desperately needed. Otto the Great, for example, was crowned emperor in 962 when he had gone to Rome in response to an appeal by Pope John XII, who had found himself unable to maintain the position acquired through his father, Alberic II. As prince and senator of the Romans, Alberic had ruled the city for two decades and then, before he died, arranged for the election of his son to the papacy in order to unite ecclesiastical and secular control in one hand. But whereas Alberic had been reasonably able and had supported needed reforms, his son was one of the vilest pontiffs of an age that taxed the descriptive capacity of the superlative. No sooner had the emperor reestablished Pope John XII in Rome and set out for Germany than the pope violated the solemn agreements he had concluded with Otto, making common cause with his enemies. Otto returned to Rome, from which John fled, and convened a special synod at which the faithless pontiff was deposed and excommunicated *in absentia*. When the emperor again left Rome, John in turn came back, denounced the synod, and took frightful vengeance on those of his enemies he could reach. Among his victims, the two clerics who had carried his initial appeal for intervention to Otto and then conducted subsequent negotiations with him were mutilated: one lost his right hand; the other, a cardinal, his nose, his tongue, and two fingers. Once more Otto turned back toward Rome, but was too late to do justice to John: he had died at the hands of an irate husband.

A distinguished Catholic historian once observed that the papacy must indeed have been divinely ordained, for no mere worldly institution could possibly have survived and flourished so long under such wretched leadership as that afforded by all too many of the Roman pontiffs. During almost a century, however — from the coronation of Otto I in 962 to the death of Henry III in 1056 — leadership of the church was not left to the popes alone, for the papacy itself was dominated by the German rulers. Emperors like Otto III and Henry III continually intervened in ecclesiastical affairs, giving the often hard-pressed reform party within the church invaluable support, thereby helping prepare the way for the dramatic resurgence of the church. The dynamic reformer Leo IX became pope with the support of Henry III, his cousin, and only three years after the latter's death the independence of the papacy from lay interference was asserted in the Lateran Decree of 1059 regulating papal elections — which had often been disastrously chaotic. Among the most radical advocates of church reform was the Italian monk Hildebrand, one of the more extraordinary figures in European history. He ascended the papal throne in 1073 as Gregory VII, and in a direct confrontation brought the German king, Henry IV, to his knees before him at Canossa in January 1077.

The conflict between them was not merely a personal one. At issue was control of the church throughout the empire. For over a century, German kings — who as emperors were also the overlords of northern Italy — had played an important and often decisive role in the selection of ecclesiastical dignitaries through their entire realm and in Rome itself. By virtue of such power over the church that even popes did not regard their elections valid without imperial approval, the emperor-kings were able to secure the services of churchmen loyal to themselves and to their dynasties. To put it in modern terms, they had a great deal of patronage at their disposal. They were able to appoint friends and relatives, able administrators, and competent soldiers to great ecclesiastical principalities such as the archbishopric of Cologne, to which, for example, Otto the Great appointed his younger brother.

Today the archbishop of Cologne, though traditionally a cardinal and one of the leading spokesmen of the Roman Catholic church in Germany, does not have political power in West German politics comparable to that of the minister-president of one of the federal states or *Länder*. During the Middle Ages, however, he and his ecclesiastical peers were leading princes of the empire who directly controlled territorial principalities on a level — in terms of political, economic, and potential military resources — with the most powerful and important German duchies. That in itself gave them great leverage. But from the king's point of view, another factor was even more important: there was a basic difference between these ecclesiastical principalities and the secular ones. When a bishop or an abbot (who had ecclesiastical rank and also often secular power corresponding to that of a bishop) died, his holdings did not remain in the family, as on the death of the ruler of an hereditary secular principality. On the contrary, the church lands he had held might now be bestowed by a powerful king upon whomsoever he deemed qualified. He could do this because an abbot or a bishop was a key official both in the ecclesiastical hierarchy headed by the pope and in the monarchical state with its strongly national church headed by the king. Consequently, German bishops were subject to the authority of the German monarch as well as that of the Roman pontiff. Nor was this merely a formally correct but somehow specious rationalization for power-hungry kings trying to undermine the pope's authority; real control over the ecclesiastical principalities was absolutely vital to the German rulers. The crown lands at their disposal were limited and they had relatively little functional authority over either the cities in northern Italy or the powerful dukes in Germany. The resources in money, soldiers, and political leverage of a loyal church organization, especially in Germany, therefore could and often did spell the difference between success and failure for a monarch. Otherwise he might well have little to depend upon but his *Hausmacht* (i.e., "house-might," the armed might of his own house) — his dynastic base of power in the principality that he controlled not as king or emperor but in his capacity as duke of Swabia, or of Bavaria, or whatever his hereditary holding before elevation to the monarchy.

If control of the church organization in Germany and northern Italy, particularly the appointment of bishops, was vital to the emperor, however, it was regarded by the ecclesiastical reformers — who took over the papacy in the second third of the eleventh century — as being absolutely essential to the head of the church in Rome. This was crucial and it was the issue which led not only to a grave breach between papacy and empire, but also to a disastrous civil war within Germany. Its significance can be suggested by a comparison with the Reformation in the sixteenth century: the reformers of the eleventh century were no less intent than those of the sixteenth on correcting widespread abuses throughout the church, but unlike the later Protestants, they succeeded in gaining control of the papacy.

They regarded this as only the beginning, however, for they held that effective reform required effective control of the entire hierarchy and that the pope could not exercise this if the bishops were primarily committed to serving as imperial administrators rather than as spiritual leaders. If the Holy Father in Rome and the Holy Roman Emperor were truly partners in the service of Christ in the widely accepted sense discussed above, the dual role of bishops subordinate simultaneously to both should not have posed a very serious problem. But the reformers saw the ruin of the church in the attempt to make this compromise work. They condemned those who held that bishops and abbots could serve both their earthly king and their heavenly king with equal diligence. They insisted that ecclesiastical dignitaries be chosen solely on the basis of their qualifications and commitment to the service of Christ in His church — under the leadership of the pope. Thus the issue was clearly drawn. By the mid-eleventh century, the authority of the emperors over the church had become so great that they had assumed an important and often determining role in the appointments of abbots, bishops, and even popes. By the decree of 1059, the papacy declared its independence of direct imperial influence in election to the supreme pontificate, and when Hildebrand became pope, he went on to assert the independence of the church from imperial interference in the selection of bishops and abbots.

The ensuing conflict was not without profound historical irony, for only with the help of the emperors had the papacy been raised to the point where it was strong enough to challenge imperial control; and the strength of the emperors, who had decisively aided the reformers in raising the papacy from an abyss of degradation so deplorable that Cardinal Baronius coined the term *pornocracy* to describe it, was derived in large measure from the support of the German church as a pillar of the monarchy. But now, in order to reform the Body of Christ in root and branch, a revolutionary on the papal throne set out on a course which would undermine the base of power of the emperor, plunge Germany into a catastrophic civil war, and change the course of European history.

In 1075, Pope Gregory VII threw down the gauntlet with a resounding declaration forbidding the king or emperor any role whatsoever in the appointment of bishops. It would have been virtually impossible for any German monarch to comply. There was certainly no question of it on the part of Henry IV. Keen, purposeful, and tenacious, he already had begun consolidating what might possibly have developed, in the course of time, into a fairly strong central government. He depended heavily on his loyal *ministeriales* — a class or category of royal official with no precise English equivalent. Often former freemen who had entered the king's service as armed knights or administrators, the *ministeriales* were frequently rewarded with substantial grants of land and honors. Nonetheless they had neither the status nor privileges of the traditional aristocracy, nor did they have the personal freedom of the feudal vassal. Already creatures of the king under the predecessors of Henry IV, they became more and more his chosen instruments until, in his attempt to establish a centralized government, he made them one of the chief pillars of his administration.

The other pillar was the German church, and Henry had no intention of compromising the traditional ecclesiastical prerogatives of the German monarchy. Therefore as "king not by usurpation but by the Holy ordination of God," he responded to the challenge from Rome, denouncing Gregory — using not the name he had just taken as pope, however, but his former name — as "Hildebrand, not pope, but false monk," proclaiming his election to have been invalid, and calling upon him to make way for someone worthy of St. Peter to ascend the papal throne: "Come down, come down, and be damned through all the ages!"

Gregory's election had indeed been open to question. Long the grey eminence of the reform party within the church, long expected to become pope, he dated his pontificate not from his canonical election according to the procedures prescribed by the Lateran Decree of 1059, but from an earlier tumultuous "proclamation" under dubious circumstances of the very sort that the Lateran Decree was presumably intended to preclude. Be that as it may, Gregory promptly excommunicated Henry, declared him deposed, and thus released his vassals and subjects from their oaths of allegiance to him.

Familiarity breeds not contempt but the comfortable inclination to take something for granted — in the case of history, familiar stereotyped accounts of "well-known" events. The textbook tale of the Investiture Contest, as this elemental struggle over the governmental structure of much of Western Christendom is euphemistically known, is hardly less familiar than the Norman Conquest of England in 1066. Consequently it is apt to be passed over, after a brief pause of passive recognition, without perception of the cataclysmic impact it had in its own time. An analogy that may seem bizarre but is not inappropriate may bring this home to us. Imagine that in the course of some shattering controversy, the interdenominational National Council of Churches and the Roman Catholic National Conference of Bishops issued a joint declaration enjoining all concerned Americans to serve neither in the armed forces nor civil service of the United States, nor to pay federal taxes or patronize the Postal Service. Imagine further that although this appeal was furiously rejected by many, nonetheless a very large proportion of the population — including a great many non-Christians — did fully support the protest action. Imagine, finally, what the long-term impact of this would be on American society and government if the crisis were to remain unresolved for years.

After the beginning of the Investiture Contest, excommunication would be used with increasing frequency and decreasing impact, for society gradually became desensitized to it, much as a patient to a drug too often administered. But in 1076 it had a stunning effect. A rebellion in Saxony, which Henry had succeeded in quelling the previous year, broke out once more and spread elsewhere as well. Some of the German princes eagerly seized upon Henry's distress as a God-given opportunity to increase their own power and prerogatives, while others, who normally would have hesitated to oppose the king openly, were moved by sincere religious convictions, or — unaffected by loyalty or convictions — simply decided that it would be most prudent to go along with their peers. The princes allied themselves with the vigorous pope, who at their invitation set out for Germany to preside personally over the election of a new monarch. Henry, however, astutely intercepted him and late in January 1077 publicly appeared on three successive days at the castle of Canossa on the northern slopes of the Apennines, beseeching the pope to receive him back into the church once more — something the pope could not and did not refuse to do.

Unlike Gregory VII, whose role as a priest would have made it unthinkable for him to have spurned a penitent sinner begging forgiveness, the German princes remained adamant. The pope counseled moderation, but they went right ahead and elected one of their number king, plunging Germany into civil war — for once Henry's excommunication had been rescinded, he regained considerable support. The ensuing strife continued intermittently for over forty years. Henry IV died in 1106, long since excommunicated again and, in the end, locked in a final bitter struggle not only with the church and the princes, but even with his own son. Mean and cunning, Henry V had gone over to the opposition, apprehensive that identification with his father and continuation of his father's policies would lead to complete alienation of the crown from the princes without any prospect of reconciliation with the church. Once on the throne, however, he found that the pursuit of his interests, as he perceived them, left him no alternative but to continue the complex struggle for years.

Its end was finally brought about in 1122 by the Concordat of Worms, whereby Henry V conceded to the papacy virtually full control over the northern Italian bishoprics. It is true that nothing in the terms of the compromise settlement formally weakened royal control over the bishops in Germany; but that was almost irrelevant. By 1122 the functional power of the German ruler had been reduced to a shadow of what it had been in the mid-eleventh century. Forty-five years of attrition from Canossa to the Concordat of Worms had gravely eroded the former strength of the monarchy. The princes had assiduously exploited what at times amounted to an interregnum to establish for themselves extensive rights and privileges at the expense of the crown and of those on whose support the crown had come to depend. Before the Investiture Contest, the German monarchs had, as noted earlier, come to depend increasingly upon the *ministeriales.* In addition to these royal officials, there remained in Germany until the time of the Investiture Contest large numbers of freemen. Most were peasants, i.e., independent farmers, not serfs in bondage to some lord, but free descendants of Germanic tribesmen who had turned to agriculture without ever forfeiting their independence. Also there had been many members of the free aristocracy who held their lands not by hereditary rights contingent upon confirmation by a higher-ranking count or duke, but rather by unconditional inherited ownership independent of any overlord. By virtue of these "allodial" holdings, as they were called, they looked, as did the peasant freemen, to the emperor alone as their lord under the law. But the Investiture Contest, which brought civil war and anarchy for almost two generations, made it dangerous for the free peasants and free aristocrats to risk the consequences of such proud independence. Vassalage might be somewhat demeaning, but feudal allegiance to a powerful lord, like an ill-tempered watchdog in a troubled neighborhood today, could afford a measure of deterrence and, if necessary, active security in times of danger. The Investiture Contest brought such times, decade after decade, with the result that the great princes were able to reduce to feudal vassalage so many of the free peasants and nobles that they could never again serve as a pillar of the monarchy.

Still more important, however, the great princes succeeded in establishing, with strong papal backing, their prerogative of electing the king. As a result of the Investiture Contest, Germany became an electoral monarchy. Since the foundation of a distinct kingdom of Germany at the beginning of the tenth century, kings and emperors had always been elected, but generally had come from the royal family in accordance with an ever stronger dynastic tradition of hereditary legitimacy. In deposing Henry IV, Pope Gregory VII had broken the trend toward hereditary monarchy, asserting that the king does not rule by virtue of birthright confirmed by his predecessor's designation, but may, like any derelict official, be ejected for cause and replaced by another person more suitable. In allying themselves with the Roman pontiff against their king, the German princes gave full support to the interpretation of the role of the king as little more than *primus inter pares* — first among equals — reinforcing that fateful dualism in German history between king and nobility which persisted into the last century.

The decisive increase in the power of the princes was manifested when, upon the death of Henry V, they did not elect his nearest heir, Duke Frederick of Swabia, a member of the southwest German house of Hohenstaufen (so named for the family seat, the Swabian castle of Staufen). They instead turned to a far weaker prince, Lothair of Supplinburg, duke of Saxony, who as king would hardly have been in a position to assert so much as the reduced measure of royal control over the church accorded in the Concordat of Worms — even had he not owed his election in large measure to strong ecclesiastical support. Although his own resources were relatively limited, he created an exceedingly strong dynasty by sealing a nuptial alliance with the Bavarian house of Welf, marrying his daughter to Duke Henry the Proud, and thereby establishing the Saxon-Bavarian pro-papal Welf (or, in Italian, *Guelph*) dynasty that long opposed the imperial house of Hohenstaufen (known in Italian as the *Ghibellines,* after their town of Waiblingen).

❧ THE HOHENSTAUFEN DYNASTY

(1138–1250)

WHEN LOTHAIR III DIED, the princes were only too mindful of the extraordinarily powerful position of Henry the Proud, the duke of Bavaria to whom Lothair had bequeathed the duchy of Saxony. Exercising their relatively new prerogative of free election, they passed over Lothair's designated heir and elected as next German king the son of the very duke of Swabia they had rejected in 1125 in favor of Lothair. Thus in 1138 the house of Hohenstaufen came to the throne, though Conrad III, like only Henry the Fowler before him, never received the imperial crown. By the time of Conrad's death in 1152, Germany had fallen into so serious a state of disarray that the princes readily accepted as successor his promising nephew, Duke Frederick of Swabia; on his deathbed he had designated Frederick, who had accompanied him on the unsuccessful Second Crusade, rather than his surviving son, a child of six.

With the thirty-year-old Hohenstaufen, closely related through his mother to the Welfs, Germany received a ruler whose combination of strength, wisdom, and longevity contributed to his achieving a place in history next to Charlemagne. Germany and the empire had been profoundly transformed during the century between the death of Henry III in 1056 and Frederick's accession in 1152. He was not fatalistic about accepting as irreversible everything that had transpired — especially where the prerogatives of the monarchy were concerned. With competent advisers he carefully assessed the situation, acquiescing where he had to, cutting his losses where he could, and rewinning considerable ground where possible — by the careful utilization, for example, of Roman law which was assiduously studied and often ingeniously applied by an able staff of legal specialists. In isolation, of course, the attempt to augment royal power by the reintroduction of at best long forgotten provisions of Roman law would not have been feasible and, if imprudently forced, might have been counterproductive. However, the reintroduction of Roman law did not stand alone; it was only one aspect of a far more sophisticated program. Whereas earlier emperors had striven to be masters of the princes and the church alike, claiming and exercising the right of deposing and appointing dukes and even popes, Frederick "Barbarossa" (as he was dubbed by the Italians because of his reddish-blond beard) wisely refrained from attempting to reestablish the kind of authoritarian, centralized regime that could have united many of the princes against him. Instead he generally recognized their newly won but in many cases already firmly held power, and he sought with considerable success to win their loyalty on what amounted to a radically different basis than had been attempted before. With their active support Frederick restructured Germany as a feudal rather than centralistic monarchy. This was illustrated and dramatized by the fall of Henry the Lion, the Welf duke of both Saxony and Bavaria.

Initially Henry had been loyal to his royal cousin, but when he refused Frederick obligatory military support on one of his half dozen Italian expeditions and thereafter defied him more and more audaciously, he made it possible and even necessary for Frederick to have him tried under feudal law. Henry was condemned by his peers as a contumacious vassal and stripped of all his fiefs. In 1182 he went into exile at the English court of his father-in-law, King Henry II; in 1185 he returned to Germany, where his allodial rights in Brunswick and Lüneburg were respected. The triumph over Henry the Lion brought Frederick Barbarossa to the height of his power, but only because he had permitted himself to be carried there by the princes, who in the long run were the chief beneficiaries of what represented nothing less than a constitutional transformation of the monarchy. Bavaria and Saxony had been the last of the great territorial duchies identified with the old Germanic tribes whose dukes once had been the chief magnates of the realm. Their place was now taken by a new class of imperial princes *(principes imperii,* in German, *Reichsfürsten)*, feudal tenants-in-chief standing in a newly established feudal hierarchy between the monarch and the lesser nobility. A century earlier Henry IV had tried to build his monarchy primarily on the *ministeriales* and the church. Frederick Barbarossa availed himself of royal *ministeriales* wherever he could, and he favored as bishops royally oriented ecclesiastical administrators rather than spiritually oriented reformers — whenever circumstances permitted him to make the choice. But these were both matters of tactics. They might be very important in individual instances, but they could not be permitted to take precedence over (or jeopardize) Frederick's fundamental strategy of restructuring the gravely weakened realm as a feudal monarchy strongly sustained by a loyal caste of imperial princes — loyal because the feudal reorganization of Germany and the special prerogatives accorded them under the new system gave them every reason to support it and oppose anyone, such as Henry the Lion, who sought to disrupt it.

The fact that their loyalty to the newly feudalized German monarchy was presumably no less self-serving than idealistic does not mean it was not sincere, but more likely the contrary. By the same token, Barbarossa's having presided over the restructuring of a disintegrating state so that its strongest princes became its strongest supporters is to his credit. Given what he

3 / THE HOHENSTAUFEN EMPIRE

The breakdown of Charlemagne's empire during the century following his death in 814 lent great importance to the eastern Carolingian duchies of Bavaria, Franconia, Saxony, Swabia, and Lorraine, though the last, because of its continuing ties with the western Carolingians, was less important in the east than the first four duchies. Shown here with solid border lines, they became the core of the emerging kingdom of Germany. Its first king, Conrad I (911–18), had been duke of Franconia. Its first dynasty was established by his successor, King Henry I (919–36), who had been duke of Saxony. It reached its height under the Hohenstaufen dynasty with Frederick Barbarossa (1152–90), who had been duke of Swabia before receiving the crowns of Germany, Italy, Burgundy, and the Holy Roman Empire, and with his son Henry VI, who added the Kingdom of the Two Sicilies (i.e., Sicily and southern Italy) to the Hohenstaufen realm. However, its very size, suggested by the superimposed silhouette of England and Wales on the inset, made it extremely difficult to rule. Between the year of his imperial coronation, 1220, and 1250, the year of his death, Barbarossa's grandson Frederick II spent only a few months in Germany. Absorbed in the south, where he named himself king of Jerusalem and his son Enzio king of Sardinia, he permitted what his predecessors had built up in the north to crumble.

had to work with at the time, his achievement was extraordinary. When we compare the territorial extent of either France or England with that of Germany toward the end of the twelfth century, and take into account, moreover, the relative stability and efficiency of their respective governments, it is understandable why Germany, despite the reverses it had suffered, was in many respects still the most powerful and most highly developed state and Frederick Barbarossa the most respected monarch in Western Christendom. It was during his reign that the term *Holy Roman Empire* first came into regular use. Considering the achievements of his lifetime, one can appreciate the old German legend that Frederick I never actually died, but

NORTH SEA

DENMARK

BALTIC SEA

POMERANIA

POMERELIA

PRUSSIA
(Teutonic Knights
in 1226)

POLAND

Vistula R.

DUCHY OF SAXONY

BRANDENBURG

Elbe R.

Weser R.

SILESIA

Oder R.

Bouvines

Aachen

Scheldt R.

Rhine R.

LOWER
UPPER
LORRAINE

DUCHY OF
FRANCONIA

Mainz

Worms

KINGDOM
OF
BOHEMIA

MORAVIA

DUCHY OF
SWABIA
(Hohenstaufen)

DUCHY
OF
BAVARIA

AUSTRIA

Danube R.

STYRIA

FRANCE

KINGDOM
OF
BURGUNDY

Rhône R.

KINGDOM
OF
ITALY

Po R.

Arles

Venice

HUNGARY

ADRIATIC SEA

PAPAL
STATES

Tiber R.

Rome

CORSICA

KINGDOM OF
SARDINIA
(Hohenstaufen
in 1242)

Naples

KINGDOM OF
THE
TWO SICILIES

Palermo

(Hohenstaufen in 1194)

Tunis

SICILIAN CHANNEL

MEDITERRANEAN

MALTA

SEA

rather went to sleep inside the Kyffhäuser Mountain, and that one day he would awaken and the empire would be restored in all its glory. The very fact that the legend originally applied to Frederick II, but subsequently came to be associated with his grandfather, merely reinforces the point: of all medieval emperors since Charlemagne, it was Frederick Barbarossa who was generally held in greatest esteem.

When Frederick died in 1190, while leading the Third Crusade to the Holy Land, he was succeeded by his son Henry VI. Ruthlessly ambitious, Henry sought to fuse the empire with southern Italy and Sicily as a single hereditary Hohenstaufen empire. Germany had been the core of the empire, to be sure, but Frederick Barbarossa, with his own dynastic base of power or *Hausmacht* in southern Germany, had already shown more concern for south European affairs than his predecessors based further north; after all, Milan was closer to Waiblingen than Hamburg or Lübeck. Barbarossa was the first emperor in well over a century to be crowned king of Burgundy. He mounted six expeditions to Italy, in the course of which he succeeded in asserting at least formal suzerainty in northern Italy, and in building up a viable imperial administration in the central part of the peninsula. Southern Italy and Sicily, which lay beyond the boundary of the empire, constituted the Norman Kingdom of the Two Sicilies, ruled by a childless king whose aunt and heir, Constance of Sicily, had been wed by Henry VI in 1186. On Christmas Day, 1194, Emperor Henry VI was crowned king of the Two Sicilies in the cathedral at Palermo; the following day, Empress Constance gave birth to the later Emperor Frederick II. Long before he came to the throne, however, his father's dream of an hereditary empire from the North Sea to the Sicilian Channel collapsed, for in September 1197, Henry VI died of malaria at thirty-one, leaving the crown to the infant Frederick and the empire to yet another struggle over the succession.

The fact that Henry VI succeeded his father had by no means marked a definitive return to hereditary succession in the German monarchy. Toward the end of his reign, Frederick Barbarossa had his son Henry crowned Caesar, reviving the ancient Roman tradition of the tetrarchy, when both East and West were ruled by an Augustus and a Caesar. In addition, before Frederick departed to lead the Third Crusade, Henry had also been formally designated regent, and was, in fact, ruling in this capacity when the news of Barbarossa's death in Asia Minor was received. Consequently there was no real opportunity for a serious challenge to the transfer of power. But Henry's sudden death in 1197 did indeed offer the princes a singular opportunity to reassert themselves, and the pressure he had brought to bear for transformation of the empire into an hereditary monarchy gave them added impetus. In 1198, moreover, Innocent III, one of the most imposing statesmen of the medieval church, ascended the papal throne and swiftly seized his chance to try to free the church from the threat of pressure from the Hohenstaufen holdings in both northern and southern Italy.

The dying emperor's plans for a regency for his son might have been realized had it not been for the vigor with which the Welf opposition pursued the candidacy of Otto of Brunswick, the younger son of Henry the Lion, who had grown up at the English court and been named count of Poitou by his uncle, King Richard the Lion-Hearted. But with the backing of the papacy and the English, the brash Welf prince was too serious a threat to be matched by a young child whose regent, no matter how able, would lack the personal moral authority of a consecrated monarch. Therefore the younger brother of the late Henry VI, the able Duke Philip of Swabia, uncle of young Frederick of Sicily, reluctantly let himself be elected by the Hohenstaufen party, while the election of his rival, Otto of Brunswick, was effected by the Welfs. Thus Germany was again plunged into a protracted civil war less than a century after the end of the destructive Investiture Contest. In view of Otto's strong support not only from the English and the papacy, but also the Danes and German Welfs, Philip renewed the Hohenstaufen alliance with France that his father Barbarossa had concluded during the previous century. The struggle over the German succession consequently became linked with the bitter conflict between France and England over Normandy, with foreign subsidies sustaining the strife in Central Europe long after it might otherwise have been ended.

By 1208, the Welf pretender's cause had become so hopeless that Innocent III was prepared to recognize his Hohenstaufen rival, when Philip was killed in a private dispute. Thereupon Otto of Brunswick, who had been willing to accept defeat and to recognize Philip, was unanimously elected king and, in 1209, crowned emperor by Innocent III. No sooner was he crowned, however, than Otto IV — who married a daughter of Philip of Swabia and recruited several of his closest advisers — set out on what was clearly a policy of Hohenstaufen imperialism, invading the Mediterranean kingdom of Sicily (which included southern Italy), over which the pope himself claimed suzerainty. This left the pope no alternative but to fall back, however reluctantly, on the original heir of Henry VI, Frederick of Sicily, the nephew of the late Philip of Swabia. The young king of Sicily, the grandson of Barbarossa and actually the pope's own ward, was the only possible rival of Otto IV with a reasonable chance of mustering the kind of support necessary to establish himself against the renegade Welf. With papal blessing and a heavy French subsidy, Frederick was once more elected king, as he had been fourteen years earlier when scarcely two years old, and was crowned king of the Romans at Mainz in December 1212. Emperor Otto IV thereupon broke off his Sicilian campaign and followed Frederick back to Germany. But the contest was not decided there. It was decided at the hamlet of Bouvines a few miles west of the Scheldt in the Lowlands, where in the summer of 1214 King Philip Augustus of France decisively defeated Otto IV and his English and Flemish allies. Otto withdrew and within five years died powerless and hardly noticed in the Harzburg, near Wolfenbüttel in Saxony. The imperial insignia he had left lying on the field at Bouvines were sent by Philip Augustus to young Frederick, who had himself elected and crowned in all due form at Aachen.

Frederick's many coronations need explanation. To begin with, when he was crowned king of Sicily at the age of three, his proxies had formally repudiated in his name his claim to be German king on the basis of his election during his father's lifetime. His hasty coronation as king of the Romans at Mainz in 1212, with the support of only a party of the princes, had been irregular and had not afforded the other princes of the empire the necessary opportunity to participate in his elevation to the monarchy and to pay him homage. Consequently, it was almost a matter of course that once his claim to the throne was undisputed, he should have been crowned king of the Germans at Aachen in 1215 and emperor at Rome in 1220. It was not a matter of course, however, that after leaving for Italy in 1220, Frederick II briefly returned to Germany only twice during his entire reign, which lasted until 1250 — for a few months in 1235 and 1237.

This German king who was born and bred a Sicilian, whose crown was won by French arms in the Lowlands, and who spent only a fraction of his reign in Germany, was one of the most remarkable monarchs in history. A man of extraordinary culture, energy, and ability — called by a contemporary chronicler *stupor mundi* (the wonder of the world), by Nietzsche the first European, and by many historians the first modern ruler — Frederick established in Sicily and southern Italy something very much like a modern, centrally governed kingdom with an efficient bureaucracy.

In Germany, however, he forfeited the hard-won progress of his grandfather Frederick Barbarossa and father Henry VI toward the development of a modern state, destroying whatever prospect there might have been that the German monarchy would keep pace with the French and the English in the development of effective royal government. Frederick II was not concerned with continuing the work of his forefathers in Germany, but merely with retaining sufficient control there to assure support in the form of men and money for his Italian and Mediterranean policies.

As early as 1213, with the Golden Bull of Eger, Frederick forfeited to the papacy the measure of control over the German church that had been reserved by the Concordat of Worms almost a century earlier, by conceding "free" elections of bishops and abbots — i.e., elections in which neither the king nor his representatives would take any part or exert any influence.

In 1220, by the terms of an extraordinary grant of privileges to the clergy *(Confoederatio cum principibus ecclesiasticis)*, Frederick exempted the German bishops and abbots from taxation and lay jurisdiction to such an extent that for all practical purposes they were made independent territorial princes. After the Investiture Contest, the church could no longer be a pillar of the monarchy; after the Golden Bull of Eger of 1213, followed by the Privilege of 1220, it could hardly be depended upon for any support whatsoever.

Little more than a decade later, Frederick II accorded the secular princes similar rights. By the Privilege of Worms of 1231 *(Statutum in favorem principum)*, Frederick made irrevocable concessions regarding administrative and legal jurisdiction, taxes and coinage, the control of roads, streams, and the like. Although still not formally sovereign, secular as well as ecclesiastical princes were thus made practically independent. It is noteworthy that Frederick II granted the princes of Germany such extensive new rights and prerogatives during the same century that the kings of France and England were concerned with extending their royal power at the expense of their vassals — and as he himself was concerned with doing in his Sicilian kingdom. Above all, by permitting individual German princes to establish their own systems of justice, Frederick II gravely prejudiced the future development of the royal judiciary, which in other kingdoms was to prove an effective means of expanding and consolidating the central power of the monarchy. Legislative power might have to be granted to a representative assembly, and executive power might be compromised by the administrative prerogatives of the aristocracy, but so long as the king retained ultimate control of the courts, his legal power was both the visible symbol and the effective instrument of his ultimate sovereignty. And this Frederick II frittered away also, as he sold off his political capital north of the Alps in order to maintain his position in the south.

The long reign of Frederick II, which ended with his death in 1250, saw the greatest territorial extension of the medieval empire. However, it was an overextension that was achieved

44

only by sacrificing control of the traditional center of the monarchy in Germany. Hence the era of Emperor Frederick II set the stage in Germany for the consolidation of the modern state not at the national level under the king, but at the regional level under the territorial princes.

2

From 1250 to 1815

AFTER 1250 THE HOLY ROMAN EMPIRE had little political weight of its own. The century following the death of Frederick II, which began with a long interregnum, saw the transformation of the empire of Otto the Great and Frederick Barbarossa into an oligarchical confederation of ecclesiastical and dynastic principalities which endured until the nineteenth century. Any initiative taken thereafter toward the reestablishment of a stable monarchy was apt to be thwarted by the opposition not only of the German princes, but also of the papacy in league with foreign powers, particularly France. German kings now concentrated more on furthering their individual dynastic ambitions than on strengthening the monarchy as such. Rudolf of Habsburg (1273–91) exploited the crown to acquire for his house no less a prize than Austria, the future *Hausmacht* of his dynasty, while the rich kingdom of Bohemia was secured by Henry of Luxemburg (1308–13) a minor vassal of the king of France from the western borderlands of the empire, who had ascended the throne largely through the influence of his brother, the archbishop of Trier. The age-old conflict of interest between the monarch and the magnates gradually subsided insofar as the king — whose royal power was no longer independent of the great princes, but largely dependent upon their cooperation as pillars of the state — more and more tended to assume their point of view. He was one of them. It was no longer feasible to think in terms of becoming king in the old sense, seeking the power of the monarchy as an end in itself. It simply did not have that kind of power any longer. It could at best be used as a means to increase the *Hausmacht* of one's own dynasty, as was attempted by princes of the houses of Habsburg and Luxemburg, and others as well.

This new political reality was reflected in a formal constitution of the empire, the Golden Bull of 1356, promulgated by Emperor Charles IV of the house of Luxemburg. It regulated the succession for 450 years by providing that the king was to be chosen by the seven prince electors — the three archbishops of Mainz, Cologne, and Trier, the king of Bohemia, the count palatine (or palsgrave) of the Rhine, the duke of Saxony, and the margrave of Brandenburg — who were accorded quasi-regal privileges and prerogatives setting them apart from the other imperial princes, not to mention the lesser nobility. (Bavaria became an electorate in the first part of the seventeenth century, and, at its end, Hanover became the ninth. Under Napoleon, at the beginning of the nineteenth century, the electorate of Mainz was transferred to Regensburg and the electorates of Cologne and Trier — which, like Mainz, were annexed by France — were abolished, but four new electorates were established: Hesse-Kassel, Württemberg, Baden, and Salzburg.)

The Golden Bull marked the conclusion of over four hundred years of German history, documenting the ultimate failure of the struggle, begun by the Saxon dynasty, to establish a unified monarchy under hereditary rule. Lord Bryce's famous verdict on Charles IV — that "he legalized anarchy, and called it a constitution" — is at best misleading. It suggests simple (or cynical) acquiescence in a lawlessness that the emperor could and (implicitly) should have mastered. Reflecting on the past, we tend to take it for granted that good leaders correct bad situations, somehow not perceiving the quality of responsible, creative statesmanship that may be required just to keep a bad situation from getting much worse. By the enlightened liberal standards of Lord Bryce's time, the Golden Bull of Charles IV

4 / THE LATE MEDIEVAL EMPIRE

After the death of Emperor Frederick II in 1250 and the extended interregnum following it, the Holy Roman Empire was little more than a fragmented confederation of literally hundreds of principalities and autonomous cities. A map on this scale can show only the larger states; light interrupted lines indicate their borders in 1356. In that year Emperor Charles IV promulgated a constitution permanently establishing detailed procedures for election of the emperor by seven prince electors: the archbishops of Mainz, Trier, and Cologne, the king of Bohemia, the count palatine of the Rhine, the duke of Saxony, and the margrave of Brandenburg. The claim of the pope (at Avignon since 1309) to have a role in the selection of the emperor was ignored. The seven electors' dominions are identified on the map with solid border lines, which also are used for a few of the larger free cities; several of these were relatively powerful city-states with considerable outlying territory, including extensive forests, pastures, and farmlands, and even dependent villages and towns. Among the most important of them were Ulm, which headed a south German league of cities, and Lübeck, the leading member of the maritime Hanseatic League. Set off with a heavy interrupted line southwest of Ulm is the Swiss Confederation; by 1356 it had grown from the original league of three forest cantons formed late in the previous century to a perpetual alliance of eight cantons, including several cities.

was a preposterous constitutional document, but it had succeeded in defining and thus, in a sense, stabilizing the *status quo* of the mid-fourteenth century. The reason it could succeed to the extent it did was that it reflected the basic political realities of its age as no enlightened "modern" constitution could possibly have done. But although it was realistic, it was not merely a pedantic blueprint of things exactly as they were. Within carefully defined limits, it introduced significant corrections in favor of the house of Luxemburg as well as other powerful parties whose support was necessary to secure formal approval of the document at the Imperial Diets of Nuremberg

CITIES AND RHINE-
LAND ELECTORATES

Cologne
Mainz
Trier
Palatinate

1. Cologne   6. Heidelberg
2. Bonn   7. Speyer
3. Mainz   8. Esslingen
4. Frankfurt 9. Rothenburg
5. Worms   10. Nuremberg

DENMARK

BALTIC SEA

NORTH SEA

Danzig
PRUSSIA
(Teutonic Knights)

Marienburg

Thorn

Vistula R.

POLAND

Lübeck

Hamburg

Bremen

BRANDENBURG

Berlin

Rhine R.

Meuse R.

Aachen

WESTPHALIA

EICHSFELD

Erfurt

Wittenberg

SAXONY

SILESIA

Oder R.

Elbe R.

Prague

BOHEMIA

MORAVIA

Trier

Verdun

Metz

Toul

Strasbourg

Basel

Besançon

UPPER
PALATINATE

Moldau R.

AUSTRIA

Regens-
burg

Augsburg

Vienna

Danube R.

Ulm

Munich

BAVARIA

HABSBURG

LANDS

STYRIA

SWISS CANTONS

FRANCE

Geneva

DAUPHINE
(French
since
1349)

Rhône R.

Milan

Po R.

Genoa

Avignon
(papal)

TYROL

Trent

CARINTHIA

CARNIOLA

Venice

PAPAL
STATES

ADRIATIC SEA

HUNGARY

MEDITERRANEAN SEA

and Metz in 1356, and to assure its subsequently being subscribed to throughout the empire.

One party was ignored, however: the pope. In epitomizing the political pretensions of the medieval papacy in the extraordinary bull *Unam sanctam* in 1302, Boniface VIII had asserted that the pope was the overlord of every earthly ruler, and that the election of the Holy Roman Emperor did not become valid without papal approval. But just as the Lateran Decree of 1059 on papal election implicitly denied the role of the German kings, the Golden Bull of 1356, in addition to ignoring papal claims, explicitly stated that the king's very first act, immediately upon election, was to confirm the privileges of the electors. This he could not do, of course, unless he had actually become king by virtue of his election, even though he had not yet been crowned, let alone endorsed by the pope. While this provision clearly obviated confirmation by the pope, it also reinforced the limitations of royal prerogatives by the prince electors. In the past, strong kings had not always immediately reconfirmed the great princes' privileges; when they did, it was often on the basis of complex political understandings that included significant commitments on the part of the individual princes. Thus the prerogative of reconfirmation — with the implicit option of refusal or delay — had represented considerable political leverage for the monarch. Consequently the Golden Bull's explicit mandate to reconfirm the privileges of the electors immediately upon election further weakened his position.

The triumph of the great princes which was signed and sealed in 1356 by no means meant that they became free to rule their respective territories as absolute sovereigns. Far later, in the seventeenth and eighteenth centuries, a number of the greater principalities would approach absolutism, but the more common pattern during the three centuries from the Golden Bull of 1356 to the end of the Thirty Years' War in 1648 was a form of regional dualism. The great princes, having denied the king the power to establish a strong central monarchy, themselves found it necessary to share their own augmented power with the estates of their respective principalities — the prelates, the nobility, and the burghers of the towns. This simply was part of the price the great magnates had to pay for their victory in their long struggle against the monarchy. To sustain themselves and to triumph in the protracted conflict with the king, they had to depend upon the loyalty of their estates. Without reliable domestic support, they could not have conducted the "foreign" policy that led to their ascendancy over the king. To win this support they had to concede prerogatives analogous to those they themselves were exacting from the monarch. As a result, the princes were far from being in a position arbitrarily to assert autocratic authority over their subjects. On the contrary, they generally found it necessary, by the mid-fourteenth century, to acquiesce in the practice of sharing power with their estates, particularly when it came to taxation.

This was only one complication, however. Even the greater principalities were shot through with independent enclaves that did not owe allegiance to anyone except the emperor. These were the free imperial cities and the imperial baronies. Scores of towns, above all in the south and west, were independent of the princes and exempt from their taxes. Yet it was precisely in these regions, especially Bavaria, Swabia, and the Rhineland, that many of the lesser principalities through division and subdivision had already been fragmented to marginal viability. Even the once proud duchy of Bavaria was reduced, soon after the death of Emperor Louis the Bavarian, to four principalities. The four Bavarian duchies — the ducal courts were at Munich, Ingolstadt, Landshut, and Straubing (and they were finally reunited at the beginning of the sixteenth century) — were reasonably viable, but the diminutive holdings of literally hundreds of free imperial knights were not. Relics of an obsolete warrior caste owing homage to none save the emperor, many of these petty barons lacked the means even to maintain their ancient castles, not to mention the archaic pretensions of an age that history had left behind. Some succeeded not merely in eking out a living by agriculture, but actually in achieving modest prosperity and reasonably good government in their lilliputian realms, but this was not generally the case. Those who were strategically located often exacted toll and transit fees so assiduously that, for their merchant victims, the ordeal differed from outright highway robbery only in style, not in effect — and sometimes not even in style.

To protect their commerce and their persons from the depredations of the often rapacious lesser nobility and endemic internal disorder verging on anarchy, many of the towns and cities of western and southern Germany banded together, in the latter half of the fourteenth century, in a swiftly expanding league of cities under the leadership of Ulm on the upper Danube, which at that very time began construction of the great minster boasting the tallest spire in Christendom. The Golden Bull of 1356 had explicitly proscribed such city alliances less than a generation before this league was organized, so imperial condemnation was promptly followed by the dispatch of imperial forces. But the cities defeated them and peace was concluded in 1377 — though it amounted to little more than a truce. The initial success of the cities gave a new impetus to the knights, themselves organized in the leagues of St. George, of St. William, and above all the League of the Lion. The petty barons regarded the city burghers as their mortal enemies. In 1382 it came to open warfare between the leagues of cities and of knights. Once more the cities succeeded in asserting themselves. But some five years later when a duke of Bavaria was kidnapped by the archbishop of Salzburg, an ally of the cities, the struggle was resumed and brought to a decisive end: all the military strength the cities could muster was annihilated in two separate battles. Thereafter they still played an important role in German intellectual, artistic, economic, and social life; for the individual many were islands of personal freedom. But their political influence on the history of Germany as a whole was virtually ended for centuries. This was all but inevitable, for Germany had no single great metropolis, like Paris or London, strong enough in its own right to be a decisive factor, let alone an arbiter in national affairs. Fragmented among themselves no less than Germany as a whole, the cities and their burghers were firmly relegated to local roles. As in so many other respects in German history, the die was cast in the Middle Ages.

The only exception was the Hanse, but precisely because the center of gravity of its interests and activities lay beyond the boundaries of Germany, it was an exception that actually proved the rule. A loosely organized commercial association, the Hanseatic League was concerned more with the promotion of foreign trade than domestic security. There was no strong German government to protect German commerce in the Baltic and North seas from Novgorod in Russia and Wisby on the Baltic isle of Gotland to Bruges in Flanders and the German steelyard in London. German cities active in overseas trade therefore joined forces in the league including over two hundred towns represented in an assembly that periodically met in Lübeck. Although the interests of the membership could normally be achieved through cooperative negotiations — eliciting trading privileges or monopolies and the like — the dangerous hostility of a Danish king in the late fourteenth century did provoke them to wage a war in the course of which they succeeded in wresting from the Danes control of the Sound, the narrow waterway between Denmark and Sweden that serves as the gateway between the Kattegat and the Baltic, much as the Straits of Gibraltar control the western entrance to the Mediterranean.

Many of the Hanseatic towns were free imperial cities, but several of the most important, particularly for the Baltic trade, lay entirely outside the empire. Both Danzig (founded by 1227) and Königsberg (the later capital of East Prussia, founded in 1255, now Kaliningrad in the Soviet Union) belonged to the great ecclesiastical principality of the Teutonic Knights. By the Golden Bull of Rimini in 1226, Emperor Frederick II had granted them title to all the lands conquered in the crusade against the Old Prussians, a heathen Lettic people after whom Prussia was named. By the third quarter of the fourteenth century, when the Teutonic Knights (and simultaneously the Hanse) reached their apogee, the monastic crusader state extended from the border of the empire, west of Danzig near the mouth of the Vistula, to the southern coast of the Gulf of Finland and inland to Lake Peipus — including, in pre-World War II terms, roughly all the territory of the Polish corridor, East Prussia, and the three Baltic States. Although the Teutonic Knights ruled the state, they themselves never constituted more than a small percentage of the population. They reached their high point at the end of the fourteenth century with about three thousand member knights — at a time when the principality included over a thousand rent-paying villages as well as over ninety incorporated towns and cities, including, in addition to Danzig and Königsberg, Riga and Reval, the future capitals of Latvia and Estonia.

This extraordinary growth was only the northernmost phase of the great eastward migration — the famous medieval *Drang nach Osten* ("drive toward the East") — which between the early twelfth and late fourteenth century almost doubled the German-inhabited area of Europe. Much of western Germany was densely populated. There the amount of land available to the peasant was generally not only small but also encumbered by heavy obligations of service to the lord of the manor. He often bore down so heavily because he in turn was condemned to a marginal existence by a system whereby individual holdings had been reduced to the threshold of viability through centuries of fragmentation in a society where primogeniture — undivided inheritance by the eldest son — was the exception to the rule. Tens of thousands of emigrants from the crowded villages of "old" Germany therefore took their heavy iron plows and experience with the three-field system of crop rotation to thinly populated areas that had never been intensely cultivated, if at all. Often recruited by *locatores,* entrepreneurs who were charged with establishing new villages in the East and who became the backbone of a new frontier aristocracy, these migrants settled in eastern Germany, Bohemia, and Austria. Many also followed the call of Polish and Hungarian lords who offered them large tracts of arable land at moderate fixed rents and free of the onerous burdens of manorial service, if only they would drain the marshes, clear the forests, and bring the heavy virgin turf under cultivation.

Although described — not without some justification — as "the greatest deed of the German people during the Middle Ages" by the nineteenth-century German historian Karl Lamprecht, the colonization of the East was certainly not a concerted national movement. Nor does it seem that the German immigration was detrimental to the original native population of the lands colonized — insofar as the areas involved had been inhabited at all. In one important way it was advantageous: the rights of the new German settlers under what came in the East to be called "German law" *(Jus Teutonicum)* were commonly conceded to the earlier inhabitants as well. In many areas, moreover, the German immigrants and the original population gradually merged through intermarriage. It was only after the great wave of colonization had subsided, late in the fourteenth century and early in the fifteenth, that growing strength and self-consciousness on the part of the eastern European peoples and their princes began to generate at least latent anti-German feelings. But even the fifteenth-century struggle between the Teutonic Knights and the Poles, ending in the former's defeat and recognition of Polish sovereignty, was anything but a nationalistic contest: the strongest ally of King Casimir IV was the Prussian Union of the German secular nobility and the German towns under the leadership of the rich and powerful city of Danzig. Most of the German burghers and barons preferred relative freedom under a Polish king at his distant court in Cracow to the pervasive bureaucracy of an ecclesiastical oligarchy of efficient tax collectors.

The triumph of the Prussian Union and the Polish king over the Teutonic Knights was sealed in the Second Peace of Thorn in 1466, just four hundred years before Prussia's victory over Austria in the second of Bismarck's three wars of German unification. It is one of the tragedies of European history that the Germany unified under Bismarck succumbed to the spell of so virulent a racist nationalism that when it was crushed, millions of descendants of the German colonists of the late Middle Ages were driven back westward with a brutality comparable to that with which the non-German population had been tormented during the Third Reich.

❦ THE IMPERIAL REFORM MOVEMENT AND THE RISE OF THE HOUSE OF HABSBURG

THE GOLDEN BULL OF 1356 formally constitutionalized the weakness of the monarchy and the fragmentation of Germany. Despite the relative insignificance of the imperial office in itself, however, it did become increasingly important to the house of Habsburg, for it gave its far-flung holdings an exalted symbol of unity and authority. From 1438 until the end of the Holy Roman Empire in 1806, the imperial crown remained with the "august house," as it came to be called, except for a single five-year interlude in the eighteenth century between the death of Maria Theresa's father and the imperial election of her husband.

During eighty of the hundred years before Albert II began the long Habsburg ascendancy in 1438, Luxemburg emperors had reigned. But when Sigismund died in 1437, he left no son to succeed him. Under the terms of a dynastic compact between the houses of Habsburg and Luxemburg, providing that on the expiration of the male line in either, the other would inherit its holdings, Albert of Habsburg became Sigismund's heir. He had married Sigismund's only daughter, he followed him as king of Bohemia and of Hungary, and soon he was also elected emperor as well. The Habsburgs temporarily lost control of Bohemia and Hungary during the bleak reign of Albert's successor, Frederick III, who combined prodigious incompetence with unusual longevity. Nonetheless Frederick's long incumbency (1440–93) saw one of the greatest triumphs of Habsburg nuptial diplomacy: the marriage of his son and successor Maximilian I (1493–1519) to the daughter of Duke Charles the Bold, bringing under Habsburg aegis the great Burgundian inheritance that included Franche-Comté and the Netherlands — the fragmented but rich and populous remains of the early medieval realm of Charlemagne's grandson Lothair. After Maximilian's son in turn wed the heiress of Ferdinand of Aragon and Isabella of Castile, who by their marriage had united Spain, not only was most of Iberia brought under Habsburg rule, but also Naples and Sicily as well as the Spanish colonial empire overseas.

The reign of Maximilian I has become relatively well known because it saw the beginning of the Reformation in Germany in 1517. Less attention has been given to a political reform movement that began during his reign and which, like the Reformation, continued under his successor. The movements for ecclesiastical and for imperial reform were closely related to each other, in many ways affected each other, and together had enormous impact on church and state in the sixteenth and seventeenth centuries — and by no means only in Germany.

In 1495, "Eternal Peace" was proclaimed by the Imperial Diet of Worms under Maximilian I. This was not some vague expression of utopian piety, but rather the equivalent, in a sense, of what in our own times might be called a proclamation calling for "Law and Order" — and providing for its enforcement by methods that would seem as drastic and unprecedented as, for example, equipping the London policemen (who traditionally have carried no firearms) with pistols plus the noxious gas dispenser "Mace." After centuries of random violence throughout much of the German countryside, the empire finally obligated itself to impose the rule of law. This meant that the incessant, openly condoned public violence of personal feuding was permanently outlawed, after having so long jeopardized the life and property of quixotic knights as well as innocent travelers, particularly merchants and their wagon trains. To be sure, it was not permanently stopped for generations, but a serious beginning was made, and after 1495 highway robbery could no longer be openly justified in the name of chivalric honor by petty barons accustomed to taking the law into their own hands — especially when their cash was low.

To assure redress of grievances under law rather than by trial of arms, the Imperial Cameral Tribunal *(Reichskammergericht)* was established by the Diet of Worms in 1495. The tribunal was to serve as a supreme court with final jurisdiction over all but the greatest principalities, which already had courts whose decisions were subject to review only by the prince exercising his sovereign power of pardon. But even though the great princes themselves too often became involved in feuding — the elector palatine with the archbishop of Mainz, for example — these larger territories were not the main problem at the grassroots level. The "Eternal Peace" and the new high court were necessitated primarily by the virtual anarchy caused by hundreds of imperial knights who acknowledged no lord except the emperor and no law but their archaic code of chivalry which, stripped of its hortatory veneer of romantic bombast, was a medieval variant of the law of the jungle. The reforms of 1495 were a loud and clear signal to the knights that the time had come to trade in their trusty squires for trustworthy advocates — or risk the consequences. Most heard and heeded it. Many who did not, learned painfully or, if they were fortunate, learned vicariously the cost of failing to do so a generation later during the Knights' War (which is taken up later).

The decree of "Eternal Peace" and the establishment of the Imperial Cameral Tribunal in 1495 were followed in 1500 by what was intended to become a new form of government for the empire. The Golden Bull of 1356 had placed the empire under an oligarchy of princes presided over by an emperor whose prerogatives were so limited that he presumably could pose no serious threat to them. But ironically, the very impotence of the imperial office contributed to its being transformed into a sort of Trojan horse. So successfully had the emperor's powers been curtailed that the imperial crown lost its attractiveness to most German princes and became interesting primarily to independent and even foreign powers; at the election of Maximilian's successor in 1519, the strongest candidates for the succession were, in fact, the kings of France and of Spain. Nineteen years earlier this could not have been foreseen in detail, but the more perspicacious of the princes, above all the archbishop-elector of Mainz, Count Berthold von Henneberg, had nonetheless been most concerned about the way things were moving under the energetic and ambitious — if also disarmingly unsystematic — Maximilian I. In order to maintain a measure of control over the conduct of policy, particularly where imperial authority might be abused to involve Germany in dynastically motivated foreign adventures, the Imperial Diet of Augsburg in 1500 established the Imperial Governing Council *(Reichsregiment)*. Emperor Maximilian gave his consent, though reluctantly, because only thereby could he even hope to win support for his proposal to raise an imperial army. The Imperial Governing Council was established as a standing executive committee of twenty, composed of the electors, other ecclesiastical and secular princes, and various prelates, nobility, and burghers representing the imperial free cities and the administrative districts of the empire (the Imperial Circles or *Reichskreise*). Constituted to serve as the executive branch of government, it was to function under the chairmanship of the emperor or his deputy, but its authority was not to depend upon his assent.

Within two years of its establishment, the Imperial Governing Council dissolved in failure, leaving Maximilian unchallenged, from that quarter, for the rest of his reign. It had not been enough for the princes to extract the emperor's grudging assent to the establishment of an agency potentially able to check and balance him. They could effectively limit his authority — in practice, not just in theory — only if they themselves responsibly assumed a substantial share of the burden of power. To do this, however, they would have had to follow through with a serious commitment to the new Governing Council — and they did not.

A constitution that defines and legitimatizes existing political arrangements, i.e., established institutions, vested interests, and accepted practices, may be viable for centuries, as was the Golden Bull of 1356 in its overall outlines. Institutional reforms brought about by decree or legislation may be the sincere expression of worthy aspirations and noble ideals. But it is not enough to sow or even plant them; if they are not carefully tended until they take root, they may wither. This is what happened to the Imperial Governing Council of 1500. It became defunct because the princes were not prepared to furnish adequate manpower and money, and the emperor himself was not about to sustain it (nor could it have controlled him effectively had he been the one to do so).

Handsome, popular, and chivalrous, Maximilian I was simply not threatening enough to most of the princes to make it seem worthwhile to devote a substantial proportion of their time, energy, and resources to building up what would at least be a watchdog agency, but ultimately would have to become a major organ of government. The picture drastically changed in 1519, however, with the death of the old emperor — "the last knight," as he was nostalgically known to a public that saw in him the romantic idealization of a more gallant and splendid age.

Because Maximilian's son Philip the Fair had already died in 1506, the Habsburg contender for the imperial throne was Philip's nineteen-year-old son Charles. King Francis I of France also assiduously sought election, and not with papal support only, for many German princes feared the growing strength of the Habsburgs. By the summer of 1517 it became apparent that Francis had no chance against Charles, so the pope and the French king's German supportors appealed to Elector Frederick III of Saxony to become emperor, an alternative that would have been unanimously adopted by the electoral college had Frederick the Wise — one of very few princes whose name bears this epithet — not categorically refused. He did so because he was already ageing and unwell, and knew he lacked the personal stamina, not to mention the base of power, to function as emperor. He gave his support to Charles of Habsburg, who thereupon became the unanimous though certainly not enthusiastic choice of all the prince electors.

The imperial election of 28 June 1519, together with his dynastic inheritances from the houses of Burgundy, Spain, Luxemburg, and Habsburg, made Emperor Charles V ruler — as he himself observed — over "an empire on which the sun never set." But as holder of no less than seventy-five titles, he was not and could never have been expected to be solely or even primarily a German king. Reared in the Low Countries, the land of his birth, and king of Spain three years before elected in Germany, he was first and last a Habsburg dynast. Earnest to the point of melancholy, diligent and intelligent but never brilliant or imaginative, keenly conscious of the sacred character of his office and always sincerely orthodox, Charles acted as though he somehow had been born to the role he had to play. He seemed to have an understanding of himself and his divine commission that he felt lesser mortals could no more comprehend or appreciate than the things he often had to do as the responsible overlord of the empire for which he was accountable to God, and to Him alone. He was sovereign in bearing and personal authority even as a teenager, but he lacked the personal charm of his grandfather Maximilian, whose easy manner was often taken as gracious poise rather than thinly veiled self-esteem — particularly by those who knew him least. Aside from the differences in personalities, however, Maximilian never had to bear his grandson's burden of having to make one decision after another, year after year, between alternatives that with harrowing frequency all seemed potentially disastrous — whether in the form of military defeat, desertion of political allies and dynastic adherents, betraying the holy Catholic faith, or some bitter combination of the three.

Never had a ruler seemed more powerful than Charles V; yet never did the inherent limitations of political power emerge more relentlessly than during the grueling reign that he voluntarily concluded with a moving act of state in the great hall of the palace at Brussels in 1555. In October of that year, he formally laid down his scepter in order to retire to a villa adjoining the monastery of San Jerónimo de Yuste in Spain, fretfully awaiting the day when he would be freed from his painfully crippling arthritis and would meet the Lord who once had made him the mightiest king in history.

Several of the more nationalistically oriented German historians of the past century have no more forgiven Charles V for having subordinated German interests to those of other parts of his dynastic empire than they have his medieval predecessors for sacrificing German interests to sustain the vain pretentions of the Holy Roman Empire. (Some Spanish historians, from their perspective, have also, for analogous reasons, been very censorious.) But if historical guilt is to be apportioned, a large measure of responsibility must be reassigned from the emperor to the German princes. We already have seen that they failed to implement potentially promising imperial reforms during the reign of Maximilian. When they elected his grandson after Frederick the Wise refused the crown, the elector of Saxony led them in eliciting from the young candidate, as a precondition of his selection, a carefully formulated list of commitments. By the terms of this "electoral capitulation," Charles explicitly agreed that he would not use the resources of the empire for dynastic purposes, not bring foreign troops into Germany, not employ foreigners in German imperial offices, and not make major political decisions without prior consultation of the estates (i.e., the prelates, princes, and imperial cities represented in the diet) — promises he eventually in every case broke. But potentially most important, Charles agreed to a new Imperial Governing Council similar to the one accepted some two decades earlier by his grandfather. To become emperor he had to accept an institution that could have held him to his electoral commitments and controlled his German policy.

The new council was set up soon after the election and initially it did prove to be an effective innovation. Its recommendations furnished the bases for a badly needed new penal code, the "Carolina," which was relatively enlightened by the unspeakably harsh standards of the day. Its governmental proposals in the areas of economic and fiscal, military, and religious policy show a quality of mature statesmanship, breadth of knowledge, and technical competence that reflects great credit on the members of the council — not so much the princes themselves, who rarely attended and participated, but their representatives, prototypes of the modern civil servant, trained in law (several at secular Italian universities), and experienced in administration.

In cooperation with the Imperial Diet, which met regularly in Nuremberg in the early 1520s, the Imperial Governing Council squarely faced the issues of the day, above all, the religious question that had come to a head following the beginning, in 1517, of what we retrospectively call the Protestant Reformation. Although the council was divided on the merits of the religious question itself, it urged, with the diet concurring, that the emperor and the pope join in convening a council of the church. This was, after all, a major ecclesiastical crisis. Just as the Council of Constance, a century earlier, had ended the Great Schism that had divided Christendom, so now once more a council was needed to consider the volatile ecclesiastical issues and grievances of the time. Charles vehemently rejected the proposal in July 1524. In an order from Burgos, Spain, in which he likened Martin Luther to Mohammed, he categorically forbade any such council of the church under pain of the most drastic sanctions. The harshness of his reaction reflects his perception of the fundamental character of the challenge represented by the proposal. It was political and institutional, threatening his sovereignty. But at the same time it was also religious, endangering the holy Catholic faith. For him, with his exalted conception of the imperial dignity as a sacred stewardship, and his fiercely uncompromising orthodoxy, the attempt to undermine his authority in Germany was simultaneously a carelessly veiled attack on the Catholic religion.

Whatever the original intention of the electors and their interpretation of the emperor's electoral capitulation, Charles clearly had no intention of sharing his sovereignty with the Imperial Governing Council. At best it might serve as a provisional organ of administrative convenience to act under the chairmanship of his representative when he was away from Germany, which he had first visited as king in 1521, returning again only in 1530. Soon thereafter the council was formally disbanded.

It is one of the tragedies of German history that the princes, who somewhat earlier might well have presented a reasonably united front to the emperor, had become so grievously divided on the religious question that, by default, they acquiesced in the imperious will of the Habsburg monarch. Thus at the very moment when a potentially effective representative governmental structure — the Imperial Governing Council working in close cooperation with the Imperial Diet — emerged and gave promise of being capable of concerted action, the Reformation divided the princes into hostile camps and set the stage for a century of religious wars that further fragmented the country and caused its people untold suffering.

❦ The Age of the Reformation and the Wars of Religion

According to venerable Protestant tradition, the Reformation was heralded by the sound of Martin Luther's hammer as on the eve of All Saints' Day in 1517 he nailed to the door of the castle church in Wittenberg his ninety-five theses — an eloquent document attacking widespread ecclesiastical abuses. There is certainly an element of truth in this account, but taken out of context it neither does justice to Luther nor even faintly suggests the character or significance of the Reformation — perhaps the most important single event in the history of western Christendom comprehensible solely within the context of German history.

Luther did not set out to start the Protestant Reformation in 1517. He was anything but a revolutionary by choice. Descended from rising peasant stock, he initially studied law. Then, in a compulsive quest for salvation, he joined the strictest of monastic orders. Before reaching thirty, he received his doctorate in theology and was entrusted with the chair in biblical studies at Wittenberg University in Electoral Saxony. As he continued his spiritual pilgrimage through prayer, meditation, and the systematic preparation of one lecture course after another on the Holy Scriptures, the granite conviction formed within him that man is saved by God's grace alone, that God in His loving mercy for the sake of Christ forgives man's sin, if he will only accept this forgiveness in faith and trust. The stunning corollary of this was that the blatantly mercenary practices of the church were not only ineffectual as means of securing salvation, but potentially dangerous to souls tempted into dependence upon them. This was the outrage against which Luther protested with all the fervor of religious genius, triggering the Reformation.

But why? Why did that particular monk raise that particular issue when and where he did? Why did it have such reverberations? Why did lightning strike in Wittenberg in the autumn of 1517? And why did this ignite so great a conflagration?

Wittenberg was the capital of Electoral Saxony, one of the major principalities of the empire. Dr. Martin Luther, as professor of biblical studies at Wittenberg University as well as preacher at the city church, enjoyed considerable prestige and prominence. Yet we must not misread these data. Luther's Saxony was relatively influential, but it was influence measured by the standards of the early sixteenth century, not the latter part of the twentieth. Moreover, it was due in no small part to the personal stature of its prince, Elector Frederick the Wise.

Thinking of the "Old World" as many of us involuntarily tend to do, it is hard to appreciate how recently settled, how sparsely populated, and how unencumbered with tradition that principality in the remote northeast of the empire was at the beginning of the sixteenth century. Luther himself spoke of Wittenberg as lying on the "frontier of civilization" and believed it never would become a real city. With only a few thousand inhabitants, it was served by a clothmaker as mayor and a tailor as judge. Wittenberg was little more than an overgrown village in the shadow of the castle — with a recently opened university. By the standards of the established schools at Heidelberg, Prague, and Vienna, which all had been in operation at least a century or more, Wittenberg University was small, new, and without tradition; the imperial charter of 1502 had been confirmed by the pope only in 1507, the year before Luther first went there.

In this setting, it was interesting but certainly not world-shaking for Doctor Martinus to have posted his ninety-five theses on the Wittenberg castle church door — the bulletin board, so to speak, at the church that was used for larger academic assemblies. It made relatively little difference whether — depending upon the weather — a mere handful of colleagues and students, or dozens at a time, stood there to study a complex theological document framed in formal Latin. It was more important that Luther's position, which soon became very widely known, did not represent, in Wittenberg, a dangerous challenge to a local establishment identified with a tradition that he somehow threatened. A very small town in the more recently conquered, Christianized, and colonized part of the empire, Wittenberg had no patrician class with deep cultural roots. Its fledgling university had just barely been founded. Far from posing a dangerous threat to the values and traditions cherished in Wittenberg, Martin Luther, more than any other one person, actually established the great Wittenberg tradition.

In any case, the fact that what he stood for spread so far

beyond Wittenberg had nothing to do with local publicity, let alone a challenge to public debate that understandably went unanswered. Nor did it really make much difference that he sent copies of the theses to the bishop of Brandenburg and to the archbishop of Mainz and Magdeburg. What was historically epoch-making was the immediate publication of his theses by the young humanists (and the printers), and their swift dissemination throughout Germany and all of Christendom. As a reasonably well-known Wittenberg theology professor, prestigious enough to have been elected his monastic order's district vicar for Meissen and Thuringia, Luther was in an exceptionally favorable position to gain a hearing, on publication, for his theses and subsequent works, which catapulted him into prominence as one of the most widely read theologians of his own or any age. As anyone who has seriously attempted to grapple with his collected works will testify, it is astounding how this man of action, during the remaining three decades of his life (born in 1483, he died in 1546), averaged — apart from his monumental translation of the Bible (the German equivalent of the King James Version) — an original treatise or pamphlet every month.

In the mid-fifteenth century the technique of printing with movable poured metal type, perfected by Johann Gensfleisch zum Gutenberg of Mainz, had made possible the large-scale production of books. Wide and intense interest in what Luther had to say meant that the potential of the press was realized on a previously inconceivable scale; at one point it required no fewer than three separate presses to keep pace with the prolific reformer: Luther himself once commented that he no sooner conceived than delivered.

Taking into account the market both for his original works and his German Bible, there is perhaps only one adequate modern analogy to suggest his impact on the reading public and the book publishing industry: the significance some four centuries later of Henry Ford and his mass-produced Model T for the American public and automobile industry. Although apparently incongruous, the comparison is valid in terms of production, marketing, and the extension of people's horizons. Ford with his production line made it possible for people to get in their own cars and drive hundreds of miles; Luther with the printers of his translation and original works made it possible for the people to get out their own Bibles, catechism, and inspirational works and chart their own course through life in the sight of God.

In terms of intellectual and spiritual content, however, Luther's ideas were individually by no means as original as their mix and intensity, not to mention the language he had the genius for framing to convey them (he was one of the greatest German poets). So far as specific issues were concerned, in England John Wycliffe and in Bohemia John Huss had long since challenged several of the teachings and practices of the church that tormented Luther over a century later. But neither Huss nor Wycliffe, whose teachings had great influence among the Hussites, is considered to have started the Reformation. The man who became known as the Great Reformer was Martin Luther.

Why?

As so often in history, the answer to the question is implicit in its definition. When we speak of the *Reformation,* we are involuntarily using a conventional term — one of those familiar code-words that may actually mean quite different things to different people, but is rarely defined and consequently permits the illusion of consensus. As used here, *Reformation* simultaneously refers to a watershed in the history of Western Christendom and to an epoch-making complex of interacting religious, intellectual, cultural, social, demographic, economic, technological, political, and military events that took place at various times and places during the sixteenth and seventeenth centuries.

But how would we refer to the Reformation in Germany if this conventional term had never been coined, or if it had already been preempted for something that had happened earlier? What other designation would we use? One possible alternative would be to think and speak in terms of the "Great Revolution of the Sixteenth and Early Seventeenth Centuries" — for it was indeed a revolution that transformed life in much of Europe, but nowhere more drastically than in the Holy Roman Empire during the 130 years between the publication of Luther's ninety-five theses and the conclusion of the Peace of Westphalia in 1648.

Luther, as already stressed, was not a revolutionary by choice; it was the discrepancy between his ideals and the hypocritical norms of his age that "got him into trouble" — to employ a common expression of our own times. He did not want to make trouble, but was not "sophisticated" enough to keep quiet when he saw the Gospel, with its promise of forgiveness of sin, reconciliation with God, and life eternal, being cynically exploited for political and economic purposes. The crisis came in 1517, when he was provoked into livid eloquence by the hard-selling campaign of an unusually aggressive team of afterlife-insurance agents pushing papal certificates of easy redemption known as "indulgences." As such, they were not actually new. Crusaders had been granted indulgences centuries earlier. Then, as a matter of fairness, persons who had been unable to go on crusades, but whose donations supported crusaders, or greatly facilitated other good works (such as building the great Gothic cathedrals), were also issued papal assurances of indulgence whereby they would be spared at least some of the pangs of Purgatory — the place where souls too good for eternal perdition but too impure for eternal bliss presumably were sent to undergo the kind of reconditioning graphically described by Dante in his record of the second part of his tour of the afterlife. Nor was the problem posed by indulgences new to Luther in autumn 1517. His own ruler, Elector Frederick the Wise, had made Wittenberg a famous center for those seeking indulgences. With no less zeal than the founders of the great collections at privately endowed libraries and museums today, Frederick devoted much time and energy to assembling a collection of relics that contained, according to catalogs of the time, a thorn from the crown of thorns (one that had pierced the Savior's brow), a nail that had fixed one of His hands to the cross, a twig from Moses' burning bush, and four strands of the Virgin Mary's hair. Between 1509 and 1520, the collection increased from a total of about five thousand relics to 19,013. By the latter date, moreover — some three years after Luther had published his initial protest against the sale of indulgences — his own patron's relic collection was advertised to enable the faithful, through prescribed devotions accompanied by stipulated good works (i.e., specified donations — which in part were used to defray the costs of operating Wittenberg University), to acquire indulgences that might reduce one's term of purgatorial trauma by 1,902,202 years and 270 days.

Luther had openly chafed under his ruler's penchant for quantification. But he did so no less vainly than many a twentieth-century scholar who may at least console himself with the thought that quantification of the essentially unquantifiable is not a bane of our times only; it seems to have an almost timeless appeal for administrators, whether of church or state, and also for the man on the street, who likes to know just what he is getting for his money — and how much of it.

This unflinchingly practical attitude was shared by the great Medici patron of the arts and architecture, Pope Leo X, the second son of Lorenzo the Magnificent, as well as by Albert of Brandenburg, archbishop of Mainz and Magdeburg, who ranked with Emperor Maximilian I as a sponsor of the arts in Renaissance Germany. But Albert and Leo had more in common than commitment to the arts. They both had grave financial problems — and one of the devices by which they jointly sought to deal with them provoked Luther's protest which triggered the Reformation in Germany.

As one of the more profligate Roman pontiffs, Pope Leo X would probably have spent his way into serious straits even if he had not inherited from his predecessor, Julius II, one of the most staggeringly expensive building projects ever undertaken in Christendom, the uncompleted basilica of St. Peter in Rome. He desperately needed whatever help he could get, and exploited to the fullest the ambitions of Albert of Brandenburg, the younger brother of Elector Joachim I. In the year of his ordination to the priesthood at twenty-three, he became archbishop of Magdeburg and also administrator of the diocese of Halberstadt. The following year, he sought in addition the senior archiepiscopal electorate of the empire, Mainz, which would not only make him archchancellor of the Holy Roman Empire, but would also enable him to join his brother in the electoral college. Although he was underage and no bishop might hold more than one diocese (not to mention three), magnaminous papal waivers were traditionally available to magnanimous donors — other things being equal. In this case, they were not equal, however, for Emperor Maximilian very strongly supported the candidacy of his nephew, a Bavarian prince, for the archbishopric of Mainz. His sense of dynastic solidarity was understandably reinforced by misgivings about the increase of Hohenzollern strength in northern Germany that the addition of Mainz to Magdeburg and Halberstadt under Albert would represent, quite apart from the complications that might result from alliance with his brother in the electoral college.

Ironically, it was precisely that factor that decided the issue in favor of Albert. With the support of Elector Joachim of Brandenburg and the resources of Mainz, in addition to the extensive holdings he already had, Albert clearly would have the kind of financial leverage necessary to overcome the pope's flexible scruples about deciding in his favor: he would be in a position to enable Pope Leo X to renew the great indulgence dedicated to the construction of St. Peter's. In 1506, his predecessor Julius II had already issued the Jubilee Indulgence, but never been able to offer it throughout northern Germany because of the resistance of so many of the princes there — who realized only too well what an economic hemorrhage it would represent. But now the matter could finally be resolved. The great Augsburg banking house of Fugger was called in to advance a huge sum to the papal treasury on behalf of Albert. He in turn was licensed to offer the special indulgence in Germany for ten years, with the understanding that half the proceeds would go directly to Rome and the other half be used to repay the house of Fugger.

The new indulgence was not offered in Electoral Saxony, for Frederick the Wise declined to permit this — less because of the kind of theological misgivings later expressed by Luther than because of its potential impact on the donations that otherwise would be made by visitors to his great collection of relics. His concern was justified, because the new indulgence was made extremely attractive, even though the carefully scaled donation rate was steep — from one gold florin for the least affluent to twenty-five for the most wealthy. Yet the benefits that were acquired by the purchaser were extraordinary. He could purchase his own papal passport to heaven and (in separate transactions) even arrange to have redemptory visas forwarded for loved ones who already had died and presumably were being tormented by the purifying flames of the Refiner's fire. In the words of the popular jingle:

> *Sobald das Geld im Kasten klingt,*
> *Die Seele aus dem Fegefeuer springt*
> [As soon as the money in the box rings,
> The soul from Purgatory's fire springs].

It is not surprising that Luther, in his dual capacity as university theologian and town preacher, should have been distraught when he heard the tales brought back about the exploitation of the faithful, and enraged when, in October 1517, he saw a copy of the archbishop's *Instructio summaria,* the sales manual for his indulgence agents. That was what provoked the ninety-five theses, which he followed with a long series of pamphlets and treatises. Some corresponded to little more than latter-day press releases; others were book-length essays. What he wrote resonated in Germany and throughout the Christian world. He addressed himself first to the church itself in the hope that, as in the eleventh century, it might again be reformed from within. But his appeal was rejected by the hierarchy; he was excommunicated by the pope and outlawed by the emperor. Elector Frederick the Wise nonetheless protected him. It was not that he was personally swayed by Luther's often audacious inspiration. Luther's prince heard him personally only on one occasion, at the Diet of Worms in 1521, where the reformer took his courageous stand before the emperor and princes, firmly refusing to disclaim any of his teachings or to disavow any of his publications held by the church to be heretical, unless and until he could be personally convinced that they were false. Elector Frederick, as custodian of one of the most famous indulgence-bearing collections of relics in Christendom, had by no means always been well pleased with everything he had heard about Luther. But he was proud of his university (he had founded it and he called it his "daughter"), undaunted by the pope (who in 1519 sought in vain to make him emperor), and unwilling to tolerate Roman persecution of one of his professors.

Such unwavering protection not only for Luther but also for his associates enabled the thwarted reformer of the old church to become the founder of a new one that spread rapidly across much of Germany and beyond its borders. It was welcomed for a number of different reasons — many of them, from Luther's point of view, wrong ones. Perhaps the most difficult task of leadership — often an all but impossible one — is to convince people not only to do the right thing, but also to do it for the right reason. Luther has been faulted for failing to succeed better than he did in this. But he never sought in the first place to be the leader of a new movement. He sought rather to correct, from within the church, unbearable abuses that jeopardized the faithful and betrayed the Gospel. When those in authority responded by ejecting him and his followers from the church, Lutheranism haphazardly emerged, without his being initially aware of its implications, as the institutionalization not just of a reform program, but of a reformed church.

Many of the princes embraced it, however, as a rationalization for directly controlling if not confiscating outright the Roman church's lands within their territories. Many patriotic Germans supported the Reformation in protest against the economic and political exploitation of their country by the venal Roman curia. Untold thousands of subjects of ecclesiastical princes adhered to it out of hatred for oppressors often more ruthless than secular princes who at least had a dynastic interest in the long-range welfare of their lands and people. Many, from all stations in life, in good faith misinterpreted Luther's profoundly religious concept of the exalted inner freedom of the spirit in grossly simplistic political terms. However bizarre such misrepresentations may have been, the combination of all these factors lent, at the very least, a vaguely idealistic aura of religious legitimacy to widespread resentment over the social and economic desperation of the period. Consequently, for many of the participants, there was divine sanction for two social risings that shook Germany in the 1520s.

The first, in 1522 and 1523, came to be called the Knights' War, though it hardly deserved the name. When petty barons had struggled against the burghers in the South German City War of the late fourteenth century, they were able, in the end, to call in the support of the great princes, and consequently to assert themselves. But the "Eternal Peace" of 1495 had outlawed the feud, which continued to serve as the rationalization for the livelihood of the remnant of those who neither turned to serious agriculture nor accepted service as functionaries of the great magnates. The most notorious of these robber barons was Franz von Sickingen, whose inherited wealth enabled him to operate on a far larger scale than most of his peers. In 1514, he began a feud with the city of Worms and greatly expanded his family fortune by "confiscating" countless merchant wagon trains. When belatedly outlawed in the empire, he moved westward, entered the service of the king of France, and pillaged his way through Lorraine with a thousand armed retainers. Rich and powerful, he was in a position actively to support the election of Charles V, and he did so. But finally he overreached himself in 1522 by starting a feud with the archbishop-elector of Trier. He claimed that his invasion of the electorate with seven thousand men, a quarter of them mounted, was a crusade to free the people from ecclesiastical exploitation and bring them the word of the Lord. But Trier was not Jericho: the walls of the city held and the siege was a failure. Forced to withdraw, Sickingen himself soon was besieged at Landstuhl and finally killed in the ruins of his castle, as it fell in the spring of 1523 to the combined forces of the elector of Trier, the elector palatine of the Rhine, and the landgrave of Hesse. In the following weeks, thirty-two more Franconian and Swabian castles were reduced. But that was about all there was to it. The majority of petty barons had wisely abstained from participation in Sickingen's perilous adventure. When the German humanist

Ulrich von Hutten, a personal friend of the rebel leader, once had suggested to Martin Luther that he should take refuge with Franz von Sickingen, Luther had emphatically refused, explaining that one must never "do battle for the gospel with violence and murder."

Incomparably more serious than the so-called Knights' War, both in its immediate impact and in its long-range implications, was the Peasants' War that engulfed much of the central and southern part of Germany from the spring of 1524 to the summer of 1526. Literally tens of thousands of peasants rose against their lords, both secular and ecclesiastical. Some did so in sheer, brutal desperation. Many did so in response to the call of natural political leaders who emerged in their midst. Some rose as followers of religious fanatics. There had been peasant risings periodically throughout the late Middle Ages, but nothing like this. By 1525, half of Germany was disrupted by roving bands of peasants — bands sometimes numbering in the thousands. Many of them claimed and probably believed themselves to be followers of Luther, but he disavowed them unequivocally. Distressed by reports of atrocious mob brutality, he called on the princes, in a searing pamphlet, *Against Robbing and Murdering Gangs of Peasants,* to "smite, strangle and stab. . . . It is just as when you must kill a mad dog; if you don't get him, he will get you."

Apologists have stressed that Luther promptly issued another pamphlet when he learned how the princes were outdoing themselves in ferocity, urging restraint, which was as little heeded as his drastic exhortation had originally been needed. But Luther requires no defense for having cried "Fire!" when he saw his world in flames, let alone for having called on the princes to extinguish them. To whom else could he have turned but the princes? He knew that he had to speak, for not only were many of the peasants rising in his name, but he was also being blamed even when they obviously were not. Aside from this, he was intensely involved by virtue of his bonafide role as a national hero, a celebrated religious leader, and an academic luminary. For him not to have spoken out on this particular issue, after having been so articulately involved in the discussion of so many others, would have been tantamount to condoning by silence the mob violence that was threatening to tear the social fabric to shreds.

Radicals have suggested that it should have been destroyed; the savage repression of the peasantry under the leadership of the great princes, who had just triumphed over the petty barons, did reinforce an already stultifyingly rigid social system. Perhaps a sustained dose of anarchy could have kept things in flux long enough for a sounder basis for stabilization to be reached than actually emerged. But this was hardly the kind of question that concerned Luther. He was not a social scientist, let alone a behaviorist or social engineer. He was a profoundly earnest religious leader. Alarmed by a nationwide epidemic of rabid mob violence threatening to sweep everything — including the prospect of reforming the church — before it, he emphatically demanded, with none of the retrospective insight inspiring his latter-day critics, that the legitimate civil authorities swiftly restore law and order. They did. Having snuffed out the last vestiges of rebellion among the petty barons in the Knights' War of 1522–23, the princes further consolidated their strength by crushing the insurgent peasantry.

Meanwhile, the Protestant Reformation swiftly spread. Luther had begun the movement, but many variations sprang up — under the leadership of Ulrich Zwingli (and later of John Calvin) in Switzerland, for example, and a number of radical sectarians. But our concern here is the mainstream of what was to become the main branch of Protestantism in Germany. Luther's brilliant young colleague at Wittenberg, Philipp Melanchthon, was virtually the co-founder of Lutheranism. At the Imperial Diet of Augsburg in 1530, where Luther, having been banned at the Diet of Worms in 1521, could not appear before the emperor, Melanchthon served as theological spokesman for the Protestants — the princes and cities whose commitment to the Reformation had led them formally to protest its prohibition throughout the empire. He formulated the lucid and conciliatory *Augustana,* the Augsburg Confession, which was not accepted by the emperor and diet, but became the classical statement of Lutheranism; on reading it, Luther admiringly commented, "I cannot walk so soft and gently."

The formulation of the Augsburg Confession as a statement

of faith setting Lutheranism apart from radical sectarianism more or less coincided with another development of fundamental importance in the history of its institutionalization as an established church: from about 1530 on, there began to be enough educated Lutheran preachers to man the village and country pulpits. Before then, Lutheranism had been established primarily in the courts and towns, and particularly the free imperial cities; thereafter it also began to take root in the countryside.

Charles V bitterly opposed the spread of heresy, as he saw it, but was far too committed to his struggle against France and the Turks to take decisive action against the Lutheran princes and cities — or, for that matter, even to dispense with their support. By 1529 the Turks under Sultan Suleiman the Magnificent (1520–66) had conquered most of Hungary and reached the gates of Vienna. To win Protestant support against the next Turkish offensive, Emperor Charles and his brother King Ferdinand (crowned in Aachen in 1531) agreed at the Imperial Diet of Nuremberg to an armistice with their Protestant adversaries, the Nuremberg "Standstill," or the Religious Peace of Nuremberg of 1532. Only with strong Protestant participation (Nuremberg, for example, supplying twice its required contingent) was it possible to raise an imperial army of 80,000, deterring the immediate threat. Soon thereafter Suleiman concluded a formal alliance with France. Not until ten years later was Charles in a position to deal with the Protestants. In 1547 he defeated Elector John Frederick of Saxony at Mühlberg on the Elbe (Frederick the Wise had died in 1525, Luther in 1546). But his victory was short-lived, for the Protestants, under the leadership of Maurice of Saxony, on whom Charles had conferred the electorate and on whom he depended to enforce the terms of peace, betrayed him and turned for aid to the Catholic French, the range of whose religious tolerance had already been demonstrated by their alliance with the sultan. The Franco-Protestant alliance secured for the French the valuable border fortresses of Metz, Toul, and Verdun, and for the Protestants imperial recognition of parity between Lutheran and Catholic princes. This was conceded by Charles in the Religious Peace of Augsburg of 1555, the year before his abdication. There was no formal recognition of Calvinism or more radical forms of Protestantism, however, nor was there any guarantee of tolerance for anyone with a different faith than that of his ruler — beyond the dubious privilege of arranging, if he could, to move elsewhere.

During the following half century, additional territorial princes embraced Protestantism. As heads of the newly established territorial church organizations, they absorbed the holdings of the Roman church within the borders of their principalities, generally leaving their subjects little choice between conversion and emigration. The Roman Catholic Counter-Reformation meanwhile dramatically stemmed and in many areas even reversed the tide of Protestantism, which at its high-water mark had engulfed almost all of Germany. Calvinism had not been recognized in the terms of the Religious Peace of Augsburg, but nonetheless it had also won numerous adherents. The religious tensions engendered by multidimensional religious division were overlaid, particularly after the first decade of the seventeenth century, by the struggle between the houses of Bourbon and Habsburg to dominate the continent of Europe — an open conflict that can be said to have begun in 1609 with a bitter contest over the succession to the strategically important northwest German agglomeration of territories composed of Jülich, Cleves, Berg, Mark, and Ravensberg, and to have been resolved (at least temporarily) only with the Peace of the Pyrenees in 1659. Within the broad context of this half-century conflict took place what in German history is conventionally known as the Thirty Years' War — actually a series of four separate wars from 1618 to 1648. Not one of the four was solely a German affair, for each involved the Habsburgs and their allies fighting foreign forces on German soil — thereby once more vindicating, if vindication were needed, the foresight of Archbishop Berthold of Mainz, Elector Frederick the Wise of Saxony, and those who, sharing their misgivings a century earlier, had joined them in seeking in vain to place limits on the extent to which Germany might be involved in Habsburg dynastic designs.

The Thirty Years' War began when, in 1618, the Protestant nobility of Bohemia rebelled against their Habsburg ruler, Ferdinand of Styria, who in 1619 was to succeed his childless cousin Matthias as emperor. The rebellion was provoked by Ferdinand's attempt to restore Roman Catholicism by employing tactics contrary to the spirit if not the letter of the conciliatory Royal Charter (*Majestätsbrief* or Letter of Majesty) issued in 1609 by Emperor Rudolf II (the predecessor and brother of Emperor Matthias). By its terms the estates of Bohemia (i.e., the great magnates, the lesser nobility, and the burghers of the cities) had irrevocably been assured both religious freedom and their traditional rights and privileges. This solemn commitment had been formally reiterated by Ferdinand himself when the Bohemian estates had elected him king of Bohemia in 1617. But Ferdinand, who had been educated by Jesuits, was a rigidly militant supporter of the Counter-Reformation. By 1618, he was ready to drop all pretense of tolerance. Not that he broke his promise casually. In the age of the Reformation and the Wars of Religion, promises made to Protestants were often regarded by Catholics, and vice versa, much as commitments to Indians were often regarded on the American frontier: "Promises made to Indians don't count." Since Protestants, by definition, had cut themselves off from civilized Christendom, they should not and indeed could not be treated as Christian gentlemen by a responsible Christian king, such as Ferdinand. Least of all could this be done — according to this narrowly fanatic but once sadly common point of view — when it was clear that honoring a commitment might retard reestablishment of the Catholic church where it had been savagely uprooted, and where nothing less was at stake than the salvation of countless souls otherwise jeopardized by dangerous heresy.

The open breach came on 23 May 1618. A delegation of Protestants entered the great Hradcany Castle in Prague to remonstrate with Ferdinand's royal governors Jaroslav von Martinitz and Wilhelm von Slavata. When they proved predictably intractable, they and a secretary were thrown out a window into a ditch fifty feet below. (Only one of the governors was injured in the incident, a conscious imitation of the defenestration that had signaled the beginning of the Hussite Wars some two centuries earlier.) In August 1619, several months after Emperor Ferdinand II had succeeded Matthias, the Bohemians, having declared the former deposed as king of Bohemia, elected in his place the German Calvinist leader, Elector Frederick of the Palatinate. Defeated at the Battle of White Mountain near Prague just over a year after taking his crown, the "Winter King" fled to Holland. While the emperor set out to extirpate Protestantism and to subjugate the traditionally independent nobility in Bohemia, his Catholic allies in Germany slowly fought their way northward to Jutland and the Baltic coast, forcing the Danes to abandon their Protestant German allies by the Treaty of Lübeck of May 1629. The Catholics' policy of reestablishing the former ecclesiastical principalities that had been secularized since the Religious Peace of Augsburg signaled a dramatic reversal of the ascendancy of Protestantism in northern Germany. Protestant Sweden, however, was not only one of the great powers of Europe in the seventeenth century but also the northern citadel of the Lutheran Reformation. Moreover, King Gustavus II Adolphus was not prepared to see his country's domination of the Baltic challenged by a powerful Catholic empire. Under his leadership, the Swedes succeeded in turning the tide against the imperial coalition. The great Swedish soldier-king fell in battle in 1632, but before long the French, who had already subsidized Gustavus Adolphus, openly entered the war; they were no more willing than the Swedes to tolerate the threat of a Germany dominated by the Habsburgs and their allies, even though preventing it meant supporting the Protestant cause once more, as they had done during the previous century.

Thus the Thirty Years' War ended as an inconclusive contest for control of Germany between the great European powers to the North, West, and East — Sweden, Bourbon France, and the Habsburg Monarchy which, although partly German, drew much of its power from non-German lands within and even beyond the periphery of the empire. Since no one of these three great powers was strong enough to control central Europe

5 / SEVENTEENTH-CENTURY GERMANY

The Thirty Years' War ended in 1648 with the Peace of West-phalia, which established the boundaries shown here. The United Netherlands left the Holy Roman Empire, as did Switzerland, leaving Savoy as a transalpine exclave. Composed of hundreds of nominally sovereign states, the empire had become an impotent zone of fragmentation serving as a central European buffer between the powers on its periphery, particularly the guarantors of the Peace of Westphalia, France and Sweden. With the duchies of Bremen and Western Pomerania, Sweden controlled the mouths of the Weser, Elbe, and Oder. France annexed the formerly Austrian Habsburg Sundgau in upper Alsace, finally acquired undisputed title to Verdun, Toul, and Metz, and assumed administrative jurisdiction over ten Alsatian cities — which it subsequently annexed outright. The Spanish Habsburgs retained the Franche-Comté (Free County of Burgundy) and the Spanish Netherlands (as well as Milan, Sardinia, and the Kingdom of the Two Sicilies). Although the Austrian Habsburgs forfeited their holdings west of the Rhine, they maintained their position to the east of it with the Breisgau on its eastern bank, backed up by their other south central German holdings known collectively as Anterior Austria. To the north, Brandenburg emerged as the strongest German power, acquiring Eastern Pomerania, Minden, and Halberstadt, as well as the right to annex the former archbishopric of Magdeburg with its exclaves, including Halle, on the death of the incumbent administrator, Augustus of Saxony, who lived until 1680.

alone, the Peace of Westphalia, concluded in 1648, perpetuated, insofar as possible, the *status quo ante bellum*. The fragile framework of the Holy Roman Empire was somewhat modified, but in its basic structure it was retained. This was done not because it was satisfactory, but rather because there was no satisfactory alternative. For the next century and a half — until the almost posthumous demise of the empire in 1806 — it would repeatedly be decried as anachronistic, superannuated, a pitiful holdover from another era. Yet it was the only constitution

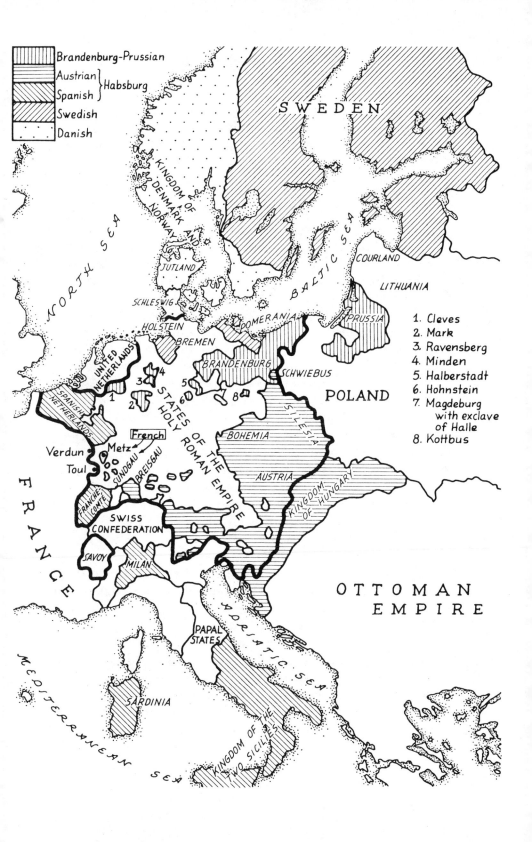

that Germany and central Europe had. Until a more viable one could be developed, or the problem somehow could be redefined and solved in entirely different terms, the tired ghost of the medieval empire was not to be permitted to sink into the pages of history.

By 1648 the princes had finally triumphed in the struggle their forefathers began by siding with Pope Gregory VII against Emperor Henry IV in 1076. The rulers of the three hundred states of the empire were all now granted most of the rights and privileges of sovereignty reserved in the Golden Bull of 1356 for the prince electors alone. They had finally won the legal right to rule over their subjects, and the practical opportunity to exploit them, without significant interference from an imperial overlord. But for many, this long-coveted sovereignty was illusory, affording anything but political independence or economic self-sufficiency, simply because they were too weak to hold their own except by sufferance (and even subsidy) of the great powers. With extensive holdings in north Germany, including much of Pomerania and the duchy of Bremen, Sweden controlled the mouths of the Weser, the Elbe, and the Oder rivers. But despite its still imposing position, Sweden by the mid-seventeenth century had passed its zenith and was to play a steadily declining role in German affairs. To the south and east, the Austrian Habsburgs became increasingly preoccupied with the Turks, who in 1683 besieged the city of Vienna for almost two months, but from whom, by the end of the century, virtually all of Hungary was liberated. Consequently, the influence of the Habsburgs in Germany declined almost as much as that of the Swedes, while that of the French steadily increased. As guarantors of the Peace of Westphalia, they had a legal right to intervene in German affairs — a right they freely exercised as guardians of German particularism.

The empire of Barbarossa had thus been broken down into three hundred principalities, most of them lilliputian fragments, though almost every one had its own army, bureaucracy, court, taxes, customs, and tolls. The empire did maintain its supreme court of law, the Imperial Cameral Tribunal, but it was so inadequately manned and supported that it developed

eighteenth-century princes perhaps as successful in individual contests in the game of power politics, whether domestic or foreign, was the deadly earnestness with which they played it. There was little of sportsmanship and less of the dilettante in any of them; they were playing for keeps. Unlike many of their happier and pleasanter counterparts on potentially as powerful thrones, they worked with withering intensity at the task of building and ruling their state, no more sparing themselves than their subordinates. They made the most even of trivial gains and redoubled their efforts in order to recoup their losses after the setbacks that befell them. They were not all endowed with genius, nor were they consistently blessed with good fortune, but each of the three contributed to the transformation, through intelligent diligence and ruthless opportunism, of a relatively destitute and defenseless collection of holdings inhabited by three quarters of a million into a rich and powerful kingdom of five million with the finest army in Europe.

When Frederick William succeeded to the electoral throne at twenty in 1640, much of Brandenburg was occupied by the Swedes, against whom his father — nominally an imperial generalissimo — had imprudently taken up arms in what was to be the last phase of the Thirty Years' War. Though handicapped by treaty commitments and the loyalty of military and civilian officials to the imperial cause, the young elector succeeded in ending hostilities with Sweden without completely breaking with the Habsburgs. He utilized the tenuous truce, during which he had to accept continued occupation of some of his territories and violation of their neutrality elsewhere, to cut back his father's unmanageable rabble of mercenaries — whose allegiance, for what it was worth, had been sworn to the emperor — to a dependable core of twenty-five hundred, around which he set out to develop a fully reliable standing army. It was only eight thousand strong by the end of the war, but even this modest force helped give him weight enough in the negotiations leading to the Peace of Westphalia in 1648 not merely to emerge unscathed, but to assert the full status of his electoral title as one of the great princes in Germany — less by virtue of overbearing strength than because of the relative weakness of other rulers in a land desolated by decades of warfare.

The core of the Hohenzollern realm that he had inherited in 1640 was, of course, the electoral margravate of Brandenburg. It had been in the Hohenzollern family since the early fifteenth century. Far to the northeast lay the duchy of Prussia. Not only was Prussia — the modern reader may think of it as East Prussia — completely detached from Brandenburg by territories then Swedish and Polish, but it lay beyond the borders of the empire and was held by the elector as a vassal of the Polish king, who had been its overlord since the defeat of the Teutonic Knights in the fifteenth century. During the Reformation, the monastic state had been secularized, on Martin Luther's personal advice, by a grand master of the Teutonic Knights, Margrave Albert of Brandenburg-Ansbach, a member of one of the junior branches of the house of Hohenzollern. But he was also a nephew of the Catholic king of Poland — without whose cooperation the controversial transformation of Prussia into an hereditary Protestant duchy could not have been effected as it was. On the death of the last of the direct heirs of the Brandenburg-Ansbach-Prussian line in 1618, the duchy was transferred to the senior member of the house of Hohenzollern, the elector in Berlin.

In addition to the margravate of Brandenburg and the duchy of Prussia, the Great Elector also inherited, when he acceded in 1640, the counties of Mark and Ravensberg as well as the duchy of Cleves. In themselves, these three principalities, which lay far to the west of his other holdings, comprised a relatively minor part of his total realm, but together they did suffice to assure the active interest in western Germany of the otherwise primarily eastern-oriented ruler of Brandenburg-Prussia.

It was neither predictable nor even probable that the widely separated dynastic holdings of the electoral house of Hohenzollern-Brandenburg — many areas of which were war-torn, impoverished, and largely depopulated in 1640 — would form the nucleus of a powerful state that eventually would incorporate most of Germany and dominate central Europe. It was far more likely that these disparate principalities would drift apart again under the rule of increasingly distant cousins, or that they would remain united only by as tenuous a bond of personal union as that which during various periods in the sixteenth century temporarily brought Spain, Austria, the Netherlands, and Portugal all under a single crown, and later brought Hanover and Great Britain under a single ruler — never, in any case, merging these very different lands into single unified states. The most important reason this never happened was that each of these other realms, like each of the principalities inherited by the young elector, already had its own sophisticated political tradition underpinned with highly enough developed constitutional institutions to resist any attempt to incorporate it into a new centralized monarchy. Although it must be heavily qualified, one can draw an analogy to the empire and the princes: much as the powers of the Holy Roman Emperor were severely circumscribed by the extensive prerogatives of the estates of the empire — the prelates, burghers, and lesser aristocracy, but particularly the greater princes with the electors at their head — the powers of Elector Frederick William were limited by the rights and privileges of the estates of his separate principalities — rights and privileges established by tradition and guaranteed under the laws of each of these states.

As it turned out, however, the Great Elector did not wish to and did not have to accept such limitations. With single-mindedness determination, he ground away at the individual institutional bases of the different states constituting his realm, ultimately imposing upon them all at least a rudimentary centralized bureaucracy. He did not do this for the sake of good government or the enforcement of law and order as such; by and large he depended upon the landed aristocracy — in the East, the *Junker* class — to handle this. The initial impetus and sustaining rationalization for the bureaucratic network he established was to raise men and money for his army. Resistance to the imposition of a centralized, authoritarian system of taxation and administration without adequate local representation took various forms. In Cleves, for example, the legitimacy of the Great Elector's basic hereditary claim to be the legitimate ruler was disputed until 1666, but even when that was settled, the estates continued to maintain their own garrisons until 1672. In short, it took the Great Elector well over thirty years to wear them down. In Prussia, to the East, the situation was if anything more critical, partly because of the peculiar importance of that land to the house of Hohenzollern. By intervening first on the one side and then on the other in a protracted conflict involving Sweden and Poland, the Great Elector secured grudging international recognition of his sole, direct sovereignty — making him ruler of Prussia, not under the king of Poland or the emperor, but under God alone. Thus in Prussia he was sovereign, a king in all but name. However, the Prussian estates did not agree to this freely. They refused homage under the terms he insisted upon as acquiescence in what was openly defined as tyranny. So long as he ruled Prussia only as a Polish duke, they had always had recourse, under the republican constitution of the Polish electoral monarchy, to higher authority. With the elector of Brandenburg as sovereign, rather than a vassal of the Polish king, they would have no recourse whatsoever. Consequently they remained adamant. Finally, in October 1662, the Great Elector landed in Königsberg with two thousand men to reinforce the garrison already there. He trained the guns of Fort Friedrichsburg (which he had already built overlooking the city) on the Prussian capital, and sent a military search party to arrest in his home the head of the Prussian opposition, Hieronymus Roth, president of the old city court and head of the city assembly. There was no open revolt. Within a year the city of Königsberg and the Prussian estates recognized the elector not as a mere Polish duke but as their sovereign under God. Fifteen years later, in 1678, Roth died, still a prisoner — not because the elector refused to release him, but because he refused to submit a formal petition for pardon, conceding guilt, that he had been assured would be granted.

Perhaps the single most important reason so few were prepared to share the fate of Roth — one of the virtually forgotten martyrs of German history — was that the Great Elector made acquiescence attractive and opposition discouraging if not impossible. He could do this by virtue of longevity. It is absurd yet suggestive to imagine, transposing this into the contemporary American frame of reference, how even the more stalwart solons of Capitol Hill might gradually become demoralized if they found themselves pitted against a man like Elector Frederick William for twelve consecutive four-year terms in the White House.

But neither longevity nor force were at work alone. Initially, the leaders of the Prussian estates had apparently not felt that they were in a position to face down the energetic and popular Roth — even had a majority of the members actually wanted to do so. But this seems unlikely, for he obviously had a strong political base in Königsberg and the other towns. As soon as the elector came with his troops and removed him from the scene, however, they showed themselves prepared to listen to the voice of reason — the single most important reason being, namely, that they knew what the estates of Brandenburg had gained by acquiescence to the elector's new regime a decade earlier: a measure of authority and freedom of action in their immediate areas of concern as extensive as that which they conceded to the elector in his. In 1653, the elector had agreed, in return for the support of the Brandenburg estates in establishing a new army on a new basis, to turn over to them virtually unconditional control of their lands and subjects. The holdings they had up to that time occupied merely as vassals were transformed into allodial estates — property they and their heirs could hold and bequeath, in absolute ownership, in perpetuity. As permanent agents of the ruler with police and judicial powers, moreover, they were granted legal control over the lives of their peasants — control so extensive that it did not preclude exercise of the archaic *jus primae noctis,* though where the prerogative was asserted, it increasingly took the form of the so-called virgin tax *(Jungfernzins),* a compensatory monetary payment by the bridegroom.

As his long reign approached its end, the old elector who had laid the foundations of Prussian absolutism aligned himself and his state with relatively liberal Calvinist Holland and its leader, William III of Orange, supporting him in the undertaking that led him to consolidate the English parliamentary monarchy in the Glorious Revolution of 1688–89. Frederick William's close ties with the Dutch dated from his youth, when he had spent several years in Holland. Subsequently he had married a princess of Orange. This policy was natural, for it was an age when political alignments were more often than not defined in religious terms; if Holland were a citadel of Calvinism, the court at Berlin had to be counted one of its most important outposts. That had come about in 1613, when Elector John Sigismund of Brandenburg had embraced Calvinism, which became the family religion of the house of Hohenzollern-Brandenburg, even though the great majority of the population remained Lutheran.* Early in the Thirty Years' War, the Calvinist leader Frederick of the Palatinate, the "Winter King of Bohemia," had lost his electoral throne. Consequently, as that long war drew to a close, Frederick William of Brandenburg was the main champion of the rights of the Calvinists in Germany. Until 1648, they had not formally been given recognition, within the empire, let alone parity with Lutheranism, and the only other Protestant elector, the Lutheran John George of Saxony, strongly opposed doing so in 1648 — but in vain. Calvinism was finally put on an equal footing with Lutheranism. When Louis XIV attacked the Dutch in 1672, their sole ally was Brandenburg; when the French king, thirteen years later, outlawed Protestantism in France, the Great Elector reacted in three weeks, issuing his famous Edict of Potsdam on 8 November 1685, whereby he offered refuge to French Protestants leav-

---

* In 1817, on the tercentenary of Luther's posting of the Ninety-Five Theses, King Frederick William III of Prussia sought to end the religious division between dynasty and people by what proved to be a very controversial state-sponsored merger of Calvinism and Lutheranism: the Evangelical Union (corresponding to the Evangelical and Reformed Church in America). The Great Elector's grandson was far more pragmatic; King Frederick William I had been untroubled by that division. He defined the situation as follows in his political testament of 1722, addressed to his heir, the later Frederick II: "I am a Calvinist, and with God's help I shall die one, but I am assured that a Lutheran who lives a godly life will achieve blessedness as well as a Calvinist, and the difference has been created only by quarrels between the preachers; so hold Calvinists and Lutherans in equal honor, do good to both religions and make no difference between them — God will bless you for it, and you will be beloved on all sides."

ing their homeland because of their faith, assuring them freedom of worship and succor in a number of specifically stated ways. Some twenty thousand Calvinist Huguenots settled in the elector's lands from Cleves to Königsberg, where direct subsidies and privileges, exemption from various services or taxes, and other special measures facilitated their integration into the economy and society of a state they greatly benefited.

In 1685, the very same year French persecution of the Huguenots culminated in Louis XIV's staggering Edict of Fontainebleau, his admirer and sometime pensioner, the Duke of York — for whom New Amsterdam had been renamed when taken by the English as French allies against the Dutch — ascended the English throne as James II. An aggressive Roman Catholic convert and advocate of royal absolutism, James was no more trusted by the great majority of staunchly Protestant Englishmen than his Bourbon mentor. But he did have a daughter who not only had remained Protestant, but had married the leader of the Dutch in their struggle against Louis XIV, her cousin William III of Orange. On his mother's side a grandson of Charles I of England, William was also a nephew by marriage of the Great Elector, with whom in 1685 he concluded a formal treaty of alliance. Frederick William died in the spring of 1688, too early to see the overthrow of James II and accession of his nephew, but his son and successor, Elector Frederick III, followed through on his commitment. At his initiative, forces of the "Magdeburg Concert" of Brandenburg-Prussia, Hanover, Hesse-Kassel, and Saxony were deployed on the Rhine, while he sent strong Brandenburg-Prussian units into the Netherlands to cover William's rear against Louis XIV's anticipated attack, as the Prince of Orange set out for England, accompanied by the Prussian general Friedrich von Schomberg.

Compared with his predecessor and his two successors, Frederick, who ruled from 1688 to 1713, did not dramatically increase either the size or strength of Prussia. He therefore has been unfavorably compared, particularly in traditional patriotic Prusso-German historiography, with the great state- and army-builders Elector Frederick William, King Frederick William I, and King Frederick II. When the Great Elector had come to the throne in 1640, only a few thousand unreliable mercenaries were at his disposal. By the end of his reign in 1688, he had built up a standing army of thirty thousand, not to mention the potential reserve represented by many discharged soldiers farming the royal domains and retired officers serving in the bureaucracy. In terms of military statistics, Frederick did make some further progress: he gradually increased the standing army to forty thousand. But this was modest, compared to the achievement of his son Frederick William I, who in 1740 left Frederick the Great a force of eighty-three thousand, the fourth strongest army in Europe, even though he ruled only the tenth largest state and the thirteenth most populous. The statistics on Brandenburg-Prussian expansion during the single century from 1640 to 1740 are in themselves so impressive that the broader European context of the relatively "unsuccessful" reign of Frederick has often been overlooked. His twenty-five years on the throne, 1688–1713, coincided almost exactly with the last quarter century of the long reign of Louis XIV and the simultaneous series of wars — the Austro-Turkish War, the War of the League of Augsburg, the War of the Spanish Succession, and the Great Northern War — which checked or turned back the French in the West, the Swedes in the Baltic, and the Turks in Hungary. As an ally of the often hard-pressed Habsburg Monarchy, Brandenburg-Prussia played a significant part in these contests that collectively set the stage for the dramatic rise of the Hohenzollern state to great-power status during the following half century.

The value of Frederick's cooperation to Emperor Leopold I (1658–1705) had important implications when he first became prince elector in 1688 and subsequently king in 1701. In 1686, two years before the Great Elector's death, Frederick William had entrusted his will to the emperor as executor. Contrary to the practice of his dynasty (not to mention his image as a modern state-builder), the old elector had left the principalities of Minden and Halberstadt, the county of Ravensberg in Westphalia, and several other substantial holdings to his younger sons. The provisions of the will were a so closely guarded secret that there is no reason to believe that Frederick was aware of them when, without his father's knowledge, he secretly came to a conciliatory understanding of his own with Leopold — on terms that would probably have enraged the Great Elector, but nonetheless served as the point of departure for Austro-Prussian relations for the next several years. Under the circumstances, it was not in the emperor's interest to raise objections when Elector Frederick III voided his father's will and provided private settlements for the disappointed beneficiaries.

Although Elector Frederick III could set aside his predecessor's will as a violation of the binding tradition of primogeniture in the house of Hohenzollern-Brandenburg, thereby assuring the continued unity of the state, he did not feel that he could risk declaring himself king independently. On the basis of his sovereignty in Prussia, he aspired to regal status, but if he were to claim this and then not be recognized, it would be a humiliating fiasco. He therefore sought the prior guarantee of recognition from the senior prince of Christendom, the emperor. Leopold was most reluctant, but finally, in autumn 1700, with the outbreak of war over the Spanish succession imminent, he agreed to a provision in the treaty renewing the Austro-Prussian alliance whereby he committed himself to recognize Frederick's royal dignity as soon as he would proclaim himself king and be crowned. Two months later, in Königsberg on 18 January 1701, Elector Frederick III crowned himself king as Frederick I and as queen his wife Sophie Charlotte, the gifted Hanoverian princess who played so fruitful a role in the cultivation of the arts of peace during his reign, which saw the founding of the University of Halle and of academies of arts and of the sciences, as well as the establishment of a gracious and cultivated court at Berlin, which, with a population of some twenty thousand, began to acquire something of the character of a city and center of culture.

Personally frail and insecure, impressive neither in body nor mind, Frederick found reassurance in the external trappings of power and the flattery of unscrupulous courtiers. The dependable officials he inherited from his father were gradually replaced by a team of avaricious favorites. As in a weak economy bad money has tended to drive out good, weak executives have tended to be more comfortable with incompetent than competent advisers. Frederick's were corrupt in addition, and in 1709 and 1710 their large-scale misappropriations and graft finally began to come to light in the wake of a severe financial crisis precipitated by widespread famine and plague. Though ineffective enough to have been duped, Frederick kept faith with his strong but tactfully respectful son, Crown Prince Frederick William, authorizing the thorough investigation he recommended. This led to changes that prepared the way for radical reform following the crown prince's accession on Frederick's death in February 1713.

As a final act of respect, King Frederick William I accorded his father a costly funeral entirely in keeping with the first Prussian king's lifelong love of solemn grandeur — but it was an act that marked the end not only of a reign but an era. King Frederick William I had found the extravagant formal court of his sire repugnant. Frederick I's costly pretensions of power had rested in large measure on foreign support. This support alone had enabled him to keep his armies in the field — and even to raise their total strength to some forty thousand; and it was this subsidized army alone that had made it possible for Frederick to secure imperial recognition as a king. Within two months of his death and Frederick William's accession, France and Spain, by the terms of the Peace of Utrecht, also formally recognized the royal title of the Hohenzollerns. But so far as Frederick William himself was concerned, it was a hollow dignity, a taunt, and a challenge — one he set out to deal with by the most draconic means. Prussia was weak and had to become independently strong. This could only be accomplished by Spartan discipline and efficiency. Well over half the court officials were dismissed and the cost of the administration was cut in half. The government was centralized under a new General Directory. Most important, however, the army was put on an entirely new basis. Under the Prussian canton system, developed under Frederick William I, each regiment was assigned its own recruiting canton, or district, from which volunteers or, if necessary, conscripts would be enlisted. This did not result in anything approximating what we today would consider an equitable system of universal military service. The soldiers recruited under the Prussian canton system were almost exclusively rural artisans or peasants. But that was intended, for the officer corps of Frederick William's army was drawn from the rural aristocracy, the *Junker* class, whose patrimonial role in rural society corresponded to the authoritarian relationship of officer to soldier in the army. The relationship of the king to the officer corps, on the other hand, was not simply authoritarian. He won the *Junker* officers' loyalty and devotion not only by building up the army, on which the greater part of the state's revenues were spent, but in a more personal sense by identifying himself with them in many ways. After 1725, for example, he was always in uniform — the same uniform as any other officer.

A gruff authoritarian at best, Frederick William could become a short-tempered tyrant when personally challenged. Never was he more directly challenged than by his own eldest son, Crown Prince Frederick. An unusually precocious boy, he developed an early love of music and the arts which his father considered frivolous. As the youth matured and the tension between them grew, Frederick became increasingly devious, his father increasingly harsh. At eighteen the crown prince finally sought to flee. The plot was betrayed to the king by a frightened page. The outraged king arrested and imprisoned Frederick as a deserting officer — which, in fact, he actually was. Moreover, the bitter monarch ordered the execution, in the courtyard of the prince's prison, of the friend who had helped him plan the flight (Lieutenant von Katte, son of a general and nephew of a field marshal, had been court-martialed and sentenced to life imprisonment, and when the court refused to "revise" its sentence, the king imposed his own "revision").

A lesser man might well have been broken by the degrading humiliations — including corporal punishment — that the crown prince endured, but on Frederick it apparently had the effect of tempering genius with a mordant contempt for mankind that intensified as he aged in increasing solitude. He provided in his testament that he be buried on the garden terrace of his palace Sans Souci alongside his little French greyhounds, the only creatures he loved.

Though once in danger of being excluded from the succession by his father, Frederick gradually succeeded in winning his confidence, complying at least outwardly with his wishes, and even being given some opportunity to try his hand at civil administration and military command before his father died in 1740.

His remarkable reign of forty-six years fell into two almost evenly divided segments. The first half was the twenty-three year period of the three Silesian wars from 1740 to 1763. The third of these wars was a part of the more general Seven Years' War, fought in America as the French and Indian War. The series of three wars began when Frederick, soon after coming to the throne, invaded — without provocation or justification — the rich Habsburg province of Silesia. By superior generalship, unscrupulous diplomacy, and extraordinarily good fortune, particularly during the Seven Years' War, he managed to escape imminent defeat by a powerful alliance of the continental European powers and even to assert his conquest of Silesia, Prussia's recognition as one of the major factors in European affairs, and his own reputation as Frederick "the Great."

His second twenty-three years on the throne were an era of reconstruction, consolidation, and growth virtually uninterrupted by war. Frederick well understood how perilously close he had come to utter destruction on the eve of the peace of 1763. Still more important, he clearly perceived how serious a threat the new might of Prussia, with her imposing army and economic resources, represented to the established powers of Europe. Rather than provoking them, therefore, into joining forces against Prussia before she became too dangerous, Frederick carefully steered a conservative course. Not only did he scrupulously refrain from further disturbing the established order, but he took the lead in thwarting Emperor Joseph II of Austria, who sought to convert the moribund empire into a modern German state under the Habsburg dynasty. Yet Frederick was not timorous. Actively cooperating with Austria

6 / EIGHTEENTH-CENTURY GERMANY

The conquest of Habsburg Silesia by Frederick the Great and the Prussian share of the partitions of Poland (between 1772 and 1795, as shown by the insets) made the Hohenzollern monarchy a major northeast European power. Less dramatic than the seizure of Silesia and northwestern Poland, but cumulatively of comparable significance, was the acquisition, especially since the early seventeenth century, of over a score of smaller territories in central and western Europe. The exclave of Kottbus south of Brandenburg had been in Hohenzollern hands since 1462, but Schwiebus, a Habsburg enclave on Brandenburg's southeastern border, was held only briefly in the late seventeenth century and not firmly secured by Prussia until the time of Frederick the Great. Northeastward from Schwiebus, along the Pomeranian border, Draheim, Bütow, and Lauenburg were incorporated into the Hohenzollern realm, although not the Holy Roman Empire, in 1657. The eastern part of Swedish West Pomerania was gained in 1720. Magdeburg and several dependencies, including Halle, came to Prussia in 1680, Neuchâtel (or Neuenburg) in 1707, and, from the last margrave of the Franconian branch of the Hohenzollern dynasty, Ansbach and Bayreuth in 1791. Other acquisitions are given, with dates, directly on the map, which also shows the Spanish Netherlands' having gone to Austria, except for Artois, taken by the French, who by the eve of the French Revolution (1789) also held Lorraine and Alsace except for a few enclaves.

and Russia in 1772, he participated in the first partition of Poland, securing the valuable province of West Prussia, which had divided the eastern and central portions of the Hohenzollern realm.

Traditionally acclaimed by Prussian-oriented patriotic historians to have been one of the most successful rulers in German history, Frederick succeeded, through conquest and negotiation, in doubling the population of Prussia. One of the finest generals of his age, he excelled no less in the arts of peace. An imaginative, dedicated administrator, he systemati-

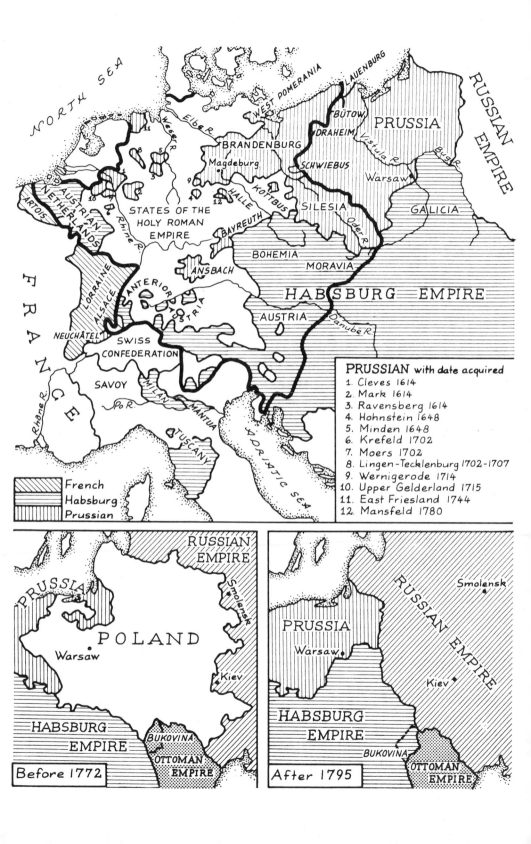

NORTH SEA

RUSSIAN EMPIRE

LAUENBURG

WEST POMERANIA

BÜTOW

PRUSSIA

DRAHEIM

Weser R.

Elbe R.

BRANDENBURG

Vistula R.

Bug R.

SCHWIEBUS

Magdeburg

Warsaw

HALLE

SILESIA

GALICIA

AUSTRIAN NETHERLANDS

STATES OF THE HOLY ROMAN EMPIRE

Rhine R.

HALLE

KOTTBUS

Oder R.

ARTOIS

BAYREUTH

BOHEMIA

MORAVIA

ANSBACH

HABSBURG EMPIRE

LORRAINE

ALSACE

ANTERIOR AUSTRIA

AUSTRIA

Danube R.

F R A N C E

NEUCHÂTEL

SWISS CONFEDERATION

SAVOY

MILAN

MANTUA

Po R.

Rhône R.

TUSCANY

ADRIATIC SEA

PRUSSIAN with date acquired
1. Cleves 1614
2. Mark 1614
3. Ravensberg 1614
4. Hohnstein 1648
5. Minden 1648
6. Krefeld 1702
7. Moers 1702
8. Lingen-Tecklenburg 1702-1707
9. Wernigerode 1714
10. Upper Gelderland 1715
11. East Friesland 1744
12. Mansfeld 1780

French
Habsburg
Prussian

RUSSIAN EMPIRE

PRUSSIA

POLAND

Smolensk

Warsaw

Kiev

HABSBURG EMPIRE

BUKOVINA

OTTOMAN EMPIRE

Before 1772

RUSSIAN EMPIRE

Smolensk

PRUSSIA

Warsaw

Kiev

HABSBURG EMPIRE

BUKOVINA

OTTOMAN EMPIRE

After 1795

cally refined the institutions of government inherited from his forefathers, introduced important economic, agricultural, industrial, and legal reforms, increased the annual revenues of Prussia almost threefold, and left a stored treasure equal to about three years' revenue to his successor.

Among the most illustrious of the enlightened despots of the eighteenth century, his collected works in French fill thirty-three volumes, aside from over forty of political correspondence. He rarely wrote in German and was oblivious to the flourishing of German literature with the works of Lessing, Goethe, Schiller, and other contemporaries. In a passage from an essay on German literature published (in French) in 1780, he observed that "to convince yourself of the bad taste that reigns in Germany, you have only to frequent the theater. You will see the awful plays of Shakespeare translated into our language. . . . Now we have a *Götz von Berlichingen* [by Goethe], a detestable imitation."

One of Frederick's historically most interesting works dates from 1739, the *Réfutation du prince de Machiavel,* in which he denied Machiavelli's contention that the inherent necessities of the exercise of power preclude a ruler, whose actions must be governed by reason of state *(raison d'état),* from observing the normal considerations of law and ethics. But when Frederick came to the throne in 1740, the year Voltaire published his edition of this treatise under the title *L'Antimachiavel,* the young king cast its moral idealism to the winds — and thereafter, throughout his forty-six-year reign, distinguished himself as one of the most unflinching practitioners of Machiavellism.

This does not mean that Frederick was wantonly or arbitrarily base, immoral, or unprincipled. It means, rather, that as king of Prussia, he felt bound neither by conventional morality, international law, nor, least of all, the fear of God, but only by what he considered beneficial to the Prussian state. For Frederick as a statesman, this was the end which justified any means his fertile genius could devise. Many Germans subsequently came to the conclusion that his very success proved beyond doubt the compelling historical validity of such amorality, an approach lent all the more dignity by the selfless dedication with which Frederick II, like his predecessors the Great Elector and Frederick William I, had served the Prussian state. If *"L'état c'est moi"* suggested Louis XIV's egocentric identification of the state with himself, Frederick more earnestly assumed the role of *"erster Diener des Staates,"* the first servant of the state, exalting it above himself, devoting his life to its service, and effectively demanding nothing less on the part of his subjects, particularly the bureaucracy and the army. Established on a solid foundation by his predecessors, these twin pillars of the state were able to carry on after Frederick's death, even under far less able monarchs. Prussia might suffer from lack of energetic leadership by an effective monarch, but its institutional bases of power were nonetheless strong enough to serve, after the humiliating defeat by Napoleon in 1806, as the foundation of a resurgent state which would, within a single lifetime, achieve the unification of Germany under its aegis.

Frederick the Great, who died in 1786, did not live to see the French Revolution, though he had been disturbed by signs of radicalism in France during the later years of his life. His nephew, Frederick William II, who ruled until 1797, was not nearly as much concerned with the epochal events in revolutionary France or their implications for Germany as with maximum aggrandizement of Prussia in the final partitions of Poland undertaken with Austria and Russia. By 1795, therefore, Prussia's halfhearted participation in the first coalition against revolutionary France was ended, Poland was completely dismembered, and Prussia withdrew to the sidelines as the map of Europe was being redrawn.

During the following decade, Napoleon virtually excluded the Habsburgs from Germany, dissolved the Holy Roman Empire and most of the ecclesiastical principalities, annexed Germany west of the Rhine, and formed a satellite confederation of the surviving German states — except for Austria, which had been defeated, and Prussia, which now stood utterly alone. Goaded into a declaration of war, Frederick William III (1797–1840) saw his armies crushed within days in two lightning

7 / THE NAPOLEONIC EPOCH

In 1812 the French Empire was composed of 152 departments (compared to France's 83 twenty years earlier) with some fifty of Europe's estimated 175 million inhabitants. It included the formerly Habsburg Illyrian Provinces on the Adriatic, Rome and much of central Italy, northern Germany as far as Lübeck on the Baltic, and the German enclaves of Erfurt and Neuhaus. In 1803, all but three ecclesiastical principalities of the empire had been abolished; scores of secular princes had lost their lands; and of the forty-eight imperial free cities, only six had survived. A still more drastic wave of reorganization and consolidation began in the summer of 1806 when Napoleon abolished the Holy Roman Empire and established the Confederation of the Rhine. Outlined here with a heavy border, it included by 1812 the four kingdoms of Württemberg, Bavaria, Saxony, and Westphalia, together with thirty-two lesser principalities, but not Austria, repeatedly defeated by Napoleon, or Prussia, which he had crushed in October 1806, driving its king to Königsberg and stripping him of all his holdings west of the Elbe. The Confederation of the Rhine did not survive Napoleon's fall, but the consolidation he brought about abruptly reversed the long trend toward territorial fragmentation in Germany, preparing the way for a more viable political order.

blows, before they could even be assembled, at the twin battles of Jena and Auerstedt in October 1806. Stripped by the Franco-Prussian Treaty of Tilsit the following year of all its territories west of the Elbe as well as the balance of its acquisitions from the partitions of Poland, the Prussian rump state remained little more than a mutilated buffer suffered to exist as a concession to the Russian emperor by his French counterpart as they divided the world from their barge on the Memel River. By 1812 Napoleon so completely dominated central Europe that overt resistance against him was all but extinguished. But he then overreached himself by invading Russia. After he suffered serious reverses there, Prussia, though initially his ally, turned against him, serving as the nucleus of German national resist-

KINGDOM
OF
SWEDEN

Stockholm

Reval

NORTH SEA

KINGDOM OF NORWAY AND

KINGDOM OF DENMARK

BALTIC SEA

COURLAND

Riga

Dvina R.

RUSSIAN EMPIRE

REPUBLIC OF DANZIG

Tilsit

Königsberg

Lübeck

Hamburg

NEUHAUS

KINGDOM OF PRUSSIA

Berlin

Niemen R.

Elbe R.

WESTPHALIA

CONFEDERATION OF THE RHINE

Waterloo

Meuse R.

Rhine R.

ERFURT

SAXONY

GRAND DUCHY
OF
WARSAW

Warsaw

Oder R.

Bug R.

Vistula R.

WÜRTEM-
BERG

BAVARIA

AUSTRIAN
EMPIRE

Danube R.

FRENCH EMPIRE

SWISS
CONFEDERATION

KINGDOM OF ITALY

ILLYRIAN
PROVINCES

Belgrad

OTTOMAN

EMPIRE

ADRIATIC SEA

Elba I.

Rome

KINGDOM OF NAPLES

MONTENEGRO

MEDITERRANEAN SEA

KINGDOM
OF
SARDINIA

Naples

CORFU

IONIAN ISLANDS
(British after 1809)

KINGDOM OF SICILY

The French Empire
The Austrian Empire
The Kingdom of Prussia
Napoleon's non-German Dependencies

ance to the French oppressor during the Wars of Liberation, and furnishing the decisive force for Napoleon's final defeat at Waterloo.

Although the great powers at the Congress of Vienna in 1814–15 attempted, where practical, to restore the old regime, they knew only too well that in Germany the clock could not be turned back. The French Revolution and Napoleon had had such great impact on Europe as a whole and Germany in particular, that in some respects the twenty-five years from 1789 to 1814–15 have come to be regarded, in all seriousness, as one of the most eventful centuries in modern European history.

Following the disaster of 1806, the vacillating Prussian king, Frederick William III, had been obliged to accept revolutionary reforms of the army, the civil administration, and even some aspects of the social structure of the Prussian state, carried out by an exceptionally able group of reformers led by Baron Karl vom und zum Stein, General Gerhard von Scharnhorst, and a number of others. As a result of their work, Prussia was able, despite its crippling losses at the hands of Napoleon, to mobilize, equip, and maintain in the field an army that would have sorely taxed the resources of other states of far greater size and population. In view of this extraordinary demonstration of residual strength and efficient leadership, Prussia was assigned the role at the Congress of Vienna of protecting Europe against any future French aggression. This was achieved by a drastic shift westward of the territorial balance of the Prussian state, which at the end of the eighteenth century had been primarily an eastern European power, the bulk of its territory consisting of what today is East Germany and Poland. But with the establishment of Congress Poland under Russia in 1815, Prussia lost most of what she had gained in the second and third partitions of that unhappy land, and was "compensated" not only by much of Saxony, but above all with a major expansion of her possessions in the Rhineland and Westphalia, making her holdings there larger even than medieval Brandenburg had been and establishing her as the dominant power in northwestern Germany. Any French aggression would consequently involve an early confrontation with the Prussian "watch on the

Rhine." Aside from this, however, the establishment of Prussian Rhineland-Westphalia had two further epoch-making results. In the first place, it made Prussia more than ever before a predominantly German state. Previously Prussia, like the Habsburg Monarchy, had been to a certain extent a peripheral power with a substantial part of her territory lying beyond the borders of the empire. But now the fate of Prussia, a divided kingdom straddling the north European plain from the upper reaches of the Mosel in the Rhineland to the north bank of the Memel in East Prussia, was more inextricably than ever involved with the destiny of Germany. In the second place, the assignment to Prussia of the large block of territory in the Rhineland and Westphalia, lands which Frederick William III and his advisers only very grudgingly accepted as a poor second choice to the entire kingdom of Saxony which they coveted, prepared the way for Prussia to become one of the most economically powerful states in Europe. Though no one knew it in 1815, Rhineland-Westphalia, including the Ruhr and the Saar, was to become in less than a century one of the most productive industrial regions in the world.

3

From 1815 to 1914

❦ The German Confederation

As Germany was reconstituted after the Revolution and the Napoleonic Wars, the influence of Prussia was second only to that of Austria, which held the permanent presidency of the German Confederation, the loosely knit league supplanting the Holy Roman Empire, which Napoleon had abolished in 1806. No attempt was made to restore the radical fragmentation of the prerevolutionary era, during which there had been literally hundreds of separate German states, not to mention well over a thousand independent estates or baronies. On the contrary, the drastic Napoleonic consolidation of the early 1800s was continued to the point that in the diet of the new German Confederation, which functioned as a standing conference of permanent emissaries with diplomatic status, only four free cities and thirty-five rulers were represented: one emperor, five kings (not including the king of the Netherlands and the king of Denmark, who were represented as a German grand duke and a German duke, respectively), one prince-elector, eleven princes, seven grand dukes, and ten dukes.

The face of central Europe had been radically altered since 1789. The revolutionary era had seen epoch-making social, economic, and legal changes. Many of these had come directly at the instigation of the French invader, but others had native roots. One of the most important in defeating Napoleon caused the restored German princes profound concern: the emergence throughout the country of a sense of collective national identity undermining particularistic regional loyalties to individual dynasties. When called upon to take up arms against the invader, countless patriots had selflessly responded — not so much out of loyalty to their individual princes as out of the will to free their fatherland, all of Germany, from the foreign conqueror. Once the Wars of Liberation, as the last phase of the Napoleonic Wars is known in German historiography, ended, many Germans were sickened to learn that their sacrifices had gone merely to secure the thrones of some three dozen princes generally opposed to liberalism and distrustful of the nationalism then widely identified with it.

As postwar disillusionment intensified, crystallizing in sporadic outbreaks of open opposition, the German Confederation was used by the princes to coordinate suppression of overt manifestations of liberalism, particularly in the press and at the universities. This policy was advocated by the influential foreign minister and later chancellor of the Austrian empire, Prince Clemens von Metternich-Winneburg. A German aristocrat from the Rhineland who had followed his father into the service of the Habsburg Monarchy and married the granddaughter of Maria Theresa's chancellor, Prince Kaunitz, Metternich had taken over the foreign ministry after Austria's crushing defeat in 1809, and gradually assumed — by virtue of great ability reinforced by at least equally great self-esteem — a leading role in shaping first the coalition that defeated Napoleon and then the so-called Metternich System that imposed a measure of stability on the continent after twenty-five years of revolution and warfare.

In America today, we tend to take many of the once controversial suppositions of classical liberalism for granted; others we are apt to regard as reactionary rather than radical. But to understand another age, we must try to understand the assumptions and criteria on which its decisions and value judgments were based. In the eyes of the leading conservative statesmen of the restoration in 1815, the previous twenty-five years had been an era of disruption, destruction, and tragedy;

8 / THE GERMAN CONFEDERATION

After the defeat of Napoleon in 1815, neither the Holy Roman Empire nor most of the hundreds of principalities composing it were restored. Instead, the progressive consolidations of the Napoleonic epoch culminated in the establishment of the German Confederation with only thirty-eight (after the addition of Hesse-Homburg in 1817, thirty-nine) states under permanent Habsburg chairmanship. Shown here are Austria, the five kingdoms, and the four free cities of the confederation, as well as two of the seven grand duchies and one of the ten duchies (Holstein). Though three of the four kingdoms of Napoleon's Confederation of the Rhine survived (Bavaria, Saxony, and Württemberg), Jerome Bonaparte's kingdom of Westphalia was divided, part going to Prussia and much of the rest to Hanover, which was reestablished as a kingdom in personal union with Britain. That arrangement had begun in 1714 with the accession in England of the elector of Hanover as King George I and was terminated on the death of King William IV in 1837. Victoria succeeded him in England but not Hanover, where, since dynastic law precluded a ruling queen, her uncle Ernest Augustus, duke of Cumberland, became king. The diet of the German Confederation, composed of emissaries of the German member states meeting in Frankfurt, was suspended during the Revolution of 1848, reestablished in 1850, and finally dissolved as a result of Prussia's triumph in the War of German Unification of 1866.

millions throughout Europe had followed the unspeakable example of the French Jacobins — the revolutionary radicals whose name then sounded as sinister as Bolshevik would later — in dispossessing their masters and deserting the church. The masses had been called to the colors, armed, and set loose to wage battles that might cost more casualties in a single day than once used to be spent in a reasonably well-managed cabinet war. Statecraft abdicated to demagoguery. Guillotines were erected for those who had not otherwise lost their heads. With impunity the mob usurped the sovereignty of the anointed king bearing his crown by the grace of God. By 1814 a measure of

KINGDOMS of
- Bavaria
- Hanover
- Prussia
- Saxony
- Württemberg

GRAND DUCHIES of
- Baden
- Luxemburg

Austrian Empire
Borderline of the German Confederation

order and stability had finally been imposed; but it had been achieved at immeasurable cost and without the slightest certainty that the frightful epidemic of revolution would not again ravage Europe. Therefore it was essential to move swiftly and decisively whenever and wherever an outbreak threatened to occur, lest it spread and start the grievous cycle once more.

Many liberals were no less concerned than restoration conservatives that the social order and the enduring values of society be sustained, but they viewed society differently. It was not a static, authoritarian hierarchy, but rather a complex body comprised of inherently free individuals participating in a dynamic process of continual, inevitable change. This made reasonable accommodation to changing circumstances an unavoidable necessity. But the thought of gradual accommodation, of change brought about in unthreateningly modest steps did not appeal to most early-nineteenth-century German liberals. Had the term then been coined, many would probably have denounced such a proposal as mere tokenism. What they had in mind was the establishment of a liberal German national state with a constitutional monarchy similar to that of Great Britain, the magnificent liberal model — and not for Germans only. All too few advocates of transplanting something like the British system to Germany seemed to understand that its balance and efficiency were the slowly achieved product of several centuries of organic development, punctuated by bitter wars of conquest in Scotland and Ireland plus a grueling civil war followed by a bloodless revolution in the seventeenth century. Their point of departure was rarely an historically sophisticated reflection on how long it had taken the British to strike an elegant institutional balance between the various political, social, and economic interests of the nation, nor how difficult it had been for the leadership of each to develop the self-imposed restraint and discipline that was necessary to keep the system viable. With a few notable exceptions they looked at the British system of government very much as outsiders, liked the design, and argued that it should be adopted in Germany too. It would require a good deal of cooperation, of course, but after all, the people and princes of Germany had proved they could join forces during the Wars of Liberation, the most exhilerating, self-fulfilling experience in living memory. Now all that was needed was to join forces once more, in order to unify Germany in a liberal constitutional monarchy.

It was understandable that they should have thought in terms of their own experiences and perceptions, remembering what they saw as an unforgettable demonstration of how the German people, the petty political boundaries dividing them notwithstanding, could effectively cooperate with each other, if only given a chance. But giving them such a chance would require forcing or finessing an unprecedented transfer of power away from the three dozen German princes who had mastered the art of holding on to it — as attested by the simple fact that they alone, of over ten times their number a generation earlier, had retained their sovereignty. They had no intention, in the years following 1815, of giving away anything that was not absolutely necessary. The thirteenth article of the constitution of the German Confederation did call for each member state to have a constitution providing for representation — to be a parliamentary monarchy, in other words. But this was a formal concession, not a serious commitment to liberalism; in relatively few states was the provision honored literally, and in still fewer honored in the spirit of liberalism as practiced on the Thames.

❧ THE REVOLUTION OF 1848

ONLY IN 1848 did the princes abruptly respond to the liberals' demands, giving them the chance they sought to design a liberal German national state. It happened in 1848 because the fever of revolution incited by the overthrow of the monarchy in France broke the spell of princely omnipotence east of the Rhine. The rulers of "the Germanies," as the confederated German states often were referred to collectively, agreed with improbable alacrity to what a generation earlier would have been unthinkable. They acquiesced in the popular election of a German National Assembly in Frankfurt, and the diet of the German Confederation formally disbanded, assigning its prerogatives to the new body. Thus Germany had its first major nationwide revolution. But whereas the English Revolution of the seventeenth century, the French Revolution of the eighteenth, and the October Revolution in twentieth-century Russia each saw the old regime overthrown and the ruler killed, the Revolution of 1848 did not topple a single German dynasty. Instead, the people elected as distinguished a parliament as the world has ever seen. It drafted an impressive liberal constitution that defined, for the first time, the liberal consensus in Germany, and described the political framework within which it was to operate. This constitution, as drafted and approved by the representatives of the people, was also recognized by twenty-eight of the thirty-nine German governments. But soon it became clear that to the most important of them it was unacceptable. Thereupon the revolutionary movement came to an end. In many areas it almost respectfully stopped. In others, it had to be halted with force at the cost of extensive bloodshed — particularly in the southwest, where many refused to bow down once more to petty princes, preferring to die or be exiled for their convictions. Their fate dramatized not only their inability to achieve in Germany what they had set out to do, but also what Germany lost, in human terms, through their suppression. Germany's loss through the wave of emigration following the debacle of the mid-century revolution is personified by no one better than Carl Schurz, who fled Germany with a price on his head and served the United States as diplomat, general, senator, secretary of the interior (where he established the civil-service merit system), and journalist (including periods as editor of the New York *Evening Post* and as chief editorial writer for *Harper's Weekly*).

There were many aspects to the fateful collapse of the Revolution of 1848. It broke out shortly after the publication of the *Communist Manifesto,* and there was considerable working-class involvement. But on the whole, the revolution was sustained by the middle classes, and in 1848 they still were relatively weak. The industrial revolution was barely getting under way in Germany. The economy remained predominantly agricultural. Even the largest cities were little more than over-grown towns by the standards that we tend to apply today — standards that make it all but impossible to picture in our minds life as it actually was lived as recently as a century and a quarter ago — not to mention before the great watershed of the French Revolution and Napoleon. (At the beginning of the nineteenth century, for example, only two German cities had more than a hundred thousand inhabitants: Berlin and Hamburg.)

The middle classes of Germany, from which the movement to unify the nation as a liberal parliamentary monarchy drew its chief support, were not in themselves strong enough to impose their will on the princes, nor were they able to redress the balance by winning sustained support from the masses for their cause. In addition to being numerically, economically, and politically weak, the German middle classes and their representatives, who overwhelmingly dominated the National Assembly at Frankfurt, were divided in terms of the perspectives and interests of their three dozen states of origin.

Under the circumstances, what is surprising is not that they achieved so little, but rather that they achieved so much. They created a liberal program and an impressive proposal for its implementation by princes uncompromisingly opposed to liberalism. Moreover, they realistically grappled with another problem that they could neither ignore nor solve: the question whether or not the new Germany should include parts of the Austrian Empire that lay within the boundaries of the German Confederation. The dream of the patriots was, after all, to unite their countrymen in one great fatherland from which they could no more wish to exclude the Austrians than the Bavarians, Westphalians, or Prussians. Yet even if only the lands of the Austrian Empire affiliated with the German Confederation were to be included in the new state, millions of non-Germans would also have to be made German citizens, for within the borders of the Habsburg Monarchy as a whole, the non-Germans by far outnumbered the German inhabitants. The non-

Germans might have been denied the right to vote, of course, but that would have been a flagrant violation of one of the fundamental principles of liberalism, which was as strong a force in 1848 as nationalism. Another theoretical possibility would have been to disregard the borders of the German Confederation that included, in the confederated area of Austria, both Bohemia (largely Czech) and southern Tyrol (largely Italian), and simply to draw a new line ethnographically redividing the entire Austrian Empire into a purely German part for incorporation into the new fatherland and a non-German part for some looser form of affiliation or association. But even had geographical partition been politically feasible, no such line could have been drawn because of the way in which both Germans and non-Germans were interlaced throughout most of the monarchy. It soon became a moot question in any case, for it became obvious that the implacable hostility of the imperial government in Vienna would preclude Austrian cooperation in the first place. The majority of the Frankfurt Assembly therefore sadly voted to exclude Austria from the new Germany and to offer an hereditary imperial crown to the king of Prussia.

They did not make this decision lightly. Certainly they did not make it because they liked King Frederick William IV of Prussia (1840–61). They offered him the crown because they had no chance whatsoever of establishing an all-German parlimentary monarchy without Prussia, and because there was no chance of Prussia being induced to enter into it if any dynasty but the Hohenzollern were to bear the imperial crown. Had Austria not been excluded, the Habsburgs would certainly have had to be considered. But as things stood, the representatives of the German people had no practical alternative but to elect Frederick William IV German emperor with the understanding that his dynasty would retain the dignity on an hereditary basis.

No matter how delicately the matter was put, however, being elected emperor by representatives of the people was an entirely different thing than being king by the grace of God. Frederick William IV had no intention of profaning the proud

was less tainted by liberalism and that would greatly have increased the influence of Prussia at the expense of Austria. This was the Prussian Union plan conceived by his able foreign minister, General Joseph Maria von Radowitz. This Prussian Union — not to be confused with the Prussian-sponsored Tariff Union or *Zollverein* — provided for a confederation of German states around Prussia in perpetual alliance with Austria, which would consequently be deprived of its dominance in Germany. The Prussian Union of 1850 was thus Berlin's answer not only to the Frankfurt Constitution of 1849 but also to the Austrian-dominated confederation established after the defeat of Napoleon. Germany should indeed be a confederation, but under the Hohenzollern rather than the Habsburg dynasty, and by the will of the princes rather than the will of the people expressed through their representatives in a national assembly. Meanwhile the Austrians recovered from the multiple shocks that in 1848 and 1849 had threatened to shatter the monarchy, reactivated the old confederation (which, as noted, was disbanded in 1848), reassumed the chairmanship, and called on the formerly participating states to send their delegations as before. Since the consolidation of the new Prussian Union was already well under way, the lines were drawn. In the fall of 1850, Austria with the old German Confederation faced Prussia with her new body of German states.

Austria and Prussia had both opposed the liberal aspirations of the Frankfurt Assembly to establish a parliamentary monarchy. But the question of nationalism was an entirely different one. The Habsburg Monarchy could no more afford to countenance nationalism than liberalism. The cement which held the multinational empire together, dynastic authority from above, loyalty to the dynasty from below, would be as quickly dissolved by nationalism on the part of the subject nationalities as by the liberalism with which they sought to rationalize their demands for autonomy or even independence. For Prussia, on the other hand, nationalism could be extremely useful. During the Wars of Liberation against Napoleon, King Frederick William III had, albeit most hesitatingly, raised the standard of German nationalism and elicited a strong response throughout much of Germany. In 1849 the representatives of the German people had turned once more to Berlin, offering Frederick William IV a German imperial crown. In Austria, nationalism was a dangerously divisive force threatening to disintegrate the Habsburg Monarchy altogether — as it ultimately did. In the rest of Germany, on the other hand, nationalism was a cohesive, integrating force that was capable of uniting the three dozen separate states around Prussia. But the attempt to achieve this in 1850 proved to be premature. When it came to a showdown between the Prussian Union and the German Confederation, the Austrians were able to secure decisive Russian backing against Prussia. Faced with the prospect of a war he could not possibly win, Frederick William IV had to accept the "Humiliation of Olmütz" (November 1850), precipitately disbanding the Prussian Union and rejoining the German Confederation. Yet despite the fact that Germany thus entered the 1850s with Austria still in the lead politically, Prussia's growing economic strength made her an increasingly serious rival. While the Austrians had been able, with Russian backing, to thwart the political organization of Germany in the Prussian Union, they were powerless to arrest the economic consolidation of Germany taking place largely within the framework of the Prussian-led Tariff Union *(Zollverein)* — from which they were excluded.

Ironically, the *Zollverein* had originated as a reluctantly accepted necessity forced upon Prussia by its geographic division. After 1814, Prussia held the Rhineland and Westphalia in western Germany, but had no land bridge between these new acquisitions and the ancient core of the kingdom in northern central Germany. The Prussian customs law of 1818, the point of departure for what developed into the *Zollverein,* was not, in its inception, a farsighted attempt to unify the non-contiguous segments of the Hohenzollern kingdom, let alone unify Germany, even economically; the fact is that in 1818, different tariff rates were introduced for the eastern and western parts of the kingdom. The goal of Prussian tariff policy, as it gradually evolved, was not to lower customs duties but rather to abolish them altogether. In the course of a number of years, the

Prussian system was extended throughout the greater part of Germany. Many of the German states joined only with the greatest reluctance, correctly apprehensive that membership would inevitably increase their economic dependence upon Prussia. But the smaller ones in particular found it impossible to operate their own customs systems at a profit, whereas they did enjoy relatively large and regular returns of revenue from the joint venture. Moreover, at a time when an extensive network of roads, canals, and railways was being planned and developed throughout central Europe, refusal to participate in dismantling tariff barriers could mean being bypassed and left to languish in economic isolation. Formal pretensions to sovereign independence notwithstanding, one German state after another found itself unable to resist being drawn into the Prussian economic sphere. The two that held out longest were able to do so because of unique circumstances; as major European entrepôts of overseas trade, the free city-states of Bremen and Hamburg not only stayed out of the *Zollverein* prior to unification, but remained aloof for another decade and a half thereafter, maintaining commercial extraterritoriality as duty-free port cities politically but not economically integrated into the German Empire.

Special as the circumstances of the two great seaports may have been, their case does illustrate the fact that economic integration and political unification are two very different matters and that in nineteenth-century Germany one by no means smoothly and inevitably accompanied the other. Economically speaking, the work of unification was well advanced when Otto von Bismarck was called to Berlin in 1862 and named minister president by William I. Since October 1857, when his brother Frederick William IV had suffered the breakdown from which he never recovered, William had ruled Prussia, first as regent, then, on his brother's death in 1861, as king. William did not name Bismarck Prussian minister president in order to have him unify Germany, nor was this Bismarck's concern when named to the highest appointive office in the state. During almost three decades in executive office, his extraordinary gifts were devoted, like those of Frederick the Great during the previous century, to furthering the welfare, as he understood it, of the Prussian state. It was to strengthen Prussia, not to gratify German nationalism, that he engineered the Prussian conquest of Germany and made the Prussian king German emperor. Before he could even concern himself with establishing Prussia's place in Germany and Germany's in the world, he had to contend with the grave domestic crisis that had led to his very unlikely appointment in the first place.

A senior diplomat, the forty-seven-year-old Bismarck had already held the three most important posts in the Prussian foreign service, representing his king in the diet of the German Confederation in Frankfurt, at the court of Tsar Alexander II, and at the court of Napoleon III. Well into his sixties, a man of strong character and integrity with a sound though not intellectually impressive mind, William was too self-disciplined, too conscientious, and too responsible not to regard it as his duty to enlist the services of the one man apparently equal to the challenges of the hour, even though he did not particularly like him.

Already a relatively well-known public figure, Bismarck was detested by many liberals as a reactionary somewhere to the right of Ivan the Terrible. His public role and reputation was not what disturbed the king and his confidants, however, but rather the imperious audacity he had shown in conferences, dispatches, and semiprivate correspondence alike. Although a loyal servant and subject of his king, Bismarck had a quality of intellectual sovereignty, and the articulateness and intensity to sustain it, that made him most uncongenial to superiors and sovereign alike. Not that he was explicitly threatening or even condescending; he was not. But by sheer force of mind and personality he had commanded attention and respect out of proportion even with the considerable status of the high diplomatic posts he had held. Evaluating one of his most striking reports, a very long handwritten letter to Baron von Manteuffel, the Prussian minister president and foreign minister, brilliantly analyzing the transformed European situation at the end of the Crimean War, one of Bismarck's most critical biographers observed that at that time "there was certainly no one in the entire German-speaking realm capable of writing an historical-political reflection of this style in this language." *

The crisis that led to his appointment had grown out of the general staff's army reform program, strongly supported by the king, an old soldier himself. The lower chamber of the Prussian legislature, the House of Delegates or the *Landtag,* dominated by a liberal majority, bitterly opposed it. When the crown refused to compromise on the key issues, the liberals blocked the budget. The king was adamant, rejecting any settlement that would weaken the army or — since this had become a test case between crown and diet — weaken the monarchy itself.

In the months during which the protracted conflict gradually came to a head, William weighed the painfully narrow range of options he considered open to him, including abdication in favor of his son and heir, Crown Prince Frederick William (who only in 1888 was finally to accede, dying of cancer, as Emperor Frederick III). A son-in-law of Queen Victoria and her late prince consort, the liberal Albert of Saxe-Cobourg-Gotha, and himself the son of a princess from liberal Weimar, the crown prince consciously identified himself with liberalism. When the crisis reached its climax with the resignations of the Prussian finance and foreign ministers, who saw no way to go on in view of the fiscal blockade of the legislature, the king summoned Bismarck and informed him that he was considering abdication rather than compromise. Neither was necessary, the *Junker* responded; the king had the responsibility and authority to see to it that the military establishment not merely be kept barely abreast of the times, but that it be thoroughly reorganized, reequipped, and professionalized.

Professionalization was the crucial issue. In the eyes of War Minister Albrecht von Roon (who had not resigned from the

---

* The distinguished liberal historian Erich Eyck, discussed in the Selected Bibliography, was referring to the so-called *Prachtbericht* — a coined term translated literally but with a trivial banality foreign to the original German as "splendid report" — published as Document 152 in the second volume of the older standard (*Friedrichsruher*) edition of Bismarck's collected works (Bismarck, *Die gesammelten Werke,* vol. 2 [Berlin: Otto Stollberg, Verlag für Politik und Wirtschaft, 1924], pp. 138–45).

cabinet with the finance and foreign ministers), Bismarck, and the king, it was necessary to eradicate all traces of "civilianization." The spirit of the "citizen in arms" had been introduced into the Prussian military system during the Napoleonic Wars. Mobilization of all human resources, irrespective of origins and character, might have been necessary then as a matter of survival, but the time had come to purge the army of unsuitable elements. When he had been crown prince (or, as he came to be known after 1848, "cartridge prince"), William himself had led Prussian units into south Germany during the mid-century revolution, and he personally had seen how ill-suited militiamen or reservists were for the rough task of suppressing civic disorder. He now was determined to build a dependable army of unquavering professionals equal to any task that might be assigned to them. In January 1861, within weeks of his brother's death and his becoming king rather than regent, William had outraged liberal opinion by separating thirty-six infantry regiments of the militia from the army and replacing them by thirty-six regiments of regulars. The vehement reaction of the liberal majority in the Prussian lower chamber only reinforced the king's determination not to compromise on his army reform program. Bismarck promised, in the spirit of "an electoral Brandenburg vassal who sees his liege lord in danger," as he put it, that, should the king have the confidence in him to vest him with the necessary authority, he would support the military reform, govern against the majority, and, if necessary, govern without a constitutionally approved budget.

Appointed minister president and foreign minister by William, Bismarck immediately sought to overcome the deadlock if possible. He was prepared to go farther in his compromise efforts than he had led the king to expect. But the olive branch he (literally) proffered the liberal opposition was refused. He then embarked on a new course. He neither compromised his differences with the liberal opposition nor insisted on a showdown. Instead, stressing that the opposition was shamelessly trying to usurp exclusive control of the budget, despite the prerogatives of the crown, Bismarck set out to govern as normally as possible but as ruthlessly as necessary. Officials were formally enjoined to show "unity of spirit and will" with the administration, or take the consequences — which were so dire in a series of exemplary cases that the bureaucracy was soon a model of efficiency and loyalty to Bismarck. A press control ordinance provided that publication of newspapers and journals might be forbidden on the basis of their "overall stance" *(Gesamthaltung)*. Tax monies were collected and allocated without legislative authority, and other fiscal resources, such as railway revenues, were tapped by the government in its determination to improvise funding.

Since neither the liberal opposition nor the Bismarck administration was prepared to compromise, the political impasse in Prussia assumed the character of an indefinite stalemate. The liberals were apparently confident that Bismarck, as a hopelessly reactionary relic of a former age, would sooner or later fully discredit himself, whereas he, singularly confident that time was on his side and that he could handle whatever it might bring, accepted the frigid deadlock as tactically advantageous for the crown.

Though he came to office because of a grave crisis in Prussia, Bismarck is remembered less for his approach to that than for the manner in which he dealt with a far older historical problem — the German question. He had no preconceived plan to unify Germany. Unification as such was not the immediate issue, but rather the Austro-Prussian rivalry in central Europe. Many a patriotic German writer has represented Bismarck as having taken office in order to realize the centuries-long thwarted aspirations of the German people, but there is very little evidence of strong nationalistic aspirations in Germany before the nineteenth century. Be that as it may, unification in the end actually evolved from year to year, from crisis to crisis, out of the struggle between Austria and Prussia to dominate Germany. By 1862, when Bismarck became Prussian minister president, the economic influence of Prussia throughout much of Germany had come to seem so ominous that many German states more than ever before looked to Vienna as a vital counterweight against political domination by the Prussian colossus in their midst. Fully conscious of this, the resourceful Austrians seized and sustained the diplomatic initiative during the early 1860s. With the support of the greater number of the German princes, who had come to feel that they had far more to fear from the house of Hohenzollern than from that of Habsburg, Vienna pressed for reforms of the German Confederation which, if implemented, would have had the general effect of strengthening the central organization as a whole and diminishing within it the influence of Prussia in relation to Austria. Only with the greatest difficulty did Bismarck succeed in persuading King William to boycott the Frankfurt Congress of Princes in August 1863, at which the Austrian reform plan was to have been agreed upon.

The Austrian project was thwarted, but Prussia remained diplomatically on the defensive, especially as its prestige throughout Germany and Europe continued to be compromised by the scandalous conflict with the legislature and, after 1863, also by Prussia's notorious Polish policy. At the beginning of 1863, a desperate Polish rising against the Russians had aroused widespread sympathy not only in western Europe, but also in liberal and in Catholic circles in Germany, including the west German provinces of Prussia on the Rhine. Bismarck, seriously concerned about the impact that any liberalization in the parts of Poland held by Russia might have in those held by Prussia, sent the king's aide-de-camp, General Gustav von Alvensleben, to the tsar on a mission of ostentatious solidarity. Thereby he dramatized unequivocal support for the diplomatically isolated Russians in their savage repression of the rebellion, but also put the seal on a new dynastic solidarity between the Romanovs and Hohenzollerns, without which the unification of Germany during the succeeding decade would have been, to say the least, far more difficult to achieve.

Back in 1850, Tsar Nicholas I had sided with Austria and forced the Prussians to accept the "Humiliation of Olmütz." The tone of Russo-Prussian relations began to change when, during the Crimean War (1853–56), Prussia had refused to go along with Austria in supporting the western powers against Russia. When Bismarck, who was known in St. Petersburg from his years as ambassador there, followed up with the Alvensleben Convention in 1863, Alexander II and his advisers knew that while it would be irresponsible to place naïve trust in the men in Berlin, they could probably be depended upon to show sound judgment in matters of mutual concern. They seemed to have a realistic understanding of the kinds of problems posed by the Austrians and the Poles. They were solid conservatives.

Later in 1863, Bismarck seized on a comparatively minor diplomatic crisis and cultivated it into a singularly favorable opportunity for Prussia to improve its weak position within Germany. Prussia was certainly not isolated, but in today's public-relations terms, it was widely felt that Berlin was in trouble, that William was gradually losing his grip, and that Bismarck was a sure loser. This bleak image, representing the opinion of many in Prussia as well as the rest of Germany, was dispelled by Bismarck's canny management of a crisis involving the Danish-German border duchies of Schleswig and Holstein, which formed what might be considered an isthmus between Germany and Denmark. Their duke was the king of Denmark, but they were not part of the Danish kingdom itself. Schleswig, which lay immediately south of the Danish border, was inhabited by many Germans as well as Danes. Holstein, adjoining Schleswig to the south and politically united with it for centuries, was predominantly German and, unlike Schleswig, a state in the German Confederation.

In November 1863, a new, nationalistically inspired constitution was promulgated for the kingdom of Denmark. It did not provide for the immediate formal annexation of the two duchies, but it included provisions that clearly pointed the way toward their eventual incorporation into the kingdom — a natural enough step, in the eyes of its advocates, considering that the Danish king was also their duke, and that so much of the population was Danish.

There was widespread sentiment in Germany in favor of transferring the united duchies, or at least Holstein, from the rule of the new Danish dynasty, which had just come to the throne in 1863 at the time the new constitution was promulgated, to that of the German house of Schleswig-Holstein-Sonderburg-Augustenburg. In terms of dynastic law, the head

of the house of Augustenburg had at least as strong an hereditary claim as the new Danish ruling house of Schleswig-Hol-
stein-Sonderburg-Glücksburg. At the initiative of Bismarck,
however, Austria and Prussia disregarded the popular Augustenburg pretender, subordinating considerations of dynastic
law to the inviolability of international compacts. In January
1864 they presented Denmark with an ultimatum to rescind the
November constitution insofar as it affected Schleswig-Holstein, and to restore the *status quo ante* in accordance with the
London Protocol of 8 May 1852, of which Denmark, Austria, and
Prussia had all been signatories — a seven-power agreement
that had ended an earlier crisis over Schleswig-Holstein which
had led to brief German-Danish hostilities. The Danes, counting on British and Russian support if necessary, refused to
comply with the January 1864 ultimatum. Thereby they seriously miscalculated. It is true that they controlled the sole gate
to the Baltic, much as Gibraltar controlled what was still the
sole gate to the Mediterranean, and that in the crisis fifteen
years earlier both Britain and Russia had shown considerable
solicitude regarding Denmark because of their economic and
strategic interest in the Baltic and North seas and the passage
between them. But by the early 1860s, the British had far more
urgent concerns than Baltic problems, while the Russians had
been strongly impressed by Prussia's benevolent neutrality
during the Crimean War, not to mention the more recent Alvensleben Convention. Bismarck, moreover, made it clear that
Prussia's only concern in the intervention was to uphold the
inviolability of past international agreements; nothing would
be done to harm the legitimate interests of the Danish monarchy as such. Consequently the Danes stood, fought, and fell
alone. By midsummer, the war was over. The Danish king was
forced to surrender the duchies, which had, of course, not been
part of Denmark, to Austria and Prussia.

The victors first ruled Schleswig-Holstein jointly, but it was
an abrasive condominium. Provisions were made by the terms
of the Austro-Prussian Gastein Convention of 14 August 1865 for
the duchies to be administered separately, Prussia occupying
Schleswig to the north, Austria Holstein to the south. This ar-

rangement was also short-lived. The Austro-Prussian comrade-ship in arms against the Danes had been prompted less by solidarity than mutual distrust. The Austrians certainly would not have wanted to risk letting the Prussians go it alone. The Austro-Prussian rivalry for domination of central Europe, which went back to the Silesian Wars between Frederick the Great and Maria Theresa, and had flared up once more in the aftermath of the revolutions of 1848, had not been resolved. Analyzing Austro-Prussian relations while still Prussian min-ister to the German Confederation, Bismarck had written in 1856 (in the famous letter to Baron von Manteuffel mentioned above) that "Germany is too small for us both; so long as no honorable arrangement has been made and executed concern-ing the influence belonging to each in Germany, we shall both plow the same disputed field, and so long will Austria remain the only state to which we can permanently lose and from which we can permanently gain."

Now that he was in charge of Prussian policy, Bismarck exploited the Schleswig-Holstein issue to bring about the final decision he regarded as inevitable in central Europe, carefully preparing the diplomatic setting for the showdown. This was essential because the vital interests of other powers than Prussia and Austria were involved. Central Europe, as struc-tured at the Congress of Vienna, had been dominated by Prussia and Austria, but less in partnership than with each as a check and balance to the other, and with the three dozen lesser states — the "middle states" or "third Germany" — as in-voluntary guarantors if not hostages of the equilibrium be-tween Berlin and Vienna. Any radical shift in the balance of power in central Europe would have serious implications for the other European powers; establishment of Prussian he-gemony in Germany at Austria's expense would represent the emergence of a potentially dangerous neighbor on the borders of France and of Russia. Sanguine French and Russian ideal-ists might vicariously rejoice with their German friends that the "German Question" was finally being given a clear answer in the Austro-Prussian war, but their less naïve countrymen could be expected to reach much the same sort of conclusion as hard-headed Americans might today if they learned of the establishment south of our border of a militant totalitarian union of all the Latin American states — with nuclear first-strike capability. Such an event would not, in itself, diminish our own armed forces by one enlisted man, but insofar as national security largely depends upon military strength, and strength is a relative thing, such an event would cause grave concern in Washington and elsewhere.

Bismarck could reasonably anticipate much the same kind of concern in the capitals of Europe, particularly if he failed to undertake careful diplomatic preparations. It was not likely that the English would feel immediately threatened, for their immediate interests were not at stake — though they certainly would be very much concerned if the overall European balance of power were gravely disrupted. Because the newly established kingdom of Italy had not yet been able to wrest Venetia — the great canal city at the head of the Adriatic, together with its rich hinterland — from Austria, it could be brought (or bought) into play. Accordingly, Bismarck negotiated a secret alliance providing for an Italian attack on the Habsburg Monarchy from the south, in return for which he would support Italian acquisition of Venetia. As for Russia, where Bismarck was known and respected, relations were such, especially in view of the Alvensleben Convention, that there would be no immediate problems.

Though he could count on a period of limited freedom of action in regard to England and Russia, Bismarck knew the situation with France was radically different. Thus he took pains to neutralize Emperor Napoleon III, whom he met in Biarritz in October 1865. As in the case of Russia, his ambassadorial experience provided personal acquaintance with the emperor and his court. No formal record of their Biarritz conference has survived, but Bismarck apparently left the impression that in case of a Prussian victory in a possible war against Austria, France might reasonably expect compensations in western Germany on her eastern border. Their gentleman's agreement was, however, not prematurely defined, for Bismarck had no intention of promising more than absolutely necessary, in case the war were quickly decided, whereas Napoleon, assuming the war could be a long one, had every intention of doing as well as he possibly could for France when the time came for intervention or mediation — either of which could fetch a very high price.

Although war was considered unavoidable in both Berlin and Vienna, neither side being willing to turn from what was clearly a collision course, it was, in a technical sense, the Austrians who actually precipitated the crisis. They did so by breaking the formal agreements they had made with Prussia regarding Schleswig-Holstein, insofar as they unilaterally turned the question over to the diet of the German Confederation and convened the Holstein diet to consider the future of the duchy. Bismarck responded by ordering Prussian troops into Holstein. Within a few days the German civil war had begun — little more than a year after the end of the American. Prussia, with a few small north German principalities as allies, faced Austria and the balance of Germany. Not only did Prussia, a state of eighteen million, oppose an empire of almost twice her population, but Hanover and Electoral Hesse, two Austrian allies, lay between the two parts of the Hohenzollern kingdom. Despite these disadvantages, the new Prussian army, which had received its baptism of fire in Denmark under the brilliant generalship of Helmuth von Moltke (who had studied the American Civil War, particularly the use of railroads and telegraph), defeated the Austrians in three weeks — to the amazement of Europe and consternation of Napoleon III. The decisive battle took place near Königgrätz in present-day Czechoslovakia. Although it was a crushing defeat for the Austrians, it need not have ended the war. The Habsburg Monarchy was by no means ready for ignominious capitulation. The Prussians would have had to fight much longer had they wanted to conclude the war with a triumphal march through Vienna. But Bismarck succeeded in persuading King William to give up all thought of further triumphs and to tender such mild terms to Austria that peace was concluded less than two months after the outbreak of hostilities.

Thus before the summer of 1866 was over, the map of Europe

had been redrawn. The Italians, though defeated in the field, received Venetia. The German Confederation was abolished and replaced by a North German Confederation under the domination of Prussia, which also annexed Schleswig, Holstein, Hanover, Electoral Hesse, and several other German states outright. But the territorial integrity of the Habsburg Monarchy was respected. So little cause for rancor was given and so perspicaciously were Austrian interests respected that Austria remained neutral during the Franco-Prussian war four years later and within another decade was prepared to conclude the Dual Alliance and become Germany's staunchest ally.

With the victory over Austria in 1866 the question of German unity was all but decided. The surviving German principalities north of the Main River were locked into the North German Confederation. Those south of the Main were economically and militarily tied to Prussia through the significantly restructured and strengthened *Zollverein* coupled with a system of far-reaching defense pacts with Berlin. Thus ended the long-standing Austro-Prussian dualism in Germany, and, with it, the freedom of the lesser princes to play the two major German powers off against each other. The surviving German princes, whatever their titles and pretensions, were now all more or less clients of the Hohenzollern king in Berlin.

The Austro-Prussian War prepared the way not only for German unity but also for settlement of the political crisis in Prussia that had not been resolved during the four years since the beginning of Bismark's ministry. Just as the Prussian *Junker* prevailed over his king in the matter of peace terms with Austria, he was also able to celebrate a fatefully historic triumph over the liberals in the lower chamber of the Prussian legislature: after governing against the *Landtag* for four years, he won by a more than three-to-one vote (230 to 75), retroactive approval of the unconstitutional budgets of the interim years. The liberals had not been defeated at the polls. The majority of the erstwhile champions of parliamentary monarchy capitulated in this decisive test of strength with the Hohenzollern autocracy because they were caught up in the rise of German nationalism triggered by the spectacular triumphs of Prussian diplomacy and arms under Bismarck and Moltke. The combined forces of nationalism and liberalism had proved unable in 1848 to solve the problem of German unity, but now Bismarck had done so through a combination of skillful diplomacy and unflinching use of the new Prussian army. The triumphant nationalists were deluding themselves, however, insofar as they automatically identified Bismarck with their ideal of a unified Germany. Although he exploited nationalist sentiment in order to manipulate public opinion, he was motivated far less by love of the German nation than by loyalty to the Hohenzollern dynasty he served and — increasingly, as the years went on — to the Hohenzollern state that he had created and that he governed.

While the Prussians during the late 1860s methodically consolidated their hegemony of Germany, the French, soon realizing how vain had been their hopes for compensations in 1866, gradually became aware also of how great a potential threat confronted them from across a frontier where only a few years before they had bordered on dozens of minor principalities neither dangerous nor hard to influence. How drastically that had changed was observed by the statesman and historian Adolphe Thiers when he said that no greater disaster had befallen France in four hundred years. Public misgivings and apprehension about Germany approached the point of frenzy when, in 1870, it appeared that the throne of Spain would be offered to a German prince descended from the south German Roman Catholic branch of the Hohenzollern dynasty. Leopold of Hohenzollern-Sigmaringen was so remotely related to the ruling house of Prussia that there was no more likelihood of Prussia and Spain being joined in personal union than of Prussia and Rumania being so joined — the latter having chosen Leopold's brother Karl as its ruler in 1866. Nevertheless, the French, haunted by the memory of Charles V, the Habsburg Holy Roman Emperor who during the sixteenth century had reigned over Austria, Germany, the Low Countries, and Spain, saw themselves once more threatened with encirclement by Germany under the aggressive leadership of Bismarck. Consequently they protested so vehemently against the renewed German threat that the Hohenzollern candidacy in Spain was abandoned. Not content with this diplomatic victory, Napoleon III went on to insist, through his ambassador, that the Prussian king give formal assurances that the matter would not be taken up again. Not having been officially involved in Leopold's candidacy, King William had no cause officially to disavow it, let alone make any assurances regarding the future. When the French ambassador, who had followed him to the resort city of Bad Ems, nonetheless sought to elicit them from him, he simply declined to discuss the matter. The king had a routine account of this initiative, and his response to it, telegraphed to Bismarck in Berlin. He in turn released an account of the incident based on the Ems telegram but edited in such a way as to give the false impression of a rude encounter at which both sides might take offense. This brought simmering French public opinion to a boil, forcing Napolean III, vulnerable through his own importunity, into a war which in the end cost him his throne.

When the French declared war in July 1870, Germany enthusiastically united behind Prussia. With the decisive military victory at Sedan in September, where Napoleon himself was captured, the stage was set for Bismarck's incorporation of the south German states into a Prussian-dominated federation — precisely what he had not been able to do before Sedan because of French objections. Thus the Franco-Prussian War prepared the way for the final step to German unification by crippling French opposition in a triumphant war that reinforced the patriotic, nationalist elements in Germany, impressed the undecided, and made it impossible for opponents of unification to prevail or even procrastinate.

Among the least enthusiastic participants in Bismarck's drama of German unification were several of the German princes. But their misgivings were overwhelmed by the manner in which Bismarck seemed prepared to use the force of German nationalist sentiment. There were, he did not hesitate to point out with sinister tactfulness, many strong voices calling for a united German kingdom. If King William I of Prussia became King William I of Germany, what then would become of the kings of Bavaria, Saxony, and Württemberg? As bitter as the prospect was, Bismarck's Prussian-led federation of princes did offer them and the lesser princes a future, while preempting other, possibly far more unsatisfactory alternatives that later might prove unavoidable. But the splendid imperial proclamation on 18 January 1871 in the Hall of Mirrors at Versailles was perhaps bitterest of all for the man hailed as emperor, King William I of Prussia. Commissioned in the Prussian army during the Napoleonic Wars, he had won the Iron Cross during the campaign in France that drove the Corsican usurper from his illegitimate throne. Over half a century later, he had led his armies back into France and crushed the self-appointed successor of the spurious pretender to imperial dignity. How could he himself now climax his own reign by subordinating the proud crown of Prussia to the improvised pretensions of an imperial title almost as spurious, in terms of the values and traditions he had lived by, as that claimed by Napoleon I or his nephew, Napoleon III? There was not and could not be any satisfactory answer to that question, but, at the same time, the old king saw no alternative to a course of action he inwardly disdained. So in the end he went through with it, because it was as necessary as it was bitter.

❦ THE GERMAN EMPIRE UNDER BISMARCK AND WILLIAM II

THE NEW GERMAN EMPIRE was a federation of twenty-five nominally sovereign states plus one over which sovereignty was jointly shared by the rest: the four kingdoms of Bavaria, Prussia, Saxony, and Württemberg; the six grand duchies of Baden, Hesse, Mecklenburg-Schwerin, Mecklenburg-Strelitz, Oldenburg, and Saxe-Weimar; the five duchies of Anhalt, Brunswick, Saxe-Altenburg, Saxe-Cobourg-Gotha, and Saxe-Meiningen; the seven principalities of Lippe, Reuss, elder line,

Reuss, younger line, Schaumburg-Lippe, Schwarzburg-Rudolstadt, Schwarzburg-Sondershausen, and Waldeck; the free cities of Bremen, Lübeck, and Hamburg; and the jointly held *Reichsland* of Alsace-Lorraine. Sovereignty over the empire as a whole rested jointly with the twenty-two monarchs and the senates of the three free cities; Alsace-Lorraine was administered by a governor who reported directly to the emperor. In time of war, the emperor was the supreme commander of all German armed forces, though in peacetime the king of Bavaria retained command of the Bavarian army. Bavaria and Württemberg also kept their individual postal systems. Citizens continued to carry passports issued by the individual states — as they would until the strongly centralistic Third Reich.

The king of Prussia presided over the new German confederation with the title German emperor and appointed the imperial chancellor. Nominally a parliamentary monarchy, the new empire had a bicameral legislature. The upper chamber was the *Bundesrat,* a federal council of the German princes or their designated representatives, who enjoyed diplomatic status in Berlin. Voting strength was unequally apportioned: larger states had more votes than smaller ones, and Prussia, the largest of all (with about a third of the area and of the population), cast almost a third of the votes, thereby so effectively dominating the *Bundesrat* that its actions were generally a foregone conclusion. In many respects it was more an administrative than legislative body.

A far more important role in the political life of the empire was played by the lower chamber, the imperial diet or *Reichstag,* composed of deputies elected by universal and equal suffrage for males over twenty-five. This was a far cry from the lower chamber of the Prussian legislature (which, of course, continued to function) with its notorious three-class electoral system requiring, for example, 600,000 votes to elect six socialists in 1908, compared with only 418,000 to secure 212 seats representing the wealthier segments of the population paying the bulk of the taxes. But Bismarck's concession to the German electorate of universal and equal manhood suffrage was largely

9 / THE HOHENZOLLERN EMPIRE

The German Empire, as shown on the upper map, was established in 1871. During the Revolution of 1848, the king of Prussia had been elected German emperor by the German National Assembly, but he had scorned a crown from the people's representatives as beneath the dignity of a king by the grace of God. German unification was brought about not by the resolutions of liberals, but by the military might of Hohenzollern Prussia, which crushed Austria and her German allies in a mercifully brief German civil war during the summer of 1866. Prussia abolished the German Confederation, ejected Austria from German affairs altogether, and annexed several of her north German allies. The few surviving north German opponents of Prussia, together with neutrals and Prussian allies, were drawn into the North German Confederation shown (except for the Prussian exclave of Hohenzollern on the upper Danube between Württemberg and Baden) on the lower map. During the Franco-Prussian War of 1870–71 the North German Confederation was extended to all non-Habsburg Germany and its head, the Prussian king, assumed the title German emperor. The empire was a federation of twenty-five co-sovereign states plus imperially administered Alsace-Lorraine, which had been conquered from France. (Luxemburg, neutral in 1866 and 1870–71, did not join the empire, but remained in the German tariff union with German-administered railways through 1918.)

a hollow one, for what the *Reichstag* gained in one respect it lost in another. It was denied direct control over the administration or government, as the chancellor was responsible not to the elected representatives of the people, but only to the emperor. Consequently he was not dependent upon parliamentary votes of confidence, but only on the confidence of the monarch. The socialist leader Wilhelm Liebknecht bitterly denounced the *Reichstag*, with its external trappings of parliamentary monarchy, as nothing but "the fig-leaf of absolutism." His great liberal contemporary, Theodor Mommsen, the German historian of Rome, went further, writing of the

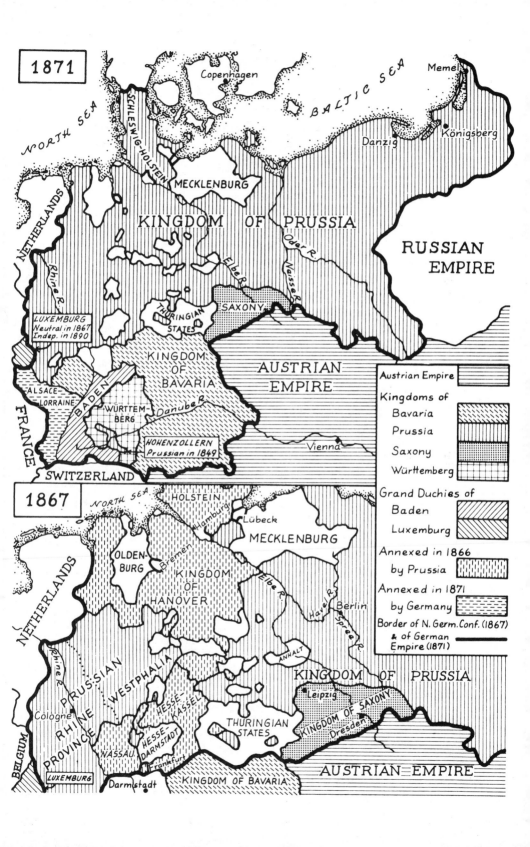

"pseudo-constitutional absolutism under which we live and which our spineless people has inwardly accepted." *

The bitter strictures of Liebknecht and Mommsen reflect the widespread frustration felt not just in socialist and liberal circles concerning the narrow limits set on political opposition, even in the *Reichstag,* during the era of Bismarck and William II. Yet it would be a gross exaggeration to say that the *Reichstag* was completely impotent or that it was categorically denied real influence on the conduct of government. Its fiscal control, though limited, was significant in that its consent was required for any new appropriations in an inflationary age during which the German economy and the German government were growing. For all practical purposes, it would have been virtually impossible for Bismarck to govern, year after year, as he had done a decade earlier in Prussia, against a solid majority. That he himself realized this is suggested by the pains to which he went to manipulate the *Reichstag* — and the compromises he was prepared to make when he found he could not otherwise scrape together a majority for some key vote.

The ultimate test of the constitutional structure of a state, however, is not how more or less routine business is transacted, but rather how fundamental conflicts on crucial issues are resolved. It is through decision-making in conflict that the essential power structure of an institution reveals itself. In Bismarck's Germany, the political contest for power which normally takes place within the traditional Anglo-American democratic system was virtually precluded. The political parties might go to the polls and win impressive majorities, but they could not thereby assure themselves the substance of power or even decisive influence on the decision-making process. With all too few exceptions, the routine administration was

* Mommsen's younger colleague, the historian Ludwig Quidde, who like him eventually became a Nobel laureate, attacked the "pseudo-constitutional absolutism" of William II in a devastating "study of Roman imperial insanity" that nominally was written about Caligula, one of the more despised Roman emperors, but in its brilliant ambivalence all too clearly, paragraph by paragraph, dealt with William II — and did so, moreover, while the emperor was still in his prime, long before he had begun to become an object almost of pity in some observers' eyes because of his obvious inadequacy for the role to which he had been born: L. Quidde, *Caligula. Eine Studie über römischen Cäsarenwahnsinn,* 20th ed. (Leipzig: Verlag von Wilhelm Friedrich, n.d. [ca. 1893]).

carried on in the spirit of bureaucratic absolutism by a self-consciously conservative, efficient civil service generally impervious to opposition criticism. Control of the higher echelons of the civil government and of the officer corps of the army, particularly in Prussia, lay in the hands of a deeply entrenched, caste-conscious aristocracy, indifferent when not indeed hostile to the very concept of parliamentary rule.

Under such circumstances, German political parties did not develop, as in Great Britain or the United States, into broad-based coalitions of heterogeneous regional and economic interests competing for power. In this sense, political power was beyond reach. There was no real incentive for pragmatic compromises of ideological principle and economic interest which might bring them into office, as in the case of the heterogeneous Republican and Democratic parties in the United States and the hardly more homogeneous Conservative and Labour parties in Britain. Since compromises for the sake of winning power were futile to begin with, German parties tended to develop into specialized pressure groups attempting to concentrate their limited leverage where it might be applied most effectively in order to support legislation or administrative policy directives of maximum benefit for their respective interests, such as free trade or protective tariffs.

Although fragmentation along economic lines was common, there were also other bases for political organization, contributing to the formation of regional, religious, or ideological parties. Two mass parties emerged which, in Bismarck's eyes, represented interests absolutely inimical to the welfare of the empire. These *"reichsfeindliche"* parties were the Center party or *Zentrum* of the Roman Catholics and the socialist party of the Marxian labor movement (known since 1890 as the *Sozialdemokratische Partei Deutschlands,* "the Social-Democratic party of Germany," or *SPD*). Although neither the *Zentrum* nor the socialists were nearly as dangerous as Bismarck represented them in the course of his bitter struggle first against the one and then against the other, they represented between them almost the full spectrum of openly declared, politically effective opposition in Germany.

In the *Zentrum* congregated the Catholics of western and

southern Germany, who remained largely unreconciled to Protestant domination from Berlin, resented Prussian suppression of Catholic Poles in the east (not to mention Bismarck's unforgotten and unforgiven support of the tsar in 1863), and generally deplored Bismarck's establishment of a German state that excluded their German Catholic brethren of the Habsburg Monarchy. In the course of the persecution of the Catholic church, primarily in Prussia, during the 1870s, hailed by many nationalistic liberals as a continuation of the ancient struggle between papacy and empire, half the bishops in the kingdom (of which Bismarck remained minister president) were imprisoned and over a thousand pastorates became vacant. But the *Zentrum* actually thrived on the persecution; the Catholics doubled their representation not only in the *Reichstag* but also in the lower chamber of the Prussian legislature. Considering the three-class electoral law in Prussia and the fact that persecution had been centered there, it was obvious that the *Zentrum* was developing increasingly strong backing among the rich, the well-born, and the able, and that the campaign against political Catholicism was becoming correspondingly counterproductive. Realizing that it would be a mistake to continue it, Bismarck seized upon the papal election in 1878 of Leo XIII as a pretext for the gradual resumption of more or less normal church-state relations. In a broader context, however, this resumption of normal church-state relations, important as it was in itself, must be seen simultaneously as part of the major political and economic reorientation that Bismarck undertook in 1878 and 1879: he broke with the National Liberals, pieced together a tenuous coalition around the *Zentrum* and the conservatives, abandoned free trade for protectionism, and substituted the socialists for the Catholics as objects of political persecution. Ever since the Prussian victory over Austria, when the liberals in Berlin had split and the majority formed a new party and endorsed Bismarck, the National Liberal party had generally cooperated with him, especially during his persecution of the Catholics and the *Zentrum*. But they had never been fully dependable; their ranks had not held firm, for example, when he needed support for the initial "septennate," the first of a series of seven-year military budgets, passed in 1874.

The septennate did facilitate long-range general-staff planning, but only at great cost. Troubled liberal parliamentarians pointed out at the time that its approval gravely compromised the capacity of the *Reichstag* to exercise meaningful legislative control over military policy by regular review of expenditures on an annual basis. It was, of course, precisely to avoid such control that the septennate was devised in the first place; the military would have preferred a permanent budget with no recurring control whatsoever (an *Äternat* rather than the *Septennat*) but settled for the sabbatical ordeal as the best available option. Despite the bitter misgivings of many in the *Reichstag,* particularly among the liberals, the septennate was approved as the maximum control that could be exercised under a system of government with neither a firm tradition of the separation of powers (the executive being balanced by the legislative) nor of the subordination of the military to the civil authorities — for in the Germany of Bismarck and William II, the military were parallel rather than subordinate to the political authorities: the chief of staff was not responsible to the chancellor, but, like him, to the emperor alone.

The immediate occasion for Bismarck's break with the National Liberals was their strong opposition to harshly antisocialist legislation which, they vehemently pointed out, was so loosely worded that it could be used against any citizen who might criticize the government. They had already opposed several earlier proposals when, following an unsuccessful attempt on the life of the octogenarian emperor in May 1878, Bismarck presented the *Reichstag* so ill-conceived an antisocialist bill that it was quashed by a vote of 251 to 57. But one week later, a second assassination attempt almost succeeded; the venerated monarch was gravely wounded. Although the second would-be assassin was no more a socialist than the first, Bismarck seized on the opportunity to exploit the widespread popular consternation and indignation, dissolved the *Reichstag,* and masterminded a ruthless electoral campaign that was directed against the socialists as well as the liberals who were "soft on socialism." Thereby he secured a *Reichstag* that was prepared not only to persecute the socialists but also to abandon free trade and to introduce protective tariffs.

The reason for this economic policy reversal was that the wave of prosperity after unification had been followed by a severe depression from which the economy could not recover without government protection. German industry, largely still in the earlier stages of the industrial revolution, made only a very slow comeback after the depression, competing as it was against the far more advanced British in the expanding free trade market of the newly unified German Empire. Meanwhile, many German farmers, above all the grain producers of the East, had continued to lose ground, even after the depression, because they could not compete with steadily increasing steamship-borne grain imports from Russia and America. Thus industry and agriculture both sought protection, and Bismarck offered it to them. In 1879, with the support of the recently reconciled Catholic *Zentrum,* conservative agrarian landowners, and business-oriented liberals to whom free trade was not sacrosanct, Bismarck mustered a *Reichstag* majority for tariffs protecting both German agriculture and industry. He thereby set the stage for the dramatic economic expansion that in less than a generation was to make Germany the most powerful industrial nation of Europe.

But this swift economic growth exacerbated social tensions, and despite harsh legislation and bitter persecution, the strength of the socialists kept pace with the rapid industrialization of Germany. "To take the wind out of their sails," as Bismarck himself put it, between 1881 and 1889 a comprehensive program of compulsory state-administered sickness, accident, invalid, and old-age insurance was enacted, generations before such protection became the rule in the United States or elsewhere. Important as this legislation was, however, it would be a misunderstanding to regard it as a manifestation of emerging liberalism in the sense that we use the word today. The German "State Socialism" of the 1880s was not conceived in the spirit of modern Western liberalism; it was an expression of old-fashioned paternalistic authoritarianism. It reflected sincere solicitude for the welfare of the subjects in general, but this was rooted, at least in part, in serious concern about the quality of the coming generation of army conscripts. With precipitous industrialization packing an increasing percentage of the population into burgeoning cities where children were often reared under unspeakable living conditions, State Socialism amounted to social insurance, on the state's behalf, against the depletion of the human resources of the nation.

Whatever the constellation of motives and expectations behind it may have been, Bismarck's social reform program did not engender political gratitude among the working people at the polls. Just as German unification had been taken out of the hands of the people and imposed upon them from above, social reforms now also were. Though first granted unification and then also a measure of financial security, the working people of Germany still had virtually no political power; they knew it; and they showed at the polls that they could not be bought off by calculated generosity. In February 1890, less than a year after the final phase of Bismarck's epoch-making program of social legislation was approved, the socialists almost doubled their strength over the previous election despite repressive laws against them, garnering almost a million and a half votes, a fifth of the total cast. The Socialist party had been driven underground, but its support at the polls could no more be suppressed than the many local sport or singing clubs established by its "former" members. Publication and sale in Germany of socialist literature had been strictly proscribed, but dissemination of material published in exile presses in England and Switzerland proved impossible to stop, if only because of the chronic color-blindness, when it came to stopping "red" propaganda, of lower-echelon officials of the state railways and postal service. The socialist leader August Bebel could be imprisoned, but the trainmen and guards could not be prevented from treating the former Leipzig turner, when he went to jail with his books and his canary in its cage, as the honored celebrity he was in their eyes — nor did it prevent his loyal constituency from returning him to the *Reichstag,* together with thirty-four of his followers, in 1890.

This election signaled the apparent bankruptcy not only of Bismarck's antisocialist campaign, but of his entire parliamentary program: the *Reichstag* coalition with which he had worked during the past years, the so-called *Bismarck-Kartell,* was slashed from 220 to 135 seats. Regarding the elections as proof of a fatal flaw not in his own policies or style of leadership, but rather in the system itself, Bismarck advocated a characteristically radical solution to the new crisis: "constructive dissolution" of the imperial constitution. The empire, he reasoned, had been constituted as a federation by a voluntary compact between sovereign princes and senates of free cities. These princes and senates consequently had the right, in case of necessity, to dissolve their compact. The empire might possibly be founded anew, but certainly without so intractable a *Reichstag,* and also — perhaps even more important a consideration — without such broad prerogatives for the emperor as those framed decades earlier with the judicious and predictable William I in mind, rather than his volatile grandson, William II, who had come to the throne in 1888.

Bismarck's precise intentions between the election on 20 February 1890 and his dismissal by the young emperor on 20 March can never be known with certainty. He habitually kept his counsel, stressing different aspects of a problem in conversations with different persons, continually seeking to identify and redefine alternative options, committing himself, even in his own mind, only to the extent necessary — and often not until the moment he had to reach a final decision. In this case, the final decision was taken out of his hands altogether. It was almost inevitable. Not only was his domestic policy becoming increasingly self-defeating, but his personality itself had become oppressive. At best, he was unconsciously overbearing; at worst, as in his vendetta against Count Arnim, he was relentlessly hateful. The bitter memory of a twenty-seven-year regime increasingly characterized by personal rancor and pettiness remained so strong, even five years after his dismissal, that what should have been a routine resolution to congratulate him on his eightieth birthday was actually defeated in the *Reichstag.* Only as the years wore on and the lingering recollections of his personal lack of magnanimity were carried into the grave by those who had suffered or seen others suffer at his hands, did the splendid legend of Prince Bismarck as a great, wise, and good man (strongly reinforced by his posthumously published memoirs) take root in Germany.

The news of the fall of Bismarck in 1890 was received with considerably more concern and with a far greater sense of loss abroad than within the empire — as epitomized by the famous *Punch* cartoon of Sir John Tenniel (best remembered as the illustrator of *Alice in Wonderland*), showing a larger-than-life Bismarck as the farsighted old pilot leaving the German ship of state to the bland, complacent little emperor. Foreign observers had a very different perspective on Bismarck than most Germans, of course, not having been involved in his domestic policies and often having had relatively little knowledge of them. Their primary concern was his foreign policy, the area in which he demonstrated truly extraordinary gifts of statesmanship.

It was no accident that on the international stage Bismarck was incomparably more effective than in the domestic arena. An aristocrat who understood and advocated the responsible exercise of legitimate sovereign power, he honored even princely adversaries, for by virtue of their standing they commanded his respect. But mere subjects of the monarchs he served did not, and he came to despise those whose pretensions to power represented a challenge, particularly in the *Reichstag,* to the immense authority delegated to him as Prussian minister president, imperial chancellor, and foreign minister. Over the years this increasingly ill-concealed attitude more and more seriously undermined his effectiveness as a domestic political leader. By the same token, however, its converse, his genuine respect for the legitimate interests of the sovereign European powers, consistently manifested in his foreign policy, won international confidence and enabled him to establish a place for the new German Empire in the European community of nations. More than most of his contemporaries, and certainly more than William II and his advisors, Bismarck realized what a potentially revolutionary and disruptive force the unified German nation represented. For centuries, "The Germanies" had been a conglomeration of relatively small and powerless principalities serving as a buffer zone in central

Europe between the great powers on the periphery — acting as a sort of continental shock absorber. But with unification this abruptly ended. Even the events of 1866 had transformed the balance of power in Europe so radically that France had felt threatened, and with the Franco-Prussian War, completing the work of German unification amid the ruins of the French Empire, Germany became superior to either France or Austria-Hungary in area, population, economic resources, and military strength. Nevertheless, these two former enemies in the wars of unification allied together, or either of them in league with Russia, might very well be able to overwhelm and dismember Germany again, restoring central Europe to its traditional fragmentation, and reducing Prussia to a third-rate power. The goal of Bismarck's foreign policy after 1871, therefore, was to prevent any possible coalition of two hostile powers which might force Germany into the "nightmare," as he put it, of a two-front war.

Bismarck prevented such a coalition by diplomatically isolating the French, who could be depended upon to make common cause with any potential enemy of Germany whenever they had the opportunity. Their implacable hostility had been assured by German annexation, following the Franco-Prussian War in 1871, of Alsace and much of Lorraine. Part of the medieval Holy Roman Empire, most of the annexed region had been German-speaking when the French had acquired it, piece by piece, during the sixteenth and seventeenth centuries. But meanwhile it had become an integral part of the modern state shaped by the French Revolution and tempered by the new spirit of nationalism that had given the French, before and above all others, an unprecedented sense of identity and even brotherhood.

Bismarck knew this well and therefore voiced serious misgivings about Field Marshal von Moltke's demand that for strategic reasons the area be annexed. But in the end he acquiesced, later rationalizing that it was less the loss of Alsace and Lorraine that had injured the French than the loss of the war itself, and therewith the loss of France's status — achieved under Louis XIV, restored with Napoleon I, and reasserted by

Napoleon III — as the first power of Europe. The French might speak of recovering lost provinces, but what rankled most deeply was loss of honor and power.

During two decades as imperial chancellor, Bismarck succeeded in preventing France from entering into any alliance that might potentially have threatened Germany. He did not use diplomatic sleight of hand or political trickery to isolate France, nor even economic leverage or the threat of force. Such tactics could achieve short-range goals, such as maneuvering Austria into war in 1866 or France in 1870, but in the long run would be counterproductive, for they inevitably would erode the basic credibility and moral authority essential for success. Bismarck knew that there was only one way for Germany to be made secure against a possible alliance of other powers: the new empire's suddenly achieved primacy had to be so firmly legitimized through the exercise of restraint and responsibility that Berlin would naturally preempt Paris or London as the diplomatic center of gravity of the civilized world. There is security in strength, but only the right kind of strength. The new German empire was so strong that it convincingly had to prove, through international leadership, that it had the right kind of strength, just as it initially had proved its military potency on the battlefield.

International leadership can no more be contrived, however, than it can be claimed — even on the basis of as great military, economic, and political power as Bismarck had at his disposal during the eighteen-seventies and eighties. Power may be a prerequisite to international leadership, but the sophisticated understanding of power is no less essential. In his conduct of foreign policy, Bismarck demonstrated an uncanny understanding of the use of power and its limitations. His contemporaries recognized this, as well as historians who refer to the quarter century he dominated the European diplomatic stage as "the Age of Bismarck." Rarely has a responsible statesman exercised great power with such restraint, circumspection, and skill.

In 1890 Bismarck was dismissed by William II, who had become emperor in 1888 on the deaths of his grandfather William I and, barely a hundred days later, of his father, Frederick III, already dying of throat cancer when he came to the throne. Almost a half century younger than Bismarck, William II was an emotionally insecure man of good intentions but immature judgment and unlimited vanity. He would hardly have been fit to rule, even had his constitutional role been more limited than that of his maternal grandmother, Queen Victoria of England. Among his extensive powers under the Bismarckian constitution was the prerogative of dismissing the imperial chancellor without formal obligation of a word of explanation to anyone. Thus no man was ultimately more responsible for his fall than Bismarck himself; as the British foreign secretary and later prime minister, Lord Rosebury, put it, he was "hoist with his own petard."

The quarter century between the fall of Bismarck and the outbreak of the First World War saw the population of Germany expand by a third to some sixty-eight million, her steel production surpass and more than double Great Britain's, and her technology and capital growth make her one of the world's leading financial and commercial powers. Under the circumstances, intense Anglo-German economic rivalry may have been inevitable, but it need not have been accompanied by the extremely costly naval arms race provoked by Germany's overt attempt to build so powerful a fleet that the British not only would never dare risk war but actually feel constrained to seek her alliance, if not indeed her friendship.

Was this even realistic? It certainly was most unlikely. The factors that made it virtually impossible, however, dramatize the fatal inadequacy of post-Bismarckian German leadership. Had industrially burgeoning Germany set out to build a strong fleet to support its overseas empire and to enable it to fulfill the world role falling to it by virtue of its power (sharing "the white man's burden" with England, so to speak); had it done so under the leadership of men who meticulously eschewed, as a matter of state policy and personal style, even the slightest suggestion of any direct naval rivalry with Britain: had all these conditions pertained, Germany might have been able to become a great naval power without provoking the increasingly bitter

Anglo-German rivalry that ensued. To spell out these conditions, of course, is to define their improbability. If nothing else, the kind of leadership required would have involved a highly cultivated style of poise and projected self-control utterly foreign to Emperor William II and many of the advocates of the new navy. It was above all to be a vehicle for achieving rank, status, and recognition, and there were few topics dearer to the heart, mind, and voice of William II. For the immature emperor of an upstart that had arrived late on the stage of world politics, the fleet seemed to offer passage to a new dimension of power and self-esteem. For the German upper middle classes, denied decisive political power within the constitutional framework of the Bismarckian pseudo-parliamentary monarchy, denied behind-the-scenes power at court by the Prussian oligarchical caste, and, up to that time, even denied military status and corresponding public recognition by the closed system of the *Junker*-dominated army officer corps, the navy finally afforded an avenue to a kind of personal success and patriotic self-realization that was previously unattainable. (As the *Luftwaffe* was being built up during the 1930s, it was often observed that Germany had a Royal Prussian army, an Imperial German navy, and a National Socialist air force.)

The self-defeating naval arms race, together with the often giddy emperor's bombastic saber-rattling, decisively contributed to bringing together in a "Triple Entente" — a three-way understanding just short of a formal military alliance — England, which only with agonizing reluctance abandoned its "splendid isolation," France, which Bismarck had successfully isolated, and Russia, whose good will had been a cornerstone of his policy. In barely two decades, the enviably strong diplomatic position Bismarck had achieved for Germany had been irrecoverably lost. This is not to say that Bismarck himself, had it somehow been possible to rejuvenate and retain him for thirty more years, could have headed off this debacle. But he would surely have been far more alert than his successors to the dangers inherent in the polarization of the European powers in two adversary alliance systems — the Triple Entente with Britain, France, and Russia, and the Triple Alliance of Austria-

Hungary, Germany, and Italy. He might well have sought to avoid the fateful rigidification represented by that system, for his diplomacy was not mechanical. A common legend to the contrary, Bismarck had not, during his long tenure in office, developed a complex web of pacts laid down over Europe like an entangling net to immobilize the powers and maintain rigid stability. He did work for stability, but knew it could not be maintained artificially. To be more than a brittle delusion, it had to function as the natural balance of vital interests guided in their interaction by sophisticated leaders.

The difference between Bismarck's conception of responsible diplomacy and that of William II and his advisors was dramatically illustrated by the change in German policy, after 1890, toward Russia and Austria-Hungary. Bismarck had found it increasingly difficult to maintain close relations with both Russia and Austria-Hungary because (among other problems) they had become bitter rivals in the Balkans. In 1887, the Russians refused to renew membership in the Three Emperors' Alliance established in 1881 and renewed for three years in 1884. Despite the fact that he regarded the Habsburg Monarchy as Germany's most dependable ally since the Dual Alliance was established in 1879, Bismarck did manage, to the very end of his chancellorship, to maintain a tenuous bond with St. Petersburg by means of a separate pact, the Reinsurance Treaty, concluded in 1887 and renewable every three years. Upon Bismarck's dismissal, however, this tie with St. Petersburg was abruptly severed. On the very evening of Bismarck's dismissal, William had personally assured the Russian ambassador that the Reinsurance Treaty would, as the tsar wished, be renewed for another three years. But within a few days he changed his mind. It is true that there were serious reasons for misgivings in Berlin: Austria-Hungary and Russia had become such keen rivals in the unstable Balkans that they might go to war with each other in the foreseeable future. Austria-Hungary was Germany's principal ally, but the Reinsurance Treaty that the Russians were seeking to have renewed until 1893 provided for German moral and diplomatic support for Russian endeavors to gain control to the entrance to the Black Sea — obviously at the cost of Turkey. It was conceivable that Austria-Hungary, supporting Turkey against Russian expansion, might be drawn into hostilities against the Russians on their way to the straits between the Mediterranean and Black seas. If this happened, Germany, under the terms of Bismarck's treaties, could theoretically be obligated to intervene militarily on the Austrian side while simultaneously supporting the Russians against Turkey, Austria's presumed ally.

The emperor's advisors convinced him that this was intolerable and that Germany had to decide one way or the other. He agreed, for neither he nor his closest advisors fully appreciated the subtlety of Bismarck's diplomacy. The same year he negotiated the Reinsurance Treaty with Russia, 1887, Bismarck had also played an important role in the formation of a "Near Eastern Entente" between Austria-Hungary, Britain, and Italy: the terms of the Mediterranean Agreements of February and December (the Russo-German Reinsurance Treaty was signed in June) provided for joint action in preventing any Russian encroachment on Turkey. Thus Bismarck tied the Russians to Berlin in part by a commitment that he simultaneously was making provisions to see would never have to be implemented. Lord Salisbury, the British prime minister at the time, perceptively referred to Bismarck's diplomacy as "employing his neighbours to pull out each other's teeth."

Within four years of being rebuffed in Berlin, the Russians were welcomed in Paris, where they concluded a diplomatic convention that became the cornerstone of the Triple Entente in World War I. There were, of course, many additional factors involved in the German decision to break with Russia, but the basic question of compatibility of obligations lies at the heart of the issue. William and his advisors were not prepared to "cheat" on Austria-Hungary by continuing Bismarck's secret liaison with the Russians. In their own way, William and his advisors felt more honorable and more honest than Bismarck. But international diplomacy, though far more serious than any game, is more like poker, where one does not show his hand, than checkers, where the pieces are out on the board. Bismarck was well aware of the hypothetical incompatibility of Germany's commitments to Vienna and St. Petersburg, but he regarded these commitments themselves as his most powerful instruments — powerful enough, in fact, to give him the leverage he would need, if a showdown ever approached, to hold the two states apart, not only preventing just the sort of conflict in wartime obligations that so profoundly concerned William, but probably also preventing war itself.

After breaking off Germany's alliance with Russia, the emperor went on to transform Bismarck's basic alliance with Austria-Hungary from a source of strength into a grave liability. For Bismarck, alliances had represented far more than security in diplomatic crises; they provided the means to prevent their getting out of hand. Consequently, the Dual Alliance between Germany and Austria-Hungary had not merely been a guarantee to Germany of support from a weaker power. For Bismarck, it had also been a vital tool enabling him to exercise a certain measure of control over the foreign policy of the increasingly distraught multinational monarchy. Bismarck had once stopped Moltke from working out contingency war plans with the Austrian general staff, because it might have made the Austrians overconfident, particularly in the Balkans; but William, as a matter of personal policy and national honor, ingenuously assured the Austrians, long before there was a serious threat of war, that he would stand beside them, no matter what the circumstances, with all the might at his disposal. Thus he not only forfeited in advance the diplomatic leverage to restrain the latently unstable Viennese leadership from ill-considered adventures, but irresponsibly encouraged them to brashness by the unconditional guarantee of full German support.

4

From 1914 to the Present

🌸 WAR AND REVOLUTION

W HEN IN THE SUMMER of 1914 the heir to the Habsburg
throne was assassinated by a pro-Serbian fanatic,
the Austrians, with strong German support, attacked Serbia,
unleashing a general war. Serbia was an ally of Russia, which
could not afford to let her fall, while Russia's alignment with
France and England, together with Germany's war plans, drew
the two western powers into the conflict. Initially there was
painful hesitation in London, for the extent to which the Anglo-
French Entente had been transformed through specific military and naval commitments from a general understanding to
an operational alliance was unknown to the public and even
to many high-level government officials. Ironically, the
dilemma of the English leaders who had secretly over-commit-
ted their country was solved by none other than the Germans
themselves through such flagrant violation of international
law that the British Parliament and public overwhelmingly
supported entry into the war: in response to Russian mobilization on their eastern border, the Germans had countered with
an attack on France, not across the heavily fortified Franco-
German frontier, but rather through neutral Belgium. This violation of Belgian neutrality was not just an act of aggression;
in an age when men took international law and gentlemen's
agreements most seriously, it was an outrage. When Belgium

had been established as an independent kingdom seventy-five years earlier, the European powers had formally committed themselves to honor Belgian neutrality — a solemn agreement freely entered into and repeatedly affirmed. The German violation of that commitment suggests the degree to which the counsel of political wisdom had been subordinated to considerations of military expediency.

This had not come about suddenly or recently. For Bismarck the specter of a two-front war had been a *cauchemar,* a nightmare, but he had managed, to the very end of his tenure, to head off an alignment of powers that would lead to such an exigency. Less than four years after his fall, however, the Franco-Russian military convention of 1894 made a two-front war a potentially serious possibility. The long-range prospects for Germany were dismal in a war in which her army would have to be divided between the two fronts, fighting against superior odds on both. In response to this challenge, the general staff of the army developed, under the leadership of Field Marshal Alfred von Schlieffen, the war plan that bore his name. It envisioned a radically different approach to the problem of a two-front war: rather than making a major effort on both fronts simultaneously, they would be mastered in sequence.

As it stood in 1905, the year after which the field marshal retired, the Schlieffen Plan provided first for an overwhelming offensive against France, employing a mobile strategy of swift encirclement and annihilation to destroy the French army in the field. In the second phase, the bulk of the German army was to be transported across Germany and hurled eastward against the Russians, who up to this point were to be held off by little more than a light screening force. Their weakness and demoralization, following the disastrous Russo-Japanese War of 1904–5 and the disruptive Revolution of 1905, led Schlieffen to the working assumption that they would be incapable of mounting a dangerous offensive in the East before the decision had been forced in the West. But this audacious design could not succeed unless French resistance were very swiftly crushed, something that obviously could not be achieved by a direct attack on the heavily fortified Franco-German frontier.

A breakthrough by frontal assault would be terribly costly in men, matériel, and probably also time; moreover, forcing the French back from the border would not lead to the swift decision necessary. That could only be brought about in a war of movement culminating in the encirclement and annihilation of the French army. The one way to achieve that was to move in from the north. In a great cartwheel movement through Belgium and northern France, an overwhelmingly powerful German right flank would move around Paris, cutting off the French capital plus the forces engaging the German left flank at the hub of the cartwheel on the Franco-German border.

The price of this plan was terribly high. To begin with, it required the violation of Belgian neutrality. Without that, there was no hope of overwhelming the French in the first weeks of the war, before turning to the Russians. But beyond that, the Schlieffen Plan gravely compromised the very possibility of maintaining German neutrality in any severe diplomatic crisis that might arise. Until 1913, the Schlieffen Plan had not been the only major war plan available. But in that year, the German general staff abandoned its converse operational plan that provided for a major build-up in the East, with a mere holding action in the West. After forfeiting that option, the Germans had virtually no freedom of action in the event of a serious threat of war. Mobilization in the West involved deployment in permanently and inviolably neutralized Belgium; mobilization in the East was not even to take place until after the military decision had been reached in France. After 1913, therefore, mobilization, for the Germans, was no longer a mere preliminary to war. Under the Schlieffen Plan, mobilization and war were merged, eliminating at the outset any possibility of a diplomatic solution to any crisis serious enough to require mobilization — not to mention precluding the option of employing mobilization as a final deterrent to war. A generation earlier, as already indicated, Bismarck had vetoed joint Austro-German general staff agreements; he even had threatened to make this a resignation issue. He went that far because he knew only too well the insidious finality of carefully developed staff recommendations. He was therefore determined to prevent their even being drawn up in the first place. He regarded it as essential to prevent this, he told the Austrian foreign minister, in order that "the prerogative of counseling our monarchs should not, for all practical purposes, slip out of our hands and be picked up by the general staffs." With the Schlieffen Plan, his worst forebodings were realized.

During the night of 4 August 1914, German forces crossed the Belgian border. The operational flaws in the Schlieffen Plan soon began to become harrowingly clear. The outermost units on the strong right flank had to cover tremendous distances as they dashed around the periphery — the outer rim of the great cartwheel rolling down through Belgium into northeastern France. This alone, aside from enemy action, subjected the right wing to the greatest attrition of any sector of the German front. At the same time, because of the amount of ground they were covering and conquering, German supply and communication lines were inordinately extended, and substantial force also had to be left in the wake of the cutting edge in order to protect the ever longer right flank as the advance continued. German units were already approaching the outskirts of Paris, when the French, together with the British Expeditionary Force, counterattacked. While French forces engaged the two outermost armies on the German right, the British marched into a gap between them, ending the immediate threat to Paris, from which the French government had fled.

The "Miracle of the Marne" had not been planned. The Western Allies had not known that the rim of the German cartwheel had parted from the wheel as the outermost German army lost contact with the next, that German headquarters, far to the rear, had all but lost control of the events at the front, or that the chief of staff, Helmuth von Moltke, the ailing sixty-six-year-old nephew and heir of the great field marshal, was at the point of a nervous breakdown. But once the French and British stopped the Germans, they pursued their advantage and drove them some twenty-five miles back from the Marne to the Aisne; there the lines were stabilized. Thus the Schlieffen Plan and with it the German concept for mastering the challenge of a two-front war had failed and the war of movement had ended in the West. The Germans consolidated their front from the North Sea to the Swiss border along a line that left them occupying the tenth of France containing half its coal and nine-tenths of its iron resources, plus most of highly industrialized Belgium: tremendous conquests, to be sure, but measured by the goals that had been established and the price that had been paid, a disaster for Germany nonetheless.

It was in the East, ironically, that the principles of swift movement, encirclement, and annihilation underlying the Schlieffen Plan were dramatically implemented in decisive German victories early in the war. These were won under the leadership of an old general who had been called up out of retirement, Paul von Hindenburg. In 1871, as a well-decorated young officer representing his regiment, he had been privileged to witness the proclamation of the German Empire in the Palace of Versailles. His great triumphs of 1914 and 1915 were in large measure due to the ability of his chief of staff, General Erich Ludendorff. The annihilation of one Russian army and the crushing defeat of a second at the battles of Tannenberg and the Masurian Lakes in late August and early September 1914 were followed, in February 1915, by the destruction of another Russian army invading Eastern Prussia in a second Masurian battle which dragged on for two weeks in the bitter cold of winter snow and ice. Far southward, however, the Russians proved more successful, inflicting a terrible defeat on the Austrians at Lemberg in a battle fought simultaneously with the momentous decisions at the Marne and the Masurian Lakes. With German support the Austrians were finally able to check the Russian advance, and the following year the Central Powers (Germany and Austria) launched a series of counteroffensives that cost the Russians Lithuania, Courland, and Poland, plus almost a million casualties.

One reason for the virtual collapse of the Russian front in 1915 had been the decision of Turkey to enter the war on the Austro-German side in November 1914. This immediately closed the vital passage from the Mediterranean to the Black Sea through which industrially backward Russia received most of her supplies from her allies; by December 1914, the

Russian commander in chief, Grand Duke Nicholas (later relieved by Tsar Nicholas II himself) warned that his armies were no longer well enough supplied to take the offensive. An amphibious operation to open the straits was attempted but failed. By the end of 1915, Bulgaria had also joined the Central Powers, while Serbia, whose dispute with Austria had initially triggered the war, had collapsed.

In the West, meanwhile, the military leaders on both sides outdid each other in appalling demonstrations of the carnage made possible by systematic application of modern industrial technology to the slaughter of disciplined masses of human beings. Trench warfare was refined; slits in the ground were transformed, particularly by the Germans, into ground-level and even subterranean fortification systems, making it advisable for attacking forces to employ sophisticated siege tactics rather than simply to advance as though one were approaching a conventional enemy force in the open field. But that lesson had still not been generally learned as late as the summer of 1916, the mid-point of the war, when the British mounted their great offensive on the Somme. The soldiers of the British Expeditionary Force, each man encumbered with his sixty-six-pound pack of ammunition and supplies, went "over the top" (of the trenches) and moved forward in orderly waves with fixed bayonets. On the first day of that offensive, 1 July 1916, the attacking British lost sixty percent of their officers and forty percent of their rank and file — a total of over sixty thousand men. Yet the attack went on, month after month, with the same sullen ferocity the Germans, for their part, had employed during the first half of 1916 in the incredible bloodletting at Verdun — and with a comparable result: Verdun and the Somme together cost each side about a million casualties, without resulting in any significant gain or loss in terrain. Over a period of three years, in fact, the line of trenches demarking the Western Front was forced less than ten miles in either direction despite the countless hecatombs offered by both sides.

When Moltke had retired in September 1914 during the First Battle of the Marne, he had been succeeded as chief of staff by the Prussian war minister, General Erich von Falkenhayn.

After having lost over a hundred thousand men in the attempt to break through the Western Allies' lines at Ypres in Flanders late in 1914, he came to the bitter conclusion that Germany simply lacked the means to win the war. With a clearcut military victory out of the question, the very best that could be hoped for would be an advantageous compromise peace, an outcome that might well be forced on the enemy by heavy attrition. As grim as this assessment was, it should have been fairly common among German military leaders, for it was compatible with the underlying rationale of the Schlieffen Plan: Germany's prospects in a protracted two-front war would be so bleak that the most desperate measures absolutely had to be employed to assure a swift victory in the West. This had been tried and had failed. Falkenhayn therefore fatalistically settled for a war of attrition, culminating in his attack on Verdun, which he sustained for month after month — though contrary to his advance calculations, the German casualty rate turned out to be nearly as high as the French. Falkenhayn had been disliked, even hated, long before Verdun because of his defeatist "no-win policy," and the Verdun operation, which was finally broken off in June, probably sealed his fate. But it was a sudden crisis in the East that triggered his fall.

Shortly before the British attack on the Somme, the Russians, whom Falkenhayn at the beginning of 1916 had all but written off as gravely crippled, began a major offensive against the Austrians; General Aleksei Brusilov's troops, though ill-equipped and poorly trained, poured through brittle Austrian lines along a two-hundred-mile front. Within five weeks, the multinational army of the Habsburg Monarchy, which had long since seen its officer corps and strongest units decimated if not destroyed, suffered three quarters of a million casualties — over half being lost as prisoners, but also a great many as deserters, reflecting the swiftly increasing disaffection of minorities conscripted into the once proud army that so long had been the principal pillar of the now obviously disintegrating monarchy. More than ever, it had become apparent to informed Germans that they were, in the macabre phrase of the time, shackled to a corpse. The Romanians, for their part, had no intention of sharing such a fate. Having long dickered with both sides, they cast their lot with the Entente and declared war on Austria.

The ghastly balance at Verdun, the steady pressure on the Somme, the portentous Brusilov offensive, and the Romanian entry into the war all contributed to the emperor's decision to replace Erich von Falkenhayn at the end of August 1916 with Paul von Hindenburg as chief of staff and, with joint operational responsibility, Erich Ludendorff as his deputy. When they arrived at German supreme headquarters, the war changed in character. Falkenhayn's grimly rational calculation that Germany and her weak allies could never force a positive decision was supplanted by unshakable faith in final victory and ironwilled determination to achieve it.

On the surface, Germany had barely been scathed when Hindenburg and Ludendorff took over the supreme command at the beginning of the third year of the war. The early Russian invasion of Prussia had been swiftly and triumphantly repulsed in the battles that had made the new supreme commanders national heroes. In the opposite corner of the country, the extreme southwest, the French had invaded Alsace-Lorraine at the very beginning of the war, but their offensive was stopped and they were driven back over the border of Lorraine, retaining to the south only a very small segment of Upper Alsace near the Swiss frontier — an area that had in any case been French before 1871. Although Germany had thus far been almost completely spared physical devastation, the cost of the war to the German people, in terms of loss of life and limb, together with the effects of steadily mounting economic deprivation, had become so great by August 1916 that the sacrifices already borne, not to mention those yet to be endured, could not be justified in the eyes of the new supreme commanders except by total victory. To ensure this outcome, they were prepared to stop at nothing, least of all sweeping aside any whose misgivings, however objective and serious, challenged their unbridled authority — which soon amounted to nothing less than military dictatorship.

The crisis in the East was mastered with the collapse of the

Brusilov offensive in late summer and the fall of Romania by winter. On the Western Front, the German lines were consolidated: as far as fifty miles behind the exposed salients and low-lying or otherwise unfavorably located front-line trenches, the substantially shorter and incomparably stronger Siegfried Line was constructed with three lines of limestone or concrete fortifications backed up by light railways for swift movement of reinforcements and supplies. The Hindenburg Line — as it was called by the Western Allies — was tested in April 1917 by a French offensive known as the Second Battle of the Aisne. On the eve of the French attack, the Germans drew back to their new line — but since an attack had been planned, it was staged nonetheless. Not only was it repulsed with over a hundred and eighty thousand casualties in ten days, but its ghastly futility brought the French army to an open mutiny that affected over fifty divisions. The crisis was brought under control only with the greatest difficulty by the new French field commander, General Henri Pétain, the hero of Verdun. More than a hundred thousand soldiers were court-martialed and about a fifth found guilty; however, only a few score were officially executed. Authority and discipline could not possibly have been restored without great forbearance, considering the frightful abuse of authority by those who even in spring 1917 had still persisted in senselessly ordering tens of thousands to certain death: small wonder that, to cite but one incident in this mutiny, one particular regiment had gone to the front bleating like sheep on their way to the slaughter. Pétain's success in reestablishing order and discipline was due in large measure to the United States entering the war: he was able to assure his French troops that the offensives would be over until the Americans arrived.

The American declaration of war was the direct result of German submarine aggression. At the beginning of the war, the Entente had imposed a naval blockade on Germany. In some respects it went beyond what was permitted by the existing rules of international law, so the United States repeatedly had occasion to protest violation of its traditional rights as a neutral. But having an American freighter stopped by a British cruiser and diverted to a British port was an entirely different matter from having it sunk by a German submarine. The German surface fleet, imposing though it was, did not directly challenge the Anglo-French blockade, let alone attempt to establish a surface blockade of the British Isles. Early in 1915, however, the German government announced a submarine blockade. In the next several months a number of ships were sunk, including the great British passenger liner *Lusitania,* which was carrying small arms and munitions from America to England. Over a thousand persons were killed, including 139 Americans. To avoid causing the United States to enter the war on the side of the Entente, the Germans sharply curtailed their submarine warfare in late summer 1915. From then on, American munitions shipments to the Western Allies greatly increased and played an important part in the protracted battles of the Western Front, in which vast quantities of ammunition were expended.

In order to win the war, Hindenburg and Ludendorff decided, it would be necessary to stop this flow of munitions. Therefore at the beginning of 1917 they insisted on resumption of unrestricted submarine warfare. Civilian misgivings about the implications of the entry of America, which had no large standing army, were brusquely dismissed, sinkings were promptly resumed, and the United States declared war.

While the war was thus being extended immeasurably in the West, it was also being transformed in the East. Just three weeks before President Woodrow Wilson's war message to Congress, the revolution of March 1917 marked the fall of the Russian autocracy. The provisional regime sought to continue the war, but was able neither to mount a successful offensive nor to consolidate its internal position. Soon after the abdication of the tsar, the German high command had obligingly furnished the exiled Russian revolutionary Lenin and a number of his Bolshevik associates transportation from Switzerland, calculating that they could be depended upon to weaken the Russian war effort. They did; after an abortive coup in the summer, the Bolsheviks succeeded in seizing power at the beginning of November. By the end of the month, they asked the Germans for peace negotiations. These dragged on, with interruptions, for some three months, concluding on 3 March 1918 with the Treaty of Brest-Litovsk. By the terms of this document, which the Russians signed only under vehement protest, the Bolshevik regime was constrained to agree to the loss of roughly a third of Russia's prewar population, arable land, and factories, a quarter of her railroads, and three quarters of her iron and coal mines. But most of the lost territory was in any case not under Bolshevik control. Even before the treaty had been signed, Estonia, Finland, Latvia, Moldavia, and the Ukraine had all declared their independence — though it was an independence clearly sponsored by Germany, as suggested by the election by the Lithuanian assembly in June 1918 of Duke William of Württemberg as king, and the proclamation of Prince Frederick Charles of Hesse as king by the Finnish assembly early in October. (With the German collapse, neither took his throne.)

The Treaty of Brest-Litovsk — and the German tactics used in forcing the Bolsheviks to sign it, which the latter widely publicized — had tremendous impact within Germany. It represented a great military conquest, to be sure, but at the same time a resounding vindication of liberal and socialist misgivings about the real character of the war. At its outset in 1914, many liberals and socialists regarded it not only as a legitimately defensive struggle to protect the fatherland, but also as a necessary stand against the most oppressively reactionary regime in all Europe: tsarist Russia. Despite their dislike of the conservative Hohenzollern monarchy and the militaristic *Junker* caste, even the socialists in the *Reichstag* had initially supported the government's war credits bill. Other considerations aside, to have voted against it would have been, in effect, to have cast a vote in favor of the hated Russian autocracy. But the fall of that regime in 1917, followed by the shocking news of the terms of the Treaty of Brest-Litovsk, completely changed this picture. No longer was it a war against the hostile Western Powers in league with reactionary Russian imperialism. It was a war to further the now unmasked designs of shameless German imperialism. How many loved ones had innocently given their lives, how much needless deprivation had been bravely suffered by those at home, merely in order to establish that broad belt of German satellite states from the Black Sea to the Baltic?

The left wing of the Socialist party had already broken with the moderate majority, establishing the Independent Socialist party (from which, in turn, the German Communist party would later break off). When the German peace terms presented to the Bolsheviks at Brest-Litovsk became known in the winter of 1918, the independent socialists led the increasingly militant workers in a number of cities, including Berlin, in a series of crippling strikes — even in the vital munitions industry. Through the personal intervention of the chairman of the moderate socialists, the *Reichstag* deputy Friedrich Ebert, the munitions strike was ended before it could jeopardize stockpiling for the forthcoming spring offensive.

Victory in the East had freed Hindenburg and Ludendorff to concentrate on forcing a decision in the West in one final offensive. But it had to be launched soon, for time was running out. The submarine campaign on which they had insisted a year earlier had at first achieved spectacular results: almost a million tons of shipping was sunk in April 1917. But the subsequent utilization of convoys so sharply reduced sinkings that by September the British and Americans were building ships as fast as the Germans could destroy them, and by the end of the year sinking submarines faster than the Germans could replace them. Like the Schlieffen Plan, unrestricted submarine warfare was a gamble that had failed disastrously: the invasion of Belgium in 1914 might indeed bring England into the war, but France was to have been so swiftly defeated that it would not have mattered — a calculation that failed. Then in 1917 unrestricted submarine warfare was to have defeated England before America could effectively enter the war. And now, a year later, it was clear that the decision to resume the submarine campaign had also been a catastrophic miscalculation. The American buildup, early in 1918, had still not really begun, but it was imminent. Consequently Hindenburg and Ludendorff decided they had no choice but to make a third and final gamble: a total offensive, employing everything available, not even withholding strategic reserves, putting the very fate of the nation at stake. It was a conscious decision; when asked on the eve of the great spring offensive of 1918 by Prince Max of Baden what would happen if it failed, General Ludendorff replied that in that case Germany would simply have to collapse.

The first phase of the offensive, which began late in March, led to a breakthrough on the Somme. By early April the Germans had advanced a total of some forty miles, threatening to split the British and French, and thereby inducing them finally to coordinate their operations under a single supreme commander, the French general Ferdinand Foch. The second blow fell toward mid-April in Flanders, far to the north, where a thirty-mile breach in the Allied lines was achieved, in part because a sector of the unexpectedly attacked front was being weakly held by a single exhausted Portuguese division awaiting rotation. The third round came at the end of May and beginning of June, bringing the Germans once more to the Marne.

Each phase of the great spring offensive had led to substantial territorial gains, but only at the cost of weakening the Germans more than their adversaries. Moreover, fresh reinforcements were beginning to arrive in large numbers from America. This became painfully obvious in the fourth and what proved to be the final stage of the last great German effort: the Second Battle of the Marne, fought in July and August 1918. On 15 July the weary Germans once more attacked. They even succeeded in crossing the Marne. But they made little further progress against strong French and American forces. Then, on 18 July, General Foch ordered a counteroffensive in which nine American divisions took part. The Germans were forced back over the Marne, beginning the slow withdrawal that would last till the end of the war. For the counteroffensive launched in the teeth of the faltering German drive did not subside after the initial thrust. Contact and pressure were generally maintained along the front, accentuated time and again by heavier blows. The Second Battle of the Marne had already raised grave doubts in the minds of the German supreme commanders about Germany's capability of forcing a military victory. These doubts were congealed into reluctant conviction by the English breakthrough near Amiens on the Somme on 8 August. In Ludendorff's words, this was "the black day of the German army." Although tanks had been used before, and just the previous month at the Marne in greater number, at Amiens 450 were concentrated for an attack that it took four days for the Germans to contain. Throughout August and September, the situation steadily worsened; sectors of the slowly but steadily yielding front nominally assigned to companies or even battalions often were held intact by a few officers with machine guns. By the end of September, it was clear to the German military leaders that the war was lost. On 29 September Hindenburg and Ludendorff suddenly demanded that the government, which until then had been excluded from meaningful authority and even from knowledge of the disastrous situation, arrange an immediate armistice. At the beginning of October, a new chancellor was appointed, Prince Max of Baden, a moderate capable of commanding reasonably broad support in the *Reichstag* and already known as an advocate of a conciliatory peace. On receiving written assurance from Hindenburg that the German front was in imminent danger of collapse and that the cease-fire must not be unnecessarily postponed a single day, Prince Max transmitted to President Woodrow Wilson a formal request for an armistice on the basis of the Fourteen Points he had spelled out in an address to the United States Congress in January 1918, an idealistic peace program including provisions for German evacuation and restoration of Belgium, the return of Alsace-Lorraine, the independence of Poland with access to the sea, impartial adjustment of all colonial claims, and the establishment of a League of Nations to assure future peace. The British and French had never officially subscribed to Wilson's peace program; several of its provisions were in fact incompatible with explicit secret treaty obligations made before or during the war. Yet however much they might regard what he idealistically advocated as potentially mischievous naïveté, they well knew that he took himself seriously and that the public in their own countries did also.

During the weeks following Prince Max's opening request for an armistice, headline publicity was given the German-

American exchange of notes defining the conditions under which President Wilson would ask the British and French to join the United States in concluding a cease-fire agreement. This publicity steadily raised public expectations of an early end of the war. Politically it would have been most imprudent for the French premier, Georges Clemenceau, or the British prime minister, David Lloyd George, to take the onus for blocking peace. Moreover, they knew that the domestic situation in Germany itself was swiftly deteriorating. Allied rigidity leading to a continuation of the war into the coming winter might well play directly into the hands of the Bolsheviks. As much as the responsible leaders in Paris and London wanted to crush Hohenzollern Germany, they did not want to do it so thoroughly as to clear the way for a German Lenin. So in the end they decided to go along with Wilson's proposal for an armistice based on the Fourteen Points, though with many reservations — two of which they made explicit. The British, still in possession of the mightiest fleet in the world, subscribed to only thirteen of the Fourteen Points; they declined to endorse the second, which provided for universal freedom of navigation. The French, for their part, had reservations concerning the question of German liability for damages suffered by the civilian population. Therefore the reparation question, insofar as it might affect payment to the civilian population for losses suffered in the war, was to be considered apart from the Fourteen Points. Wilson agreed that the armistice, though otherwise based on his program, should include explicit reservations in these two areas — and it did. The American president also agreed with the British and French that in order to prevent the cease-fire serving merely as a device to afford the Germans a respite, enabling them subsequently to resume hostilities, the British naval and French military authorities should determine the armistice provisions that would be necessary to prevent this. Consequently the terms of the armistice, as finally presented to the Germans, provided that literally thousands of artillery pieces, machine guns, aircraft, locomotives, railway cars, and motor trucks were to be surrendered, as well as two dozen battleships and cruisers, fifty destroyers, and all of Germany's submarines. Moreover, the blockade was to remain in force and German ships on the high seas would remain subject to seizure.

No less important than the actual terms of the armistice was the question of precisely with whom it was to be concluded. In the third of the American notes in the exchange begun by the initial German request for a cease-fire, the United States secretary of state asserted that the power of the Prussian monarchy and military establishment was so great that the German people through their representatives could obviously do nothing to wrest democratic control from the entrenched military-monarchical establishment. There could be no question of negotiating peace terms with Germany under rulers with contempt for international law. From their initial violation of Belgian neutrality to the recent sinking by submarines, during this current exchange with Washington, not only of passenger ships but also their lifeboats, the present masters of Germany had clearly proven that they could never be trusted to abide by any international agreement to which, following the armistice, they might subscribe. Consequently, should they remain in power, it would not be possible to end the war with a negotiated peace: Germany could only surrender unconditionally. This virtual ultimatum provoked Hindenburg and Ludendorff to demand that the emperor order the armistice negotiations with Washington broken off immediately. William himself was enough stung by the third American note to have commented (in English) to Prince Max that it was "a piece of unmitigated frivolous insolence." But William himself, for all his flaws, was not so frivolous as to demand the ultimate sacrifice of countless tens of thousands in a struggle utterly devoid of any rationale. He faced down Ludendorff, whom he had so long let dominate him, refused to order Max to break off negotiations with Wilson, and when the general angrily proffered his resignation as deputy chief of staff, accepted it, offering him a prestigious field command as an army group commander. Ludendorff categorically refused. William did not accept the refusal as stated; he pointed out that it was up to him, as monarch and commander in chief, to decide who served where. But he did not insist on Ludendorff's further service. In the end, with dark glasses and a false beard as disguise, Ludendorff made his way incognito to Sweden, returning to Germany only long after the war. During the stormy exchange between his deputy and the emperor, Hindenburg had been silent; he long since had learned the value of keeping his counsel — especially in situations like this. After it was over, he also offered his resignation, but calmly, almost perfunctorily. As counseled by Prince Max, William ordered him to stay, and the field marshal acknowledged with a conventional slight bow of assent. The new deputy chief of staff succeeding Ludendorff was not a Prussian but a Württemberger, General Wilhelm Groener, who was to play a crucial role during the following months. Groener commanded Hindenburg's confidence and consequently, like Ludendorff before him, exercised his authority; but unlike Ludendorff he was politically sophisticated enough to understand what was going on in Berlin and later at Weimar and was therefore able to function as a constructive link between the army and the civilian government during the delicate processes of demobilization, restoration of the economy, and reestablishment of civil authority. His competence and the reputation he established is suggested by his having subsequently served during the Weimar Republic as minister of transport in four early cabinets from 1920 to 1923 and then as minister of defense in four later cabinets from 1928 to 1932 (during the last two years simultaneously holding the portfolio of the interior ministry as well). These data are in themselves less important at this point than what they signify: under Hindenburg and Groener the supreme command was not only as unequivocally committed to ending the war as the civil government under Max of Baden, but it also finally had adroit enough leadership to cooperate in facing the challenge of ending a war while simultaneously establishing a republic.

Under the chancellorship of Max of Baden there had already been major reforms that had gone a long way toward making Germany a parliamentary monarchy. But the interaction of wartime defeat, foreign pressure, and domestic turmoil made it necessary, within little over a month, for the new parliamentary regime of Prince Max to step down and for Germany to be declared a republic — even before the armistice was finally signed. Thus the background of the Weimar Republic not only overlapped that of the armistice, but was historically identical with it. In a broader context, both the Weimar Republic and the Versailles Treaty, as well as the revolution and the armistice preceding them, grew out of the war, the way it was conducted, the way it was concluded, and the cumulative impact of all these factors within Germany itself when word of the catastrophe suddenly swept the land during the final weeks of the war.

The sudden demand for an armistice and the sequel exploded into a political vacuum in Germany. The optimistic expectations of the press, the people and their *Reichstag* representatives, and even the vast majority of government officials, had so systematically been nurtured by misleading propaganda that they were totally unprepared, after victory in the East and the dramatic gains of spring and early summer, for the sudden admission of defeat — something that even under the best of circumstances would have been extremely hard to take.

On 30 September a general staff major from the operations section at headquarters, Baron Erich von dem Bussche-Ippenburg, candidly briefed conservative party leaders of the *Reichstag* on the desperate military situation, and held a second briefing for the remaining party leaders on 2 October. (Bussche, incidentally, was one of two generals who, early in 1933, personally implored then President Hindenburg, shortly before he did so, not to appoint Hitler chancellor.) The impact of Bussche's exposé was staggering. The chairman of the Socialist party, Friedrich Ebert (whose role in the munitions strike early in 1918 has already been noted) left the second of Bussche's briefings to participate in negotiations with Prince Max on the formation of the new cabinet. Ebert's *Reichstag* colleague, Philipp Scheidemann, chairman of the Socialist caucus, slated to become a member of Prince Max's cabinet, was most reluctant to enter it. Without going into all too great detail, Max had, of course, indicated that the situation was very serious. For the socialists now to step in would, in Scheidemann's opinion, have tended to implicate the party, at the very last minute, in the impending crisis — something for which it certainly did not need to share responsibility. But then Ebert came in, as the negotiations proceeded, chilled to the marrow by Major Bussche's report. Pallid, he told his friend Scheidemann that it was not merely a question of defeat, but of catastrophe. It was not a question of political loss or gain, but of the fatherland's survival. No matter what the consequences might be for the party, they had to do whatever they possibly could. Scheidemann accepted this and took the post in Prince Max's cabinet, which the socialists loyally supported.

Although the supreme command of the army posed no problems with Groener having relieved Ludendorff, the fleet remained under Admiral Reinhard Scheer, who had been in command during the only major Anglo-German naval engagement of the war, the inconclusive Battle of Jutland in 1916. The war was not to end without the proud German surface navy having fully vindicated itself, whatever the cost! The government was not consulted about Scheer's plans; Ludendorff (just before his dismissal) was personally informed, but only in strictest confidence, which he honored. As Scheer set out to assemble the fleet off the coast, however, sailors on several ships extinguished the fires in the boilers. They had heard rumors of a planned suicide attack on the English coast — or, at the very least, of attempts somehow to thwart the government's well-publicized efforts to negotiate an armistice. Realizing that an undetermined number of ships were undependable for combat because of the mutiny that was simmering on some, already boiling over on others, Scheer abandoned his plan. When the fleet returned to port, the dock workers made common cause with the mutinying sailors. An attempt to free imprisoned mutineers resulted in violence with deaths on both sides. The news of this reinforced the rebellion. The sailors hoisted the red flag of revolution on the warships; the captain of the battleship *Koenig* was the only one to defend the imperial colors to the death.

Kiel and other port cities were soon dominated by councils

of workers and sailors. The movement swiftly spread inland as well, where deserting soldiers returning from hospitals, being transferred, or due back at the front from leave, joined the snowballing movement to form councils, seize power, and join in strikes. In one city after another, the councils claimed power — consciously following the model of the Russian soviets (a word actually meaning councils) of workers and soldiers. On 7 November Bavaria was declared to be a republic. Calmer heads in Berlin and at headquarters, where William had isolated himself, urged that the emperor and the crown prince — notorious for having taken after his father in many ways — both immediately abdicate in favor of the emperor's twelve-year-old grandson, Prince William, in order to save at least the monarchy and the dynasty. But William refused to desert in time of crisis. He was, however, prepared to compromise. He agreed to issue a proclamation abdicating as emperor, but retaining his crown as king of Prussia. This was wildly unrealistic. Events had overtaken the monarchy altogether. Already a general strike had been called to force the abdication and free the way for the armistice that would end the war and for the revolution that would break the power of the hated militaristic oligarchy. At noon on the ninth, Prince Max announced in Berlin that both William and the crown prince had decided to renounce the Prussian-German throne. By phrasing his announcement as he did, without actually stating that they had abdicated, he hoped to make it possible for the emperor's grandson to accede and thereby to save the institution of the monarchy itself. He explicitly stated in his proclamation that he intended to set up a regency, and that once the regency was established, he himself would resign, recommending that his successor as chancellor be the socialist leader Friedrich Ebert. But events had overtaken Prince Max also. He was no longer even nominally in control. The radical Independent Socialists were on the point of proclaiming a proletarian republic. Once they did that, given the temper of the masses swarming in Berlin, there is no telling what might have happened. So Philipp Scheidemann took it upon himself to head off the radicals by proclaiming the German Republic from a window of the

Reichstag building at two in the afternoon. At four, from the balcony of the Berlin Palace, the radical Independent Socialist (and later Communist) leader Karl Liebknecht nonetheless went ahead and proclaimed the "Free Socialist Republic." But Scheidemann had stolen his thunder. Friedrich Ebert had not known of Scheidemann's proclamation in advance; like Max, he was personally committed to a regency. After Liebknecht's move, however, any appearance of pro-monarchist vacillation on the part of the moderate socialists would have driven many of their supporters into the arms of Liebknecht and the extremists. There was nothing for Ebert and his followers to do but to move to the left and to try to co-opt the radical leaders and their supporters insofar as possible, meanwhile appealing to the conservative forces to hold themselves in check. Prince Max acquiesced, realizing Friedrich Ebert had no more latitude than he himself, and designated the former saddle-maker's apprentice to be his successor. This enabled Ebert to draw the radicals with him into a coalition that they would never have considered joining had the prince remained chancellor. Ebert immediately issued a public appeal for quiet and order, so that, as he put it, the people could be provided the food and services they needed to live. The general strike ended. People returned to work.

Meanwhile, the decision to accept the armistice had been made by Prince Max's cabinet three days before it fell. The Catholic *Zentrum* leader, State Secretary Matthias Erzberger, had crossed the lines, accompanied by Count Alfred von Oberndorff, an experienced diplomat. The crushing terms were presented by Marshal Foch. Erzberger and Oberndorff were stunned; this was no mere cease-fire, nor even an armistice on condition of withdrawal, but virtual unilateral disarmament on the part of Germany. Yet Marshal Hindenburg, when consulted on how to proceed, advised negotiations for any modifications possible, but reiterated that the armistice had to be signed even if there were no changes. Erzberger did seek modifications, but in vain, except for insertion of a clause to the effect that despite the blockade there would be, "as shall be necessary," consideration of Germany being provided foodstuffs. By the time he reported this and sought formal authorization to sign or instructions to the contrary, there was technically no longer a constitutionally legitimate government in Germany, for Prince Max had not actually had the constitutional power to invest Friedrich Ebert with the authority of the imperial chancellorship. Consequently the supreme command, when it relayed Berlin's authorization to sign the armistice to the German delegation at Compiègne, simply concluded its radio message with the nameless signature "Imperial Chancellor." Early on the morning of 11 November, the armistice was signed. Before noon the guns were finally silent.

❧ THE WEIMAR REPUBLIC

THUS ENDED HOSTILITIES in the Great War, as it was to be known until its still greater sequel. But the proclamation of the republic and the signing of the armistice did not end deprivation at home or hostilities abroad. Large numbers of German forces remained in the East, under the terms of the armistice, because of the Bolshevik threat, where they often were engaged by partisans. For years there were sharp clashes, often involving relatively large units of German irregulars, especially along the bitterly contested Polish border. The naval blockade not only continued but tightened, for after the armistice Allied ships were able to patrol the Baltic, from which they previously had been excluded. Hunger intensified as millions of demobilized soldiers were cast onto the civilian economy. Desperate shortages were further exacerbated by the loss of rolling stock: under the terms of the armistice, Germany forfeited 150,000 freight cars and 5,000 locomotives in addition to 5,000 trucks. In the armistice, as modified, the victors had indicated a willingness to provide relief "as . . . necessary," but serious negotiations concerning food deliveries began only in January 1919 and the first cargoes of food to pass through the blockade did not reach German ports until late in March. The winter of

1918–19 was consequently the worst of the war, even though it was nominally over.

The widespread starvation, particularly in the large cities, was not so much due to a lack of good will or integrity among the victors or vanquished as to their almost inevitably working at cross purposes, however sincerely they purported to cooperate. Even among themselves, the western leaders sharply differed in their understanding of the problems confronting them. The November armistice, by which the Germans sought a cease-fire, was regarded by Wilson no less as a vehicle for ending hostilities than for eliciting from the warring powers briefly dependent upon the United States their irrevocable commitment to his new design for a just and peaceful world order and its institutionalization in a League of Nations, as stated in the last of his Fourteen Points. The Allied leaders had gone along with his program not only because they had seen no practical alternative, but also because they had appreciated the ideological appeal of its soaring democratic liberalism and cosmopolitan idealism as counter-propaganda against the competitive schemes for world peace being propagated among the working classes in Germany and elsewhere by Lenin's Bolshevik agents. While paying lip service to Wilsonianism, however, Prime Minister David Lloyd George and Premier Georges Clemenceau had never lost sight of their own priorities and had been determined (especially the latter) that, if there were to be an early cease-fire, then the terms of the armistice and the subsequent peace treaty must secure what might otherwise be forfeited by prematurely discontinuing hostilities: the crushing defeat of Germany.

The period from the armistice until the German signing and ratification of the Treaty of Versailles the following summer was consequently one of cold war during which the Germans were reduced to the impotent defiance personified by the fledgling republic's foreign minister, Count Ulrich von Brockdorff-Rantzau, when he headed the German delegation summoned to Versailles early in May 1919 to receive the 440-article treaty prepared by the victors. Count Brockdorff did not rise to respond to the remarks addressed to him by Premier Clemenceau, who had stood to speak. Instead, the overtly hostile German foreign minister, a monocled aristocrat of rather haughty demeanor at best, lashed out from his seat at the victors with snarling indignation, above all for continuing the murderous blockade. His sustained outburst caused Clemenceau to flush with unconcealed rage, Lloyd George to break the letter opener before him into pieces in his hands, and Wilson to comment after the session that "the Germans are really a stupid people. They always do the wrong thing. . . . This is the most tactless speech I have ever heard. It will set the whole world against them." At least they saw to it that their own navy would not be set against them. On 21 June 1919 at Scapa Flow, the vast anchorage sheltered by the Orkneys north of Scotland, over one hundred and seventy-five interned German warships, including ten battleships and more than a hundred submarines, were scuttled by their crews to forestall the ultimate shame of the fleet falling permanently into the hands of the enemy. Two days later, 23 June 1919, under the pressure of an ultimatum threatening resumption of hostilities, the German delegation was instructed to sign the Versailles Treaty under protest — yet explicitly without reservations. The very same day, the twenty-third, the French flags and colors taken as trophies during the Franco-Prussian War of 1870–71 and due for return to France under Article 245 of the Treaty, were burned in Berlin. (The subsequent provision, Article 246, provided that Germany "hand over to His Britannic Majesty's Government the skull of the Sultan Mkwawa which was removed from the Protectorate of German East Africa and taken to Germany.")

Under the territorial provisions of the treaty, Germany lost her overseas colonies, despite the commitment to impartial adjustment of all colonial claims specified in the fifth of Wilson's Fourteen Points, as well as between a seventh and an eighth of her continental land area with about a tenth of her prewar population, including Alsace-Lorraine, conquered from France a half century earlier, and much of Posen and West Prussia, including Danzig, largely seized by Prussia in the course of the eighteenth-century partitions of Poland. Germany west of the Rhine was occupied. The German army was reduced to a token force of one hundred thousand, with a maximum of four thousand officers, and the navy to a total of fifteen thousand. Potential paramilitary officials, such as customs officers, forest guards, and coastguardsmen, were not to exceed the number in service in 1913, while the number of police was not to be proportionally larger to the population than in 1913.

Especially resented was Article 80, binding Germany to respect the "inalienable independence" of German Austria, the republic comprising the tenth of the former Habsburg Monarchy still under Vienna after the disintegration of the multinational empire. Stripped of the vast non-German holdings and the great-power interests that had precluded Bismarck's unifying Germany except by excluding it, Austria was now a rump state of under ten million with a disproportionately large metropolis of some two million which had lost its great southeast European hinterland, but which still might hope to flourish within Germany. Both the Weimar constitution and that of the Austrian Republic provided for union with Germany, but this was blocked with what seemed to many Germans and Austrians to be maliciously selective disregard of the principle of democratic self-determination that had undermined the Habsburg empire.

From the point of view of Clemenceau, self-determination was not the important thing, but the security of France. As a young man, he had seen the French Empire crushed in 1870, and in his old age watched his country once more brought to the brink of collapse. His mission was now to assure that the Frenchmen who had given their lives — almost a million and a half of them — should not have done so in vain. He was determined to secure at the conference table what they had died to make possible: peace with security from future German aggression against France. Germany already outnumbered France by twenty million. For him not to prevent the annexation of Austria, which would have more than restored the relatively little, as Clemenceau saw it, that Germany had lost in the Treaty of Versailles, would have been unthinkable. The very fact that Germany did not actually have to forfeit substantially more was due only to Anglo-American resistance, compensated

10 / THE WEIMAR REPUBLIC

Early in 1918, the last year of World War I, the Central Powers under German leadership seemed far from defeat; as shown on the lower left map, the Allied and Associated Powers had managed to capture only a small district in southern Alsace, which the Germans had taken from France forty-seven years earlier. Germany's unexpectedly swift capitulation in the fall of 1918 came simultaneously with the establishment of the Weimar Republic, which bore the onus of accepting the staggering terms of the armistice and the Treaty of Versailles. As shown on the upper map, Germany ceded territory to France, Belgium, Denmark, Lithuania, Poland, Czechoslovakia, and the League of Nations, which administered the Free City of Danzig, totalling a loss equivalent in area to the prewar kingdom of Bavaria. Germany's principal inland waterways were internationalized. Luxemburg was withdrawn from the German tariff union and economically unified with Belgium. German territory west of a line fifty kilometers (about thirty miles) east of the Rhine was permanently demilitarized; in addition, German territory west of the Rhine was temporarily occupied, together with substantial bridgeheads east of Cologne, Koblenz, and Mainz, as well as a smaller area across the river from Strasbourg. In January 1923, the French and Belgians also occupied the industrial heartland of Germany, the Ruhr district. The Allied occupation of the Rhineland ended in 1930.

by Wilson's and Lloyd George's willingness to conclude security pacts with France at the same time the peace treaty was being concluded with Germany; otherwise France would have had to insist on dismemberment of Germany — detachment of the Rhineland, at the very least, as a separate state under French protection, a sort of satellite buffer state.

As it turned out, President Wilson was no more able to secure United States Senate approval of the French security pact he had signed with France than of the peace treaty with Germany, and as the terms of the Anglo-French pact only were to become effective concurrently with the Franco-American pact,

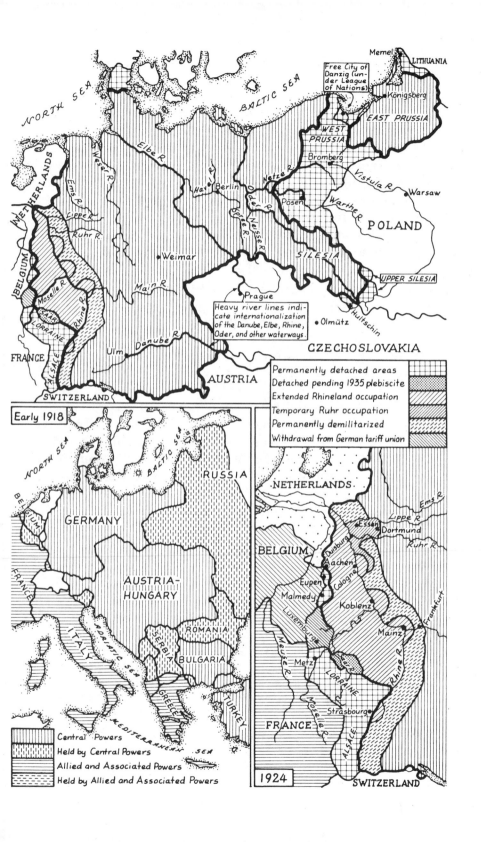

NORTH SEA

BALTIC SEA

Memel

LITHUANIA

Free City of Danzig (under League of Nations)

Königsberg

EAST PRUSSIA

WEST PRUSSIA

NETHERLANDS

Weser R.

Ems R.

Lippe R.

Ruhr R.

Elbe R.

Havel R.

Berlin

Oder R.

Spree R.

Netze R.

Bromberg

Posen

Warthe R.

Vistula R.

Warsaw

POLAND

BELGIUM

Mosella R.

SAAR

LORRAINE

ALSACE

Rhine R.

Weimar

Main R.

Neisse R.

SILESIA

UPPER SILESIA

Prague

Heavy river lines indicate internationalization of the Danube, Elbe, Rhine, Oder, and other waterways.

Olmütz

Hultschin

FRANCE

Ulm

Danube R.

SWITZERLAND

AUSTRIA

CZECHOSLOVAKIA

Permanently detached areas
Detached pending 1935 plebiscite
Extended Rhineland occupation
Temporary Ruhr occupation
Permanently demilitarized
Withdrawal from German tariff union

Early 1918

NORTH SEA

BALTIC SEA

RUSSIA

BELGIUM

GERMANY

FRANCE

AUSTRIA-HUNGARY

ROMANIA

ITALY

ADRIATIC SEA

SERBIA

BULGARIA

GREECE

TURKEY

MEDITERRANEAN SEA

Central Powers
Held by Central Powers
Allied and Associated Powers
Held by Allied and Associated Powers

NETHERLANDS

Ems R.

Lippe R.

Essen

Dortmund

Ruhr R.

Duisburg

BELGIUM

Aachen

Eupen

Malmedy

Cologne

Koblenz

Luxemburg

Saar R.

Mainz

Frankfurt

Mosel R.

Metz

LORRAINE

Rhine R.

Moselle R.

Strasbourg

ALSACE

FRANCE

1924

SWITZERLAND

the French wound up with neither a Rhenish satellite nor its substitute, the security pacts with America and England. French chagrin at having been — from their point of view — cruelly disappointed if not betrayed by their former comrades in arms goes a long way toward explaining the gratuitously harsh and ultimately self-defeating postwar policy of the French toward Germany, particularly during the early twenties. They were determined to use the Versailles Treaty to do what no diplomatic treaty alone can be expected to do: to hold down a great power that has not been thoroughly defeated long after the war is over, even after the allies who turned the tide are gone and, what is worse, when the treaty itself is not only onerous to the defeated nation, but even morally offensive.

Many Germans regarded a number of the provisions of the Versailles Treaty as implicitly invidious and punitive, but Part VIII, dealing with reparation, was explicit and devastating. On the basis of French reservations regarding Wilson's Fourteen Points, the final American note to Berlin in the pre-armistice exchange in 1918 had already strongly emphasized Germany's full liability for reparation of all damages to the allied civilian population caused by German aggression by land, by sea, and from the air. In Article 19 of the armistice of 11 November 1918, Germany had explicitly accepted that commitment. Its implications were ominous, for in terms of the standards of international law generally considered valid on the eve of the First World War, an all but incontrovertible case could be made that Germany was guilty of grossly illegal aggression by land in Belgium, by sea through unrestricted submarine warfare, and from the air by the bombing of England (since 1915 Zeppelins and since 1916 airplanes had mounted increasingly frequent air raids that had been militarily trivial, yet had caused a number of unfortunate civilians loss of life, limb, and property). But it was Article 231, which opened the reparation section of the Versailles Treaty, that went far beyond anything for which the Germans had been prepared by the Fourteen Points, the American notes, or the armistice. It stated that the "Allied and Associated Governments affirm and Germany accepts the responsibility of Germany and her allies for causing all the loss and damage to which the Allied and Associated Governments and their nationals have been subjected as a consequence of the war imposed upon them by the aggression of Germany and her allies."

On examining the treaty, when it was presented to them for comment in May 1919, the Germans immediately singled out Article 231 as its crowning outrage: an extorted confession, to be wrung from them by force, that they and their former allies bore sole guilt for the war. A distinguished committee of internationally recognized authorities in their respective fields, including the military historian Hans Delbrück and the sociologist Max Weber, drafted a memorandum emphatically rejecting Article 231 as a one-sided moral denunciation lacking archival documentation or intellectual objectivity. Their memorandum was only one of a number of expert statements hastily drawn together, in the three weeks permitted for the task, to form a book-length "note" stating the German government's position on the treaty. In effect it was a recommendation that much of the treaty be entirely reworked, article by article — a recommendation that was not accepted. Nonetheless, a few provisions were modified, despite strong French misgivings, on the initiative of Lloyd George. He initially had taken a politically popular hard line against the Germans, but then gradually came to realize that in the long run it could prove terribly self-defeating to attempt to achieve by treaty what had not been accomplished on the field of battle.

War, as Clausewitz observed, is the continuation of politics by other means; to try to carry this one step further and utilize a peace treaty as a continuation of the war by diplomatic means would in the end make peace impossible. It would not be peacemaking at all, but rather self-delusion resting on a fundamental misconception, still very common today, concerning the nature of international agreements. They never have been regarded as eternal and rarely as permanent compacts -- except perhaps for certain treaties imposed by the United States on American Indian tribes (whose claim to nationhood, other than for the purpose of concluding such treaties, has been disputed no less than many Indians' claim to the rights of

American citizenship). In his memoirs, Bismarck pointed out that "the binding character of all treaties between great states is conditional as soon as . . . put to the test in 'the struggle for existence.' No great nation will ever be able to be moved to sacrifice its existence on the altar of fidelity to treaties, when forced to choose between the two. No clause in a treaty can suspend the *ultra posse nemo obligatur* [the implicit reservation that no one can be obligated beyond his means]." Moreover, Bismarck stressed, "in state treaties involving obligations, the *clausula rebus sic stantibus* is silently taken for granted" — the clause whereby each party considers itself obligated by the terms of the treaty only insofar as circumstances remain essentially as they were at the time the treaty was concluded.* This does not mean that international commitments may be broken at will. The irresponsible statesman who capriciously does so will lose, as did Hitler, all credibility as a treaty partner. The key to successful diplomacy between sovereign states has always been to conduct relations in terms of mutually respected self-interest, whereby — in an inevitably changing world — the terms are periodically reexamined and redefined as appropriate. When this has been left undone, and agreements have no longer reflected the respective interests of the contracting parties, they often have become dead letters and actually impeded good relations. In this context, the Treaty of Versailles was no mere diplomatic impediment; it was virulent poison. Not only did it poison German foreign relations, however; it also poisoned the Weimar Republic.

Territorial losses, occupation, and even disarmament were grim realities which might hardly be acceptable, but with which Germany might at least have been able to come to terms. Even a reasonably heavy indemnity, moreover, such as Germany had levied on France in 1871, and France on many a country earlier, could be dealt with: the loser in a war has generally had to pay. But the gratuitously humiliating guilt clause was beyond discussion for even relatively moderate Germans — the more so as it served to introduce the provisions of

*Otto von Bismarck, *Gedanken und Erinnerungen* (Stuttgart and Berlin: J. G. Cotta'sche Buchhandlung Nachfolger, n.d.), pp. 530, 537.

the treaty assigning Germany formal liability for reparation payments, in cash and in kind, which until 1921 were not yet calculated: a total, as finally announced on 1 May 1921, of thirty-three billion dollars, plus the entire Belgian war debt as well as the costs of maintaining occupation forces in the Rhineland. No German could feel morally bound to the terms of the *"Versailler Diktat,"* and even those statesmen who led Germany to comply with its terms did so primarily in the hope of thereby winning international credibility and confidence enough to achieve, in gradual steps, the favorable revision that in time would become politically feasible. In point of fact, that time came far earlier than the most sanguine optimist of 1919 would have thought likely: in 1932, the year before the fall of the Weimar Republic, it was agreed at an international conference in Lausanne that German reparation payment should be ended; and at the Disarmament Conference in Geneva that same year, Germany's claim for parity in armaments was recognized in principle by several of the powers. The achievement in less than fourteen years of what would have been unthinkable in 1919 required statesmanship of the highest order — above all the courageous leadership of the Nobel peace laureate Dr. Gustav Stresemann, whose foreign policy, together with that of his French counterpart Aristide Briand, largely reconciled France and Germany, and enabled the latter to enter the League of Nations. But the unflinching realism with which he achieved so much for Germany led not merely to angry opposition, but to intense hatred and vilification. Throughout the brief span of the Weimar Republic, 1918–33, Stresemann and other "fulfilment politicians" were defamed as traitors for their allegedly cowardly fulfilment of the terms of the treaty by demagogues who themselves well knew that there was no practical alternative.

The ordeal of Stresemann and those who realized that Germany had no choice but to accept the awful consequences of defeat, demonstrated the fatal weakness of the Weimar Republic: from its very origin it had lacked broad popular backing or even the strong support of the elite. Determined commitment on the part of either the masses or leadership classes would have facilitated the development of a broad political consensus, affording a positive framework within which political leaders could operate, doing the often difficult things that have to be done, particularly in times of crisis and national disaster. But such a framework was never firmly established. In a formal sense, to be sure, it was; the Weimar Constitution defined the basic rules under which the business of state would be conducted. But it was a politically contrived instrument, never commanding deeply rooted loyalty, never defining a true national consensus, and therefore never setting effective limits on radical opposition, whether from left or right, that was prepared to stop at nothing in order to seize political power. Consequently the German Republic, precariously improvised to assure the armistice while heading off Bolshevik revolution, was racked for especially its first five years by political riots and murders, Communist uprisings, separatist plots, and attempted *coups d'état*, notably the Kapp *Putsch* of 1920 which drove the government from Berlin to Stuttgart and was broken only by a general strike, after the army had refused to move against the right-wing insurgents, and the abortive National Socialist *Putsch* in Munich in 1923, led by Adolf Hitler, a self-educated Austrian anti-Semite with uncanny powers of demagogic persuasion.

With the social, political, and economic fabric of the nation already under almost unendurable stress due to the external defeat and internal dissension, the moderate socialist leaders who had assumed office during the fall and winter of 1918 and 1919 considered themselves in no position to consider implementing the radical reforms explicit in their Marxist ideology. Far from being genuine revolutionaries, they consciously decided, once in power, to preserve what remained of the existing social and economic order. Thus they took on themselves the thankless task of liquidating the bankrupt Hohenzollern empire, accepting, on the one hand, the peace settlement imposed by the victorious enemy, and on the other, the odium of crushing, in league with the returning German army, the radical movement which threatened to engulf Germany in a Communist revolution comparable to that which had overthrown the provisional government in Russia the year before. The strength of the socialist cadres was sufficient to assure Friedrich Ebert, already the designated successor of Prince Max of Baden as head of the government, the crucial parallel revolutionary position in Berlin of cochairman of the "Council of People's Commissars," and then to secure, by an overwhelming majority, the endorsement by the revolutionary councils of nationwide elections in January 1919 to a German National Assembly that would provide a new German constitution and conclude the peace treaty ending the war (both of which it ultimately did). Meeting in the provincial city of Weimar, safe from the revolutionary turmoil and bloodshed of the capital (where on 31 December 1918 the German Communist party had been founded), the assembly drew up a new constitution that proclaimed the German Reich to be a republic and retained the general structure and organization of the Bismarckian empire with the difference that the constituent principalities became republican states and the empire as a whole a republic under a popularly elected president. The chancellor was normally responsible to the *Reichstag*. The basis for a democratically responsible parliamentary regime seemed to be assured.

By the end of 1923, which had brought the French occupation of the Ruhr, right radical, Communist, and separatist rebellions, together with an inflation which destroyed the value of the mark, ultimately worth less than a quarter trillionth of a dollar, the Weimar Republic finally became stabilized enough to enter a half decade retrospectively considered by some to be at least a brief silver age — though at the time it was perceived as a time of almost continual crisis. It was during these five years, from 1924 to 1929, that Foreign Minister Stresemann succeeded in bringing the pariah Germany back into the community of nations. It was a period of cultural creativity and economic growth, even though the latter rested on the dubious foundation of short-term American private loans financing reparations installments that were used partly or, in the case of England, almost wholly for payment of American war debt — a dangerous cycle if not, as Churchill observed, an "insane" one.

But the five good years of the Weimar Republic afforded far too little time for a people who had always been denied political responsibility to transform themselves from obedient subjects to active citizens. In all too many ways, little changed after 1918, least of all the mentality of the upper classes. There was, to be sure, no longer an imperial court, but after the death in 1925 of the socialist president, Friedrich Ebert, the almost eighty-year-old Hindenburg was elected to replace him, his apparently scarcely tarnished prestige almost fully restored by the nefarious legend he himself helped propagate, that the war had been lost because the German army, undefeated in the field, had been "stabbed in the back" by traitors at home. Yet the irony of the election to the presidency of an imperial field marshal was compounded when, after the expiration of his seven-year term in 1932, he was reelected, not by the conservatives and reactionaries who had first installed him, but by the votes of the socialists and liberals whom he inwardly disdained, yet who saw in him the last possible bulwark against a dictatorship of the right or, less likely but more frightening, of the left.

With the collapse of the world economy in 1929, Germany was particularly hard hit. Under the pressures of the emergency, parliamentary government broke down and after mid-1930 the country had to be ruled, as it had been during the crisis of 1923 during Stresemann's ninety-nine-day chancellorship, by emergency decrees. Under the impact of economic misery, moreover, the tenuous loyalty of the people to the Weimar Republic crumbled. *Reichstag* elections in September 1930 and again in July 1932 saw the Communist popular vote rise from 10.6 to 13.1 to 14.6 percent, while that of Hitler's National Socialists surged from 2.6 to 18.3 to 37.4 percent. Thus by the summer of 1932, the Weimar Republic had been repudiated by the majority of Germans, 52 percent of them supporting radicals either of the left or the right who scorned democracy and openly acknowledged that they were using its instrumentalities only to gain power and destroy it. The question in people's minds was therefore not whether, but in which direction, the tottering republic would fall, to the right or to the left. As the strength of the Hitler movement first surpassed and then greatly exceeded that of the Communists, it was more and more widely felt that the coming dictatorship would be National Socialist. An eloquent demonstration of this has been preserved in the published correspondence of the distinguished Berlin historian Friedrich Meinecke. In a letter written early in December 1931, almost fourteen months before Hitler's appointment as chancellor, he informed a friend how he had attempted to find eight prominent colleagues to support a public statement taking a democratic as opposed to a National Socialist stand on a controversial issue vitally affecting the university. It had been in vain; too many people were already accommodating themselves to the "coming Nazi regime." *

❧ THE THIRD REICH AND THE SECOND WORLD WAR

AFTER HIS UNSUCCESSFUL Munich *Putsch* in 1923, the leader of the National Socialist German Workers' Party (*Nationalsozialistische Deutsche Arbeiterpartei* or NSDAP), Adolf Hitler, was convicted of high treason and sentenced to a fine of 200 gold marks and five years' detention. In its verdict, the court stressed his "patriotic motives and honorable intentions" and waived deportation — though obligatory under German law for the convicted Austrian citizen — because it would have been inappropriate in the case of a man "who thinks and feels in such German terms." Late in 1924 Hitler was released on parole from Landsberg Fortress, where he had written the first volume of his programmatic autobiography, *Mein Kampf* (published in 1925, and followed by the second volume the following year). Although the treatment Hitler received was lenient, General Ludendorff, who had marched with him in the abortive *Putsch* and had also been a defendant in the trial, was

* Letter of 4 December 1931 to W. Goetz in his *Ausgewählter Briefwechsel*, ed. Ludwig Dehio and Peter Classen (Stuttgart: K. F. Koehler Verlag, 1962), p. 131.

acquitted. Given the independence of the largely reactionary judiciary inherited from the empire by the Weimar Republic, treason from the right was generally treated as mildly as that from the left was treated harshly.

On his release, Hitler soon regained control of the NSDAP, which had all but disintegrated during his Landsberg sabbatical (he ironically referred to it as his "university at state expense"), and built up the party organization on a nationwide basis, working, watching, and waiting for his time to come, as it did in 1929 with the onset of the Great Depression, the collapse of the German economy, and soaring unemployment. Ever wider popular support catapulted Hitler into national prominence. Playing with breathtaking virtuosity on the sensitivities of the masses, cultivating the bourgeois terror of the Communist revolution, interweaving the most violent anti-Semitism with virulent denunciation of the "November criminals" who had "stabbed the army in the back" and treacherously shackled Germany to the *"Versailler Diktat,"* Hitler sustained his crudely vulgar and yet perversely sophisticated demagogy with a fanatically intense belief in himself and the mission assigned him by destiny. He would not have been able to mesmerize his listeners by the tens of thousands without this infectious conviction that he could not and would never be able to fail, a conviction sustained by a force of will bordering on the demonic.

The bestial depravity Hitler ultimately revealed was by no means apparent at the beginning. Much that he said and wrote was simply dismissed by the intelligent and critical either as insincere rhetoric to influence the masses, or immature sentiments he would soon enough cast off once burdened with the responsibility of office. Thus it was possible for Hitler, despite the staggering candor with which he compulsively proclaimed both his intentions and the techniques by which he would achieve them, to gain the support not only of the rabble and the lunatic fringe, but also of a substantial segment of the German elite. The intellectual primitiveness of his pseudoscientific racist ideology notwithstanding, Hitler enjoyed strong backing among the established professional classes and also among university students, who in turn could point to many highly respected intellectuals of the day as followers of his movement. Such prominent figures as the existentialist philosopher Martin Heidegger, the legal scholar Carl Schmitt, the dramatist Gerhart Hauptmann, and the musician Richard Strauss, men of distinction in their fields, gave National Socialism, through their emphatic support, a certain legitimization in the eyes of the general public which it might otherwise never have acquired. But this was less important than another more fundamental consideration: the Germans had tried democracy and found it wanting. Since the emperor had entrained for exile in Holland, a people nurtured on the international prestige, economic expansion, social rigidity, and efficient authoritarianism of the Bismarckian empire had suffered too much national humiliation, economic misery, social disintegration, and political instability. Now at last the fate of the nation could be confidently placed in the hands of a dynamic leader with unquestioning faith in himself and the ability to generate fervent loyalty in others, a man who promised to lead Germany once more to an era of prosperity, stability, strength, and respect in the eyes of the world. He was certainly no democrat in the sense of the Weimar constitution, but the people of Germany had long since clearly repudiated the republic at the polls. A democracy is no stronger than the will of its citizens to live and if need be die for it. The past fourteen years had shown the Germans that democracy was not worth either. Now they were ready to exchange the hollow rhetoric of liberty, equality, and fraternity, for the stirring realities of bold leadership, national discipline, and systematic rearmament. First Prussia and then Germany had been led to greatness by men of indomitable will and unswerving purpose followed by a people prepared to give their all, doing their duty, obeying orders, and even laying down their lives for the fatherland. Now once more, after years of drifting and despair, the German people were summoned by a man prepared to lead them.

But Hitler did not come to power because of the response of the population at large or because of the strength of his movement in the *Reichstag,* where the NSDAP became the strongest party in 1932. He would not have been appointed chancellor in January 1933 had he not seemed a likely tool to serve the various purposes of a number of ambitious conservatives led by Franz von Papen, a confidant of the now senile president. Chancellor from June through mid-November 1932, Papen was a proud and sensitive man who had been profoundly embittered at having been displaced in that office by his defense minister, General Kurt von Schleicher, ostensibly for having been unable to deal simultaneously with the extremist challenges of Communism and National Socialism. By arranging for Hitler to become a sort of figurehead chancellor in a cabinet to be completely dominated by himself and his colleagues, Papen revenged himself on Schleicher, regained at least indirect power, and harnessed the Nazi demagogue who would dispose once and for all of the Communist threat. In their facile complacency, he and his associates regarded it as a safe assumption that the revolutionary character of the Hitler movement would slowly but surely be toned down to respectability by the fetters of responsibility. However, what to one man is the burden of responsibility is to another the elixir of power. Hitler was possessed of an elementary instinct for power which neither his coalition partners nor more than a few of his contemporaries possessed or even perceived. Hardly had the cabinet list been drawn up than Hitler began gathering into his hands the reins of power in Germany. The crafty barons and business magnates who dreamed of using him awoke to discover he had made them almost helpless pawns in a game they never quite understood.

Yet Hitler's appointment to the chancellorship on 30 January 1933 was not the full-blown seizure of power *(Machtergreifung)*, into which retrospective National Socialist propaganda sought to transform it. That was a legend. No one knew better than Hitler himself that the chancellorship was just the first step. Even before he was sworn into office, he had set to work on the second, staking the inauguration of his coalition on prior consent to prompt national elections, enabling him to use the public impact of his appointment, and the authority it would bring him, to strengthen his parliamentary position. On

5 March 1933 the National Socialists received 43.9 percent of the vote and Hitler's conservative coalition partners 8 percent. But their combined *Reichstag* majority of 51.9 percent, narrow though it was, afforded Hitler all the leverage he needed: on 23 March the representatives of the German people formally abdicated their constitutional responsibility. The Communists having already been excluded by force, only the socialists voted in opposition. But even the votes of the eighty-one absent Communists would not have sufficed to block the fateful *Ermächtigungsgesetz* (Enabling Act), for the final tally was 441 to 94, well over the two-thirds majority required for a law suspending provisions of the constitution.

By the end of 1933 all the political parties in Germany had either been dissolved or outlawed except for the NSDAP, which by the law of 1 December 1933 was "insolubly tied" to the state. But it was not absorbed into it. Quite the contrary, the National Socialist party was accorded the status of a public corporation under its leader, the *Führer*, who alone determined its statutes; its disciplinary courts were recognized as having special jurisdiction; and cabinet rank was bestowed on Hitler's party deputy, Rudolf Hess, as well as Ernst Röhm, chief of staff of the SA (for *Sturmabteilungen*), the party militia of brownshirted paramilitary storm troopers. The sanction of law was thereby given to a German party-state dualism analogous to the dualism in Russia of the Communist party and the Soviet state.

The implications of this were keenly appreciated by the leaders of the German armed forces, the *Reichswehr*, for they were the custodians of the Prusso-German tradition of a very different sort of dualism: a dualism approaching parity between the civilian and military authorities, permitting the latter to remain aloof from party politics and to maintain the military establishment on a semi-independent basis. Their privileged status had hardly been diminished by the twenty fragile coalitions of the Weimar Republic from 1918 to 1933, especially not after the election to the presidency of Field Marshal von Hindenburg in 1925. But close Russo-German military ties during the twenties had given the leaders of the *Reichswehr* opportunity to become quite familiar with what it could mean for a professional officer corps to be subjected to the authority of a totalitarian party and its secret police — such as the *Cheka.* Concern about the danger of a similar system emerging in Germany had been an important factor in Hitler's rise to power. He was militantly anti-Communist. Whatever the shortcomings of the National Socialist chancellor, the military-industrial-landowning establishment generally felt he could be depended upon to stop bolshevism and, presumably, the threats it implied.

The elevation on 1 December 1933 of SA Chief of Staff Röhm to cabinet rank on a par with the defense minister, General Werner von Blomberg, came as a rude shock. It did not challenge the privileged position of the armed forces in the same way establishment of a cabinet-level secret police authority would. But it was serious nonetheless because of the implicit threat that the professional military establishment might be engulfed by the plebeian horde of party storm troopers. In February 1934, *Reichsminister* Röhm made this explicit with his proposal to the cabinet that the SA be used as the basis for swift expansion of the army, and that this expansion program be carried out under the aegis of a single minister (obviously himself), who would be in charge of the regular armed forces as well as the paramilitary and veterans' organizations.

Limited to 100,000 by the Treaty of Versailles, the German army was a finely honed professional elite force that would have lost its identity in an amalgamation with Röhm's militia of millions. The SA proposal was immediately side-tracked, not only because of an emphatic army protest directly to Hindenburg, the supreme commander, but also because Hitler himself grasped its implications. Röhm's brownshirts had been indispensable during the years he was storming the gates, but now he had no need for coarse street fighters. His future plans called for as sophisticated a striking force as the professional competence of the general staff, modern military technology, and the economic and human resources of the nation could provide. Röhm's continuing pressure during the spring of 1934 provoked increasing concern in the German military hierarchy, for the army's obviously failing eighty-six-year-old protector, President Hindenburg, could not be expected to live longer than a few more months. Hitler intended to succeed him as head of state and supreme commander of the armed forces, but he realized this would not be feasible without at least the acquiescence of the tightly knit military hierarchy. With his uncanny instinct for power, Hitler well knew the difference between titles of office and real control — and also understood the peril of underestimating this difference.

Machiavelli once observed that one does not maintain power with the same following used to gain it. A month before Hindenburg's death, Hitler gave a ruthless demonstration of this axiom by ordering Röhm and scores of his associates shot in a series of actions retroactively proclaimed, by a special law, to have been "legal as acts of self-defense by the state." Röhm and his "accomplices" had allegedly been caught red-handed in the process of staging a *coup d'état*. This was untrue. While the SA chief of staff and many of his supporters had been dissatisfied with the government, they had not sought to overthrow it, but rather to gain greater influence within it. Scores of others who obviously had nothing to do with the fictional "Röhm Revolt" were simultaneously murdered in a nationwide settling of old accounts that took perhaps two hundred lives and possibly more. Among the victims on the "Night of the Long Knives" were Father Bernhard Stempfle, a former editorial reader of Hitler's *Mein Kampf,* Papen's ghost-writer Edgar Jung, Erich Klausener, the head of Catholic Action in Berlin, and Hitler's predecessor as chancellor, General Kurt von Schleicher, together with his wife as well as one of his close associates, General Kurt von Bredow.

Not Röhm was guilty of a *coup d'état* in the summer of 1934, but Hitler. The Röhm purge was the first step in a triple *coup* by which Hitler made himself Germany's highest judge, head of state, and supreme commander of the armed forces on an extraordinary basis.

The dictator's usurpation of ultimate judicial authority was already implicit in the law by which the cabinet on 3 July 1934 retroactively condemned to death as traitors the victims of the purge. But in his *Reichstag* speech ten days later, Hitler went on to proclaim that he had acted as "the supreme judge of the German people." The legislative branch had forfeited its authority by passing the Enabling Act sixteen months earlier; now Hitler placed himself above the judiciary as well. This was in no way related to the exercise of the power of pardon, a traditional and constitutional prerogative of the sovereign head of state, an office which Hitler in any case did not yet hold. What he claimed, having already blatantly exercised it, was unbridled authority to order executions without due process of law or even the most peremptory of formal convictions.

On the death of President Hindenburg at the beginning of August 1934, Hitler immediately succeeded him as head of state and supreme commander of the armed forces. Despite the explicit inviolability of the presidency under the Enabling Act, that office was now united with the chancellorship in Adolf Hitler as *Führer* and Reich chancellor by a law decreed by the cabinet on 1 August and endorsed by some 85 percent of the voters in the plebiscite of 19 August. On the second, meanwhile, Defense Minister Blomberg had ordered a sacred oath of personal obedience administered to all members of the armed forces. Earlier forms of the *Reichswehr* oath, previously required only of new personnel, had been solemn avowals of loyalty and obedience to the constitution and the fatherland, but the new oath, sprung without warning on all, was a commitment, under God, "to render unconditional obedience to the *Führer* of the German Reich and people, Adolf Hitler." Unsanctioned by law or precedent, this vow subordinated those who took it to the status of personal subjects if not vassals of Hitler. Yet it was accepted, despite strong misgivings on the part of many, because Hitler, for his part, had freed the German armed forces from the threat posed by the party militia with one stunning blow and had subsequently pledged, in his *Reichstag* speech of 13 July, that just as the National Socialist party would be the sole bearer of the political will of the nation, the *Reichswehr* would be the sole bearer of arms.

The apparent triumph of the professional military establishment over the party militia was a pyrrhic victory. The killings had largely been carried out by Heinrich Himmler's

SS (*Schutzstaffeln,* defense echelons) and Gestapo (*Geheime Staatspolizei,* secret state police). On 20 July 1934, exactly one week after his unequivocal pledge to the armed forces, Hitler rewarded the SS for its "great services" in connection with the "Röhm Revolt" by severing its affiliation with the SA, of which it had been a subdivision initially charged with the personal protection of the *Führer.* Henceforth reporting directly to him, *Reichsführer-SS* and Gestapo Chief Himmler would be in a position to develop a combined palace guard and secret police incomparably more dangerous to the army and other established interests in Germany than Röhm's SA could ever have become. This did not happen without early warning. A more resounding challenge to the caste-like solidarity and rigid code of honor of the officer corps, particularly unyielding among the army generals, could hardly have been contrived than the cold-blooded murder of Bredow and the Schleichers. Nonetheless, the military leadership corps was prepared to accept the lead of General von Blomberg, who observed that the Prussian officer's honor had consisted in being stringently proper, but from now on, the German officer's honor had to consist in being cunning.

For over three years this approach seemed to pay off. The German military establishment prospered, as never before in its history, under leadership of Blomberg, one of very few senior members of the officer corps who had become a dedicated National Socialist. In 1935 Hitler introduced universal military training, secured British recognition of German rearmament in the Anglo-German Naval Agreement, and reorganized the *Reichswehr* of the Weimar Republic, consisting of the army and navy, into the *Wehrmacht* of the Third Reich, which included an independent third service branch, the air force *(Luftwaffe)* under Hermann Göring, a fighter ace and squadron commander in World War I who had been at Hitler's side since before the Munich *Putsch.* In 1936 Blomberg, now minister of war rather than defense, was promoted to field marshal. By late 1937, however, serious problems had begun to arise in the allocation of raw materials. Shortages had been brought about largely by the precipitate rearmament program. Göring ruthlessly exploited his position as general plenipotentiary for the Four-Year Plan (for economic mobilization) to the advantage of the air force at the expense of the other service branches. After postponing a showdown as long as he could, Blomberg asked Hitler for a joint conference with himself and the three service chiefs, not seriously expecting to bridle the powerful Göring, but possibly to establish more equitable guidelines he could be expected to honor. Hitler consented to the meeting, setting it up for the afternoon of 5 November 1937. To Blomberg's surprise, Hitler summoned the foreign minister, Baron Konstantin von Neurath, in addition to Göring, the commander in chief of the army, Baron Werner von Fritsch, and the head of the navy, Admiral Erich Raeder. To the war minister's greater surprise still, Hitler used the topic of raw materials merely as a launching pad for an extended explanation of his plans for increasing Germany's living space *(Lebensraum)*. First Austria and Czechoslovakia would be taken; then, with the flanks of the Reich secured, France could be dealt with as the major enemy. Göring was already prepared for what was coming. Admiral Raeder was reserved, not only because of his habitual reticence regarding matters outside his immediate area of professional responsibility, sea warfare, but also because he tended to underestimate the seriousness of what he regarded as mere rhetorical excursions on Hitler's part. Blomberg, Fritsch, and Neurath were astounded but far from speechless; they challenged Hitler's judgment on the spot, and the latter two followed up with subsequent individual conferences. Hitler refused to reconsider his plans, and all three dissenters were removed from office. Three months later to the day, on 5 February 1938, it was announced that the prominent NSDAP foreign affairs functionary Joachim von Ribbentrop had been named foreign minister and General Walther von Brauchitsch commander in chief of the army. The office of minister of war had been abolished, Field Marshal von Blomberg relieved, and General Wilhelm Keitel named chief of a newly established supreme staff directly under Hitler.

Blomberg had no direct successor because his former functions, much like those of the presidency in 1934, were taken over by Hitler, who converted the ministry of war into the "High Command of the Armed Forces" (*Oberkommando der Wehrmacht* or OKW). Through the OKW, which took precedence over the general staff organizations of the individual service branches, Hitler personally preempted the direct command previously exercised by the war minister. General Wilhelm Keitel, whom the dictator inherited as administrator of his new supreme staff, had been virtually assured the post by Blomberg's remark to Hitler that he had merely served as his *"chef de bureau"* (office manager) in the war ministry.

Hitler subsequently made light of the removal of Blomberg and Fritsch, and of the conversion of the war ministry into the OKW, which assured him personal control of the armed forces, remarking that the generals were cowardly. The totalitarian dissimulator had very good reason to trivialize the matter: he wanted to cover up the grave internal crisis triggered by this last major *coup* in the series that finally brought him unchecked power within Germany, thereby freeing his hands for the mad career of conquest that ultimately led to the destruction of the German Reich and his own suicide in the bunker beneath the ruins of his Berlin chancellory. Perhaps Hitler had thought, or at least hoped, that he had achieved full control over the armed forces with the oath of unconditional personal obedience in August 1934. If so, he realized the contrary after the historic November conference in 1937 at which his authority was categorically challenged by none other than the war minister who had ordered administration of that oath and the commander in chief of the army who had dissuaded his chief of staff, General Ludwig Beck, from resigning in protest against it. So they had to be removed. But though he did have formal authority to replace them, he realized that he could not afford to do so arbitrarily, least of all in the context of an open conflict over plans for aggression that could be implemented only with the dependable support of the very organization of which they were the senior members.

Just at this juncture, Blomberg, a sixty-year-old widower, blundered into a *mésalliance* with a former nude model with a police record, including at least one conviction. Once that became known, he would have been completely unacceptable to the straitlaced officer corps with its rigid code of ethics, even had Hitler wished to keep him. But his successor would almost inevitably have had to be the highly esteemed commander in chief of the senior service branch, the army's General Werner von Fritsch. A conservative, reticent bachelor, he was personally as well as professionally above reproach. The Gestapo produced a dossier on him nonetheless, based on perjured allegations of homosexuality by a professed blackmailer and occasional police informer.

When Hitler and Göring made known the charges against the top two officers of the army, there was, as anticipated, no serious effort in the military hierarchy to spare Blomberg the consequences of his unfortunate marriage. But so strong was the support for Fritsch that the only way Hitler could remove him was to consent to a court martial, in which the charges against him would have to be thoroughly tested (with the result that he was ultimately proven innocent), and, in addition, to agree that his post as head of the army be taken over by an acceptable senior general. As fate would have it, General Walther von Brauchitsch, the man most acceptable both to Hitler and the generals turned out, unbeknown to the latter, to have serious marital problems also. For this reason he resisted being made commander in chief, but Hitler would not hear of letting a mere personal impediment, that he would only too gladly solve personally with a gift of 80,000 marks (for a lump-sum alimony payment) to Brauchitsch, stand in the way of what thereby became an ideal solution: the appointment of a highly respected officer with an excellent record, yet secretly beholden to Hitler, and therefore as pliable a tool as the tractable Keitel, whose reassignment as chief of the OKW was grudgingly accepted by the military hierarchy.

It was in the court martial of Fritsch that the emerging SS-Gestapo state within the state unmasked itself most compromisingly. The key defense witness was detained and badly manhandled by the Gestapo, and only freed from its "protective custody" when Hitler was personally confronted with the issue under circumstances precluding refusal or cover-up. Baron

von Fritsch was ordered to a Gestapo interrogation at an outlying villa which, it was learned, had been especially staffed for
the occasion by SS veterans of execution squads who had distinguished themselves during the Röhm purge four years earlier;
Fritsch went as ordered, but his adjutant stayed with the staff
car before the door in contact with a tank company under dependable officers that just happened to be holding an exercise
conspicuously near the villa — a circumstance that made it virtually impossible for the awkward affair to be resolved, from
the National Socialist point of view, by Fritsch's alleged suicide
due to despondency over his disgrace.

The complete exoneration of Fritsch at his court martial
should have represented a grave setback to the Hitler regime,
especially as more and more details about the mendacity of the
SS-Gestapo plot were carefully leaked out by the members of
the military hierarchy and by their allies in the ministry of
justice and elsewhere, for they could feel not only vindicated
but strengthened by the outcome — particularly in relation to
the SS and Gestapo; Himmler's sinister lieutenant Reinhard
Heydrich, for example, was actually talking about his career
being ruined by the turn of events. But they suddenly turned
yet again on the very eve of the court martial verdict: Hitler
annexed Austria, a bloodless triumph of such magnitude that
it completely overshadowed the disturbing implications of the
Fritsch affair, a matter that seemed completely irrelevant, but
was not. The fact is that Hitler's triumph in Austria in March
1938, just five weeks after the installation of Ribbentrop in the
Foreign Office and of Keitel and Brauchitsch in charge of the
OKW and the army, had in part been made possible by the
appointment of these three men. Unlike Neurath, Blomberg,
and Fritsch, they were dependable instruments through whom
the dictator could orchestrate at will diplomatic duress and
military blackmail in combination with propaganda in Germany and agitation in Austria by the National Socialists there.

The "reunification" of Austria with the Third Reich represented the fulfilment of genuine aspirations of both the German and the Austrian people. They had shown this earlier but
had been thwarted by the victors in the immediate aftermath

of the First World War. Hitler had meanwhile built up the power to achieve what even Bismarck had not been able to bring about, and he used it unflinchingly and successfully. The basic legitimacy of his *coup,* in terms of the right of a people to national self-determination, seemed fundamentally so justifiable, even to many of those who were shocked by his means, that Hitler's stunning *fait accompli* was accepted as a final step in his vigorous foreign policy of undoing what had been done to Germany in the Treaty of Versailles and during the period after its forcible imposition.

Incomparably more perilous than the annexation of Austria was its sequel later the same year: the Sudeten crisis. The Sudeten Mountains, which formed Czechoslovakia's natural border with Germany, had a large German population, but any attempt to incorporate them into the Third Reich involved the serious risk of war with Czechoslovakia's ally, France. Hitler's reckless determination to pursue the course he had outlined at the secret conference early in November 1937, as reflected in military preparations for an invasion of Czechoslovakia, led a small group of senior *Wehrmacht* officers and civilian officials who had drawn together in the Fritsch crisis to make preparations of their own for a *coup d'état* if Hitler ordered a military attack on Czechoslovakia. But it never came to this, for at the end of September 1938 the heads of the British, French, and Italian governments met him in Munich and agreed that Germany should be awarded the Sudetenland. The Czechs, who had not participated in the crucial deliberations, were given no choice but to acquiesce immediately.

At the Munich Conference, Neville Chamberlain, the British prime minister whose consciousness of the injustice done Germany at Versailles, whose appreciation of the role of a conservative Germany as a bulwark against communism, and whose determination to avert war Hitler had exploited beyond measure, elicited from the German dictator a personal assurance in writing that with cession of the Sudetenland Germany's territorial demands were satisfied, so that there was now the assurance, as the prime minister triumphantly announced on his return to England, of "peace in our time." On the international scene there was indeed a brief respite, but the momentum of the National Socialist movement had by no means been stayed. The month after the German march into the Sudetenland, the civilized world was shocked to learn that on the night of 9 to 10 November throughout Germany a nationwide pogrom had been staged. According to Gestapo chief Heydrich's report, seventy-five hundred Jewish business establishments were demolished and about two hundred and fifty synagogues burned. Countless Jewish houses and apartments were wrecked and cemeteries desecrated. Dozens of Jews were murdered, hundreds beaten, and thousands thrown into concentration camps. The Jews were subsequently forced to repair the damages they suffered independently, as their insurance claims were confiscated, and to pay in addition a collective fine of a billion marks. Several years earlier Germans with at least three Jewish grandparents — irrespective of religious affiliation — had been stripped of their citizenship and made mere subjects of the state. Marriage between Jews and other Germans had been forbidden. Jews had been excluded from a large number of occupations, the list of which continually grew. Long before the Second World War, thousands had already died in concentration camps, but with the wartime establishment of the extermination camps, supplemented by mobile extermination teams, the Third Reich embarked on what was euphemistically termed the "Final Solution" — ultimately resulting in the murder of millions.

The hideous plan for administrative murder was not worked out until the early years of the war, and its implementation was a closely guarded wartime secret in a society which even during peacetime had not enjoyed freedom of information. The press, radio, cinema, and theater had long been under the rigid control of Hitler's cunning minister of popular enlightenment and propaganda, Joseph Goebbels. For years he had filtered and carefully rationed detrimental news while brilliantly manipulating the media of public information to create an atmosphere of frenzied approbation for the new regime's restless and in some respects quite imaginative and constructive public activity. There were, of course, many too critical,

II / THE THIRD REICH

In March 1935, just over two years after Adolf Hitler came to office, Germany recovered the highly industrialized Saar Basin as the result of a plebiscite conducted by the League of Nations in accordance with provisions of the Treaty of Versailles. A year later, in defiance of that treaty and subsequent German treaty commitments, Hitler ordered his troops into the permanently demilitarized Rhineland. In March 1938 he seized Austria. Half a year later he annexed the Sudetenland with the sanction of the powers represented at the Munich Conference — which did not include the victim, Czechoslovakia. As indicated on the upper map, Poland and Hungary joined in the predatory undertaking. In March 1939, six months after the Munich Conference, where Hitler had made a personal pledge in writing to go no further, he dismantled the defenseless rump state and also annexed the Memel District north of East Prussia. At the beginning of September 1939 he launched his invasion of Poland, unleashing the Second World War. Within three years, Hitler's "Greater German Reich" stretched from the annexed portions of prewar Belgium and France into Yugoslavia and the Ukraine, as shown on the lower map, which also indicates the farthest advances made by the armed forces of the Third Reich and its Axis partners.

suspicious, or intellectually scrupulous to be caught up in the tide of popular enthusiasm, but for them awaited the twin brother of Dr. Goebbels' raucous propaganda, Heinrich Himmler's stealthy terror. Little was generally known in Germany of the organs of control, least of all the concentration camps, but the efficiency of the secret police was an almost ubiquitous deterrent, even to muted opposition, under a system which did not hesitate to train young children to spy on their parents. Yet there were certain limits beyond which Hitler and his minions could not go, as they had learned in 1938 when they tried to remove General von Fritsch without the court martial that exonerated him, and again in 1941, when they were forced to end their mass euthanasia program.

At the beginning of the war, Hitler ordered that the incura-

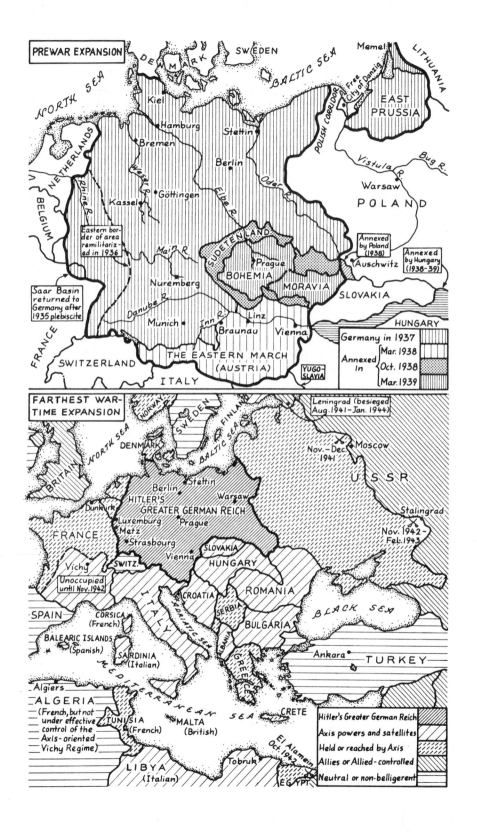

PREWAR EXPANSION

NORTH SEA

SWEDEN

BALTIC SEA

DENMARK

Memel

LITHUANIA

Kiel

Hamburg

Stettin

POLISH CORRIDOR

Free City of Danzig

EAST PRUSSIA

Bremen

NETHERLANDS

Rhine R.

Berlin

Oder R.

Vistula R.

Bug R.

Warsaw

POLAND

BELGIUM

Weser R.

Kassel

Göttingen

Elbe R.

Eastern border of area remilitarized in 1936

Main R.

SUDETENLAND

Prague

BOHEMIA

MORAVIA

Annexed by Poland (1938)

Auschwitz

Annexed by Hungary (1938-39)

Saar Basin returned to Germany after 1935 plebiscite

Nuremberg

Danube R.

Munich

Inn R.

Braunau

Linz

Vienna

SLOVAKIA

HUNGARY

FRANCE

SWITZERLAND

THE EASTERN MARCH (AUSTRIA)

ITALY

YUGO-SLAVIA

Germany in 1937

Annexed In | Mar. 1938
Oct. 1938
Mar. 1939

FARTHEST WAR-TIME EXPANSION

Leningrad (besieged Aug. 1941–Jan. 1944)

NORWAY

SWEDEN

FINLAND

BALTIC SEA

NORTH SEA

DENMARK

Moscow

Nov.–Dec. 1941

BRITAIN

Berlin

Stettin

Warsaw

U S S R

Dunkirk

HITLER'S GREATER GERMAN REICH

Luxemburg

Prague

FRANCE

Metz

Strasbourg

Stalingrad

Nov. 1942–Feb. 1943

Vienna

SLOVAKIA

Vichy

SWITZ.

HUNGARY

Unoccupied until Nov. 1942

ROMANIA

ITALY

CROATIA

SERBIA

BLACK SEA

SPAIN

CORSICA (French)

ADRIATIC SEA

ALBANIA

BULGARIA

BALEARIC ISLANDS (Spanish)

SARDINIA (Italian)

GREECE

Ankara

TURKEY

MEDITERRANEAN SEA

Algiers

ALGERIA

(French, but not under effective control of the Axis-oriented Vichy Regime)

TUNISIA (French)

MALTA (British)

CRETE

El Alamein Oct. 1942

LIBYA (Italian)

Tobruk

EGYPT

Hitler's Greater German Reich

Axis powers and satellites

Held or reached by Axis

Allies or Allied-controlled

Neutral or non-belligerent

bly ill throughout Germany be put to death as worthless parasites. Within two years the secret compulsory euthanasia program took the lives of some seventy thousand. Then, on 3 August 1941, the Roman Catholic bishop of Münster, Count Clemens August von Galen, proclaimed from his pulpit in St. Lambert's that throughout his Westphalian diocese, on state orders, lists of incurables were being drawn up in hospitals and sanatoria. They were all to be murdered. During the previous week the first transport, from nearby Marienthal, had already been taken away. "Woe unto mankind," the bishop thundered, "and woe unto the German people, when the holy commandment of God, 'Thou shalt not kill,' . . . not only is violated, but when this violation is even tolerated and goes unpunished." Nor did Bishop Galen stop there; with the militancy of his seventeenth-century predecessor, Baron Christoph Bernhard von Galen, the prince-bishop of Münster who in 1664 had been a director of the imperial army mobilized against the pagan Turks, he went over to the offensive, lashing out with example after example of how the Germans under Hitler had shamelessly violated other commandments as well.

The wrathful sermon had an electrifying effect. There had been courageous protests against the euthanasia program, but they had not been made in public. There had also been public opposition to the regime from the churches, epitomized by the Barmen Declaration of 1934 from Protestant circles identified with Karl Barth, Dietrich Bonhoeffer, and Martin Niemöller, and the German encyclical of Pope Pius XI in 1937, *"Mit brennender Sorge"* ("With Burning Concern"), but neither the declaration nor the encyclical had been intended or interpreted as a withering denunciation of a criminal regime. The public impact of Bishop (later Cardinal) von Galen's indictment was magnified because it came completely unexpectedly in a closed society under heightened wartime censorship just as the great German offensive in Russia was hitting its stride (the attack on the Soviet Union had been launched six weeks earlier). The text was secretly duplicated and copies distributed not only throughout Germany but also in occupied territories and among the troops on the front — men to whom Galen directly addressed the terrible question what they or their comrades, if wounded and permanently disabled, might ultimately expect from a state prepared to take the lives of those no longer able to be productive.

Several prominent National Socialist leaders urged Hitler to have Galen hanged as a traitor, but Dr. Goebbels, his shrewd propaganda minister, originally from the Catholic Rhineland-Westphalia region himself, argued that "the population of Münster could be regarded as lost during the war, if anything were done against the bishop, and in that fear one safely could include the whole of Westphalia." Rather than risk compromising morale in one of the most important industrial areas of Germany for the rest of the war, Hitler acquiesced in the inevitable: within a month of Galen's courageous sermon, he ordered the operation to be halted. Like the *Wehrmacht* crisis of early 1938, the Galen case serves to illustrate the outer limits of Hitler's power. The officer corps of the army and the hierarchy of the Roman Catholic church, each highly elitist, tightly knit, and informed with clearly defined values and traditions, were incomparably less vulnerable to National Socialism than German society at large, where Hitler enjoyed overwhelming support.

One of the most important reasons for the genuine enthusiasm throughout Germany for the Hitler regime was the fact that through strength and initiative it had succeeded, within less than six years, in doing more to restore Germany's place as a world power than would have seemed imaginable under the timorous politicians of the Weimar Republic in a lifetime. During the first half of the National Socialist dictatorship, the six years ending early in 1939, Hitler proved able to achieve hardly less spectacular gains than Frederick and Bismarck. Unlike them, however, he did not know when to stop. By the end of the Seven Years' War, Frederick had expanded Prussia as far as feasible, just as Bismarck had done with Germany by the end of the Franco-Prussian War. Both Frederick and Bismarck clearly perceived these limits, realizing that further expansion would almost certainly provoke their neighbors into uniting against them. Not understanding this, Hitler plunged

Germany and Europe into the Second World War within a generation of the first, conjuring into existence a hostile coalition against which he could not possibly prevail in the end, no matter how imposing his territorial conquests had become by late 1942.

Although Hitler unleashed the Second World War, he did not plan it and did not prepare Germany to wage it. At least since the mid-twenties, he had envisioned war, writing in *Mein Kampf* that National Socialists "turn their gaze toward the land in the East" and unambiguously affirmed that the only possible way for modern Germany to survive was to resume the eastward march of the medieval Teutonic Knights "in order to provide with the German sword land for the German plow and thereby daily bread for the nation."* However, he was thinking in terms of anything but a long war of attrition comparable to the First World War. He was determined to avoid that kind of conflict, as he explained to Dr. Hermann Rauschning, the National Socialist president of the senate of the Free City of Danzig who later went over to the opposition, emigrated, and published his conversations with Hitler: "Whoever experienced the war at the front will not want to cause more bloodshed if it can be averted." This did not mean he wanted to avoid war, as such, at all costs. Quite the contrary, he considered it necessary. As Rauschning reconstructed their conversation, the dictator continued:

Who says that I will begin a war like the fools of 1914? Aren't we doing everything we possibly can to prevent just that? Most people have no imagination. They can visualize what is coming only in terms of their own limited experience. They do not see the new and surprising. The generals are also sterile. They are trapped in their own professional expertise. The creative genius is always an outsider so far as the professionals are concerned. I have the gift of reducing the problems to their essential core. . . . What is war but cunning, swindle, delusion, assault, and surprise? People have resorted to killing only when there was no other way

* Adolf Hitler, *Mein Kampf,* 41st ed. (Munich: Eher-Verlag, 1933), pp. 742, 154.

to get ahead. . . . There is such a thing as strategy in an extended sense; there is war with intellectual means. What is the object of war . . . ? That the enemy capitulate. Once he does that, I have the prospect of destroying him entirely. Why should I demoralize him militarily when I can do it more cheaply and effectively in other ways? . . .

When I wage war . . . , one day in the middle of peacetime I will have troops in Paris. They will be wearing French uniforms. They will march through the streets. No one will stop them. Everything is prepared down to the smallest detail. They march to the general staff headquarters. They occupy the ministries, the parliament. Within a few minutes France, Poland, Austria, Czechoslovakia are robbed of their leading men. An army without a general staff. All political leaders taken care of. The confusion will be unprecedented. But long since I have been in touch with men who will form a new government — a government which suits me. We find such men. We find them in every land. We do not have to buy them. They come on their own. Ambition and delusion, party strife and intrigue drive them. We will have a peace treaty before we have war. I guarantee you, gentlemen, that the impossible will always succeed. The most improbable way is the surest.*

It was precisely by such revolutionary techniques that Hitler first annexed Austria and then dismembered Czechoslovakia without having to resort to overt hostilities in the traditional sense. In both cases he was clearly willing to risk war, and this alone — the fact that he was not bluffing but ready to fight — made it unnecessary for him to do so. When in March 1939, however, he went on to seize the "Protectorate of Bohemia and Moravia" (what was left of the Czech part of Czecho-Slovakia after Munich) and to sponsor the establishment of Slovakia as a separate state, Hitler went too far. The extraordinary concessions made to him at Munich a half year earlier had been linked to a personal pledge to the chief architect of the policy of appeasement, British Prime Minister Neville Chamberlain. Hitler now violated his personal pledge to the

* Hermann Rauschning, *Gespräche mit Hitler* (Zurich: Europa-Verlag, 1940), pp. 12–13.

prime minister, who had taken on the role of arbiter of Europe and had crippled Czechoslovakia in order to save the peace and rectify the wrong done Germany at Versailles. Twenty years after the end of the Great War, serious advocates of appeasement could in good faith argue that what had been done to Germany at the Paris Peace Conference of 1919 had been a grave mistake, that Hitler's coming to power, rearming Germany, and threatening war over the Sudetenland had grown out of that mistake, and that peace could be preserved only by one final act of reconciliation: sacrificing Czechoslovakia's natural frontier. Grim as this was, it would be preferable — it seemed to many in the autumn of 1938 — to permitting the Sudeten crisis to lead to a general war in which Czechoslovakia would in any case probably be entirely overrun by the Germans. If Hitler, after Munich, had kept his word, the Munich Pact might well have been regarded, in the long run, as the final correction of the Treaty of Versailles; because he did not, it turned out to be only one more step down a long road leading to a war that vindicated opponents of appeasement and those who had argued that the Treaty of Versailles had been far too lenient.

When Adolf Hitler betrayed Chamberlain and those who backed Chamberlain's policy of appeasement — the policy that had sanctioned his foreign policy triumphs through 1938 — he almost irrevocably committed Germany and Europe to war. It was not merely that his flagrant violation of international treaty and personal promise was morally offensive or ungentlemanly — though this was certainly the case — but rather that by his almost cynical ruthlessness Hitler convincingly demonstrated that never, under any circumstances, could a reasonable settlement be reached with him on the basis of mutual understanding. He ruled this out by clearly proving that he could not be bound in the least by even the most solemn personal agreements. He apparently had never grasped the elementary principle that, as a matter of enlightened self-interest, a statesman must respect the vital interests of his treaty partners: he must do this in order to establish credibility and thereby command reciprocal respect. By flaunting his capricious infidelity as a treaty partner and his scornful contempt for those who had taken him at his word, Adolf Hitler succeeded in so completely isolating himself and the Third Reich that he made Germany, even before the outbreak of the Second World War, hardly less a pariah than it had been under the early Weimar Republic. This was not immediately obvious, of course, because of Germany's great strength in 1939. But it accounts for the fact that when Hitler, after having unmasked himself in March 1939, took his next step, he unexpectedly found himself in a war to the death. There was no alternative to this, for there was no way to make peace with him. Driven by the forces he himself had unleashed, Hitler was, in a peculiar sense, a prisoner of his own diabolical momentum. This has perhaps never been more clearly perceived and described than by the former League of Nations high commissioner for the Free City of Danzig from 1937 to 1939, the late Swiss historian Carl Jacob Burckhardt, who repeatedly negotiated with Hitler personally during the immediate prewar period, and who as a biographer of Cardinal Richelieu was himself a master analyst of the manipulation of power. Burckhardt (who, as president of the Committee of the International Red Cross, also played an important role in postwar Europe) described in his Danzig memoirs how swiftly Hitler would adapt his actions to changing circumstances, but how in doing so, he simultaneously divested himself of freedom of choice despite the great power that he possessed — yet which also possessed him:

> In his almost total lack of freedom . . . he was very close to those whom he ruled. Between himself and the overpowering circumstances a mechanical force was at work to which he succumbed as did all those he had bound to himself. The German word *Verhängnis* (fate) is a very expressive word. It suggests the conception of a chain reaction which, once begun, can no longer be stopped. Once unleashed, the course of events mechanically pursued its contradictory way through Hitler's decisions. Whatever happened outside the scope of his will seemed to become an act of this same will. His constant vision was striking, the goal of his dream; from the very beginning he had always, in the most uncanny way,

said what he finally did do after countless detours, feints, and contradictions. It is not entirely unreasonable to assume that the insatiable hatred that burned in him was related to the suppressed but always present conviction in his subconsciousness that in the end there would be the most frightful failure and a personal fall just such as awaited him in the Reich Chancellery on 30 April 1945.*

Although Britain and France declared war on Germany when Hitler ordered the invasion of Poland, they were unprepared to wage it, so that Hitler was able, undisturbed by distractions from the West, to stage his first great demonstration of *Blitzkrieg,* literally "lightning war," as German armies took western Poland by storm. From the East, the unhappy country was invaded by the Russians, for on the eve of the attack, Hitler and the Communist dictator, Joseph Stalin, had seen fit to suspend their ideological principles and to conclude the Nazi-Soviet pact providing for the partition of Poland.

Not until May 1940 was Hitler able to mount his attack on France, though in April he took Denmark and Norway. When the western offensive came, it found the French internally divided and seriously demoralized. Within six weeks the Low Countries and France collapsed — although 140,000 French troops escaped to England with the 200,000 men of the British Expeditionary Force who were plucked at the very last minute from the beaches at Dunkirk. In less than a year, Hitler had become master of Europe from the Pyrenees to beyond the Vistula. Then, on 22 June 1941, the first anniversary of the French capitulation, he turned on his Soviet treaty partner with Operation Barbarossa, *Blitzkrieg* on so vast a scale that Hitler was almost right in his prediction that the world would hold its breath. By the end of September, with victory in sight, "the greatest warlord of all times" (as Goebbels was wont to call him) actually went so far as to order a substantial reduction in armaments production. Only the grim Battle of Moscow and the formal entry of the United States into the war brought home to Hitler, at the end of 1941, that his astounding series of

* Carl J. Burckhardt, *Meine Danziger Mission 1937–1939* (Munich: Callwey, 1960), pp. 269–70.

triumphs by armed diplomacy, coercion, subversion, and *Blitz-krieg* had finally come to an end and that he was now indeed engaged in the long war of attrition for which he had not seriously prepared the Third Reich because he had neither wanted it nor thought it would be necessary. Deluded by his own extraordinary chain of successes, he had failed to make adequate provisions for a turn of fate against him. The German armed forces, which he had hastily built up during the six prewar years, did have a tremendous initial advantage against Germany's weaker adversaries, but the Third Reich was not prepared for the war, and even when Hitler began it, he adamantly refused to give the orders for full-scale economic mobilization urged by the responsible specialists in the OKW. As a matter of fact, he went so far as to resist the establishment of fixed priority schedules or stable production guidelines within the framework of existing directives. Only on 7 September 1939, a week after ordering the attack on Poland, did Hitler agree to set up a war production priority schedule, giving top classification to munitions and replacement of destroyed weapons and equipment. But then on 4 October he revised this to include, at equally urgent top priority on a competitive basis, a number of additional programs, including submarine construction, which had not even been on the prior schedule — though the submarine force was so weak that during the early part of the war it was hardly possible to keep a dozen U-boats at combat station in the Atlantic. On 10 October, however, Hitler suddenly established super-priority (over the previous top-priority programs) for motorization; and in mid-November, just as German industry was being retooled for that latest shift, he gave super-super-priority to munitions production — a decision forced by the alarming shortages resulting from Germany's having entered the war, despite repeated warnings from the OKW, with only a four- to six-weeks' supply of ammunition. (Had the French attacked Germany immediately after the Polish campaign, many German units would have had little more to fight with than bayonets.)

In the U.S. Strategic Bombing Survey, a major postwar study to ascertain the impact of aerial bombardment on Germany, it was found that the economy of the Third Reich was not fully mobilized before 1942, when the Second World War was already half over:

> There can be no doubt that Germany started the conversion of her economy to a wartime footing far too late. Had Germany's leaders decided to make an all-out war effort in 1939 instead of 1942, they would have had time to arm in "depth"; that is, to lay the foundations of a war economy by expanding their basic industries and building up equipment for the mass production of munitions. Starting their armament program as late as 1942, they could only arm in "width"; that is, accept their equipment and material base as given and expand munitions production on the basis of available capacity.*

Germany, in other words, was not economically prepared for total war in 1939 and did not actually begin to convert her economy "to a wartime footing" until 1942. When this finally was done, the results were dramatic. By July 1944, German munitions production peaked at 322 percent of the level of January–February 1942. "Despite the damage wrought by air attack and territorial loss," according to the Strategic Bombing Survey, "and despite the general drop in production in the second half of 1944, total industrial output for the year was the highest in the war."

But by 1944, the war had been irrevocably lost. The triumphs of the early years had been followed by a titanic stalemate on the Russian front that finally was broken at Stalingrad — an unprecedented catastrophe for the German army. The success of the Anglo-American landing in Normandy in 1944 sealed the fate of the Third Reich: Hitler himself had earlier acknowledged that if the Americans and British established a western front, the war would be lost. But when it actually happened, he refused to draw the consequences. Others did, however, lending strength to the opposition, which had by no means ended with the thwarted conspiracy of 1938; the crises of 1938 had rather served to crystallize a clandestine movement that gradually involved persons from all walks of life drawn together in the

---

* U.S. Strategic Bombing Survey, *The Effects of Strategic Bombing on the German War Economy* ([Washington, D.C.:] Overall Economic Effects Division [Dir.: J. Kenneth Galbraith; Asst. Dir.: Burton H. Klein], 1945), p. 7.

realization that in a land where even loyal opposition was prosecuted as crime, those seriously opposing a criminal regime had no alternative but conspiracy. "We must act," said Count Claus von Stauffenberg, "for this man is evil incarnate." But as by a miracle, Hitler survived with only minor injuries the bomb that Stauffenberg, a general staff colonel, planted in his conference room on 20 July 1944, killing four of his closest associates and seriously wounding several others. Thus he was able to lead the German people who, with few exceptions, faithfully followed him to the end; thereupon he eluded his enemies by taking poison. Only then was the infernal spell finally broken. Only then did the great majority of Germans begin to apprehend the dimensions of the catastrophe that had befallen them and their nation: a thousand years after the coronation of Emperor Otto the Great, Germany was once more fragmented. The consolidation of the medieval empire as a German national state had been thwarted by the princes in league with the church. The attempt to establish a parliamentary monarchy in 1848 had collapsed because of the weakness of the liberal movement and the opposition of Prussia and Austria. Prussian unification had established a national state at the price of excluding Austria from Germany and the people from a reasonable share of power. The Weimar Republic had brought democratic government to a unified Germany, but only with the stigma of defeat and the burden of reparations. Finally, Hitler's Third Reich, which had replaced the democracy of Weimar with totalitarian dictatorship and the Prussian unification of Germany without Austria with an imperialism which led not only to the annexation of Austria and Bohemia, but to the conquest of most of continental Europe, had culminated in the worst disaster in German history.

🌸 POSTWAR GERMANY

THE WARTIME COALITION provoked by Hitler's aggression barely survived his defeat. At the end of the war, Germany was partitioned among the victors, America, Britain, France, and

Russia. The eastern provinces of Prussia were annexed by the Soviet Union or Poland. Although central Germany was occupied by the Russians, Berlin, in the heart of their zone, was divided into four sectors for joint occupation by the four powers. The Russians soon demonstrated that they had no intention of cooperating with the efforts of the western powers to restore economic and thus social stability to Germany as a whole. The economic integration of the western zones of occupation began early in 1948; in June a monetary reform was introduced not only in West Germany but also in the western sectors of Berlin. The Russians promptly sealed off the land routes between the western zones of occupation and West Berlin. The United States and Great Britain responded with the Berlin airlift, which in the course of about a year sustained the beleaguered city with supplies brought in on over a quarter of a million flights. The Berlin blockade and the airlift, which both ended in 1949, dramatized the fact that victory over the Third Reich in the Second World War had led not to peace, but to the division of Berlin, Germany, and Europe by the Iron Curtain, and to a cold war between the Russian-led Communist bloc and the western powers under the leadership of the United States. This polarization gave impetus to the establishment in 1949 of the two postwar German states.

The western zones, with about half the area of the former Weimar Republic, were organized, under Allied tutelage, as a democratic confederation, the Federal Republic of Germany. The Soviet zone of occupation—once considered the central part of the country, but later known as East Germany—was organized as the German Democratic Republic. A communist dictatorship less than half the size of West Germany, it was initially inhabited by over eighteen million, but by the beginning of the seventies had dropped to seventeen million, about equal to the West German state of North Rhine-Westphalia. The decline in East Germany's population (during a period when that of West Germany increased from less than fifty to over sixty million) was largely due to the flight of refugees from the German Democratic to the Federal Republic. This was partly in response to the forced collectivization of agriculture and industry, but reinforced by the heavy-handed totalitarianism of the regime of Stalinist East German party chief Walter Ulbricht. An active member of the German Communist party since its establishment in 1919, he had been trained at the Lenin School in Moscow in the early twenties and elected to the *Reichstag* in 1928. When Hitler came to power, he went into exile, served in the Spanish Civil War, returned to Moscow, survived Stalin's purges that claimed the lives of four members of the German Communist party's Politburo and ten of its Central Committee, and on 30 April 1945, the day of Hitler's suicide, was flown by the Russians back to Germany to lay the foundations of the German Communist state. In the wake of Stalin's death early in 1953, he resisted strong Soviet pressure to modify his hard-line policy, but before he could be disciplined or possibly even removed, it provoked a popular uprising that began in Berlin and spread like wildfire throughout the major urban centers of the German Democratic Republic. The Russians intervened, and having saved the Ulbricht regime with their bayonets, could not topple it without vindicating the challenge to his and their own authority and giving the dangerous impression that they had been forced to make a major concession from weakness.

Ulbricht stayed on, but over four hundred thousand fled East Germany for the West in 1953 alone. The rate of flow varied during the following years, but the number of refugees never dropped below one hundred seventy thousand annually and sharply increased during the summer of 1961, until, in early August, it reached some five thousand daily. The long border between East and West Germany having been transformed into an all but impassable "death strip," the émigrés went through Russian-controlled East Berlin, from which they could take public transportation to West Berlin, register at the reception centers set up by the Bonn government, and be flown to the Federal Republic with impunity. But early on the morning of 13 August 1961, the East German government assumed "state control" of the border between the Soviet and western sectors of the city and abruptly sealed the last remaining gap in their

12 / CONTEMPORARY GERMANY

Following the collapse of the Third Reich in 1945, Germany was partitioned. As shown on the lower right inset, the eastern provinces (with a total area of some forty-four thousand miles) were lost outright: East Prussia was split between Russia and Poland; Germany east of the Oder-Neisse line as well as the Stettin area west of the Oder were annexed by Poland. The remainder of Germany was divided into American, British, French, and Russian occupation zones, and Berlin, the capital, into four corresponding sectors. As the Cold War polarized Europe, the division of Germany was institutionalized by the two German states shown on the upper map, the German Democratic Republic, with East Berlin as its capital, and the Federal Republic of Germany, with its seat of government in Bonn. In addition to the provisional capital, the map shows the two city-states of West Germany and the eight other states with their respective capital cities. West Berlin had non-voting representatives in the Bonn parliament without being a full voting member state of the West German federation. In 1990 it merged with East Berlin to form the city-state of Berlin, which on 3 October of that year acceded to the Federal Republic, together with all of East Germany. On 20 June, 1991, the German parliament voted to move the seat of government from Bonn to Berlin.

"death strip" by building the Berlin Wall.

Denied the possibility of following the more than two and a half million who had fled westward since 1949, the East Germans made the best of the situation in which they found themselves—knowing, for the first time in years, that not one of the office colleagues or supervisors, mechanics, teachers, physicians, or pharmacists they saw on a Friday evening would be in West Berlin the following Monday morning. This enforced stabilization of the population roughly coincided with the final phase of the "Construction of Socialism," a ten-year "internal class struggle" proclaimed by Ulbricht in 1952, in the course of which every area of the party, state, economy, and

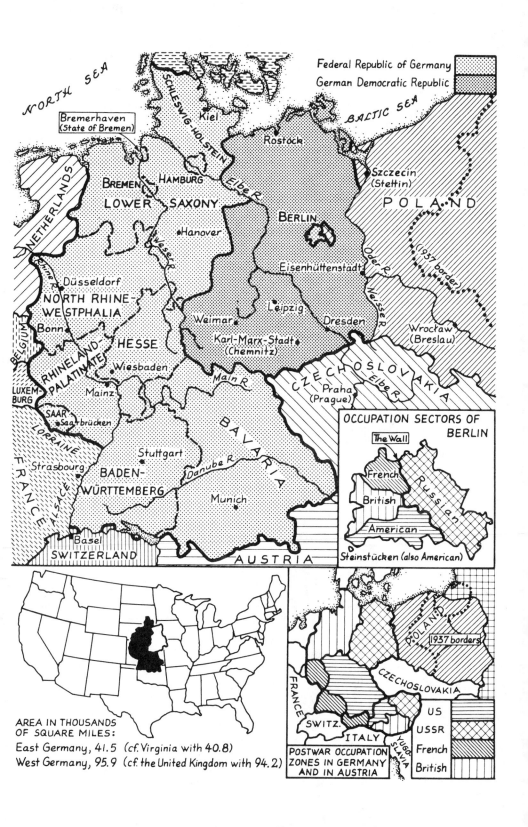

NORTH SEA

BALTIC SEA

Federal Republic of Germany
German Democratic Republic

Bremerhaven
(State of Bremen)

Kiel

Rostock

Szczecin
(Stettin)

P O L A N D

SCHLESWIG-HOLSTEIN

BREMEN

HAMBURG

LOWER SAXONY

Hanover

BERLIN

Elbe R.

Weser R.

Eisenhüttenstadt

(1937 border)

NETHERLANDS

Düsseldorf

Rhine

NORTH RHINE-
WESTPHALIA

Bonn

BELGIUM

Weimar

Leipzig

Dresden

Oder R.

Neisse R.

Wrocław
(Breslau)

HESSE

Karl-Marx-Stadt
(Chemnitz)

RHINELAND-
PALATINATE

Wiesbaden

Mainz

LUXEMBURG

SAAR

Saarbrücken

LORRAINE

Main R.

BAVARIA

C Z E C H O S L O V A K I A

Elbe R.

Praha
(Prague)

FRANCE

ALSACE

Strasbourg

Stuttgart

Danube R.

BADEN-
WÜRTTEMBERG

Munich

OCCUPATION SECTORS OF
BERLIN

The Wall

French

British

American

Russian

Steinstücken (also American)

Basel

SWITZERLAND

A U S T R I A

AREA IN THOUSANDS
OF SQUARE MILES:
East Germany, 41.5 (cf. Virginia with 40.8)
West Germany, 95.9 (cf. the United Kingdom with 94.2)

POLAND

1937 borders

CZECHOSLOVAKIA

FRANCE

SWITZ.

ITALY

YUGOSLAVIA

US

USSR

French

British

POSTWAR OCCUPATION
ZONES IN GERMANY
AND IN AUSTRIA

society (except for the churches) was subjected to reexamination and restructuring. At the end of the war, during the period of direct Soviet military rule, prior to the establishment of the German Democratic Republic, the largest estates and economic enterprises had been expropriated for subdivision or state administration, but during the nineteen-fifties and early sixties, the East German authorities systematically dealt with the pre-socialist remnants of the capitalist structure in agriculture, commerce and industry, and even the small-scale crafts and trades.

Early in 1963 Ulbricht introduced the "New Economic System of Planning and Management of the People's Economy," providing for an unprecedented degree of decentralization of authority on a cost-accounting but profit-sharing basis for management, coupled with realistic production incentives for workers, including recognition and rewards for quality as well as quantity. The New Economic System was not simply a rerun, embellished with different rhetoric, of the counterproductive form of control exercised in the past, when rational economic considerations were subordinated to the current exigencies of ideological orthodoxy. The heavy hand of the party-state apparatus was withdrawn, at least temporarily, to the next higher echelon, relinquishing operational decisionmaking in an increasing number of economic enterprises and related government agencies to competent professionals. Many of these had been representatives of a new generation of case-study-trained and computer-oriented technocrats whose mentors had included a group of "institutionalized revisionists" who had ingeniously adapted cybernetic systems theory to communist ideology, gaining wide acceptance of their approach to scientific management as the direct outgrowth of the faithful application of the basic principles of Marxism-Leninism to the socioeconomic challenges of the contemporary world.*

* "'Dialectical' systems theory begins by transposing whole categories from the [Marxist] philosophy of history to the field of technology, and then applies them to the interpretation of history and society under the pretext of greater exactitude (in the form of feedback)" (Peter C. Ludz, *The Changing Party Elite in East Germany*, trans. Israel Program for Scientific Translations [Cambridge, Mass.: MIT Press, 1972], pp. 411–12).

The decade following the construction of the Berlin Wall saw the moderation of the internal class struggle, the implementation of the New Economic System through the mid-1960s, and a dramatic increase in East German production. By 1971, when Ulbricht was replaced as party chief by Erich Honecker, the German Democratic Republic had claimed a place in the ranks of the world's leading industrial powers and its citizens enjoyed the highest standard of living in the Communist world, though far from equal to that in the Federal Republic. Throughout the 1970s and into the 1980s, the East German standard of living gradually rose under the Honecker regime, which gave high priority to consumer goods and housing, assuring freedom from want and, for many, an unprecedented measure of comfort and leisure. This striking material success did not bring with it the quality of personal freedom afforded the individual in the western democracies, but it probably helped to reconcile many with the system and to make life bearable for those remaining inwardly alienated from what the Constitution of 1968, as amended in 1974, described as a "socialist state of the worker and the farmer."

The counterpart to internal consolidation was the achievement, by the mid-1970s, of general international recognition. East Germany had remained relatively isolated, largely as a result of the West German policy of conducting diplomatic relations only with states that did not recognize the German Democratic Republic (with exceptions such as the Soviet Union and, after January 1967, Romania). This policy was abandoned, however, in December 1972, when the Federal Republic, in conjunction with its new, conciliatory approach to relations with the East, concluded a "Treaty on the Basis of Relations" with the German Democratic Republic, formally recognizing it—not, to be sure, as a foreign country, but as a second German state. In September 1973 (the month after Walter Ulbricht, still East German head of state, had died at eighty), the German Democratic Republic was admitted to the United Nations as its 133rd member, followed by the Federal Republic as the 134th.

Whereas East Germany underwent a Communist revolution after World War II, West Germany saw what was in some ways a restoration, under the aegis of the occupying powers, of state and society as they had existed during the Weimar Republic. The chief German architect of the West German postwar political restoration was an elderly but still vigorous veteran of the Weimar era, Konrad Adenauer. Adenauer had become lord mayor of Cologne in 1917 and a member of the Prussian State Council (the upper house) in 1920. A prominent member of the Catholic *Zentrum*, he had been considered for the chancellorship of the Weimar Republic. His primary political role had not been in Berlin, however, but his native Rhineland. The third son of an administrative official of the appeals court in Cologne (a retired soldier whose outstanding military record had facilitated his appointment), young Adenauer had studied law and passed his examinations around the turn of the century. (He never studied for the doctorate; his many doctoral degrees were honorary, beginning with the early one from Cologne University in recognition of his decisive role as mayor in its reestablishment, after 120 years, in 1919.) Throughout the twenties, Cologne flourished under Adenauer's effective leadership, but the National Socialists expelled him from the mayor's office when they came to power in 1933. Thirteen years later, in 1946, at seventy, Adenauer became chairman of the newly established Christian Democratic Union (CDU) in the British-occupied zone of West Germany; in 1948–49 he presided over the Parliamentary Council that drew up the Basic Law (the constitution) of the Federal Republic; and in 1949 he was elected to the chancellorship, in which he served until his retirement as head of government (though not as a member of the West German parliament) in 1963, at eighty-seven.

A stern patriarch, shrewd and tough, Adenauer single-mindedly clove to the West. He was bitterly attacked for pursuing a "western" rather than "German" policy, but he succeeded in preparing the way for the economic and political emergence of the Federal Republic as a major West European power. Particularly controversial was his determination to reestablish the German armed forces and to provide for their being equipped with tactical nuclear weapons—even though these were not to be produced by the Federal Republic and would remain under United States control within the framework of the NATO alliance, which West Germany joined on receiving virtual sovereignty in 1955.

Those who opposed Adenauer—both socialists and reactionary nationalists—maintained that unification might somehow have been brought closer had he only taken a more neutral course rather than striving to build a strong enough West German defense establishment to make the Federal Republic the European pillar of the Atlantic alliance, while simultaneously integrating the West German economy into the European Common Market. But from the early fifties onward, the Russians were obviously bent on militarily and economically incorporating the German Democratic Republic into the Soviet empire. Any demonstration on Adenauer's part that he was less than a stalwart supporter of the Atlantic alliance and West European integration could well have shaken the confidence of the western powers—a precondition for West Germany's heavily subsidized economic recovery—without bringing unification nearer or ameliorating the situation of the Germans under Communist rule.

During the nineteen-fifties and even in the sixties there was considerable public discussion in the Federal Republic of the hope of reunification with the territories beyond the Iron Curtain that were the native homelands of over a fifth of the West German population—and to which many of them long hoped to be able to return, bearing in mind the explicit constitutional mandate of the Basic Law of the Federal Republic, the preamble of which called upon the German people "to achieve, by self-determination, the unity and freedom of Germany." But meanwhile the burgeoning free market economy, which eventually made West Germany the fourth-, if not third-ranking industrial power in the world, afforded an ever higher standard of living in the Federal Republic, and the older refugees were gradually supplanted by a younger generation far less concerned about the lost lands of their own or their forefathers' birth.

With an increasingly large segment of the West German public realizing that there was no foreseeable solution to the division of their country, a new coalition formed in Bonn in 1969 initiated negotiations that led not only to interim settlements with Germany's former enemies in the East, but to the establishment of relations between the two German states. This was begun and all but completed under Willy Brandt, a very different sort of leader than the Rhenish patriarch Adenauer. A courageously tenacious man from the opposite end of the political and cultural spectrum, Brandt had been born out of wedlock to a Lübeck salesgirl in 1913 and reared by her working-class father. Unusually precocious and articulate, he joined the Socialist party at seventeen, soon made a name for himself as a radical youth leader, and went into exile, not yet twenty, a few months after Hitler came to power. A successful multilingual author and journalist, he returned after the war to Berlin—where ten years earlier he had been an anti-Nazi underground agent—as Norwegian press attaché with the Allied Control Council. Brandt relinquished his Norwegian citizenship, acquired in 1940 after having been stripped of German citizenship by the National Socialists in 1938, was renaturalized, and entered German politics as a member of the Social Democratic party (SPD). In 1957, he became mayor of West Berlin; from 1966 to 1969, he served as foreign minister of the Federal Republic in a coalition led by the CDU; and in 1969, he became chancellor of the Federal Republic, heading a coalition of the SPD with the small, liberal Free Democratic party (FDP).

Following up on initial steps taken during the late sixties, such as the recognition of Romania in 1967, Brandt instituted a conciliatory *Ostpolitik*, a policy of accommodation toward the East. During the four and a half years of his chancellorship, he succeeded in resolving a staggering accumulation of complex problems by coordinating an interlocking network of diplomatic accords: treaties with the Soviet Union, with Poland, and with Czechoslovakia; the comprehensive American-British-French-Russian agreement on Berlin; and, as noted above, the "Treaty on the Basis of Relations," tantamount to reciprocal recognition between East and West Germany, followed by the admission of the two German states to the United

Nations. For his achievement, Willy Brandt was awarded the Nobel Peace Prize in 1971—just a hundred years after Bismarck's triumphant proclamation of the German Empire at Versailles.

In May 1974, Brandt was succeeded as chancellor by his able party and cabinet colleague Helmut Schmidt, who successfully maintained a moderately liberal course for over eight years, contending with the financial and social consequences of the quadrupling of oil prices in 1973–74 and with the impact of the second oil shock that triggered the global recession at the end of the 1970s. But in mid-September 1982 the business- and industry-oriented FDP insisted upon curtailment of social welfare expenditures that were unacceptable to the SPD and the coalition collapsed. Two weeks later, the FDP joined with the conservative caucus of the Christian Democratic Union and its still more conservative Bavarian counterpart, the Christian Social Union (CDU/CSU) in a constructive no-confidence vote, electing in place of the incumbent a new chancellor, Dr. Helmut Kohl of the CDU. A pragmatic conservative, Kohl had become prime minister of his native state of Rhineland-Palatinate in 1969, before he was forty, and had moved on to Bonn in 1976 as parliamentary opposition leader. On becoming chancellor in fall 1982, Kohl formed a coalition committed to fiscal retrenchment in domestic policy, but to continuity in intra-German and international relations—a continuity personified by the reappointment as foreign minister of Hans-Dietrich Genscher, the head of the Free Democratic party, who had held the same portfolio from May 1974 until mid-September 1982 under Helmut Schmidt.

By the early eighties, Bonn's policy of calculated cooperation with East Berlin had come to be widely accepted even in initially reluctant conservative West German circles, as illustrated by the extension in summer 1983 by a Bavarian banking consortium of over DM 1 billion in credit to the East German government, on the basis of an agreement initiated by the leader of the Christian Social Union, Franz Joseph Strauss, and formally underwritten by the government of the Federal Republic. This was followed in November 1983 by a postal and telephonic communications agreement that increased annual West German support to East Germany from DM 85 million to DM 200 million (well over a hundred million dollars), in July 1984 by a credit agreement for a further DM 950 million, and in July 1985 by Bonn's agreement permanently to increase East Germany's interest-free credit line (the "swing," as it was known) from DM 600 million to DM 850 million.

This financial support was provided only in the context of a series of other intra-German accords that in May 1986 culminated in a five-year cultural agreement that provided for artistic, educational, and scientific cooperation, which led, in practice, to events such as the first West German book fair in East Berlin, at which some three thousand publications from over four hundred publishers were displayed in an exhibition that subsequently went on to be shown in Dresden, Rostock, and Weimar.

Increasingly close intra-German relations during the 1980s, epitomized by Erich Honecker's visit in 1987 to the Federal Republic, where he was received not only in Bonn, but in several West German states, did, however, not lead to a resolution of the fundamental disagreement between Bonn and East Berlin regarding the question of German nationality. When initially established in 1949, both states had affirmed that there was only one German citizenship. Germany might be divided, but German nationality was indivisible. But in 1967, in its quest for recognition as a separate, sovereign state, East Germany, disavowing its earlier position, enacted a restrictive law making East Germans citizens of the German Democratic Republic. The Federal Republic, which remained constitutionally committed to German unity, continued to recognize German nationality alone and to issue passports identifying the bearers as German (rather than "West German") not only to citizens living in the Federal Republic, but also to their fellow countrymen from the German Democratic Republic and ethnic Germans from Poland or Russia settling in the Federal Republic. And East Germans knew that if they went west, they could count on receiving a German passport—and the security afforded by a generous network of social and educational programs.

❧ THE REVOLUTION OF 1989

RELATIONS BETWEEN THE TWO GERMAN REPUBLICS were conducted not in a vacuum, but in the context of the division of Berlin, Germany, and Europe as a whole along the Iron Curtain. By the late 1980s, however, the character of that division was in the process of transformation as a consequence of the far-reaching reforms initiated under Mikhail S. Gorbachev, who had come to power in Moscow in 1985. Through *perestroika*, restructuring, he set out to rebuild and modernize the Soviet Union's centrally-planned, government-managed economy, encumbered by inefficient, often redundant state and party bureaucracies. Through *glasnost*, openness or transparency, he facilitated the free flow and exchange of information and data indispensable for a viable modern economy—not only in the Soviet Union, but also among its economic partners in Comecon (the Council for Mutual Economic Assistance), including the German Democratic Republic.

East Germany's leaders in the 1960s had by no means opposed limited technical modernization, as they had demonstrated by introducing the New Economic System, but their successors in the 1980s had no intention of going overboard with Gorbachev. They were convinced that the introduction in East Germany of the reforms that he advocated would involve relinquishing control and permitting the socialist system as they knew it to unravel before their very eyes. Their counterparts in Warsaw or Budapest might risk such experiments, trusting that Polish or Hungarian nationalism, if nothing else, might assure the survival of their respective regimes, even if radically modified, but East Berlin could not fall back on nationalist patriotism. The only rationale for the existence of the German Democratic Republic as a sovereign state was that it represented the communist German alternative to capitalist West Germany, with which it shared a common language, a common history, and a common border, and to which since the mid-1970s it had also become increasingly tightly linked by cultural, economic, and commercial agreements. If East Germany did not remain a socialist state of workers and farmers, it was sooner or later bound to be absorbed by the Federal Republic. In autumn 1988 the Honecker regime's adamant rejection of *glasnost* was unambiguously illustrated by the withdrawal from East German cinemas of five controversial Soviet films and by the East German postal service discontinuing delivery of the German edition of the Soviet political journal *Sputnik*, because of its "distortion of history," effectively banning it from circulation in the German Democratic Republic.

On 1 January 1989 new travel regulations went into force that spelled out in minute detail the conditions under which East Germans might justify applications for exit visas (stamps in their passports required as documentation of official permission to leave the country) for personal travel to West Germany or West Berlin. Such burdensome rules would have been resented even had they not been suddenly imposed after a long period during which intrusive controls had gradually been relaxed. Coming when they did, however, they were particularly demoralizing, for they clearly represented an unmistakable sign of the East German leaders' rejection of the reform movement that was gradually bringing increased individual freedom to so many throughout much of the Communist world.

The new visa regulations did not pertain to vacation travel to Hungary, where, by the late 1980s, tens of thousands were spending affordable summer holidays in the wooded hill country of western Hungary, on the Platten-See (Lake Balaton), the largest inland body of water in Central Europe, or further west in the foothills of the Austrian Alps along the Hungarian border. Until May 1989 that border was a fortified segment of the Iron Curtain, but then the reformed Hungarian government began dismantling it as a "gruesome anachronism." This enabled East Germans to hike across the "green frontier" into Austria, from which they could go on to the Federal Republic, register as German citizens, and count on state support as they started their new lives. They did so in steadily increasing numbers, abandoning their cars as they bypassed the official border crossings where Hungarian officials, until August 1989, continued to honor their government's commitment to East Berlin to stop East Germans attempting to go west without proper exit visas, stamping an indelible entry into their passports that they had been turned back at the border and that they would be allowed to leave Hungary only in order to return to the German Democratic Republic, where the border guards, on inspecting returning East Germans' passports, would find the incriminating stamp. But on 9 August the Hungarians announced that they would discontinue stamping East Germans' passports, even though they would still stop them from crossing into Austria, and a month later, on 10 September (after the prime minister and the foreign minister of Hungary had secretly flown to Bonn for a meeting with their West German counterparts), Budapest announced that as of midnight that night, East Germans would no longer be turned back at the Austro-Hungarian border. As though a dam had burst, the steadily growing stream suddenly became a deluge. Within three days some fifteen thousand East Germans arrived in the Federal Republic, followed by an additional nine thousand by the end of the month.

This dramatic exodus through Hungary coincided with the equally unprecedented emergence within East Germany of an articulate, highly visible political opposition. On 10 September, thirty prominent dissidents drew up a manifesto proclaiming the establishment of New Forum (*Neues Forum*)—not as a political party, but as an association for public dialogue on political reform, and on the twelfth, another activist group, Democracy Now (*Demokratie Jetzt*), surfaced with a program linking its demand for electoral reform with a bitter protest against the Socialist Unity party's blatant electoral manipulation in the past. On 4 October 1989, leaders of New Forum, Democracy Now, and several other politically active associations, including human-rights advocacy committees and church-affiliated pacifist circles, met and formed a collaborative opposition contact group. Two days later, almost a thousand of their supporters meeting at the East Berlin Church of the Redeemer adopted a joint declaration calling for UN-supervised East German elections. Potentially newsworthy at any time, this appeal commanded particularly wide coverage because of its timing, having been issued just as representatives of the international press and broadcast media (together with political delegations from throughout the Communist world) were converging on East Berlin for the celebration the next day, Saturday, 7 October 1989, of the fortieth anniversary of the founding of the German Democratic Republic.

As the ranking guest of honor at the East Berlin ceremonies, President Gorbachev expressed his confidence that the German Democratic Republic's problems would be resolved not in Moscow but in Berlin, a statement widely taken to mean that although he would not impose reforms on East Germany, should the rigidity of the Honecker regime lead to an uprising against it, there would be no Soviet intervention—unlike during the rising against the Ulbricht regime in 1953. According to Gorbachev's memoirs, he attempted during a private meeting of some three hours with Honecker to discuss the crisis gripping the German Democratic Republic (on which the Soviet president was well informed), but found the German leader unwilling or perhaps unable to acknowledge the gravity of the situation. Before returning to Moscow, he wrote, he met with the members of the East German Politburo and urged reform, warning that "in politics, whoever comes late will be punished by life," and concluding with the admonition that "life calls upon you to make courageous decisions."

On the streets of Berlin, meanwhile, the East German authorities had exercised relative restraint during the day of the anniversary celebrations, but during the evening of Saturday, 7 October, as the thousands who had participated in the demonstration at the Alexanderplatz left the center of town, the police arrested well over a thousand and injured scores in a show of brutal violence reminiscent of the tactics of Hitler's brownshirts during the first year of the Third Reich. But no firearms were used and there were no fatalities.

In Leipzig, a full-scale showdown if not a bloodbath seemed imminent on Monday, 9 October. For years, prayer services for peace had been held on Mondays at 5:00 P.M. at the *Nikolaikirche* (the Church of St. Nicholas). These had been followed by political demonstrations that had become larger each Monday in September. On the twenty-fifth, when an estimated five thousand took part, the outnumbered police had hesitated to move against them. A week later, however, on Monday, 2 October, the police, reinforced by Working-Class Combat Group troops (armed reservists in a kind of proletarian East German National Guard), had brutally dispersed over fifteen thousand demonstrators. With tension in and around Leipzig having steadily escalated during the first week of October, the turnout on Monday the ninth was sure to be greater than ever. To contend with it decisively, armed units of the Ministry of the Interior and mechanized forces of the Ministry of State Security were deployed in and around Leipzig, prepared to crush all hostile activity, taking special care to isolate its instigators.

Heartsick at the likelihood of a catastrophe, which would be virtually certain to follow the slightest provocation, Leipzig's most famous citizen, Kurt Masur, conductor of the Leipzig Gewandhaus Orchestra, invited Dr. Peter Zimmermann, a Protestant pastor and member of the CDU (East) National Committee, the popular entertainer Bernd Lutz Lange of the Leipzig cabaret "Akademixern," and three senior Leipzig officials of the Socialist Unity party, Kurt Maier, Jochen Pommert, and Roland Wötzel, to his home, where they drew up an urgent appeal for calm (*Besonnenheit*), in order that a peaceful dialogue on the future course of socialism in East Germany might be conducted, committing themselves to ensure that this dialogue would take place, "not only in the district of Leipzig, but with our government as well." The appeal of the "Leipzig Six," as they came to be known, was immediately reproduced and posted, locally broadcast, and read over loudspeakers in the city and from church pulpits. Moreover, it was telephoned to Egon Krenz in East Berlin by the ranking party official in the Leipzig district. Among the most powerful men in the East German oligarchy, a member of the small West Slavic Sorbian (or Wendish) minority, tall, articulate, and self-confident, Krenz, the youngest of the Politburo's twenty-six members, was Erich Honecker's heir apparent. Most important, he was the Politburo member responsible for security affairs throughout East Germany. Considered a hardliner, he had been severely criticized during a visit to West Germany in summer 1989 for characterizing Beijing's brutal suppression of the democracy movement at Tiananmen Square as an internal security matter of the People's Republic of China. He clearly realized that the crisis in the German Democratic Republic had gone too far to be mastered even by a ruthless "Chinese solution" and he deserves as much credit as anyone for the absence of massive bloodshed in East Germany in fall 1989. From secret opinion surveys, Krenz knew that the credibility of the Socialist Unity party leadership had been gravely eroded, even among party members, and that the people's sense of identification with the German Democratic Republic had virtually dissolved. He therefore had orders sent to all forces deployed in Leipzig that violence was to be avoided unless there were provocation on the part of the demonstrators—and there was none. Consequently some seventy thousand participated in a demonstration held without interference by the authorities. To assure restraint the following week as well, Krenz persuaded a very reluctant Honecker to sign an order that during the demonstration anticipated on Monday, 16 October, the strong forces still deployed in Leipzig were to be used only to forestall violence, and that firearms were in no case to be used. Well over a hundred thousand participated and not only were there no incidents, but live coverage was provided by the East German media.

The following morning, Tuesday the seventeenth, as Erich Honecker convened the Politburo for its weekly meeting, he was interrupted while presenting the first item on the agenda by Prime Minister Willi Stoph, whom he had displaced as East German head of state in 1976. Stoph bluntly proposed that Honecker "be released from his function" as secretary general of the Socialist Unity party of Germany. Once he saw that he stood alone, Honecker acquiesced. The next day it was announced that Erich Honecker had retired due to ill health and that Egon Krenz had succeeded him as secretary general. On the following Monday, 23 October, the East German parliament elected Krenz chairman of the Council of State, making him head of state of the German Democratic Republic, and, on the twenty-seventh, the Council of State issued an amnesty for all who had defected from the German Democratic Republic and been declared criminals *in absentia* (*Republikflucht* ["flight from the Republic"] having been a serious felony), and for those who had been found guilty of attempting to leave illegally.

Meanwhile, having called upon the director of the State Planning Commission to prepare a candid analysis of the economic situation of the German Democratic Republic (forbidden by Honecker), Krenz learned, at the end of October 1989, that East Germany was at the point of bankruptcy. In order to meet current obligations without incurring further foreign debt, the standard of living would have to be reduced in 1990 by 25 to 30 percent. This would entail cutbacks in consumer goods and services that would at any time be deeply resented, but that, considering the atmosphere prevailing in fall 1989, would make the country virtually ungovernable. It was therefore clear that extensive reforms would be needed—but also very substantial foreign aid on an emergency basis.

At the beginning of November 1989, Krenz flew to Moscow for a conference with Gorbachev, after which, on Friday, 3 November, he appealed in a radio and television address to the people of the German Democratic Republic for their support of a reform program that included the establishment of a supreme court and the introduction of alternative national service for those unwilling to be conscripted into the armed forces. Above all, Krenz appealed to the citizens not to leave their country, but to have confidence in the reforms and to help make them successful: "Your place, dear fellow citizens, is here. We need you." Yet if they decided otherwise, he assured them, they were free to go and should have no misgivings about turning to the appropriate government authorities.

The next day, Saturday, 4 November, at a spectacular rally attended by over half a million in East Berlin, and carried live on East German radio and television, over two dozen speakers, including prominent writers, artists, politicians, and government officials, called for freedom of the press, free elections, and freedom to travel abroad. In several other East German cities there were also demonstrations involving tens of thousands demanding freedom and democracy. On Monday the sixth, the government released for public comment its long-awaited proposal for a new law liberalizing foreign travel, only to have it rejected the very next day as completely inadequate by the Constitutional and Legal Affairs Committee of the East German parliament. Had this law providing that citizens might spend thirty days abroad annually been proposed a year earlier, it might have been seen as a sign of accommodation, but, in the first week of November 1989, it was taken to demonstrate nothing but the inability of the old guard, even after Honecker's fall, to understand the crisis.

The regime's lack of credibility was dramatized more effectively by the exodus. At the beginning of November, the Czech border, which had been closed when Hungary had opened its western border to East Germans, had once more been opened, and in the first seven days of the month, thirty-five thousand more East Germans had moved west. Responding to the urgent need for a highly visible change of the guard, coupled with a radical change in policy, Egon Krenz and his allies in the beleaguered East Berlin hierarchy moved quickly to regain the initiative.

On Tuesday, 7 November, the East German Council of Ministers, including Prime Minister Willi Stoph, resigned as a body.

On Wednesday the eighth, at a special meeting of the Central Committee of the Socialist Unity party, the old Politburo, over two dozen strong, resigned as a body and was replaced by a new team of eleven, still headed by Krenz as secretary general, but now including the Dresden district party chief, Dr. Hans Modrow, whom Honecker had kept at arm's length as an articulate advocate of Gorbachev-style reform. Not only was Modrow brought into the Politburo, but also designated as Willi Stoph's successor as prime minister (i.e., as head of government, as opposed to Krenz, who was to remain head of state as well as being head of the party).

Early on the evening of Thursday the ninth, finally, while the new Politburo and the new government were still being organized, a spokesman of the Central Committee, speaking live before television news cameras, announced, with reference to the recently rejected draft travel regulations, that the government had decided to open the borders of the German Democratic Republic. Asked if this meant that every East German could freely go to the West, the spokesman responded that there would be no requirements and that the authorities were being instructed to issue passports and visas "fast and unbureaucratically," adding that the new regulations were going into effect "at once." The decision had been so recently reached that provisions for its implementation had not yet been made, but thousands of East Germans took what they saw on television at face value and went to border-crossing points demanding to be let through. Perplexed guards turned to their superiors for instructions. When Krenz was telephoned at home that evening by the minister of state security and asked what orders to give, he answered, "Let them pass."

Thus the ninth of November became a triple anniversary. That date in 1918 had seen the fall of the German monarchical system and the proclamation of a republic that, within fifteen years, would be supplanted by the most catastrophic regime in German history. Twenty years after the 1918 revolution, on 9 November 1938, the terrible pogrom known as the "Night of Broken Glass," the National Socialist *Reichskristallnacht*, foreshadowed the Holocaust. But 9 November 1989 turned out to be a landmark on the road to the most successful revolution in German history, for the opening of the border represented the turning point in East Germany's peaceful liberation from a once ruthless and—in the fall of 1989—still heavily armed regime.

During the long weekend following that electrifying Thursday evening announcement, well over a million East Germans took advantage of a freedom of movement most of them had never known in their entire lives. The international media focused its coverage on Berlin. But in West German towns and villages all along the intra-German border, an extraordinary reunion was spontaneously celebrated by Germans from the two republics. While hundreds of thousands crossed through the openings in the Berlin Wall along the border between the Soviet and western sectors of Berlin, tens of thousands more set out via the eighteen border crossings between East and West Germany, traveling in endless columns of Trabant and Wartburg subcompacts (with low-powered, two-stroke motors burning an emission-rich mixture of gasoline and oil), visiting childhood friends and relatives from whom many had been cut off for decades, sightseeing in a land that a week earlier they had seen only on the television screen, and shopping in stores with a variety and quality of merchandise that was available in East Germany, if at all, only to members of the party oligarchy and to those whose connections in the West enabled them to patronize the government-operated chain of stores that sold Western merchandise for Western currency only.

The East Germans were welcomed with enthusiasm and, because East German money was almost worthless in the West, with a cash subvention. Town halls and financial institutions were kept open over the weekend to disburse the hundred-mark allowance of West German government "welcome funds" (the equivalent of approximately sixty U.S. dollars)—and the opportunity to spend it was provided by the relaxation of the strict West German regulation of store hours that would otherwise have kept the stores closed from late Saturday afternoon until Monday morning.

On Monday, 13 November, Hans Modrow, the sixty-one-year-old Dresden reformer brought into the Politburo only the week before, was elected prime minister of East Germany. An unpretentious Pomeranian with a doctorate in economics from the Humboldt University in Berlin, respected for personal integrity, administrative ability, and the advocacy of desperately needed reforms, he had been harshly criticized in the official East German press during the last phase of the Honecker regime, but survived in his post as chief of the party organization in the Dresden region (one of the fifteen major administrative districts of the republic) not only because of his steady competence, but because of his reputation abroad, especially in the Soviet Union. In organizing his government, the new premier formed a coalition cabinet that he called a "National Front." It included as ministers several deputies who had been elected to the East German parliament as members of the small non-Communist parties that had been permitted by the Honecker regime to have token representation in the legislature beside the ruling Socialist Unity party—including, as minister for church affairs, a prominent lawyer who had recently become chairman of the Eastern CDU, Lothar de Maizière. To an extent not possible for Krenz, whose credibility had been irreparably undermined by his conspicuous role in the Honecker regime, Modrow succeeded in commanding respect and generating loyalty in an atmosphere still reeking of corruption, servility, fear, and hatred. On Friday, 17 November, Modrow presented a straightforward program to the East German parliament, in which he announced drastic reforms and a policy toward the Federal Republic that he hoped would lead to a contractual community (*Vertragsgemeinschaft*) between the two German states.

Chancellor Kohl in his landmark address to the West German Parliament in Bonn on 28 November not only responded to Modrow but defined his policy in terms of a ten-point program to deal with the immediate crisis, to coordinate the development of intra-German relations with European integration, and eventually to bring about German unity through free self-determination, under circumstances taking into account the interests of all involved and guaranteeing peace in Europe. For many, in both German republics and abroad, Kohl's speech came as a somewhat unwelcome surprise. There had been widespread jubilation over the liberation of East Germany from a detested regime, but Kohl's agenda leading to German unification, even though he set no target dates for the stages by which it was to be reached, step by step, was hardly welcome in London or Paris, where Kohl's speech was received with reservations. In Washington, however, the reception of the German chancellor's initiative was comparatively positive. President George Bush and Secretary of State James Baker both regarded German unification as inevitable and by no means undesirable.

In East Berlin, meanwhile, the remaining shreds of state authority had been gathered by Modrow's coalition government, which was firmly committed to reform. The East German parliament formally terminated the communist monopoly of power on 1 December by deleting from the East German constitution the provisions declaring the German Democratic Republic to be a "socialist state of the worker and the farmer" and institutionalizing the leadership of the Socialist Unity party. The same day, a special parliamentary commission's report on misappropriation of funds and other corruption in the East German hierarchy was telecast, triggering a grave crisis. Within five days over half a million Socialist Unity party membership books were turned in by resigning members.

The Central Committee of the party was hastily convened for what would be its final meeting on Sunday, 3 December 1989. Erich Honecker and eleven of his closest associates were expelled from the party. Several of them were arrested on charges of corruption. General Secretary Egon Krenz and all the members of the Politburo and the Central Committee resigned. An emergency party congress was convened within a week. Prime Minister Modrow headed off plans for the dissolution of the party by appealing to the delegates to sustain the government coalition that had been established with the confidence and support of all the parties in the East German parliament. Dissolving the party, which held a majority in the parliament, could bring down the government, with unforeseeable consequences. Modrow's call to duty was effective. Instead of being dissolved, the party was taken into a kind of political receivership and given new leadership, a new program, a new name, and, insofar as possible, a new image. Gregor Gysi, a forty-one-year-old lawyer of Jewish descent was elected, with the support of over 95 percent of the delegates, as new chairman, with Prime Minister Modrow and his able colleague from Dresden, Mayor Wolfgang Berghofer, as deputy chairmen. The party's name was changed from "Socialist Unity Party of Germany" to "Socialist Unity Party of Germany–Party of Democratic Socialism," designated by the German initials, SED-PDS (but the first part of the compound name soon was dropped and it went into the 1990 elections as the PDS). The Politburo and Central Committee were abolished, new statutes were drafted, and many of those associated with the old regime were expelled from the party, including Egon Krenz.

On Tuesday, 19 December 1989, Chancellor Kohl flew for his first meeting with Prime Minister Modrow to Dresden, where his host had served for over fifteen years as regional party chief. Committed to the preservation of the German Democratic Republic within a loose confederation, Modrow made it clear that despite his reservations about Kohl's long-term goal of full unification in a single state, East Germany urgently needed, to forestall collapse, a kind of *Lastenausgleich* (an "equalization-of-burdens" payment) of DM 15 billion, as a compensation for having suffered incomparably greater deprivation in the aftermath of World War II than West Germany. Kohl brushed aside the idea of an equalization of burdens as inappropriate, but agreed in principle to consider a major West German infusion of capital as an emergency solidarity measure as soon as appropriate terms and conditions could be worked out. The day-long conference ended with a joint declaration by the two heads of government announcing their agreement to establish a contractual community of the two German states through a treaty to be signed in spring 1990. Modrow also announced that before Christmas the East German government would open the Brandenburg Gate in Berlin for pedestrians; that, as of 24 December, Germans entering the German Democratic Republic from West Berlin or the Federal Republic would no longer need to have entry visas; that the East German criminal law code was being reformed; and that all political prisoners were to be released, if possible, before Christmas.

Although the agenda for the Dresden meeting had not included a public address by the chancellor, the pilgrimage of tens of thousands to the Saxon capital, as though for a papal visit, with special trains from all over the German Democratic Republic, led to a last minute change of plans. After the meeting and the ensuing news conference, Kohl gave a televised address to a throng estimated at a hundred thousand from an improvised podium set up before the ruins of Dresden's *Frauenkirche* (the Church of Our Lady, destroyed in the February 1945 bombing). In a low key, carefully avoiding anything that might arouse false expectations, the chancellor expressed his admiration for the peaceful revolution in the German Democratic Republic and assured his East German listeners of West German solidarity on the long and difficult road ahead.

The extraordinarily moving response left no doubt in Kohl's mind (nor in the minds of many of those who were present or watched the telecast of the event) of the enormous groundswell in East Germany for immediate, full unification with the Federal Republic. In his memoir of German unification, Kohl stated that Dresden was decisive. With his ten-point program he had drawn up the itinerary for a journey, but carefully avoided writing in the dates. At Dresden he saw that, as far as the East Germans were concerned, the train had already left the station.

Three days later, on the afternoon of Friday, 22 December, Kohl joined Modrow in Berlin, participating with him in the formal reopening of the Brandenburg Gate, a ceremony that symbolized the end of the division of the city, of Germany, and of Europe as a whole.

German Unification

THE EAST GERMAN REVOLUTION of fall 1989 had set the stage for German unification, but it was brought about only through complex multilateral negotiations in which the presidents of the Soviet Union and the United States played key roles. During Gorbachev's visit to Bonn in June 1989, Kohl had established rapport with the Russian leader. At the beginning of December 1989 at Malta, Bush had informed Gorbachev of America's support for Kohl's ten-point plan for the gradual achievement of German unity and urged him to accept the changes inevitably coming in Germany. Two days later, in his speech at a NATO summit meeting in Brussels, Bush endorsed German unification, provided that Germany remain a member of the Atlantic alliance. Later in December, support for unification was expressed in a joint statement of the NATO foreign ministers in Brussels and in a joint declaration of the Council of Europe in Strasbourg on behalf of the heads of state and government of the European Community.

Meanwhile, the alarming disintegration of East Germany continued, dramatized and further exacerbated by a renewed surge in migration to West Germany in January 1990. With the opening of the intra-German border and the Berlin Wall early in November, the number of resettlers to West Germany had soared from 57,024 in October to 133,429 in November. There was a brief decline to 43,221 in December (the total for 1989 was 34⊃,854), but in January 1990, 73,729 more resettlers registered with West German authorities. The inexorable mass exodus, continuing at a rate of over two thousand daily during the early weeks of the new year, reflected the catastrophic collapse of the East German economy and, moreover, dramatized the failure of its government to generate public confidence. To broaden his political base, Modrow in mid-January turned for support to the Round Table. Established early in December 1989, this was a kind of *ad hoc* steering committee in which leaders of the major opposition groups and parties, including the Liberal Democratic and Social Democratic parties and the various citizens' movements, had improvised a well-publicized forum for serious public consideration of current issues in a land in which open political discussion in civil society had been suppressed for decades. After Modrow agreed to advance the date for parliamentary elections from May to mid-March 1990, eight members of the Round Table became ministers without portfolio in his broadened coalition.

With the fabric of East Germany's state, economy, and society unraveling before him, Modrow realized by the end of January 1990 that he had no alternative but "to combine the stabilization of the German Democratic Republic with the gradual unification of the two German states." To this end, on 29 January he announced to the East German parliament a proposal for the federation (and military neutrality) of the two German republics and flew to Moscow the next day, where he elicited Gorbachev's agreement, in principle, to his plan for German unification. When Modrow informed Kohl, whom he met on 3 February at a World Economic Forum in Davos, Switzerland, of the urgent need for emergency support, they agreed to confer in Bonn ten days later, after Kohl had returned from a trip to Moscow. While he was there, the Soviet president confirmed that he considered it up to the Germans to decide when, how, and under what circumstances they would realize their unification. On 13 February, Kohl met with Modrow, who was accompanied to Bonn by his seventeen-member cabinet. Modrow presented a Round Table position paper that called for the Federal Republic to provide East Germany, as a matter of solidarity, between ten and fifteen billion marks "immediately, independently of all further negotiations (*sofort, unabhängig von allen weiteren Verhandlungen*)." Kohl responded to the East German request by pointing out that his government had already allocated over DM 5 billion in aid and credits in a supplementary budget for 1990 to meet the immediate needs of the East Germans. Considering the gravity of the crisis of the German Democratic Republic, he was unwilling to administer a further fiscal transfusion. Instead, he proposed what amounted to the equivalent of a heart transplant, i.e., a full-scale currency union. Under the terms of the plan approved by the Bonn cabinet on the eve of the Modrow visit, West German currency would on the day of implementation replace East German currency as legal tender throughout the German Democratic Republic, where the East German government would meanwhile have created "the necessary legal conditions for the introduction of a social market economy."

Modrow and his colleagues were deeply disappointed not to receive the requested emergency aid, but the East German prime minister agreed without delay to begin the negotiations that, as it turned out, were concluded under his successor following the March elections.

While Kohl and Modrow were setting the stage in Bonn for negotiations for a currency union, U.S. Secretary of State James Baker coordinated with the foreign ministers of France, the Soviet Union, the United Kingdom, and the two German republics, in Ottawa for a long-planned NATO and Warsaw Pact conference on open skies, an agreement to hold a series of working conferences on the "external aspects" of German unity, including the question of the status of Berlin, which remained under four-power occupation. The Two-Plus-Four Talks, as these meetings were called, were held on 5 May in Bonn, on 22 June in East Berlin, on 17 July in Paris, and on 12 September in Moscow, where the Treaty on the Final Settlement with Respect to Germany was signed. Under its terms, the four powers relinquished the authority they had exercised in Berlin since 1945 and acknowledged Germany's "full sovereignty over its internal and external affairs." Moreover, they affirmed that "the right of the united Germany to belong to alliances, with all the rights and responsibilities arising therefrom, shall not be affected by the present treaty." Thus the Soviet Union not only agreed to give up the position it had held in East Berlin since the end of the war and to withdraw its forces from eastern Germany, but also to accept united Germany's membership in the Atlantic alliance.

Soviet acquiescence in Germany's NATO membership had not come easily. It was elicited, with active support from Washington, by Chancellor Kohl and Foreign Minister Genscher in six months of negotiations with President Gorbachev and Soviet Foreign Minister Eduard Shevardnadze, beginning with Kohl's and Genscher's trip to Moscow on 10 February and culminating in a bilateral Soviet-German agreement reached in mid-July in the Caucasus that paved the way for the final settlement of 12 September 1990. Under the terms of the Caucasus accord, Gorbachev agreed that the Soviet Union would give up its control of East Berlin and withdraw its forces from a Germany that would remain in NATO, while Kohl agreed that Germany, once unified, would cut its military establishment by over a third and that it would conclude agreements with the Soviet Union to fund not only the cost of maintaining the Soviet forces in Germany during the period from the economic union of the two German states in July 1990 until their final departure to the Soviet Union (completed in August 1994), but also the cost of their relocation in the Soviet Union.

By the time the German and Soviet leaders announced their accord at a joint press conference at the Zheleznovodsk sanatorium in the Caucasus Mountains on 16 July 1990, the March 1990 elections in East Germany had led to the formation of a coalition committed to swift unification, and the two German republics had concluded and implemented the monetary union noted above. The East German elections had turned out to be a referendum on whether unification should take place by accession in a matter of months, under the terms of Article 23 of the Basic Law, the process whereby the Saarland had joined the Federal Republic on 1 January 1957, or whether unification should take place under a new constitution, which, as stipulated in Article 146 of the Basic Law, would supersede the Basic Law on the day it came into force through the freely enacted decision of the German people. Prime Minister Modrow, his colleagues in the Party of Democratic Socialism, many members of the Round Table, and most East German Social Democrats (as well as a number of their counterparts in the Federal Republic) urged gradual unification, under a new constitution. They realized that the process of unification would be protracted because of the time that it would take to draft and ratify a new constitution, but they thought the delay might spare many East Germans at least some of the dislocations and hardships of an abrupt shift from the centrally directed East German economic system to the Federal Republic's capitalistic social market economy. The average standard of living in East Germany was far lower than in West Germany, and many modern appliances, not to mention luxuries, were unattainable for the average citizen, but everyone was assured food, clothing, shelter, a job, and medical care. By West German or American standards, public transportation, housing, postal service, and basic food and clothing were very cheap, but the enormous subventions that had kept down the cost to consumers of the basic necessities of daily life had contributed substantially to the East German government's horrendously mounting deficit throughout the 1980s.

Chancellor Kohl and the coalition for which he actively campaigned in East Germany, the "Alliance for Germany," led by the chairman of the East German CDU, Lothar de Maizière, advocated immediate accession to the Federal Republic under the terms of Article 23 of the Basic Law. Kohl acknowledged that quick unification would inevitably entail difficulties in adjustment, but argued that protracting the process would only increase the economic costs and might well be political folly. He was convinced that the prospect of cooperation of the Soviet Union under Gorbachev represented a unique and possibly fleeting historic opportunity, one that it would be irresponsible not to seize. The victory at the polls on 18 March 1990 of the "Alliance for Germany," led, on 12 April 1990, to de Maizière's election as prime minister; to the signing, on 18 May, of the treaty establishing a monetary, economic, and social union, which went into force 1 July; and to the signing, on 31 August, of the Unification Treaty, which provided for unification by accession of the five states on the territory of the former German Democratic Republic, together with the city-state of Berlin, on 3 October 1990.

Thus German unity was formally achieved under the terms of three treaties: the two German republics' treaties of economic union signed in Bonn on 18 May and of unification signed in Berlin on 31 August, and the treaty on the final settlement signed in Moscow on 12 September by the two German states and the four powers. However, as President Richard von Weizsäcker stressed on the Day of German Unity, 3 October 1990, the work had only just begun: "The form of unity has been determined," he said. "Now we must give it substance."

This was anything but a rhetorical exaggeration, for the unification process had been handled in such a way that much of East Germany's governmental bureaucracy as well as its economic infrastructure would, for all practical purposes, have to be rebuilt from the ground up. The reason for this was that, unlike the Saarland, which acceded to the Federal Republic in 1957, or the Republic of Texas, which was admitted to the United States of America in 1845, the German Democratic Republic did not, on 3 October 1990, become a constituent state of the Federal Republic. Had it done so, it would have become the largest state in the Federal Republic, with half again the area of the next in size, Bavaria, and a population roughly equal to that of Rhineland-Westphalia, the most populous and productive West German state.

Instead, the Treaty of Unification provided for the dissolution of the German Democratic Republic and the accession to the Federal Republic, on 3 October 1990, of Berlin and of the states of Brandenburg, Mecklenburg-West Pomerania, Saxony, Saxony-Anhalt, and Thuringia. These states had comprised the German Democratic Republic when it was established in 1949, but in 1952 they had been supplanted, as governing bodies, by fourteen administrative districts (together with a fifteenth, East Berlin, which was not recognized as part of East Germany by Britain, France, or the United States). Thirty-eight years later, on 22 July 1990, the five states were, in effect, resurrected (with minor boundary changes from 1952) on the eve of German unification. Only on 14 October, after their formal accession to the Federal Republic on 3 October 1990, did they hold initial parliamentary elections, enabling them to establish state governments and elect minister-presidents. This fresh start-up entailed a great deal of work and expense, but it had the advantage that the new eastern German states were not automatically encumbered with the established regional bureaucracy of the administrative districts through which the Socialist Unity party had governed the German Democratic Republic for the past thirty-eight years. The new state governments consequently enjoyed far more freedom than they would otherwise have had to draw selectively on the pool of experienced and readily available civil servants employed by district governments being phased out, while also recruiting suitably qualified applicants from western Germany (particularly for the many positions that required detailed knowledge of West German and European Community laws and regulations with which most East German officials were unfamiliar).

Because education in the Federal Republic is under the aegis of state governments, the restoration of the five new states in the East, together with the organization of Berlin, the capital, as a sixth new state, also had profound impact on institutions of higher learning in eastern Germany. The East German universities and institutes of technology and of sports were transferred to new state governments with the authority to continue their programs and to reappoint their faculties and staff—or to decline to do so. Virtually every institution was faced with what could be compared, in American terms, to a process of reaccreditation, rechartering, and, in many cases, reorganization, whereby, apart from political considerations, the transfer to the new state governments not infrequently led to drastic cutbacks constrained by deep cuts in fiscal support.

These changes were not, of course, imposed immediately on unification in 1990, but only in its aftermath, as the "new states" gradually were restructured after the economic unification treaty came into force on 1 July and the political unification treaty on 3 October, followed by the state elections in October and national elections in December 1990.

In the initial parliamentary elections held on 14 October in the five recently reestablished East German states, Chancellor Kohl's Christian Democratic Union won a plurality of seats in three states and an absolute majority in a fourth, while the liberal Free Democratic party led by his coalition partner, Foreign Minister Genscher, cleared the five-percent hurdle, assuring representation in all five state parliaments. Seven weeks later, on 2 December, in national parliamentary elections held throughout the Federal Republic, the governing coalition won a clear victory, reflecting widespread appreciation for the achievement of unification. Four years later, however, in the national elections on 16 October 1994, Kohl was returned to the chancellorship by only a narrow margin.

The marked decline in the chancellor's majority reflected dissatisfaction during the years following unification with its unexpectedly high costs and their consequences, whether in the form of levied taxes, curtailed services, or disappointed expectations. The fundamental problem was that German unification not only required the imposition throughout eastern Germany of the Federal Republic's tax, banking, social security, medical care, and welfare systems, but also the conversion of East Germany as a whole from a communist to a social market economy. This entailed the privatization of nationalized businesses and industries, as well as the restitution to their original, legal owners of confiscated property, including real estate, factories, and farms, after more than four decades of communist rule.

The first step had been taken back in March 1990, when the Modrow government established an office under the prime minister to function as a public trustee of the "People's Assets." This Trust Office (*Treuhandstelle*) was charged with responsibility for thousands of "People's Enterprises" (*Volkseigene*

Betriebe or *VEB*), ranging from relatively small plants to industrial conglomerates, as well as a vast amount of real estate held in the name of the people of the German Democratic Republic by the communist regime. On 17 June 1990, two weeks before the economic unification treaty signed a month earlier went into force, the East German parliament, at a special session attended by Chancellor Kohl, passed a law transforming the Trust Office from an executive department charged with the administration of government property into a virtually autonomous public holding company mandated to restructure the economic assets of the failed East German bureaucratic command economy, privatizing whatever it could and liquidating the rest as humanely and efficiently as possible. The rechartering of the Trust Agency (*Treuhandanstalt*) was followed, on 29 June, two days before economic unification, by Prime Minister de Maizière's announcement of the appointment to its chairmanship (with the power of a virtual economic tsar of East Germany) of the liberal West German industrialist Detlev Karsten Rohwedder. A Social Democrat who had served in Bonn for a decade as secretary of state in the economics ministry during the Brandt and Schmidt administrations and, since 1979, in Dortmund as chairman of the board of Hoesch Steel, Rohwedder was widely respected for his ability to nurse languishing enterprises back to viability. (The largest state conglomerate in history, the Trust Agency was assigned in Germany a role comparable in some respects to that in the United States of the Resolution Trust Corporation established by the U.S. government, during the same period, as a huge holding company taking into receivership failed American savings and loan associations.)

In mid-August 1990, Rohwedder took charge of the agency and early in September issued his first bleak progress report. Some twenty-eight hundred Western companies had entered into joint venture agreements with East German firms, but fewer than a hundred were on a large enough scale to have major economic impact, and there were very few prospects for buyouts or applications for shareholdings. The reason for this was that few of eastern Germany's antiquated, inefficient enterprises had been found, on close inspection, to be promising investments. Before investment capital could be attracted, far more extensive restructuring and retrenchment would be necessary than anticipated, and the initial estimate of the agency's assets, at between DM 800 billion and DM 1 trillion, was cut back to DM 200 billion. On 4 October 1990, the day after unification, the heads of the fifteen regional branches of the *Treuhandanstalt*, none of whom had brought to their positions Western-style management skills, were replaced with carefully chosen executives from the Federal Republic. Later that month, the agency announced its first major shutdown: the Dresden camera maker Pentacon was closed and some three thousand workers were laid off, insofar as there was no prospect for the firm to survive in the camera-making business, as the agency spokesman put it, "against overwhelming competition from Asia." In the automobile industry, on the other hand, the outlook was better. Before the end of 1990, the Volkswagen corporation concluded an agreement with the Trust Agency to develop a subsidiary employing six thousand and plans were announced by Daimler-Benz to invest in a truck production plant and by Opel, the German subsidiary of General Motors, to invest in an assembly plant.

When Rohwedder fell victim, at the beginning of April 1991, to a terrorist assassination, the board of the *Treuhandanstalt* unanimously elected as his successor his former deputy, Birgit Breuel. A Christian Democrat with over a decade of experience as minister first of economics and then of finance in the State of Lower Saxony before going to the agency, she announced, on her appointment to its chairmanship, that she would hold the course set by Rohwedder: to "privatize quickly, restructure resolutely, shut down carefully." The agency, which at its peak, late in 1993, had more than three thousand employees in its Berlin headquarters and branches throughout eastern Germany, returned thousands of properties to their original owners or their heirs, sold many others, and dissolved some 3700 plants or businesses. Many of the sales were made possible only by the agency writing off (i.e., assuming) the old debt of a business or enterprise, or by sharply discounting its purchase price to allow for modernization costs and, in many cases, severance pay for redundant employees. This liability represented the hidden cost of East Germany's vaunted full employment, which turned out to have been achieved by putting everyone on one payroll or another, whether there was work to be done or not. In Eisenach, for example, where, by 1995, 1800 employees were producing 150,000 autos per year, a production rate of eighty-three cars per worker annually, it had taken 10,000 employees to make 80,000 cars per year in the late 1980s, at an annual rate of only eight cars per worker.

At the end of 1994 the agency was finally dissolved, having privatized 14,500 properties, of which 855 had been sold to foreign investors. But the liquidation of the East German economy had been extremely expensive. Because of costs such as the subventions that had been required to keep many enterprises in operation until they could be sold and the old debts assumed by the agency in order to make potentially viable enterprises attractive to investors, the Trust Agency, notwithstanding proceeds of DM 65 billion from sales, was dissolved with a net deficit of DM 256 billion, which was added to the German national debt.

Enormous though it was, the investment through the Trust Agency represented no more than a fraction of what was needed in the east during the first few years after unification. A substantial amount was also made available through the European Recovery Program, which had not simply given away the millions of dollars of Marshall Plan aid with which it had been entrusted over four decades earlier, but had institutionalized it as a permanent revolving fund to provide long-term, low-interest capital for qualified development projects. The greatest portion of the burden, however, has fallen directly on the German taxpayer in the form of supplemental taxes. Huge sums have been expended to repair and upgrade the eastern German infrastructure, which in many areas had only been patched together after World War II, and in which modernization by late-twentieth-century standards had barely been commenced with the aid of West German credit in the 1980s.

Among the greatest investments were those being made by

the German government itself as a consequence of the parliament's narrowly enacted decision in 1991, to move from Bonn to Berlin. The resolution was passed after an eleven-hour debate conducted not on party lines, but as a matter of individual conviction. Speaking as a "simple deputy," Chancellor Kohl urged the move to Berlin (for which his mentor, Adenauer, had not infrequently expressed disdain), and his position was shared by former chancellor Willy Brandt and by Foreign Minister Genscher. Some prominent opponents to the move opposed it as an enormous extravagance, while others advocated remaining in Bonn as a center of Western-oriented German democracy, rather than moving to a city long identified with militarism and authoritarianism. But forty-two years earlier, in 1949, when Bonn rather than Frankfurt was selected as West Germany's provisional seat of government, the parliament of the Federal Republic, in the spirit of the Basic Law's mandate for unification, had explicitly linked its choice of the town on the Rhine with a solemn commitment to move to Berlin once free elections had been held there and in East Germany. This commitment, together with an enduring sense of solidarity with Berlin and eastern Germany as a whole, evidently tipped the scales in favor of the German parliament's decision, by a vote of 338 to 320 with one abstention, to leave Bonn, restoring Berlin as the principal seat of government for Germany (though part of the federal bureaucracy was to remain in the Rhineland indefinitely).

❧ GERMANY IN THE EUROPEAN UNION

THE MOVE TO BERLIN from Bonn did not mean that united Germany was turning away from Western Europe. Quite the contrary, the Federal Republic was not only firmly embedded in the European Community, but played a leading role in the integration of its twelve member states into the European Union in 1993. It was no accident that the negotiations that led to that milestone in European integration coincided with those that brought about German unification; the process of European integration in the early 1990s was as closely related to German unification in 1990 as West Germany's economic recovery in the 1950s had been to the establishment of the European Coal and Steel Community in 1952 and the formation of the Common Market five years later. The French occupation of the Ruhr in 1923, half a decade after the end of World War I, had poisoned relations between France and Germany, but the integration of the Ruhr into the European Coal and Steel Community (ECSC), under the terms of the Treaty of Paris of 18 April 1951, established a practical basis for German economic collaboration with Belgium, France, Italy, Luxemburg, and the Netherlands, and thereby set the stage for the establishment of the European Economic Community (EEC or Common Market) and the European Atomic Energy Community (Euratom) by the Treaties of Rome of 25 March 1957.

In July 1967 the ECSC, the EEC, and Euratom merged to form a single European Community (EC). The accession of Denmark, Ireland, and the United Kingdom in 1973, Greece in 1981, and Portugal and Spain in 1986 raised the membership to twelve countries.

In June 1983, meanwhile, the member states had formally resolved to strengthen the institutional basis of the EC. On the basis of a draft approved in 1984 by the European Parliament (based at Strasbourg, with members directly elected, since 1979, for five-year terms), the community's charter, the treaties of Paris and of Rome of 1951 and 1957, was amended by the Single European Act, signed in December 1986 and effective in July 1987. It authorized the council of ministers, the main decision-making body of the EC, to take action in many cases by majority rather than unanimous vote, and it established the goal of creating by the end of 1992 a single European market, with free movement of persons, goods, services, and capital across the boundaries between the member states.

Early in 1990, when it became evident that German unification was imminent, the European Community, on the joint recommendation of President François Mitterand of France and Chancellor Kohl, resolved to accelerate the process of European integration by the beginning of 1993, further developing institutions of the EC and renaming the strengthened community the European Union (EU). This initiative, which led to the Treaty of Maastricht of February 1992 and, under its terms, the establishment of the EU in 1993, was vigorously advocated by Mitterand in particular because, seeing that German unification was inevitable, he considered it imperative for France to enmesh as thoroughly as possible her more powerful eastern neighbor in a network of European regulations and commitments—in short, to see to it that united Germany would be as thoroughly Europeanized as possible. Just as the postwar recovery of West Germany had been acceptable and unthreatening to France within the Common Market, German unification could be accepted in conjunction with the formation of the European Union.

For his part, Kohl regarded the acceleration of European integration to be no less in the interest of Germany than of France, not only for political reasons (there was strong domestic support in Germany for European integration), but also in order to assure the viability of a Europe (in which Germany would be playing a leading role) in the global economy, in competition with the area covered by the North American Free Trade Agreement (NAFTA) and with the emerging economic powers of Asia and the Pacific.

German unification involved no change in the membership of the European Community because it took the form of the East German states' accession to the Federal Republic, a charter member. Moreover, East German goods had been traded, through the Federal Republic, in the Common Market for years. Ever since the improvement in relations between the two German republics in the 1970s, goods from East Germany had increasingly been imported through West Germany into the Common Market on a duty-free basis (i.e., sold in the Common Market as though they had originated in the Federal Republic), making East Germany a significant trading partner in the Common Market. The competitive impact of relatively low-cost East German goods in the markets of the Low Countries led the Belgian and Dutch governments to turn to the European Court of Justice in Luxemburg with a complaint about the dumping of East German imports introduced into their markets through

West Germany. On 21 September 1989, the European Community's court ruled that West Germany had the right to continue this practice, which was permissible under the terms of the Protocol on Intra-German Trade signed by the founding members of the European Economic Community on 25 March 1957. Under the terms of the protocol, a supplemental agreement to the Treaty of Rome of the same date establishing the Common Market, the members of the Common Market had agreed that trade between the two German states was intra-German rather than foreign trade. West German imports from East Germany, the court of the European Community therefore ruled in 1989, were not imports from a third (i.e., foreign) country at all, and were thus not subject to import duties. The court in 1989 accepted the German view that the Federal Republic, in joining the Common Market, had acted on behalf of Germany as a whole.

On 21 December 1992, Article 23 of Germany's constitution, on the "Jurisdiction of this Basic Law," the provision for accession under which first the Saarland and then the five East German states and the city-state of Berlin had joined the Federal Republic, was deleted and a new Article 23 inserted that provides for Germany's participation in the development of the European Union, mandating the transfer of sovereign powers to the European Union. On 13 October 1993, the day after the Federal Constitutional Court in Karlsruhe, Germany's supreme court, ruled that the Treaty of Maastricht was not incompatible with the German Basic Law, the German government, as the last of the signatory powers, ratified the treaty, enabling it to go into force at the beginning of the following month. Thus the European Community became, on 1 November 1993, the European Union, an association of states committed to establishing not only a common market but also a common currency, to coordinating their foreign and defense policies, and to developing joint standards and guidelines in agriculture, ecology, education, human rights, and law enforcement.

With the accession of Austria, Finland, and Sweden on 1 January 1995, the European Union was expanded to include fifteen states with a total population of some 368 million. Two and a half years later, following the evaluation of its provisions called for in the Maastricht Treaty, it was amended by the Treaty of Amsterdam, approved by the member countries' heads of state and government meeting as the European Council on 17 June 1997, and signed on 21 September 1997. Maastricht II, as the revised and expanded edition of the Treaty on European Union came to be known, included a section on social policy not in the body of the original treaty because it had been unacceptable to the conservative government in power in Britain in the early 1990s. The new Treaty on European Union increased the powers of the European Parliament and of the president of the European Commission; it extended the jurisdiction of the European Court of Justice in the area of human rights; and it incorporated the provisions of the Schengen Accords, named for the Luxemburg town in which Germany, France, and the Benelux countries initially concluded a 1985 agreement on the gradual abolition of border controls, to which most other states of the EU adhered.

Contemporary German Society

During the half century since the end of the Second World War, the rigid divisions that once characterized German society have to a striking degree been reduced. By American standards, many Germans, particularly those of the older generation, may still seem rather class-conscious, socially inflexible, and personally formal. But Hitler's social revolution, wartime attrition, social mobility, and increasing educational and economic opportunity, not to mention, in East Germany, the drastic socialization program considered above, have interacted to bring about changes that can best be appreciated in the overall perspective of modern German social history.

In comparison with France, Britain, and the United States, Germany never had a powerful middle class. In the English and French revolutions of the seventeenth and eighteenth centuries, the bourgeoisie had seized a very substantial share of power in the state, whereas the German revolution of the mid-nineteenth century was a tragic failure. Consequently the rapid industrialization of Germany in the later nineteenth century did not contribute, as in the western democracies, to the consolidation of further power on the part of the middle classes, together with the gradual extension of political influence to ever broader circles of the population. In Germany, on the contrary, a modern industrial economy was superimposed on a largely unreconstructed authoritarian class system. At the beginning of the twentieth century, Germany was in many respects less a typical bourgeois capitalist than an anachronistic feudal-industrial society in which the traditional ruling class of soldiers, bureaucrats, and landowners had maintained their authority relatively intact. They had been able to do so because the political opposition remained severely limited in the means by which it could influence policy: the *Reichstag*, for example, had sharply limited prerogatives, and the Prussian diet, with its three-class electoral system, reinforced the oligarchical tendencies of the Hohenzollern monarchy.

Aside from the working classes and an articulate but relatively uninfluential middle-class liberal minority, the balance of the German population seemed to find the system acceptable—if not indeed gratifying. The personal aspirations of the rising new industrialist or businessman, for example, were generally apt to be more social than political, so that he was far less interested in a seat in parliament or a government post than the coveted patent of nobility entitling him to preface his surname with the aristocratic *von*—not to mention the recognition implicit in the bestowal of an honorary commission in the army or the award of a prestigious decoration such as the *Wilhelmsorden*, which was instituted by William II in honor of his grandfather on the twenty-fifth anniversary of the proclamation of the new German Empire at Versailles.

The fall of the monarchy and the establishment of a republic following the First World War might ultimately have led the German middle classes to assume a decisive political role. Certainly the Weimar constitution did provide a basic, institutional framework for responsible parliamentary government to an extent that never came into question under the constitution of the Bismarckian Reich. But no strong parliamentary tradition was developed during the fourteen and a quarter years of the ill-fated republic, November 1918 through January 1933. The period began with what amounted to an anti-revolutionary coalition between the moderate socialists and the German Army, and it ended with the destructive polarization of the country between left and right radicalism during a terrible depression that reduced large segments of the middle classes to economic misery and political desperation. The short half decade from 1924 to 1929, between the end of the tenuous initial stabilization of the republic and the beginning of its ultimate dissolution, was simply too brief an interlude for the middle classes to emerge as a self-confidently dominant political force in the face of the tenacious old establishment, the more so as the bureaucracy had remained relatively intact and the wartime head of the army, Field Marshal von Hindenburg, soon became *Reichspräsident*—the only popularly elected president in German history.

It would be an exaggeration to say that the power of the officer corps, the civil service, and the great landowners of central and eastern Germany had not been challenged during the Weimar Republic. They were indeed challenged, but they responded vigorously and held on to their prerogatives with a resilient resourcefulness that only began to falter under the pressure of the totalitarian dictatorship of Adolf Hitler—for despite his rhetorical appeals to tradition, he actually had little sympathy for or patience with the conservative values of the old establishment. But it was less Hitler's social revolution than his war that shattered the pillars of the old order. By mid-1945, the great estates east of the Elbe were occupied by the Red Army, the Prussian-German bureaucracy had been disbanded, and the leadership corps of the armed forces had been virtually annihilated—with over seven hundred generals and admirals dead or missing in action.

This is the background against which the unprecedented changes in the social and political structure of postwar Germany took place. We have already seen how socialism was imposed on East Germany under Soviet sponsorship. In the Federal Republic, with Dr. Konrad Adenauer, the middle classes finally came into power for the first time in German history. (There had been middle-class chancellors during the Weimar Republic, to be sure, but none with even remotely comparable power, duration of tenure, or historical impact; and though Hitler had a middle-class background, he did not represent or personify the class of his origin.) *Der Alte*—as Adenauer was known with far more respect than affection—brought with him many of the old values and all too much of the authoritarianism of the old order, and his heavy-handedness in domestic politics led to his being compared to Bismarck, not only for sagacity in the conduct of foreign policy, but also in a penchant for undermining the parliamentary tradition of the new state he had so important a role in founding. But the institutional foundations of responsible parliamentary democracy in West Germany have proven to be incomparably stronger than in the Weimar Republic, the more so as in the Federal Republic there is a powerful high court that has broad jurisdiction to function as "supreme guardian of the Constitution" and has demonstrated itself quite capable of doing so.

One of the more controversial aspects of Adenauer's political style was the character of his attacks on the opposition Social Democrats, which at times hardly fell short of Bismarck's venomous denunciations of them as enemies of the state. But far from letting themselves be driven into isolation by his attacks, the Social Democrats, under the charismatic leadership of Berlin mayor Willy Brandt and the gifted political strategist Herbert Wehner, firmly abjured the remnants of their nineteenth-century ideology and assumed a more pragmatic stance, one still consonant with the interests of the prosperous workers of West Germany, but at the same time attractive to many middle-class liberals disenchanted with the clerically tinged, business- and industry-oriented conservatism of the Christian Democratic Union and its Bavarian counterpart, the Christian Social Union. In 1966, as noted, the Social Democrats entered into a broad coalition with the CDU and CSU, and then, in 1969, with the support of the small liberal party, the FDP, they established a new coalition under Brandt as chancellor—the first Social Democrat elected to head a German national government since 1930.

The thirteen years of the social-liberal coalition, 1969–1982, saw extensive domestic reforms. The civil and criminal law codes, parts of which had become very antiquated, were revised. West Germany's already extensive network of welfare programs was further developed. Educational opportunities, particularly at the college and university level, were greatly expanded. In 1976, as a matter of cardinal importance to the labor movement, a federal codetermination law, enacted in 1976, mandated employee representation on the supervisory boards of corporations with over two thousand employees.

From the beginning of the Brandt chancellorship, Social Democratic planners had been constrained to temper their reform agenda out of consideration for the traditional, laissez-faire liberalism of their coalition partners of the Free Democratic party; with strong backing in professional, commercial, and financial circles, the FDP had grave reservations about the expansion of the welfare state. The most serious limits on reforms under the social-liberal coalition did not have their origins in domestic politics, but in international economics. The "oil shock" that followed the Near Eastern war of 1973, when the price of crude oil quadrupled by the end of the year, triggered an international recession that broke the rising curve of West German prosperity. For the first time since the founding of the Federal Republic, overall production declined in 1975, while unemployment rose to more than a million. It was reduced by the end of the 1970s, but only temporarily, and went on to exceed two million by the mid-1980s.

This relatively high level of unemployment (representing between 8 and 10 percent of the work force) was the result not only of the oil shock of 1973 (followed by a second round of oil price increases in 1979, after the revolution in Iran); other interacting factors included high German labor costs, structural unemployment due to industrial modernization, and loss of export and, to a certain extent, domestic markets to foreign competition, particularly from Japan, Taiwan, and other recently industrialized countries.

One response to the oil shock of 1973 was the decision of the West German government to accelerate the development of nuclear power as an alternative energy source. By the end of the decade, over a dozen nuclear plants were in operation and others under construction, but the bitter controversy they generated made them a severe political liability for their proponents and contributed to the crystallization, in the 1970s, of a new kind of political party, The Greens (*Die Grünen*). Established in 1978 as a task-oriented association of environmentalists, opponents of nuclear power and the nuclear arms race, and proponents of a number of local, regional, national, and international causes, they have succeeded since 1979 in winning seats in the parliaments of several of the West German states and in the European Community's Parliament of Europe. When the Greens first nominated candidates for the Federal parliament in Bonn, in the national elections of 1980, they received only 1.5 percent of the vote, well below the 5 percent threshold for representation. But in 1983 they cleared the hurdle and entered the parliament as a fourth party, where they won representation again in the 1987 elections, and, following unification, in the first two all-German elections, in 1990 and 1994. The active role this loosely organized movement has come to play in German political life has been a significant demonstration of the capability of the German political system to provide effective representation for a controversial, innovative minority constituency.

An important minority that remains without formal representation in Germany is comprised of foreign workers and their families. An acute labor shortage during the swift economic expansion of West Germany that began in the 1950s led to the recruitment of labor from southern Europe and Turkey. By the mid-1960s, there were over a million "guest workers" in West Germany and West Berlin; by the early 1970s, over two million. Their numbers declined following the recessions triggered by the oil shocks of 1973 and 1979, but by the mid-1990s had increased to about three million. Taking into account their families as well, a total of over seven million foreigners lived in Germany in 1996 (including some two million from Turkey and over a million from former Yugoslavia), constituting 8.9 percent of Germany's total population of 82 million. Concentrated largely in the urban centers of western Germany, the foreign workers dwell, for the most part, in de facto ghettoes—not because of legally mandated segregation, which does not exist, but as a matter of convenience if not economic necessity. In Frankfurt am Main, for example, where a quarter of the population was non-German in 1990, over three-quarters of the residents of the downtown district around the main railroad station (the *Bahnhofsviertel*) were foreign.

Roughly a sixth of the foreigners in Germany are schoolchildren. Because German citizenship is not automatically acquired by being born on German soil, they inherit the citizenship of their non-German parents. By the early 1990s, over nine percent of the schoolchildren in Germany, over one in eleven, were foreign. Because many entering elementary school had been unable to understand or speak German, increasing numbers of schools in districts where they comprised a large percentage of the enrollment offered supplementary instruction in their native languages. By the mid-1990s fewer than a fifth of the foreign workers' children were dropping out of school without graduating, and over a third were in commercial or industrial apprenticeship programs linked with instruction in vocational schools, assuring graduates of the qualifications needed for employment in skilled trades.

Many of the foreigners are engaged in low-paying labor for which insufficient numbers of Germans—even in times of high unemployment—have proved to be available. Considering Germany's negative birth rate (deaths having exceeded births since the 1970s), it is likely that there will be a continuing need for their services. In spite of their relatively menial status, the foreign workers have generally not perceived themselves as an oppressed minority. Often culturally segregated from German society as a whole in neighborhoods where they live, speak, eat, and watch videocassettes from home together, the foreign workers in Germany may seem, to those observing them from a German or European perspective, to constitute a kind of permanent underclass, but insofar as they live together in communities in which they remain rooted in the traditions and values of their homelands, the older generation, at least, evidently appreciates being able to enjoy the tangible benefits they can earn by making an indispensable contribution to Germany's increasingly pluralistic society without having to give up their language, culture, or family ties.

A more acute social problem is the high level of unemployment. In West Germany, it began, as noted, with the recession of the mid-1970s, and it substantially increased in the 1980s, notwithstanding the general recovery of the economy as a whole. An important factor was the elimination, through automation, of many workplaces in business and industry—a process that has continued in western Germany, since unification, throughout the 1990s. But unification has greatly compounded the problem because of the dilapidation and inefficiency of the eastern German economy. To overcome this structural unemployment, retraining is being offered to those whose skills are no longer marketable. Moreover, a concerted effort is being made to prepare the young people entering the marketplace year by year for fields in which long-term openings are likely. This effort is centered in Germany's complex state-owned and -operated educational system, which has been dramatically expanded in western Germany since the 1960s and in eastern Germany since unification, providing substantially greater educational opportunity, particularly at the college and university level.

The Federal Republic was established under the political guardianship of the Western Allies, subsidized by an American aid program massive enough to start what amounted to a new industrial revolution, militarily insulated from the threat of Soviet imperialism and the fate of the eastern half of prewar Germany, and thus spared the ultimate wages of the Third Reich's defeat. It was encumbered with neither the burden of a peace treaty such as Versailles nor the economic liabilities that contributed to the failure of the Weimar Republic. That the Federal Republic was able to mature undisturbed was a case of extraordinarily good fortune. Far sooner than would have been considered possible fifty years ago, a semidesolate wasteland of endless battlefields, smoldering cities, and bombed-out or dismantled factories became the base for the strongest economy in Europe.

East Germany's postwar recovery was far slower, but by the

mid-1970s it had emerged as a significant trading partner in the Communist bloc with increasingly close ties to the Federal Republic, with which, despite the Iron Curtain, it came to be linked, since the 1970s, by common interests beyond the common heritage and language. The extent to which East and West Germany grew apart during forty-four years of separation became more obvious in the course of the 1990s than it had been at the time of the accession of the eastern German states to the Federal Republic. Above all, the cost of rebuilding—or salvaging—the infrastructure of eastern Germany proved to be so staggering that the German government, even after raising taxes and cutting back expenditures in many other areas, saw no choice but to resort to an unprecedented level of deficit financing. The necessity of severe fiscal retrenchment has, of course, triggered intense partisan controversy in Germany, but the unexpectedly costly challenges posed by unification have not weakened the consensus favoring fulfilment of Germany's leading role in the European Union's program of European integration, while continuing to honor the Federal Republic's commitments to the Atlantic Community (NATO), the Organization for Security and Cooperation in Europe (OSCE), and the United Nations.

A Brief Chronology

A Selected Bibliography

Index

A Brief Chronology

Antiquity

First Millennium B.C. Migration of Germanic tribes into the area of present-day Germany.

A.D. 9   Battle of Teutoburg Forest: annihilation of three Roman legions under Varus by Germanic insurgents under Arminius.

A.D. 16   Defeat of Arminius by Germanicus, followed by heavy Roman losses of seaborne troop transports in a North Sea storm and subsequent abandonment of Roman colonization of central Germany between the Rhine and the Elbe.

The Frankish Period (Early Middle Ages)

431–751   Merovingian Dynasty.

752–911   Carolingian Dynasty.

768–814   Emperor Charlemagne (Charles the Great; Karl der Grosse; Carolus Magnus), king of the Franks in 768; king of the Lombards in 774; emperor in 800.

814–840   Emperor Louis I (the Pious), son of Charlemagne.

843   Division of the Carolingian Empire among three grandsons of Charlemagne under the Treaty of Verdun (with subsequent redivisions).

843–876   King Louis II (the German), son of Louis the Pious.

876–887   Emperor Charles III (often referred to as "the Fat," an epithet given him only centuries later), king of much of Germany in 876; emperor in 881; king of France in 884; deposed in 887.

887–899 Emperor Arnulf (of Carinthia), nephew of Charles III, king of Germany in 887; emperor in 896.

900–911 King Louis IV (the Child), son of Arnulf, died without issue.

911–918 King Conrad I (of Franconia), duke of Franconia; elected king by the magnates after the extinction of the eastern line of the Carolingians.

The Saxon and Salian Dynasties (919–1125)

919–936 King Henry I (the Fowler), duke of Saxony; designated by Conrad I and elected by Frankish and Saxon magnates as Conrad's successor.

936–973 Emperor Otto I (the Great), son of Henry I, king in 936; emperor in 962.

955 Otto's decisive defeat of the Hungarians at the Battle of the Lechfeld.

973–983 Emperor Otto II, son of Otto I.

983–1002 Emperor Otto III, son of Otto II.

1002–1024 Emperor Henry II (the Saint), great-grandson of Henry I, second cousin of his immediate predecessor, and last of the emperors of the Saxon dynasty.

1024–1039 Emperor Conrad II (the Salian) of the Franconian (or Salian) house, descended in the female line from Otto the Great, by election.

1039–1056 Emperor Henry III (the Black, so called because of his grimly earnest disposition), son of Conrad II.

1056–1106 Emperor Henry IV, son of Henry III.

1076 Confrontation of Henry IV with Pope Gregory VII at Canossa (Investiture Contest and intermittent civil war until 1122).

1106–1125 Emperor Henry V, son of Henry IV.

1122   Concordat of Worms (papal-imperial compromise resolving the Investiture Contest).

The House of Welf

1125–1137   Emperor Lothair III (of Supplinburg), duke of Saxony, elected with ecclesiastical support, rather than the nephew of Henry V, whom Henry had designated as his successor, Duke Frederick of Swabia, of the house of Hohenstaufen or Waiblingen (in Italian, *Ghibelline,* referring to the pro-imperial, anti-papal party); nuptial alliance of Lothair with the Bavarian house of Welf (in Italian, *Guelph,* referring to the pro-papal, anti-imperial party), resulting in his son-in-law, Henry the Proud, duke of Bavaria, also becoming duke of Saxony when Lothair died in 1137, having designated him as his imperial successor. (Some authorities, not counting the Carolingian Lothair II, 855–69, list Lothair of Supplinburg as the second rather than third monarch of this name.)

The Hohenstaufen Dynasty (1138–1250)

1138–1152   King Conrad III, son of the above-mentioned Hohenstaufen Duke Frederick of Swabia who had been passed over in 1125 for Lothair III; elected king in preference to Lothair's designated heir, Henry the Proud, but never crowned emperor.

1152–1190   Emperor Frederick I (Barbarossa), nephew of Conrad III.

1180   Condemnation of Henry the Lion, Welf duke of Saxony and Bavaria, son of Conrad III's rival in 1138, Henry the Proud.

1190–1197   Emperor Henry VI, son of Frederick Barbarossa.

1198–1214   Civil war over the succession, following the untimely death of Henry VI, between the Hohenstaufen Philip of Swabia (younger brother of Henry VI) and the Welf Otto of Brunswick (son of Henry the Lion).

1208   Death of Philip of Swabia.

1210   General recognition and coronation of Philip's Welf rival, Emperor Otto IV.

1214   Crushing defeat of Otto and his Anglo-Welf allies by the French at Bouvines.

1212–1250   Emperor Frederick II, son of Henry VI, with support of the pope and the Hohenstaufen party.

1213   Golden Bull of Eger, by which Frederick II relinquished a large measure of the monarchical control over the German church.

1220   *Confoederatio cum principibus ecclesiasticis,* a compact with the ecclesiastical princes by which Frederick II granted them unprecedented privileges in their territories.

1226   Golden Bull of Rimini, by which Frederick II granted the Teutonic Knights whatever territory they might conquer from the heathen inhabitants of what was to become East Prussia.

1231   *Statutum in favorem principum,* by which Frederick II granted the secular princes far-reaching rights similar to those conferred upon the ecclesiastical princes in 1220.

1250   Death of Frederick II.

1250–1273   The Great Interregnum, in the course of which Frederick's son Conrad IV (1250–54) was no more able to consolidate his position than the Welf contenders, William of Holland (1247–56) and Richard of Cornwall (1257–72), or than Alfonso X of Castile (1257–84).

The Habsburg Dynasty (1273–1806)

1273–1291   *King Rudolf of Habsburg* (so named for "Hawk Castle," the *Habichtsburg,* the original family seat) elected king, but never crowned emperor.

1292–1298 King Adolf (of Nassau), elected in preference to the designated heir of Rudolf, but deposed without ever having been crowned emperor.

1298–1308 King Albert I, son of Rudolf of Habsburg, elected king but never crowned emperor.

1308–1313 Emperor Henry VII (of Luxemburg), founder of a dynasty which seriously rivaled the Habsburgs from its base of power in Bohemia (which he acquired by nuptial diplomacy), until the two families merged through nuptial diplomacy.

1314–1347 Emperor Louis IV (the Bavarian) of the house of Wittelsbach, a second major dynasty challenging the Habsburgs in the fourteenth and again in the eighteenth century.

1347–1378 Emperor Charles IV (of Luxemburg), grandson of Henry VII, son and heir of King John of Bohemia.

1356 The Golden Bull of Charles IV, basic constitution of the empire.

1378–1400 King Wenceslas (of Bohemia), son of Charles IV, never crowned emperor; deposed as king of Germany in 1400; remained king of Bohemia until his death in 1419.

1400–1410 King Rupert of the Palatinate, elected to replace Wenceslas but never crowned emperor.

1410–1437 Emperor Sigismund, brother of Wenceslas, last non-Habsburg emperor until 1742.

1415 Frederick of Hohenzollern, burgrave of Nuremberg, made margrave and elector of Brandenburg, beginning the five-hundred-year rule of the Hohenzollern dynasty in north Germany.

1438–1439 King Albert II (of Habsburg), great-great-grandson of Albert I, son-in-law and heir of Emperor Sigismund (merger of the patrimony of the houses of Habsburg and Luxemburg), never crowned emperor.

1440–1493   Emperor Frederick III, second cousin of Albert II.

1493–1519   Emperor Maximilian I, son of Frederick III; adoption, with papal sanction, of title "Roman Emperor-elect," assuring recognition of imperial dignity even without papal coronation.

1517   Beginning of the Protestant Reformation in Germany (Luther's Ninety-Five Theses).

1519–1556   Emperor Charles V, grandson of Maximilian I, who had his brother Ferdinand made German king in 1531, announced his abdication and retired to Spain in 1555 (the month after the Religious Peace of Augsburg), sent formal notification to the prince electors of his abdication in 1556, and died in 1558.

1556–1564   Emperor Ferdinand I, brother of Charles V, German king since 1531.

1564–1576   Emperor Maximilian II, son of Ferdinand I.

1576–1612   Emperor Rudolf II, son of Maximilian II.

1612–1619   Emperor Matthias, brother of Rudolf II.

1618   Beginning of the Thirty Years' War, traditionally divided into four phases: the Bohemian period, 1618–25; the Danish period, 1625–29; the Swedish period, 1630–35; the Swedish-French period, 1635–48.

1619–1637   Emperor Ferdinand II, cousin of Matthias.

1637–1657   Emperor Ferdinand III, son of Ferdinand II.

1640   Accession in Brandenburg-Prussia of Frederick William of Hohenzollern (the Great Elector), who ruled until 1688.

1648   The Peace of Westphalia: treaties of Münster with France and Osnabrück with Sweden.

1658–1705   Emperor Leopold I, son of Ferdinand III.

1688   Accession in Brandenburg-Prussia of Elector Frederick III, son of the Great Elector; assumed the title of king in 1701; ruled until 1713.

1705–1711   Emperor Joseph I, son of Leopold.

1711–1740   Emperor Charles VI, brother of Joseph.

1713   Accession in Prussia of King Frederick William I, son of Frederick I.

1740   Accession in Austria of Archduchess (later Empress) Maria Theresa, daughter of Charles VI, queen of Hungary and of Bohemia, and spouse of Grand Duke Francis Stephen of Lorraine, who unsuccessfully sought the imperial crown in 1740 but was elected only in 1745.

1740   Accession in Prussia of King Frederick the Great, who ruled until 1786, and who began his reign with an attack on Austria, triggering the three Silesian wars (1740–42; 1744–45; and 1756–63, the third being known in Europe as a whole as the Seven Years' War).

1742–1745   Emperor Charles VII (of Bavaria), twelfth lineal descendant of the fourteenth-century emperor Louis the Bavarian, and the only non-Habsburg to have been elected emperor after 1438.

1745–1765   Emperor Francis I of the house of Habsburg-Lorraine (spouse of Maria Theresa).

1765–1790   Emperor Joseph II, son of Francis and Maria Theresa.

1786   Accession in Prussia of King Frederick William II, nephew of Frederick the Great; ruled until 1797.

1790–1792   Emperor Leopold II, brother of Joseph.

1792–1806   Emperor Francis II, son of Leopold, who laid down the crown of the Holy Roman Empire on its dissolution in 1806, though retaining the title of emperor as ruler of the possessions of the house of Habsburg-Lorraine.

1797   Accession in Prussia of King Frederick William III, son of Frederick William II.

The Nineteenth Century

1797–1840   In Prussia, King Frederick William III (as noted above).

1804–1835   In Austria, Emperor Francis I (who as noted above had acceded in 1792 as Francis II, but relinquished the title of Holy Roman Emperor on the dissolution of the empire in 1806) with Metternich as his foreign minister since 1809 and chancellor since 1821 (an office he held until 1848).

1806   Dissolution by Napoleon of the Holy Roman Empire and establishment under French sponsorship of the Confederation of the Rhine (excluding Austria and Prussia), which was disbanded when Napoleon was defeated.

1814   Convocation of the Congress of Vienna (which ended the following year) at which the map of Europe was largely redrawn and the German Confederation of thirty-nine states under the presidency of Austria established.

1834   Organization of a Prussian-sponsored tariff union *(Zollverein)* which gradually came to embrace most German states (but excluded Austria).

1840–1861   In Prussia, King Frederick William IV, son of Frederick William III, in his last years so incapacitated that his younger brother William (later Prussian king and then German emperor) became regent.

1848–1850   Revolution throughout much of Europe, leading in Germany to the unsuccessful attempt of a nationally elected representative assembly at Frankfurt to establish a German constitutional monarchy, and the subsequent attempt of Prussia to establish a measure of unification under her own hegemony (the "Humiliation" of Olmütz at the hands of Austria and Russia).

1848–1916   In Austria, Emperor Francis Joseph I, nephew of Ferdinand I, whose abdication, together with Metternich's retirement, had been brought about by the revolution.

1861–1888   In Prussia, King William I, brother of Frederick William IV, regent since 1858; German emperor in 1871; with Bismarck as foreign minister and Prussian minister president after 1862 and imperial chancellor after 1871.

1863   The Alvensleben Convention between Russia and Prussia regarding the Polish question.

1864   The war of Austria and Prussia against Denmark.

1866   The Austro-Prussian War, resulting in Prussian hegemony of Germany.

1867   Establishment of the North German Confederation under Prussian domination.

1870–1871   The Franco-Prussian War, incited by circumstances surrounding the candidacy of a Hohenzollern prince for the Spanish throne, and resulting in the fall of the French Empire and establishment of the German Empire by proclamation at Versailles in January 1871 (William I emperor, Bismarck chancellor).

1879   In domestic policy, establishment of an alliance of agrarian and industrial interests; in foreign policy, establishment of the Dual Alliance between Germany and Austria, initially concluded for five years but regularly renewed to the end of the First World War.

1881   The Three Emperors' Alliance between Austria, Germany, and Russia, a tenuous alignment initially concluded for three years but renewed only once, permanently lapsing in 1887.

1881   Inauguration of comprehensive social legislation program with the enactment, by the end of the decade, of provisions for sickness, accident, invalid, and old age insurance.

1887   Conclusion of a three-year but renewable Russo-German Reinsurance Treaty, by which Bismarck maintained as close a relationship as possible with the Russians after their refusal to renew the Three Emperors' Alliance due to tension with Austria.

1888   Emperor Frederick III, son of William I, already dying of cancer at his accession.

1888–1918 Emperor William II, son of Frederick III.

1890 Dismissal of Bismarck by William II, whose subsequent chancellors were General Leo von Caprivi (1890–94), Prince Chlodwig zu Hohenlohe-Schillingsfürst (1894–1900), Count (later Prince) Bernhard von Bülow (1900–1909), Dr. Theobald von Bethmann Hollweg (1909–17), Dr. Georg Michaelis (1917), Count Georg von Hertling (1917–18), and Prince Max von Baden (1918).

1898 German Navy Bill, beginning the naval arms race with Britain.

The Twentieth Century

1914–1918 The First World War, ending with the fall of the monarchy, the proclamation of the republic, and the armistice of 11 November 1918.

1919 Adoption of the Weimar Constitution and submission to the Treaty of Versailles.

1919–1925 Friedrich Ebert, first president of the German Republic; originally named provisional president by the constitutional assembly in Weimar (February 1919) but never confirmed by general election, he died in office.

1923 Franco-Belgian occupation of the Ruhr (ostensibly because of deliberate German refusal to comply with economic obligations under the reparations provisions of the Treaty of Versailles), followed by passive resistance, disruption of the German economy, and political crises, including the abortive National Socialist *Putsch* in November; relative stability restored during the ninety-nine day chancellorship of Gustav Stresemann (August–November), who stayed on, after the fall of his own cabinet, as foreign minister during the subsequent seven, until his death in 1929.

1925   On 26 April, following the death of Ebert, election to the presidency of the retired First World War field marshal, Paul von Hindenburg (elected to a second seven-year term in 1932).

On 1 December, signing of the treaties of Locarno, setting the stage for Germany's admission to the League of Nations in September 1926.

1930–1933   Following the onset of the Great Depression in 1929, bringing rapidly increasing unrest and instability, government by presidential decree under the emergency provisions of the Weimar Constitution, with Dr. Heinrich Brüning as chancellor from March 1930 to May 1932, Franz von Papen from June through November 1932, General Kurt von Schleicher from December 1932 through January 1933, and, as of 30 January 1933, Adolf Hitler.

1933   Following parliamentary elections in March, in which the Hitler coalition won with a 51.9% total, passage of the Enabling Act (by 441 to 94), granting the government dictatorial powers for four years.

In October, Germany's withdrawal from the League of Nations, followed by parliamentary elections conducted as a plebiscite on withdrawal, with 92% voting National Socialist.

1934   On 30 January, the German states are stripped of autonomy and their parliaments abolished.

1934–1945   On the death of Hindenburg (at eighty-seven), Hitler head of state and supreme commander of the armed forces with the title of *Führer* (leader) and Reich chancellor (by dictatorial decree, subsequently endorsed by ca. 85% of the German electorate in the plebiscite of 19 August 1934).

1935   In January, return of the Saar basin to Germany as called for by 91% of participants in a League of Nations plebiscite.

In March, Hitler's repudiation of the disarmament clauses of the Treaty of Versailles and announcement of Germany's open resumption of rearmament.

In June, Anglo-German naval agreement.

In September, proclamation of the "Nuremberg Race Laws" stripping Jews of the rights of citizenship and forbidding marriage between Jews and persons of "German blood."

1936   In March, Hitler's repudiation of the Locarno pacts and remilitarization of the Rhineland (to have remained permanently demilitarized under the terms of the treaties of Versailles and of Locarno).

In July, German intervention in the Spanish Civil War.

1937   Hitler's conference of 5 November with heads of the armed forces and ministers of war and foreign affairs, in which he outlined his agenda for aggression, provoking explicit misgivings on the part of Generals Blomberg and Fritsch and Foreign Minister Neurath.

1938   Reorganization of military and diplomatic command in February, with removal of Blomberg and replacement of Fritsch, Neurath, and others, followed by the annexation of Austria in March and that of the Sudetenland (after the Munich Conference) in October.

1939   Dismemberment of the restructured rump state of Czecho-Slovakia with the annexation of Bohemia and Moravia in March; conclusion of the Hitler-Stalin Pact in August; invasion of Poland in September.

1939–1945   The Second World War and the Holocaust, ending with Hitler's suicide and the division of Germany between Russia and the western powers.

1945–1946   Trial of major war criminals before the International Military Tribunal.

1947   In January, economic fusion of the American and British occupation zones.

On 25 February, formal dissolution of Prussia by Allied Control Council Law No. 46.

1948   Establishment in April of the Organization for European Economic Cooperation (the Marshall Plan).

In June, currency reform in the American, British, and French occupation zones of Germany and the western sectors of occupied Berlin (replacement of the *Reichsmark* [RM] by the German mark [*Deutsche Mark* or DM]), followed by the introduction of a different currency in East Germany; Russian imposition of the blockade of Berlin (terminated the following year after its failure due to the Berlin airlift).

1949   On 23 May, establishment of the Federal Republic of Germany, initially composed of the states in the French, British, and U.S. zones of occupation.

On 7 October, establishment of the German Democratic Republic in the Soviet zone under the dictatorial leadership of Walter Ulbricht, head of the Socialist Unity party (SED).

1949–1963   Dr. Konrad Adenauer, head of the conservative Christian Democratic Union (CDU) and its Bavarian counterpart, the Christian Social Union (CSU), chancellor of the Federal Republic of Germany.

1951   Treaty establishing the European Coal and Steel Community (ECSC, the Schuman Plan) signed on 18 April by Belgium, the Federal Republic of Germany, France, Italy, Luxemburg, and the Netherlands.

1952   Contractual agreement with the occupying powers in West Germany granting the Federal Republic internal autonomy.

1953   In June, popular rising in East Germany suppressed by the Russian Army.

1954–1955   Treaties of Paris, signed in October 1954 and ratified in May 1955, providing for the sovereignty of the Federal Republic (with reservations) and its adherence to the North Atlantic Treaty Organization (NATO).

1955   In May, establishment of the Warsaw Pact, to which the German Democratic Republic accedes in 1956.

In September, Chancellor Adenauer establishes diplomatic relations with the Soviet Union and negotiates the release of German prisoners of war.

1957   On 1 January, accession of the Saarland to the Federal Republic of Germany (following 1955 plebiscite).

1958   On 1 January, on the basis of the Treaties of Rome signed 25 March 1957 by the six states of the European Coal and Steel Community, the European Economic Community (EEC or Common Market) comes into force.

1959   In November, the Social Democratic party of Germany (SPD) adopts a non-Marxist liberal democratic program.

1961   On 13 August, occupation of the Soviet sector of Berlin by East German forces who seal off the western sectors, erecting the Berlin Wall and terminating a mass exodus of East Germans to West Germany via West Berlin.

1963   "New Economic System" introduced in East Germany.

1963–1966   West German chancellorship of Dr. Ludwig Erhard (CDU/CSU).

1965   The executive organs of the Common Market (EEC), the European Coal and Steel Community (ECSC), and European Atomic Energy Community (Euratom) merge to form the European Community (EC).

1966–1969   West German chancellorship of Dr. Kurt Georg Kiesinger (CDU/CSU), as head of a broad coalition, with SPD leader and former Berlin mayor Willy Brandt as vice chancellor and foreign minister.

1968   Establishment of the European Community Customs Union, eliminating duties on intra-Community trade and introducing a common customs tariff to replace national customs duties in trade with the rest of the world.

1969–1974   West German chancellorship of Willy Brandt (SPD), in a coalition with the small, liberal Free Democratic party (FDP).

1970   West German treaties with Russia and Poland.

1971   Erich Honecker successor of Walter Ulbricht as East German party chief.

Quadripartite Agreement on Berlin between France, the

Soviet Union, the United Kingdom, and the United States (signed in September 1971, effective in June 1972, on the signing of the Final Quadripartite Protocol, formalizing the status of the four occupying powers).

1972 Conclusion of Treaty on the Basis of Relations (the Basic Treaty) between East and West Germany (effective on 21 June 1973 after being sustained by the Federal Constitutional [supreme] Court).

1973 On 1 January, accession of Denmark, Ireland, and the United Kingdom to the European Community (raising its membership to nine).

On 18 September 1973, admission of the two German states to the UN.

On 12 December, West German treaty with Czechoslovakia.

1974–1982 West German chancellorship of Helmut Schmidt (SPD), succeeding his party and cabinet colleague Brandt as head of the SPD-FDP coalition.

1975 Helsinki Final Act chartering the Conference on Security and Cooperation in Europe.

1976 Federal Codetermination Law for West German firms with over 2000 employees.

1978 Establishment in West Germany of The Greens.

1982 Election as federal chancellor of Dr. Helmut Kohl (CDU/CSU), heading a coalition with the Free Democratic party (FDP), after the latter's withdrawal from the coalition with the SPD.

1983 In June, West German credit of over DM 1 billion for the East German government.

In November, an intra-German postal and telephonic communications agreement raising annual West German support to East Germany in this sector alone from DM 85 million to DM 200 million.

1984 In July, West German credit of over DM 915 million for East Germany.

1986 On 6 May, conclusion of a five-year intra-German cultural agreement providing for exchanges in the sciences, cinema, theater, music, painting, sports, and publishing.

1987 In July, the Single European Act goes into force, under the terms of which the European Community sets out to integrate its members into a single market.

On 7–11 September, the Chairman of the East German Council of State, Erich Honecker, visits West Germany.

1989 On 2 May, Hungary begins dismantling its fortified frontier with Austria, facilitating escape of East Germans to West Germany.

On 17 May, East German municipal elections with officially reported 98.85% support for the *Einheitslisten* (i.e., the officially nominated candidates).

By July, hundreds of East Germans seek asylum in West German legations in East Berlin, Prague, and Budapest.

On 9 September, establishment in East Germany of "New Forum," whose manifesto is before long signed by 200,000.

On 11 September, Hungary formally opens its border crossings to East Germans, tens of thousands of whom flee to West Germany.

In September, October, and early November, increasingly large, nonviolent demonstrations in Leipzig and elsewhere for reform.

On 3 October, East Berlin bans visa-free travel to Czechoslovakia in order to stop the mass flight of East Germans through that country to West Germany.

On 6 October, several East German opposition groups publish a joint appeal for UN-supervised elections in East Germany.

On 7 October, Soviet President Mikhail S. Gorbachev, in Berlin on the 40th anniversary of the founding of the German Democratic Republic, says the Soviet Union will not intervene in East German affairs.

On 18 October, Honecker resigns and is replaced by Egon Krenz.

On 8 November, East German Politburo restructured to include reformers.

On 9 November, opening of the intra-German border and the Berlin Wall.

On 13 November, Dr. Hans Modrow, a reform-oriented communist, becomes East German prime minister.

On 17 November, Modrow proposes a contractual community between the two German states.

On 28 November, Chancellor Helmut Kohl proposes establishment of a confederation of the two German states, eventually to lead, by gradual implementation of a ten-point program synchronized with European integration, to the unification of Germany.

On 3 December, resignation of Egon Krenz, the Politburo, and the Central Committee, ending party control, leaving Prime Minister Modrow, as head of government, in authority.

On 12 December, formation of the Round Table.

On 19 December, Chancellor Kohl visits Prime Minister Modrow in Dresden, where they agree on negotiations to form a contractual community, and Kohl afterwards gives a very warmly received speech.

1990 From January through March, continuation of the mass exodus from East to West Germany.

In February, Modrow takes representatives of the Round Table into his cabinet as ministers without portfolio in a broadened "government of national responsibility," having agreed to hold elections on 18 March.

In early March, establishment under Modrow of a trust agency to serve as a government-owned holding company to manage the nationalized (i.e., collectivized) assets (estimated at ca. 600 billion East–German marks).

On 18 March, first free parliamentary elections in the history of the German Democratic Republic, leading to the replacement of the Modrow government by a coalition committed to the immediate accession of East Germany to the Federal Republic, led by Prime Minister Lothar de Maizière (head of the East German CDU).

On 17 June, enactment under de Maizière of legislation mandating the Trust Agency (*Treuhandanstalt*) to privatize as quickly as possible not only thousands of East German companies, but also farmland and forest with an area comparable to that of the state of West Virginia.

On 1 July, implementation of the economic and social union of the two German republics, as provided in the intra-German state treaty signed in Bonn on 18 May.

On 31 August, second intra-German state treaty signed in Berlin, providing for dissolution of the German Democratic Republic and accession to the Federal Republic on 3 October 1990 of the five states of Brandenburg, Mecklenburg-West Pomerania, Saxony, Saxony-Anhalt, and Thuringia, as well as the city-state of Berlin (the German capital, where the occupying powers retained sovereignty until the eve of unification).

On 12 September, in Moscow, signing of the Treaty on the Final Settlement with Respect to Germany (the "Two-Plus-Four Treaty") by representatives of the two German republics and the four victorious powers of World War II, America, Britain, France, and the Soviet Union, whereby these powers agree to relinquish all rights and responsibilities relating to Berlin and to Germany as a whole and to acknowledge Germany's full sovereignty.

On 13 September, initialing by the Soviet and the West German foreign ministers of a German-Soviet Treaty on Good-Neighborliness, Partnership, and Cooperation (signed by Gorbachev and Kohl on 9 November), providing DM 12 billion in direct assistance,

plus interest-free credit of DM 3 billion, to the Soviet Union to cover such expenses as the withdrawal
of Soviet forces from East Germany.

On 3 October, unification of Germany through accession of the formerly occupied city-state of Berlin and
of the five states formerly constituting the German
Democratic Republic.

On 14 October, German-Polish treaty signed confirm-
ing the existing Oder-Neisse border.

On 2 December, first all-German elections, leading to
the reelection of Chancellor Kohl and his coalition
partners.

1991 On 25 February, dissolution of the Warsaw Pact.

On 20 June, legislative decision (by a vote of 338 to
320 with one abstention) to move the German seat of
government from Bonn to Berlin.

In December, at Maastricht (Netherlands), fundamental agreement reached by the Council of the European Community on integration of the EC into a
European Union (with a single currency).

1992 On 17 February, signing of the Treaty of European Union
(Treaty of Maastricht).

On 21 December, following approval of the Treaty of
Maastricht by the German parliament, deletion from
the German constitution of the provision for accession to the Federal Republic and insertion in its place
(as Article 23) provision for the transfer of sovereign
powers to the European Union.

1993 In March, agreement on a "solidarity surcharge"
(*Solidaritätszuschlag*) involving a 7.5% tax surcharge
to spur the lagging eastern German development.

On 12 October 1993, Germany's accession to the European Union upheld as constitutional by the German
supreme court, enabling Germany on 13 October to
certify its ratification (the last member state so to do)
and enabling the Treaty of Maastricht to go into effect at the beginning of the following month.

On 1 November, implementation of the Treaty of European Union, whereby the twelve signatories, Belgium, Denmark, France, Germany, Greece, Ireland, Italy, Luxemburg, the Netherlands, Portugal, Spain, and the United Kingdom, give the European Community (EC) a new name, the European Union (EU), in conjunction with the treaty's program to develop an integrated market with a single European currency and to coordinate European defense and security policies.

1994   On 31 August, withdrawal of the last of some 340,000 Russian troops from Germany since unification in late 1990.

On 16 October, second all-German elections, leading to the retention of the CDU/CSU-FDP coalition under the continuing chancellorship of Dr. Helmut Kohl.

At the end of December, the Trust Agency, having substantially completed the privatization of the East German economy, is dissolved, with its remaining responsibilities, assets, and liabilities transferred to other bodies, including the Federal Agency for Unification-Related Special Tasks (*Bundesanstalt für vereinigungsbedingte Sonderaufgaben* or *BvS*), and with its closing deficit of DM 256 billion being assumed as part of the national debt by the German government.

1995   On 1 January, Austria, Finland, and Sweden accede to the European Union.

On 15/16 December, the European Council approves the establishment of the European Monetary Institute, the future central bank of the European Union, in Frankfurt am Main, and resolves that the future single European currency is to be the *Euro*.

1997   On 21 September, the heads of state and government of the fifteen countries of the European Union sign the Treaty of Amsterdam (Maastricht II), revising the provisions of the Treaty of European Union of 1992 and strengthening the institutions of the EU.

A Selected Bibliography

GENERAL WORKS

FOR AN ANNOTATED BIBLIOGRAPHY, including standard works in languages other than English (not included here), see Hajo Holborn's "Germany, Austria, and Switzerland" in George Frederick Howe et al., eds., *The American Historical Association's Guide to Historical Literature* (New York: Macmillan, 1961). Like the present bibliography, Holborn's section of the *Guide* focuses on German history in a narrow sense. Works concerning Germany in the broader context of European diplomatic or economic history, for example, are given in the sections "Europe (General), 1450–1914" by Walter L. Dorn and "Recent History" by Walter C. Langsam and Reginald C. McGrane. There is corresponding coverage to that in the *Guide* in John Roach, ed., *A Bibliography of Modern History* (Cambridge: At the University Press, 1968). For detailed treatment see, for the medieval and early modern periods, Jonathan W. Zophy, *An Annotated Bibliography of the Holy Roman Empire*, Bibliographies and Indexes in World History, no. 3 (Westport, Conn.: Greenwood Press, 1986), and, for more recent German history, two bibliographical essays of some fifty pages each: Norman Rich, *Germany, 1815–1914* (Washington, D.C.: American Historical Association, 1968), and Henry Cord Meyer, *Five Images of Germany: Half a Century of American Views of German History* (2d ed., Washington, D.C.: American Historical Association, 1960), which stresses the twentieth century. Many additional titles on German history can be found in an unannotated inventory of Harvard University Library holdings, *General European and World History*, Widener Library Shelflist 32 (Cambridge: Harvard University Press, 1970), in which some 37,000 titles are listed first by category in shelflist order, then chronologically by year of publication, and finally, in a single alphabetical sequence, by author and title.

For a general bibliography of the Federal Republic and West Berlin, with consideration of the German heritage as a whole, see

A Selected Bibliography

Donald S. Detwiler and Ilse E. Detwiler, *West Germany: The Federal Republic of Germany*, World Bibliographical Series, vol. 72 (Oxford and Santa Barbara: Clio Press, 1987). Written for the English-speaking reader, the extensively annotated entries provide across-the-board coverage from flora and fauna to education and law. On postwar East Germany, see Ian Wallace's companion volume *East Germany: The German Democratic Republic*, World Bibliographical Series, vol. 77 (Oxford and Santa Barbara: Clio Press, 1987). Larry L. Richardson's *Introduction to Library Research in German Studies: Language, Literature, and Civilization* (Boulder, Colo.: Westview, 1984) includes a systematic introduction to bibliographical access systems (catalogues, bibliographies, data bases, etc.).

On postwar Germany, Anna J. Merritt and Richard L. Merritt, *Politics, Economics, and Society in the Two Germanies, 1945–75: A Bibliography of English-Language Works* (Urbana: University of Illinois Press, 1978) is an unannotated, computer-generated, topically divided listing of 8,548 book and article titles, followed by an alphabetical index of the 5,116 authors. Gisela Hersch, *A Bibliography of German Studies, 1945–1971* (Bloomington: Indiana University Press, 1972), also unannotated, is a listing based on holdings at Indiana University. Margrit B. Krewson, *The German-Speaking Countries of Europe: A Selective Bibliography* (Washington, D.C.: Library of Congress, 1985), cites titles (in German as well as English) published since Arnold H. Price compiled *The Federal Republic of Germany: A Selected Bibliography of English-Language Publications* (2d ed., Washington, D.C.: U.S. Government Printing Office for the Library of Congress, 1978) and *East Germany: A Selected Bibliography* (Washington, D.C.: U.S. Government Printing Office for the Library of Congress, 1967).

Three volumes in the Garland Reference Library of Social Science focus on German military history, but include among the citations many works providing coverage of related areas as well: Keith W. Bird, *German Naval History: A Guide to the Literature* (New York: Garland, 1985); Edward L. Homze, *German Military Aviation: A Guide to the Literature* (New York: Garland, 1984); and Dennis E. Showalter, *German Military History, 1648–1982: A Critical Bibliography* (New York: Garland, 1984). A fourth volume published in the same series, Dieter K. Buse and Juergen C. Doerr, *German Nationalisms: A Bibliographic Approach* (New York: Garland, 1985), deals with a central question in German history from the period before 1800 to the present in a well-structured bibliography including 769 in part extensively annotated entries.

Selective coverage of the vast periodical literature on German history can be found in John C. Fout, *German History and Civilization, 1806–1914: A Bibliography of Scholarly Periodical Literature* (Metuchen, N.J.: Scarecrow Press, 1974), and in three annotated bibliographies of journal articles: *The Weimar Republic: A Historical Bibliography, The Third Reich, 1933–1939: A Historical Bibliography,* and *The Third Reich at War: A Historical Bibliography,* ABC-Clio Research Guides 9, 10, and 11, respectively (Santa Barbara, Calif.: ABC-Clio Information Services, 1984).

William Harvey Maehl's *Germany in Western Civilization* (University, Ala.: University of Alabama Press, 1979) includes in the "Sources and Aids" section of the bibliography a concise introduction, addressed to the English-reading student, to the standard reference works on German history published in German and (primarily for the Middle Ages) in Latin. Like the earlier textbook by John Rodes, *Germany: A History* (New York: Holt, Rinehart and Winston, 1964), which also has an extensive bibliographical essay, Maehl's 833-page volume is a college history text substantial enough to provide reasonable coverage of the medieval and early modern periods without slighting the past century. For more detailed treatment of cultural history, see Malcolm Pasley, ed., *Germany: A Companion to German Studies* (London: Methuen, 1972), with introductory essays on German language, literature, music, and philosophy, as well as history.

For general reference, see Richard F. Nyrop, ed., *Federal Republic of Germany: A Country Study* (2d ed., Washington, D.C.: U.S. Government Printing Office, 1983), and Eugene K. Keefe, ed., *East Germany: A Country Study* (2d ed., Washington, D.C.: U.S. Government Printing Office, 1982), two volumes in the Department of the Army Area Handbook Series compiled at the American University, Washington, D.C.; Robert E. Dickinson's seven-hundred-page *Germany: A General and Regional Geography* (2d ed., London: Methuen; New York: Dutton, 1961); and the uniquely comprehensive yet readable Geographical Handbook on Germany prepared at Cambridge during World War II by a team of leading specialists: Great Britain, Naval Intelligence Division (H. C. Darby, general editor), *Germany,* vol. 1: *Physical Geography;* vol. 2: *History and Administration;* vol. 3: *Economic Geography;* vol. 4: *Ports and Communications* (London: His Majesty's Stationery Office for the Admiralty, 1944–45).

A Selected Bibliography

On the interpretation of German history, see Georg G. Iggers, *The German Conception of History: The National Tradition of Historical Thought from Herder to the Present* (rev. ed., Middletown, Conn.: Wesleyan University Press, 1983), Andreas Dorpalen, *German History in Marxist Perspective: The East German Approach* (Detroit, Mich.: Wayne State University Press, 1985), and four complementary papers on a century of German historiography in America: Fritz Stern, "German History in America, 1884–1984," *Central European History*, vol. XIX (1986), pp. 131–163; Charles E. McClelland, "German Intellectual History," *ibid.*, pp. 164–173; Gerald D. Feldman, "German Economic History," *ibid.*, pp. 174–185; and Konrad Jarausch, "German Social History—American Style," *Journal of Social History*, vol. 19 (1985), pp. 349–359.

In *The Origins of Modern Germany* (2d ed., Oxford: Blackwell, 1947; rpt., New York: Norton, 1984), Geoffrey Barraclough focuses on the Middle Ages; less than a quarter of this standard work is devoted to the modern period. His book therefore dovetails with Hajo Holborn's three-volume *History of Modern Germany*, vol. 1: *The Reformation;* vol. 2: *1648–1840;* vol. 3: *1840–1945* (New York: Knopf, 1961, 1964, and 1969, respectively; rpt., Princeton, N.J.: Princeton University Press, 1982), which may be supplemented by his *Germany and Europe: Historical Essays* (Garden City, N.Y.: Doubleday, 1970) and by the selection from his more important studies published together with a bibliography of his works in *Hajo Holborn: Inter Nationes Prize 1969* (Bonn: Inter Nationes, 1969).

Cultural history is emphasized by Franz H. Bäuml in *Medieval Civilization in Germany, 800–1273* (New York: Praeger, 1969) and by Kurt F. Reinhardt in *Germany: 2000 Years* (2 vols., rev. ed., New York: Ungar, 1961). Four works offering relatively balanced coverage of modern German cultural, political, social, and economic history are Ernest K. Bramsted's *Germany,* in the Modern Nations in Historical Perspective series (Englewood Cliffs, N.J.: Prentice-Hall, 1972); Koppel S. Pinson's *Modern Germany: Its History and Civilization* (2d ed., New York: Macmillan, 1966), with a final chapter on the Bonn republic by Klaus Epstein; Golo Mann's *History of Germany since 1789,* translated by M. Jackson (New York: Praeger, 1968), a best-seller with considerable impact, on the basis of its literary as well as historiographical merit, when first published in the Federal Republic of Germany; and Gordon A. Craig's *Germany, 1866–1945* (New York: Oxford University Press, 1978), in the Oxford History of Modern Europe series. See also H. W. Koch, *A Constitutional History of*

Germany in the Nineteenth and Twentieth Centuries (London: Longman, 1984); Gustav Stolper, Karl Hauser, and Knut Borchardt, *The German Economy, 1870 to the Present*, translated from the second German edition by Toni Stolper (New York: Harcourt, Brace and World, 1967); the general survey of German history since 1890 by A. J. Ryder, *Twentieth-Century Germany: From Bismarck to Brandt* (New York: Columbia University Press, 1973); V. R. Berghahn's *Modern Germany: Society, Economy and Politics in the Twentieth Century* (2d ed., Cambridge: Cambridge University Press, 1987), with fifty-five statistical tables; and the account of German-American relations in the context of the history of both countries, with a very useful bibliographical essay, by Hans W. Gatzke, *Germany and the United States: A "Special Relationship"?*, The American Foreign Policy Library (Cambridge: Harvard University Press, 1980).

Though by no means focused on Germany alone, authoritative coverage of modern German military history will be found in *Makers of Modern Strategy from Machiavelli to the Nuclear Age*, a 941-page volume edited by Peter Paret with the collaboration of Gordon A. Craig and Felix Gilbert (Princeton, N.J.: Princeton University Press, 1986). The twenty-eight contributions include essays on Frederick the Great, Guibert, and Bülow by Robert R. Palmer; on Carl von Clausewitz by Peter Paret; on Helmuth von Moltke and the rise of the General Staff by Hajo Holborn; on Moltke, Alfred von Schlieffen, and the doctrine of strategic envelopment by Gunther E. Rothenberg; and on the military historian Hans Delbrück by Gordon A. Craig. Michael Geyer's well-structured, extensively annotated seventy-page analysis of "German Strategy in the Age of Machine Warfare, 1914–1945" is supplemented, in a six-page segment of the "Bibliographical Notes" at the end of the volume, by a wide-ranging critical review of the literature. Considered together, the bibliographical notes pertaining to the essays on German topics comprise the equivalent of a well-informed, up-to-date bibliographical essay on German military history, with sophisticated consideration of related aspects of modern German political and intellectual history as well.

A convenient selection of documents on German history is available in Louis L. Snyder's six-hundred-page *Documents of German History* (New Brunswick, N.J.: Rutgers University Press, 1958), which also includes several appendices with statistical and other data.

A Selected Bibliography

Antiquity and the Middle Ages

Germania, an account by the Roman writer Tacitus of Germany during antiquity, is available, together with his *Agricola* on Roman Britain, in an annotated translation by Hugh Mattingly (Baltimore: Penguin Books, 1960). The clash between Rome and the Germanic tribes early in the first century and their subsequent relations until the third, is treated in the first and fourth chapters of Theodor Mommsen's classic Roman history, selections from which are reprinted in *The Provinces of the Roman Empire from Caesar to Diocletian,* translated by William P. Dickson, edited with an introduction by T. Robert S. Broughton (Chicago: University of Chicago Press, 1968).

A detailed review of available sources and their interpretation is given by William A. Oldfather and Howard Vernon Canter in *The Defeat of Varus and the German Frontier Policy of Augustus* (Urbana: University of Illinois, 1915; rpt., New York: Johnson, 1967). For more recent scholarship, see C. M. Wells, *The German Policy of Augustus: An Examination of the Archaeological Evidence* (Oxford: Clarendon Press, 1972), a study based in part on relatively recently discovered archeological evidence, and Edward N. Luttwak, *The Grand Strategy of the Roman Empire from the First Century A.D. to the Third* (Baltimore: Johns Hopkins University Press, 1976). Accounts of the movement of the Germanic tribes into the Roman Empire are given in J. B. Bury's *The Invasion of Europe by the Barbarians* (London: Macmillan, 1928; rpt., New York: Norton, 1967) and E. A. Thompson's *The Early Germans* (New York: Oxford University Press, 1965). In addition to Katherine F. Drew, ed., *The Barbarian Invasions: Catalyst or New Order?* (New York: Holt, Rinehart and Winston, 1970), which presents a cross section of standard interpretations, see the recent monograph by Patrick J. Geary, *Before France and Germany: The Creation and Transformation of the Merovingian World* (New York: Oxford University Press, 1988), which concludes with a concise bibliographical essay citing studies and source materials available in English, as well as the most important works of Continental scholarship.

An early medieval record of the rise of the Franks is the *History of the Franks* by Gregory, Bishop of Tours, selections translated with notes by Ernest Brehaut (New York: Columbia University Press, 1916; rpt., New York: Norton, 1969). Lewis Thorpe has translated medieval biographies of Charlemagne by Einhard and Notker the

Stammerer, *Two Lives of Charlemagne* (Baltimore: Penguin Books, 1969). Heinrich Fichtenau's study, *The Carolingian Empire: The Age of Charlemagne*, translated by Peter Munz (Oxford: Blackwell, 1957; rpt., New York: Harper Torchbooks, 1964), and the selections (with bibliography) in Richard E. Sullivan's *The Coronation of Charlemagne — What Did It Signify?* (Boston: Health, 1959) are complemented by François Louis Ganshof, *Frankish Institutions under Charlemagne*, translated by Bryce and Mary Lyon (New York: Norton, 1970), and Eleanor S. Duckett, *Carolingian Portraits: A Study in the Ninth Century* (Ann Arbor: University of Michigan Press, 1962).

Lord Bryce's nineteenth-century classic, *The Holy Roman Empire* (rev. ed., New York: Macmillan, 1904; rpt., abr. ed. with intro. by Hans Kohn, New York: Schocken, 1961) is complemented by Friedrich Heer's interpretive synthesis of the same title, translated by Janet Sondheimer (New York: Praeger, 1968), and by Dietrich Gerhard, *Old Europe: A Study of Continuity, 1000–1800*, Studies in Discontinuity (New York: Academic Press, 1981), an essay that is not focused exclusively on Germany, but that illuminates one of the least understood aspects of German history: how and why many of the institutions and ideas of the Middle Ages persisted into the nineteenth century, and did so not as moribund anachronisms, but as enduring, viable aspects of a society and culture whose continuity had been far less disrupted by the Renaissance and Reformation than by the French and industrial revolutions.

Geoffrey Barraclough, the medieval focus of whose *Origins of Modern Germany* was noted above, provides a brief introduction to a central theme of the history of the Middle Ages in his pamphlet entitled *The Medieval Empire: Idea and Reality* (London: The Historical Association, 1950). In his Studies in Mediaeval History series, Barraclough has made available in English the findings of otherwise largely inaccessible German scholarship. The first and second volumes were published under the title *Mediaeval Germany, 911–1250: Essays by German Historians* in his translation with an extensive introductory essay (2 vols., Oxford: Blackwell, 1938; rpt., 1961); the third and fourth volumes have been reissued as paperbacks: (vol. 3) Gerd Tellenbach, *Church, State and Christian Society at the Time of the Investiture Contest*, translated by R. F. Bennett (London: Blackwell & Mott, 1959; rpt., New York: Harper Torchbooks, 1970); (vol. 4) Fritz Kern, *Kingship and Law in the Middle Ages*, translated by S. B. Chrimes (New York: Praeger, 1956; rpt., New York: Harper Torchbooks, 1970). The fifth volume in this series is Michael Seidlmayer's *Currents of Medieval Thought with Special Reference to Germany,* translated by D. Barker (Philadelphia: Dufour Editions, 1961).

A standard German account is Karl Hampe's *Germany under the Salian and Hohenstaufen Emperors,* translated by Ralph F. Bennett from Friedrich Baethgen's 11th rev. ed. (Totowa, N.J.: Rowman & Littlefield, 1973). Concise compilations of authoritative selections with bibliography are Robert E. Herzstein, ed., *The Holy Roman Empire in the Middle Ages: Universal State or German Catastrophe?* (Boston: Heath, 1966); Boyd H. Hill, Jr., ed., *The Rise of the First Reich: Germany in the Tenth Century* (New York: Wiley, 1969); and Karl F. Morrison, ed., *The Investiture Controversy: Issues, Ideals and Results* (New York: Holt, Rinehart and Winston, 1971; rpt., Malabar, Fla.: Krieger, 1976). Morrison also provided the historical introduction to *Imperial Lives and Letters of the Eleventh Century,* translated by Theodore E. Mommsen and K. F. Morrison and edited by Robert L. Benson (New York: Columbia University Press, 1962). For the Hohenstaufen period, see the account by Bishop Otto of Freising, continued by Rahewin, of *The Deeds of Frederick Barbarossa,* translated and annotated with an introduction by C. C. Mierow (New York: Columbia University Press, 1953; rpt., New York: Norton, 1966) and the work by Peter Munz, *Frederick Barbarossa: A Study in Medieval Politics* (Ithaca, N.Y.: Cornell University Press, 1969); and *Frederick the Second, 1194–1250* by Ernst H. Kantorowicz, translated by E. O. Lorimer (New York: R. R. Smith, 1931; rpt. New York: Ungar, 1957). See Benjamin Arnold, *German Knighthood, 1050–1300* (New York: Oxford University Press, 1985), for the role of the German knights in the Holy Roman Empire, and Charles C. Bayley, *The Formation of the German College of Electors in the Mid-Thirteenth Century* (Toronto: University of Toronto Press, 1949), on an important institutional development of the late Middle Ages. F. R. H. Du Boulay, *Germany in the Later Middle Ages* (New York: St. Martin's Press, 1983), deals with the late medieval period as a whole.

D. J. A. Matthew translated Fritz Rörig's *The Medieval Town* (Berkeley and Los Angeles: University of California Press, 1967); see also Helen Zimmern's *The Hansa Towns* (New York: Putnam's, 1891; rpt., Ann Arbor, Mich.: University Microfilms International, on demand) and Philippe Dollinger's *The German Hansa,* translated by D. S. Ault and S. H. Steinberg (Stanford, Calif.: Stanford University Press, 1970). Heinrich von Treitschke's *Origins of Prussianism,* translated by Eden and Cedar Paul (London: Allen & Unwin, 1942;

rpt., New York: Fertig, 1969) is a brief history of the Teutonic Knights. A symposium bearing on several aspects of German eastward expansion, including an article on "Slavs and Germans" by Frantisek Graus and contributions by Karl Bosl, Ferdinand Seibt, M. M. Postan, and Alexander Gieysztor, has been edited with an introduction by Geoffrey Barraclough under the title *Eastern and Western Europe in the Middle Ages* (New York: Harcourt Brace Jovanovich, 1970).

The Early Modern Period

Two leading figures in Germany during the first half of the sixteenth century were Emperor Charles V and Martin Luther. The standard biography of the great Habsburg is Karl Brandi's classic, *The Emperor Charles V: The Growth and Destiny of a Man and a World Empire,* translated by C. V. Wedgwood (London: Jonathan Cape, 1939; rpt., Atlantic Highlands, N.J.: Humanities Press, 1968). With Luther, a good place to begin is the biography by Roland H. Bainton, *Here I Stand: A Life of Martin Luther* (New York and Nashville: Abingdon Press, 1950; rpt., both Apex and Mentor Books, n.d.). A concise introduction and bibliography is given by Harold J. Grimm in his pamphlet, *The Reformation* (Washington, D.C.: American Historical Association, 1972). The relationship between the Renaissance and the Reformation is elucidated in *The Renaissance and Reformation Movements* (Chicago: Rand McNally, 1971) by Lewis W. Spitz, whose recent volume in the Rise of Modern Europe series, *The Protestant Reformation, 1517–1559* (New York: Harper & Row, 1985; rpt., Harper Torchbooks) includes an extensive bibliography. In his compilation of a number of representative articles and extracts illustrating different schools of thought, *The Reformation: Basic Interpretations* (2d ed., Lexington, Mass.: Heath, 1972), Spitz includes his translation of an article entitled "Why Did the Reformation Happen?" by Joseph Lortz, an ecumenically oriented Roman Catholic historian respected by German scholars of all religious persuasions, one of whose major works was translated by Ronald Walls as *The Reformation in Germany* (2 vols., New York: Herder, 1968). See also Abraham Friesen, *Reformation and Utopia: The Marxist Interpretation of the Reformation and Its Antecedents,* Publications of the Institute of European History, vol. 71 (Wiesbaden:

Steiner, 1974); Erwin Iserloh, *The Theses Were Not Posted: Luther between Reform and Reformation,* translated by Jared Wicks, S.J., introduction by Martin E. Marty (Boston: Beacon Press, 1968); and, for a vivid eyewitness approach, Hans J. Hillerbrand's *The Reformation: A Narrative History Related by Contemporary Obervers and Participants* (New York: Harper & Row, 1964).

On social history, see Gerhard Benecke, *Society and Politics in Germany, 1500–1750,* Studies in Social History (London: Routledge & Kegan Paul; Toronto: University of Toronto Press, 1974), and Eda Sagarra, *A Social History of Germany, 1648–1914* (London: Methuen, 1977). On a crucial episode during the Reformation, Kyle C. Sessions edited a compilation of various interpretations, with a bibliography, *Reformation and Authority: The Meaning of the Peasants' Revolt* (Lexington, Mass.: Heath, 1968). Friedrich Engels gives a Marxist interpretation of the same topic in *The German Revolutions—The Peasant War in Germany, and Germany: Revolution and Counter-Revolution,* edited with an introduction by Leonard Krieger (Chicago: University of Chicago Press, 1967), a volume in the Classic European Historians series. Urban history is the focus of studies by Bernd Moeller, *Imperial Cities and the Reformation,* translated by H. C. Erik Midelfort and Mark U. Edwards, Jr. (Philadelphia: Fortress Press, 1972), and Gerald Strauss, *Nuremberg in the Sixteenth Century* (New York: Wiley, 1966).

A concise account of the long conflict that concluded the Age of the Reformation is provided by Georges Pagès in *The Thirty Years' War, 1618–1648,* translated from the French by David Maland and John Hooper (New York: Harper Torchbooks, 1971). S. H. Steinberg stresses the broader European context in *The Thirty Years' War and the Conflict for European Hegemony, 1600–1660,* (New York: Norton, 1966). *Wallenstein: His Life Narrated* by Golo Mann, translated by Charles Kessler (New York: Holt, Rinehart and Winston, 1976), a monumental historical biography by one of postwar Germany's most esteemed historians, brings to life one of the most powerful and interesting figures of the Thirty Years' War. For further interpretations and bibliography, see Theodore K. Rabb's compilation *The Thirty Years' War* (2d ed., Lexington, Mass.: Heath, 1972; rpt., Lanham, Md.: University Press of America, 1981).

The Rise of Brandenburg-Prussia to 1786 by Sidney B. Fay, revised by Klaus Epstein (New York: Holt, Rinehart and Winston, 1964; rpt., Malabar, Fla.: Krieger, 1981) is a brief introduction. F. L. Carsten treats the early period in *The Origins of Prussia* (Oxford:

Clarendon Press, 1954). Standard biographies are *The Great Elector* by Ferdinand Schevill (Chicago: University of Chicago Press, 1947); Robert R. Ergang, *The Potsdam Führer: Frederick William I, Father of Prussian Militarism* (New York: Columbia University Press, 1941; rpt., New York: Octagon, 1973); and Chester Easum, *Prince Henry of Prussia: Brother of Frederick the Great* (Madison: University of Wisconsin Press, 1942; rpt., Westport, Conn.: Greenwood, 1971). On Frederick himself, George P. Gooch's *Frederick the Great: The Ruler, the Writer, the Man* (New York: Knopf, 1947; rpt., Hamden, Conn.: Archon, 1962) is a collection of studies rather than an integrated biography; but Peter Paret translated Gerhard Ritter's extended biographical essay *Frederick the Great: A Historical Profile* (Berkeley and Los Angeles: University of California Press, 1968) and complemented it with a dozen articles, essays, and contemporary accounts, over half not previously available in English: *Frederick the Great: A Profile* (New York: Hill and Wang, 1972). In addition, see the volume edited by Thomas M. Barker, *Frederick the Great and the Making of Prussia* (New York: Holt, Rinehart and Winston, 1972; rpt., Malabar, Fla.: Krieger, 1976), which also includes much previously untranslated material; John Clive's abridged edition of a monument of nineteenth-century British historical literature, Thomas Carlyle's *History of Friedrich II of Prussia Called Frederick the Great* (Chicago: University of Chicago Press, 1969); and *Frederick the Great on the Art of War*, translated and edited by Jay Luvaas (New York: Free Press, 1966).

From an essay on absolutism by the German authority Fritz Hartung, H. Otto and G. Barraclough translated and published the pamphlet *Enlightened Despotism* (London: The Historical Association, 1957). A volume of documentation on the two most important German monarchies of the period was edited by C. A. Macartney, *The Habsburg and Hohenzollern Dynasties in the Seventeenth and the Eighteenth Centuries* (New York: Harper & Row, 1970). Other major German states, including Bavaria, Hesse, Saxony, and Württemberg, are the subject of a study by F. L. Carsten, *Princes and Parliaments in Germany: From the Fifteenth to the Eighteenth Century* (New York: Oxford University Press, 1959). See also the detailed study of a single southwest German duchy by James Allen Vann, *The Making of a State: Württemberg, 1593–1793* (Ithaca: Cornell University Press, 1984).

Biographies of three important figures in early modern Germany: Erwin Panofsky, *The Life and Art of Albrecht Dürer* (4th ed.,

Princeton, N.J.: Princeton University Press, 1955); Albert Schweitzer, *J. S. Bach*, translated with a foreword by Ernest Newman (2 vols., Leipzig: Breitkopf and Härtel, 1911; rpt., New York: Dover Publications, 1966); and Ernst Cassirer, *Kant's Life and Thought*, translated by James Haden (New Haven, Conn.: Yale University Press, 1981).

Further works on state and society during the early modern period: Henry F. Schwarz, *The Imperial Privy Council in the Seventeenth Century*, with a supplement on its social structure by H. F. Schwarz and J. I. Coddington (Cambridge: Harvard University Press, 1943); William O. Henderson, *Studies in the Economic Policy of Frederick the Great* (London: Cass, 1963), Herman Weill, *Frederick the Great and Samuel von Cocceji: A Study in the Reform of the Prussian Judicial Administration, 1740–1755* (Madison: State Historical Society of Wisconsin, 1961); Hans Rosenberg, *Bureaucracy, Aristocracy and Autocracy: The Prussian Experience, 1660–1815* (Cambridge: Harvard University Press, 1958; rpt., Boston: Beacon, 1966); three essays by Otto Hintze on Prussian history through the eighteenth century, included in *The Historical Essays of Otto Hintze*, edited with an introduction by Felix Gilbert (New York: Oxford University Press, 1975), pp. 33–154; two political studies by Reinhold A. Dorwart, *The Administrative Reforms of Frederick William I of Prussia* and *The Prussian Welfare State before 1740* (both Cambridge: Harvard University Press, 1953 and 1971, respectively); and three sociocultural studies, Walter H. Bruford's *Germany in the Eighteenth Century: The Social Background of the Literary Revival* (Cambridge: At the University Press, 1935; rpt., 1965), his *Culture and Society in Classical Weimar, 1775–1806* (Cambridge: At the University Press, 1962), and Henri Brunschwig's *Enlightenment and Romanticism in Eighteenth-Century Prussia*, translated by Frank Jellinek (Chicago: University of Chicago Press, 1974).

GERMANY, 1789–1945

Two approaches to the interpretation of modern German history in light of the cataclysms of the First and Second World Wars are Friedrich Meinecke's *The German Catastrophe: Reflections and Recollections*, translated by Sidney B. Fay (Cambridge, Mass.: Harvard University Press, 1950; rpt., Boston: Beacon, 1963) and Gerhard Ritter's *The German Problem: Basic Questions of German Political*

Life, Past and Present, translated by Sigurd Burckhardt (Columbus: Ohio State University Press, 1965). On the significance of Prussia in German history, see E. J. Feuchtwanger's *Prussia: Myth and Reality — The Role of Prussia in German History* (Chicago: Regnery, 1970) and Rudolf von Thadden's *Prussia: The History of a Lost State,* translated by Angi Rutter (Cambridge: Cambridge University Press, 1986).

Hans Kohn, *The Mind of Germany: The Education of a Nation* (New York: Scribner's, 1960; rpt., New York: Harper Torchbooks, 1965), is an introduction to German cultural and intellectual history. The following studies provide insight into the lives and works of the leading figures they portray, as well as the times in which they lived: Paul R. Sweet, *Wilhelm von Humboldt: A Biography* (2 vols., Columbus: Ohio State University Press, 1978 and 1980, respectively); Richard Friedenthal, *Goethe: His Life and Times* (London: Weidenfeld and Nicolson; Cleveland, Ohio: World Publishing Co., 1965), and Georg Lukács, *Goethe and His Time,* translated by Robert Anchor (New York: Howard Fertig, 1978); Alexander Wheelock Thayer, *Thayer's Life of Beethoven,* rev. and ed. by Elliot Forbes, (rev. ed., 2 vols., Princeton, N.J.: Princeton University Press, 1967); Jeffrey L. Sammons, *Heinrich Heine: A Modern Biography* (Princeton, N.J.: Princeton University Press, 1979); Joachim Remak, *The Gentle Critic: Theodor Fontane and German Politics* (Syracuse, N.Y.: Syracuse University Press, 1964); Andreas Dorpalen, *Heinrich von Treitschke* (New Haven, Conn.: Yale University Press, 1957; rpt., Port Washington, N.Y.: Kennikat Press, 1973); Martin Gregor-Dellin, *Richard Wagner: His Life, His Work, His Century,* translated by J. Maxwell Brownjohn (San Diego: Harcourt Brace Jovanovich, 1983); and Nigel Hamilton, *The Brothers Mann: The Lives of Heinrich and Thomas Mann, 1871–1950 and 1875–1955* (London: Secker & Warburg, 1978; New Haven, Conn.: Yale University Press, 1979).

On German cultural, social, and intellectual history, see also Ernest K. Bramsted, *Aristocracy and the Middle Classes in Germany: Social Types in German Literature, 1830–1900* (rev. ed., Chicago: University of Chicago Press, 1964); W. H. Bruford, *The German Tradition of Self-Cultivation: "Bildung" from Humboldt to Thomas Mann* (Cambridge: Cambridge University Press, 1975); J. G. Legge, *Rhyme and Revolution in Germany: A Study in German History, Life, Literature and Character, 1813–1850* (London: Constable, 1918; rpt., New York: AMS, 1970); Erich Heller, *The Disinherited Mind: Essays in Modern German Literature and Thought*

(New York: Farrar, Straus and Cudahy, 1957; rpt., Cleveland: Meridian Books, 1959); Karl Löwith, *From Hegel to Nietzsche: The Revolution in Nineteenth-Century Thought,* translated by David E. Green (New York: Holt, Rinehart and Winston, 1964; rpt., Garden City, N.Y.: Anchor, 1967); Reinhard Bendix, *Max Weber: An Intellectual Portrait* (Garden City, N.Y.: Doubleday, 1960; rpt., Anchor Books, 1962); Wilhelm Pauck, *Harnack and Troeltsch: Two Historical Theologians* (New York: Oxford University Press, 1968); and Peter Gay, *Weimar Culture: The Outsider as Insider* (New York: Harper & Row, 1968; rpt., Harper Torchbooks, 1970), and also his *Freud, Jews and Other Germans: Masters and Victims in Modernist Culture* (New York: Oxford University Press, 1978; paperback rpt., 1979).

Germany Confronts Modernization: German Culture and Society, 1790–1890 by Robert Anchor (Lexington, Mass.: Heath, 1972) is an introductory essay that deals with the relationship between sociocultural change and political and institutional history. Various aspects of this relationship and related questions, including the emergence of German nationalism and Germanic ideology, are dealt with in Reinhold Aris, *History of Political Thought in Germany from 1789 to 1815* (London: Allen & Unwin, 1936; rpt., New York: Russell, 1965); Henry C. Meyer, *Mitteleuropa in German Thought and Action, 1815–1945* (The Hague: Nijhoff, 1955); Leonard Krieger, *The German Idea of Freedom: The History of a Political Tradition* (Boston: Beacon, 1957); Donald G. Rohr, *The Origins of Social Liberalism in Germany* (Chicago: University of Chicago Press, 1963); Klaus Epstein, *The Genesis of German Conservatism* (Princeton, N.J.: Princeton University Press, 1966); Vernon L. Lidtke, *The Alternative Culture: Socialist Labor in Imperial Germany* (New York: Oxford University Press, 1985); Walter Z. Laqueur, *Young Germany: A History of the German Youth Movement* (New York: Basic Books 1962); Fritz K. Ringer, *The Decline of the German Mandarins: The German Academic Community, 1890–1933* (Cambridge: Harvard University Press, 1969); Fritz Stern, *The Politics of Cultural Despair: A Study in the Rise of the Germanic Ideology* (Berkeley and Los Angeles: University of California Press, 1961; paperback rpt.), and by him also, *The Failure of Illiberalism: Essays on the Political Culture of Modern Germany* (New York: Knopf, 1972); Hannah Arendt, *The Origins of Totalitarianism* (new ed. with added prefaces, New York: Harvest Books, 1973); George Mosse, *The Crisis of German Ideology: Intellectual Origins of the Third Reich,* and also his *Nazi Culture: Intellectual, Cultural and Social Life in the Third Reich,* with translations by Salvator Attanasio et al. (both New York: Grosset's Universal Library, 1964 and 1968, respectively); Klemens von Klemperer, *Germany's New Conservatism: Its History and Dilemma in the Twentieth Century* (Princeton, N.J.: Princeton University Press, 1957; paperback rpt. with a new postscript, 1968); and Jeffrey Herf, *Reactionary Modernism: Technology, Culture and Politics in Weimar and the Third Reich* (Cambridge: Cambridge University Press, 1984), with consideration, among others, of Oswald Spengler, Ernst Jünger, and Werner Sombart.

Concise orientation, with bibliography, on the political history of the early nineteenth century is provided in three textbooks: Arthur J. May, *The Age of Metternich, 1814–1848* (rev. ed., New York: Holt, Rinehart and Winston, 1963); Henry F. Schwarz, ed., *Metternich, the "Coachman of Europe": Statesman or Evil Genius?* (Boston: Heath, 1962), a selection of essays with differing historical interpretations; and Mack Walker, ed., *Metternich's Europe* (New York: Harper & Row, 1968), with early nineteenth-century documentation in translation. Enno E. Kraehe, *Metternich's German Policy*, vol. 1: *The Contest with Napoleon, 1799–1814;* and vol. 2: *The Congress of Vienna, 1814–1815* (Princeton, N.J.: Princeton University Press, 1963 and 1983, respectively) provides detailed coverage of the Napoleonic wars and the restoration that followed them. John R. Seeley, *Life and Times of Stein: or Germany and Prussia in the Napoleonic Age* (3 vols., Cambridge: At the University Press, 1878; rpt., New York: Greenwood, 1969), though dated, remains worth reading. On this period, see also Richard C. Raack, *The Fall of Stein* (Cambridge: Harvard University Press, 1965); Peter Paret, *Yorck and the Era of the Prussian Reform, 1807–1815* (Princeton, N.J.: Princeton University Press, 1966); Eugene N. Anderson, *Nationalism and the Cultural Crisis in Prussia, 1806–1815* (New York: Farrar and Rinehart, 1939); Walter M. Simon, *The Failure of the Prussian Reform Movement* (Ithaca, N.Y.: Cornell University Press, 1955; rpt., New York: Fertig, 1971); and J. E. d'Arenberg, *The Lesser Princes of the Holy Roman Empire in the Napoleonic Era* (Washington, D.C.: Georgetown University Press, 1950; rpt., Ann Arbor, Mich.: University Microfilms International, on demand).

On nineteenth-century Germany through the period of unification, see Theodore S. Hamerow's three volumes, *Restoration, Revolution, Reaction: Economics and Politics in Germany, 1815–1871* and *The Social Foundations of German Unification, 1858–1871*, vol. 1: *Ideas and Institutions;* and vol. 2: *Struggles and Achievements*

A Selected Bibliography

(Princeton, N.J.: Princeton University Press, 1958, 1969, and 1972, respectively).

On the mid-century revolution, the account in Veit Valentin's *1848: Chapters from German History,* translated and abridged by E. T. Scheffauer (London: Allen & Unwin, 1940; rpt., Hamden, Conn.: Archon, 1965), and the selected interpretations, with bibliography, in Melvin Kranzberg, ed., *1848: A Turning Point?* (Boston: Heath, 1959), are complemented by the vivid panorama of men and events painted by Priscilla Robertson in *Revolutions of 1848: A Social History* (Princeton, N.J.: Princeton University Press, 1952). See also the more recent study by Frank Eyck, *The Frankfurt Parliament, 1848–1849* (New York: St. Martin's, 1968), and the Marxist classic on the German revolution and counter-revolution by Friedrich Engels, originally published in the *New York Tribune* (in 1851–52), included with his account of the sixteenth-century Peasant War in his already cited volume on *The German Revolutions* (Chicago: University of Chicago Press, 1967).

Lothar Gall, *Bismarck: The White Revolutionary,* translated by J. A. Underwood (2 vols., London: Allen & Unwin, 1986) is biography at its best—a readable synthesis of historical scholarship and humanistic insight. For a concise introduction to Bismarck and the literature on him, see George Kent, *Bismarck and His Times* (Carbondale and Edwardsville: Southern Illinois University Press, 1978). An abridged translation of Bismarck's *Reflections and Reminiscences* (New York: Harper Torchbooks, 1968) was edited by Theodore S. Hamerow, who also edited a concise collection of articles and extracts from longer works, *Otto von Bismarck: A Historical Assessment* (2d ed., Lexington, Mass.: Heath, 1972). On the crisis that led to Bismarck's appointment as Prussian prime minister, and his subsequent role in it, see Eugene N. Anderson, *The Social and Political Conflict in Prussia, 1858–1864* (Lincoln: University of Nebraska Press, 1954; rpt., New York: Octagon, 1968), and the first volume of a projected full-length biography, Otto Pflanze, *Bismarck and the Development of Germany,* vol. 1: *The Period of Unification, 1815–1871* (Princeton, N.J.: Princeton University Press, 1963). Pflanze also edited a fine collection of articles presenting differing views on *The Unification of Germany, 1848–1871* (New York: Holt, Rinehart and Winston, 1968; rpt., Malabar, Fla.: Krieger, 1979).

William II, emperor from the last years of Bismarck's chancellorship to the end of the First World War, is the subject of a standard biography by Michael Balfour, *The Kaiser and His Times* (Boston:

A Selected Bibliography

Houghton Mifflin, 1964; rpt., with an afterword, New York: Norton, 1972). Though basically unchanged, the picture of the man is sharpened in *Kaiser Wilhelm II, New Interpretations: The Corfu Papers*, ed. by John C. G. Röhl and Nicolaus Sombart (Cambridge and New York: Cambridge University Press, 1982). On the first decade of William's reign, see John C. G. Röhl's *Germany without Bismarck: The Crisis in Government in the Second Reich, 1890–1900* (Berkeley and Los Angeles: University of California Press, 1967). One of the most influential figures in late Bismarckian and early Wilhelminian Germany was Holstein, whose biography by Norman Rich, *Friedrich von Holstein: Politics and Diplomacy in the Era of Bismarck and William II* (2 vols., Cambridge: At the University Press, 1965), is complemented by *The Holstein Papers*, edited by Rich together with M. H. Fisher (4 vols., Cambridge: At the University Press, 1955–1963). See also Frederic B. M. Hollyday, *Bismarck's Rival: A Political Biography of General and Admiral Albrecht von Stosch* (Durham, N.C.: Duke University Press, 1960); Fritz Stern, *Gold and Iron: Bismarck, Bleichröder, and the Building of the German Empire* (New York: Knopf, 1977); William Harvey Maehl, *August Bebel: Shadow Emperor of the German Workers* (Philadelphia: American Philosophical Society, 1980); Stanley Zucker, *Ludwig Bamberger: German Liberal Politician and Social Critic, 1823–1899* (Pittsburgh, Pa.: University of Pittsburgh Press, 1975); Erwin H. Ackerknecht, *Rudolf Virchow: Doctor, Statesman, Anthropologist* (Madison: University of Wisconsin Press, 1953), on the father of cellular pathology, who served for decades in the Prussian legislature; Konrad H. Jarausch, *The Enigmatic Chancellor: Bethmann Hollweg and the Hubris of Imperial Germany* (New Haven, Conn.: Yale University Press, 1973); and Margaret Lavinia Anderson, *Windthorst: A Political Biography* (New York: Oxford University Press, 1981), on the head of the Center Party. See also Ellen Lovell Evans, *The German Center Party, 1870–1933: A Study in Political Catholicism* (Carbondale and Edwardsville: Southern Illinois University Press, 1981), and James J. Sheehan, *German Liberalism in the Nineteenth Century* (Chicago: University of Chicago Press, 1978).

A pioneering work on the Wilhelminian period is Eckart Kehr's *Battleship Building and Party Politics in Germany, 1894–1901: A Cross-Section of the Political, Social, and Ideological Preconditions of German Imperialism*, edited, translated, and with an introduction by Pauline R. Anderson and Eugene N. Anderson (Chicago: University of Chicago Press, Midway Reprints, 1973). See also the collection of Kehr's essays edited by Gordon A. Craig and translated by Grete Heinz, *Economic Interest, Militarism, and Foreign Policy: Essays on German History* (Berkeley and Los Angeles: University of California Press, 1977). In addition to Woodruff D. Smith, *The German Colonial Empire* (Chapel Hill: University of North Carolina Press, 1978), see, for Germany's loss of the overseas colonies, Mary Evelyn Townsend, *The Rise and Fall of Germany's Colonial Empire, 1884–1918* (New York: Macmillan, 1930; rpt., New York: Fertig, 1966).

For German economic history, see, in addition to the standard work on the period since 1870 by Gustav Stolper et al., *The German Economy*, cited in the first part of this bibliography: J. H. Chapham, *Economic Development of France and Germany 1815–1914* (4th ed., Cambridge: At the University Press, 1935; paperback rpt., 1966); William O. Henderson, *The Rise of German Industrial Power, 1834–1914* (Berkeley and Los Angeles: University of California Press, 1975); Alexander Gerschenkron, *Bread and Democracy in Germany* (Berkeley and Los Angeles: University of California Press, 1943; rpt., with a new preface, New York: Fertig, 1966); and James Harold, *The German Slump: Politics and Economics, 1924–1936* (New York: Oxford University Press, 1986). The origins of the Prussian tariff union are traced in Arnold H. Price's *The Evolution of the Zollverein: A Study of the Ideas and Institutions Leading to German Economic Unification between 1815 and 1833* (Ann Arbor: University of Michigan Press, 1949; rpt., New York: Octagon, 1973); its subsequent history is recounted in William O. Henderson's *The Zollverein* (Cambridge: At the University Press, 1939; rpt., London: Cass, 1968).

Evelyn Anderson's *Hammer or Anvil: The Story of the German Working-Class Movement* (London: Gollancz, 1945) and Helga Grebing's more recent *History of the German Labour Movement: A Survey*, abridged but with a chapter on foreign policy by Mary Saran, translated by Edith Körner (London: Oswald Wolff, 1966), may be supplemented by several monographs dealing with different phases and aspects of the subject: Richard W. Reichard, *Crippled from Birth: German Social Democracy, 1844–1870* (Ames: Iowa State University Press, 1969); W. L. Guttsman, *The German Social Democratic Party, 1875–1933: From Ghetto to Government* (London: Allen & Unwin, 1981); Vernon Lidtke, *The Outlawed Party: Social Democracy in Germany, 1878–1890* (Princeton, N.J.: Princeton University Press, 1966); S. H. F. Hickey, *Workers in Imperial Germany: The Miners of the Ruhr* (New York: Oxford University Press, 1985); Peter Gay, *The Dilemma of Democratic Socialism: Eduard Bernstein's*

Challenge to Marx (New York: Columbia University Press, 1952; rpt., New York: Collier Books, 1962); Carl E. Schorske, *German Social Democracy, 1905–1917: The Development of the Great Schism* (Cambridge: Harvard University Press, 1955; rpt., New York: Harper Torchbooks, 1972); Ben Fowkes, *Communism in Germany under the Weimar Republic* (New York: St. Martin's, 1984); and Richard N. Hunt, *German Social Democracy, 1918–1933* (New Haven, Conn.: Yale University Press, 1964; rpt., Chicago: Quadrangle, 1970).

Gordon A. Craig, *The Politics of the Prussian Army, 1640–1945* (New York: Oxford University Press, 1955; paperback rpt., 1964), a standard history of the Prussian-based German military tradition, devotes relatively little space to the period from the end of the First World War to the end of the Second, the subject of John W. Wheeler-Bennett, *The Nemesis of Power: The German Army in Politics, 1918–1945* (2d ed., London: Macmillan; New York: St. Martin's, 1964). Martin Kitchen's *A Military History of Germany from the Eighteenth Century to the Present Day* (Bloomington: Indiana University Press, 1975) gives a concise overview. Telford Taylor's *Sword and Swastika: Generals and Nazis in the Third Reich* (New York: Simon and Schuster, 1952; rpt., Chicago: Quadrangle, 1969) critically examines the period 1933–1945. For a socialist indictment from the first decade of the twentieth century, see Karl Liebknecht, *Militarism and Anti-Militarism*, translated by Alexander Sirnis, with an introduction by Philip S. Foner (New York: Dover, 1972).

Studies dealing with German military social history, with particular attention to the officer corps, are Karl Demeter, *The German Officer-Corps in Society and State, 1650–1945*, translated by Angus Malcolm, introduction by Michael Howard (New York: Praeger, 1965); Martin Kitchen, *The German Officer Corps, 1890–1914* (New York: Oxford University Press, 1968); and Holger H. Herwig, *The German Naval Officer Corps: A Social and Political History, 1890–1918* (New York: Oxford University Press, 1973). Many aspects of military history are dealt with at considerable length in the narrative (i.e., explanatory) sections of three titles cited in the first part of this bibliography: the volumes on naval, aviation, and military history bibliography, respectively, by Keith W. Bird, Edward L. Homze, and Dennis E. Showalter.

Gerhard Ritter's classic study of the German military tradition was translated by Heinz Norden as *The Sword and the Scepter: The Problem of Militarism in Germany*, vol. 1: *The Prussian Tradition, 1740–1890;* vol. 2: *The European Powers and the Wilhelminian*

Empire; vol. 3: *The Tragedy of Statesmanship—Bethmann Hollweg ,as War Chancellor, 1914–1917;* vol. 4: *The Reign of German Militarism and the Disaster of 1918* (Coral Gables, Fla.: University of Miami Press, 1969–1973).

In connection with his work on the German military tradition, Gerhard Ritter wrote *The Schlieffen Plan: Critique of a Myth,* translated by Andrew and Eva Wilson, foreword by B. H. Liddell Hart (New York: Praeger, 1958), analyzing the operational plan that provided for the German violation of Belgian neutrality. An introduction to the extensive literature on the origins of the First World War is provided by Dwight E. Lee's compilation of interpretive and bibliographical material in *The Outbreak of the First World War: Causes and Responsibilities* (4th ed., Lexington, Mass.: Heath, 1975). Lee's volume also touches on the closely related question of German war aims, the central problem dealt with in a volume edited by Gerald D. Feldman, *German Imperialism, 1914–1918: The Development of a Historical Debate* (New York: Wiley, 1972). On the controversy regarding Imperial Germany's responsibility for the First World War, see three books by the Hamburg historian Fritz Fischer: *War of Illusions: German Policies from 1911 to 1914,* translated by Marian Jackson, foreword by Alan Bullock (New York: Norton, 1975); *Germany's Aims in the First World War,* abridged by the author, introductions by Hajo Holborn and James Joll (New York: Norton, 1967); and *World Power or Decline: The Controversy over Germany's Aims in the First World War,* translated by Lancelot L. Farrar et al. (New York: Norton, 1974). Fischer's contribution is taken into account in Andreas Hillgruber's *Germany and the Two World Wars,* translated by William C. Kirby (Cambridge: Harvard University Press, 1981), a ninety-eight-page comparative analysis of Germany's role in the events preceding the two great wars of the twentieth century. A well-written narrative of the background and the course of the First World War from an urbane German perspective by a widely read industrialist turned publicist is *The Lamps Went out in Europe* by Ludwig Reiners, translated by Richard and Clara Winston (Cleveland: Meridian Books, 1966).

Ivo J. Lederer edited a volume of evaluative interpretations with bibliography on the treaty imposed on Germany after the war, *The Versailles Settlement: Was It Foredoomed to Failure?* (Boston: Heath, 1960). On the fall of the German monarchy at the end of the war and the establishment of the republic, see A. J. Ryder's pamphlet, *The German Revolution, 1918–19* (London: The Historical Association, 1959), the text of which is available also in *From Metternich to*

A Selected Bibliography

Hitler—Aspects of British and Foreign History, 1814–1939: Historical Association Essays, edited by W. N. Medlicott (New York: Barnes & Noble, 1966), a collection including essays by Erich Eyck on Bismarck, Bernadotte E. Schmitt on the origins of the First World War, and Medlicott on the origins of the Second. The twentieth century and also earlier periods of German history are considered in Leonard Krieger and Fritz Stern, eds., *The Responsibility of Power: Historical Essays in Honor of Hajo Holborn* (Garden City, N.Y.: Doubleday, 1968; rpt., Anchor Books, 1969); Ludwig Dehio, *Germany and World Politics in the Twentieth Century,* translated by Dieter Pevsner (London: Chatto & Windus, 1959; rpt., New York: Norton, 1967); and two volumes by Gordon A. Craig, *From Bismarck to Adenauer: Aspects of German Statecraft* (rev. ed., New York: Harper Torchbooks, 1965) and *War, Politics, and Diplomacy: Selected Essays* (New York: Praeger, 1966).

In addition to A. J. Ryder's Historical Association pamphlet and his scholarly monograph on *The German Revolution of 1918: A Study of German Socialism in War and Revolt* (Cambridge: At the University Press, 1967), see a widely read, scathing account of the upheaval that ended the monarchy in Germany, but left the social structure that had sustained it largely intact, Sebastian Haffner's *Failure of a Revolution: Germany 1918–19,* translated by Georg Rapp (London: André Deutsch; New York: Library Press, 1972). For detailed treatment, see Ralph H. Lutz's basic *Fall of the German Empire, 1914–1918* (2 vols., Stanford, Calif.: Hoover Institution Press, 1932; rpt., New York: Octagon, 1969) as well as his edition of *The Causes of the German Collapse in 1918* (Stanford, Calif.: Hoover Institution Press, 1934; rpt., Hamden, Conn.: Shoe String Press, 1969), and, jointly edited with Charles B. Burdick, *The Institutions of the German Revolution 1918–1919* (New York: Praeger, 1966).

A lucid interpretation of German history during the era of the two world wars is given in Hannah Vogt's *The Burden of Guilt: A Short History of Germany, 1914–1945,* translated by Herbert Strauss, with an introduction by Gordon A. Craig (New York: Oxford University Press, 1964; paperback rpt.); originally written as a school text for the postwar generation, it is organized in twelve chapters to deal with problems such as whether Germany was indeed responsible for World War I, why the Weimar Republic failed, what life was like in the Third Reich, and "the fate of our Jewish fellow-citizens." For concise documentation on this period as a whole, see Henry Cord Meyer, ed., *The Long Generation: Germany from Empire to Ruin, 1913–1945*

A SELECTED BIBLIOGRAPHY

(New York: Harper & Row, 1973); and on the latter part of it, Joachim Remak, ed., *The Nazi Years: A Documentary History* (Englewood Cliffs, N.J.: Spectrum Books, 1969). For more extensive documentation, see Jeremy Noakes and Geoffrey Pridham, eds., *Nazism 1919–1945: A Documentary Reader*, vol. 1: *The Rise to Power 1919–1934;* vol. 2: *State, Economy and Society 1933–1939*, Exeter Studies in History, no. 6 and no. 8, respectively (Exeter, England: The University of Exeter; Atlantic Highlands, N.J.: Humanities Press, 1983 and 1984, respectively). See also Louis L. Snyder's *National Socialist Germany: Twelve Years That Shook the World* (Malabar, Fla.: Krieger, 1984), a 209-page Anvil paperback with an extended introductory essay and a wide-ranging selection of readings, including the Hossbach Memorandum and Hitler's political testament.

Arthur Rosenberg's *Imperial Germany: The Birth of the German Republic, 1871–1918*, translated by Ian F. D. Morrow (New York: Oxford University Press, 1931; rpt., Boston: Beacon, 1964) analyzes the background of the establishment of the republic, particularly from the beginning of the war; his sequel deals with the subsequent period: *A History of the German Republic*, translated by Morrow and L. M. Sieveking (London: Methuen, 1936; rpt., New York: Russell, 1965). See also Erich Eyck, *A History of the Weimar Republic*, translated by Harlan P. Hanson and Robert G. L. Waite (2 vols., Cambridge: Harvard University Press, 1962 and 1963, respectively; paperback rpt., New York: Atheneum, 1970). More recent than Eyck or Rosenberg, and considerably shorter—but still more detailed in its coverage than the surveys by Holborn, Craig, and others, mentioned earlier in this bibliography—is S. William Halperin's *Germany Tried Democracy: A Political History of the Reich from 1918 to 1933* (New York: Crowell, 1946; rpt., Ann Arbor, Mich.: University Microfilms International, on demand).

The republic's crisis-ridden first half decade, 1918–1923, culminated in the economic catastrophe dealt with in Fritz K. Ringer's *The German Inflation of 1923* (New York: Oxford University Press, 1969). Accounts of two key figures during the Weimar Republic are Andreas Dorpalen, *Hindenburg and the Weimar Republic* (Princeton, N.J.: Princeton University Press, 1964), and Henry Ashby Turner, Jr., *Stresemann and the Politics of the Weimar Republic* (Princeton, N.J.: Princeton University Press, 1963). On Stresemann, see also Henry L. Bretton, *Stresemann and the Revision of Versailles: A Fight for Reason* (Stanford, Calif.: Stanford University Press, 1953), and Hans W. Gatzke, *Stresemann and the Rearmament of Germany* (Baltimore:

Johns Hopkins Press, 1954; rpt., New York: Norton, 1969). Further aspects of the period are considered in Klaus Epstein, *Matthias Erzberger and the Dilemma of German Democracy* (Princeton, N.J.: Princeton University Press, 1959; rpt., New York: Fertig, 1971); Herman Lebovics, *Social Conservatism and the Middle Classes in Germany, 1914–1933* (Princeton, N.J.: Princeton University Press, 1969); Lewis Hertzman, *DNVP: The Right-Wing Opposition in the Weimar Republic, 1918–1924* (Lincoln: University of Nebraska Press, 1963); Harold J. Gordon, Jr., *The Reichswehr and the German Republic, 1919–1926* (Princeton, N.J.: Princeton University Press, 1957); George Mosse, *Germans and Jews: The Right, the Left, and the Search for a "Third Force" in Pre-Nazi Germany* (New York: Fertig, 1970; rpt., New York: Grosset's Universal Library, 1971); Istvan Deak, *Weimar Germany's Left-Wing Intellectuals: A Political History of the "Weltbühne" and Its Circle* (Berkeley and Los Angeles: University of California Press, 1968); Robert G. L. Waite, *Vanguard of Nazism: The Free Corps Movement in Postwar Germany, 1918–1923* (Cambridge, Mass.: Harvard University Press, 1952; rpt., New York: Norton, 1969); and Earl R. Beck, *The Death of the Prussian Republic: A Study in Reich-Prussian Relations* (Tallahassee: Florida State University Press, 1959).

Documentation on the rise of the National Socialist movement during the Weimar Republic is available in the Meyer, Remak, and Noakes and Pridham volumes cited above, but the basic contemporary text was published by Hitler himself during the mid-twenties: *My Struggle. Mein Kampf,* as it usually is cited, was edited by Alvin Johnson et al. and published in an unabridged and heavily annotated translation under the editorial sponsorship of a representative committee including the historians Sidney B. Fay, Carlton J. H. Hayes, and William L. Langer (New York: Reynal and Hitchcock, 1939); in the Ralph Manheim translation, it was published as a paperback (Boston: Houghton Mifflin, 1943; rpt., Sentry Edition, 1962).

Harold J. Gordon, Jr., has produced a comprehensive study of the National Socialists' first attempt to seize power, the abortive Munich *Putsch* of November 1923, *Hitler and the Beer Hall Putsch* (Princeton, N.J.: Princeton University Press, 1972). See also *The Hitler Trial before the People's Court in Munich,* translation by H. Francis Freniere, Lucie Karcic, and Philip Fandek, introduction by Harold J. Gordon, Jr. (3 vols., Arlington, Va.: University Publications of America, 1976), a record of the twenty-five days of proceedings, between 26 February and 1 April 1924, against Hitler, Ludendorff, and others.

A Selected Bibliography

The rise of National Socialism in the northernmost part of Germany, Schleswig-Holstein, is illuminated in Rudolf Heberle's *From Democracy to Nazism: A Regional Case Study on Political Parties in Germany* (Baton Rouge: Louisiana State University Press, 1945; rpt., New York: Fertig and [paperback] Grosset's Universal Library, 1970); the English edition is an abridged version of Heberle's pioneering work in sociography, which eventually was published in full in Stuttgart in 1963 by the Institute for Contemporary History. How the National Socialists went about the cultivation and consolidation of power at the local level is the subject of a community study by William Sheridan Allen, *The Nazi Seizure of Power: The Experience of a Single German Town, 1922–1945* (rev. ed., New York: Franklin Watts, 1984). Three regional studies on National Socialism are Jeremy Noakes, *The Nazi Party in Lower Saxony, 1921–1933* (London: Oxford University Press, 1971); Geoffrey Pridham, *The Nazi Movement in Bavaria, 1923–1933* (New York: Harper & Row, 1973); and Johnpeter Horst Grill, *The Nazi Movement in Baden, 1920–1945* (Chapel Hill: University of North Carolina Press, 1983). That the German business and finance community did not generally support Hitler before he came to power is shown by Henry Ashby Turner, Jr., in *German Big Business and the Rise of Hitler* (New York: Oxford University Press, 1985), which has extensive discussion of the sources and the literature in the notes and a detailed bibliography. See also the memoirs of the businessman who in 1929 became chief of staff of the storm troopers, Otto Wagener, *Hitler: Memoirs of a Confidant,* edited by H. A. Turner, Jr., translated by Ruth Hain (New Haven, Conn.: Yale University Press, 1985).

Milton Mayer, *They Thought They Were Free: The Germans, 1933–1945* (Chicago: University of Chicago Press, 1955; rpt., with a new foreword, 1966), based on the stories of ten persons interviewed by the author, is a book about what National Socialism actually meant to the average German. See also the account by the West German journalist Bernt Engelmann, *In Hitler's Germany: Daily Life in the Third Reich,* translated by Krishna Winston, with a foreword by Studs Terkel (New York: Pantheon Books, 1986). An early study of the grass-roots appeal of the Hitler movement was the sociologist Theodore Abel's *Why Hitler Came into Power: An Answer Based on the Original Life Stories of Six Hundred of His Followers* (New York: Prentice-Hall, 1938); it was reprinted under the title *The Nazi Movement: Why Hitler Came to Power* (New York: Atherton, 1966). The autobiographical statements solicited by Abel in 1934 and used as the

304 �

basis for his book were later statistically analyzed by Peter H. Merkl, who published his findings under the title *Political Violence under the Swastika: 581 Early Nazis* (Princeton, N.J.: Princeton University Press, 1975). There are more recent studies by Thomas Childers, *The Nazi Voter: The Social Foundations of Fascism in Germany, 1919–1933* (Chapel Hill: University of North Carolina Press, 1983), and Michael H. Kater, *The Nazi Party: A Social Profile of Members and Leaders, 1919–1945* (Cambridge, Mass.: Harvard University Press, 1983).

The Hitler movement emerged in large measure as a response to the threat from the Left, of which several aspects are considered in *Stillborn Revolution: The Communist Bid for Power in Germany, 1921–1923* by Werner T. Angress (Princeton, N.J.: Princeton University Press, 1963); the previously cited study of Communism in Germany by Ben Fowkes (New York: St. Martin's, 1984); *Revolution in Bavaria, 1918–1919: The Eisner Regime and the Soviet Republic* by Allen Mitchell (Princeton, N.J.: Princeton University Press, 1965); *Revolutionary Hamburg: Labor Politics in the Early Weimar Republic* by Richard A. Comfort (Stanford, Calif.: Stanford University Press, 1966); and *Nazis and Workers: National Socialist Appeals to German Labor, 1919–1933* by Max H. Kele (Chapel Hill: University of North Carolina Press, 1972).

The Nazi Revolution: Hitler's Dictatorship and the German Nation, edited by John L. Snell and revised by Allan Mitchell (2d ed., Lexington, Mass.: Heath, 1973), introduces a wide range of interpretations (with accompanying biography) regarding the origins and significance of the Third Reich. For ten important articles from the leading German journal on contemporary history, see *Republic to Reich: The Making of the Nazi Revolution,* edited with an introduction by Hajo Holborn, translated by Ralph Manheim (New York: Pantheon, 1972). Another symposium, translated by John Conway and published with an introduction by Fritz Stern, is composed of ten broadcasts by North German Radio on *The Path to Dictatorship, 1918–1933* (Garden City, N.Y.: Anchor, 1966).

Though dated, the biography of Hitler by Alan Bullock, *Hitler: A Study in Tyranny* (rev. ed., New York: Harper & Row, 1962; rpt., Harper Torchbooks, 1964), suffers surprisingly little by comparison with later attempts. Many of these do take into account more recent research, but the accumulation of additional data does not necessarily lead to a better overall understanding of Hitler. In his ambiguity and ambivalence, he posthumously seems to elude some biographers and historians as readily as he once confounded politicians and statesmen. Among the more recent works that can be recommended are Joachim Fest's full-length biography *Hitler,* translated by Richard and Clara Winston (New York: Harcourt Brace Jovanovich, 1974; paperback rpt., New York: Vintage Books, 1975), and Norman Stone's biographical essay, *Hitler* (London: Hodder and Stoughton, 1980).

The challenge posed by Hitler's elusive complexity was itself a central concern of the late Göttingen historian Percy E. Schramm. Assigned to Hitler's headquarters as war diary officer, he defied orders to destroy the diary in 1945 and subsequently published it in four massive volumes. In an extended introductory essay to the war diary, he analyzed Hitler's performance as a warlord. In a corresponding introductory essay to a German edition of Hitler's transcribed wartime table conversations, Schramm evaluated in contemporary context the dictator's statements about himself, his ideas, and his historical role. These two essays form the core of Percy Ernst Schramm, *Hitler: The Man and the Military Leader,* edited and translated with an introduction by Donald S. Detwiler (Chicago: Quadrangle, 1971; paperback rpt., Malabar, Fla.: Krieger, 1986). The table conversations themselves are available in English as *Hitler's Secret Conversations, 1941–1944,* translated by Norman Cameron and R. H. Stevens, with an introduction by H. R. Trevor-Roper (New York: Farrar, Straus and Young, 1953, rpt., New York: Signet Books, 1961). The complete edition of the war diary of the High Command of the German Armed Forces (commonly referred to as the OKW, for *Oberkommando der Wehrmacht*) is available only in German, but extensive draft segments were compiled in English translation for the U.S. Army after the war, when Schramm and his associates were prisoners of war, and the typescript of this translation was published, in facsimile, as a five-volume segment of a 24-volume collection: Part IV, "The OKW War Diary Series," vols. 7–11, *World War II German Military Studies,* D. S. Detwiler, ed., C. B. Burdick and J. Rohwer, assoc. eds. (New York & London: Garland, 1979). See also *Blitzkrieg to Defeat: Hitler's War Directives, 1939–1945,* edited, with an introduction and commentary, by H. R. Trevor-Roper (New York: Holt, Rinehart and Winston; London: Sidgwick & Jackson, 1964). Studies of the history of the war are cited below. For selections from the extensive literature on the dictator and further bibliography on him see, in addition to the Snell and Mitchell volume cited above, George H. Stein, ed., *Hitler* (Englewood Cliffs, N.J.: Spectrum Books, 1968).

A Selected Bibliography

Karl Dietrich Bracher, *The German Dictatorship: The Origins, Structure, and Effects of National Socialism,* translated by Jean Steinberg, with an introduction by Peter Gay (New York: Praeger, 1970), is a balanced synthesis of postwar scholarship on Hitler's Third Reich; it also has an extensive bibliography. For a brief introduction (with bibliographical notes), addressed to the student, see Jeremy Noakes, ed., *Government, Party and People in Nazi Germany,* Exeter Studies in History, no. 2 (Exeter: University of Exeter; Atlantic Highlands, N.J.: Humanities Press, 1980). See also Martin Broszat's *The Hitler State: The Foundation and Development of the Internal Structure of the Third Reich,* translated by John W. Hiden (London and New York: Longman, 1981); Dietrich Orlow, *The History of the Nazi Party* (2 vols., Pittsburgh, Pa.: University of Pittsburgh Press, 1969 and 1973, respectively); David Schoenbaum, *Hitler's Social Revolution: Class and Status in Nazi Germany, 1933–1939* (Garden City, N.Y.: Doubleday, 1966; rpt., New York: Norton, 1980); Helmut Krausnick, Hans Buchheim, Martin Broszat, and Hans Adolf Jacobsen, *The Anatomy of the S.S. State,* translated by R. Barry, M. Jackson, and D. Long, introduction by Elizabeth Wiskemann (New York: Walker, 1968); and Robert Lewis Koehl, *The Black Corps: The Structure and Power Struggles of the Nazi SS* (Madison: University of Wisconsin Press, 1983).

On the background of anti-Semitism during the Third Reich, see Peter G. J. Pulzer, *The Rise of Political Anti-Semitism in Germany and Austria* (New York: Wiley, 1964) and Solomon Liptzin, *Germany's Stepchildren* (Philadelphia: Jewish Publication Society of America, 1944; rpt., Cleveland, Ohio: Meridian Books, 1961). The institutionalized anti-Semitism of the prewar Third Reich is analyzed by Karl A. Schleunes in *The Twisted Road to Auschwitz: Nazi Policy toward German Jews, 1933–1939* (Urbana: University of Illinois Press, 1970). A concise introduction to the systematic genocide program implemented during the war is given in Jacob Robinson et al., *Holocaust,* Israel Pocket Library (Jerusalem: Keter Publishing House, 1974), a booklet with material originally published in the *Encyclopaedia Judaica,* including a 57-page history of the Holocaust and articles on the attitude of the Christian churches and on Jewish partisans. Martin Gilbert, *The Macmillan Atlas of the Holocaust* (New York: Macmillan, 1982) includes a concise narrative and a detailed index. Yehuda Bauer, *A History of the Holocaust* (New York: Franklin Watts, 1982) is readable, well documented, and includes a bibliography and a dozen of Martin Gilbert's maps. A heavily annotated study based on original source materials is *The Destruction of the European Jews* (rev. ed., 3 vols., New York: Holmes & Meier, 1985) by Raul Hilberg, who edited, with commentary, *Documents of Destruction: Germany and Jewry, 1933–1945* (Chicago: Quadrangle, 1971).

A sense of both the reality and the enormity of what was done to the Jewish people from 1933 to 1945 is conveyed by an extensive collection of contemporary records (some two-thirds in English or English translation) compiled from the Nürnberg Trial files and other holdings at the U.S. National Archives, and published in facsimile, John Mendelsohn, ed., D. S. Detwiler, advisory ed., *The Holocaust: Selected Documents*, 18 vols. (New York: Garland, 1982). On the role of Hitler in the Holocaust, euphemistically referred to in National Socialist jargon as the "Final Solution to the Jewish Question," see Gerald Fleming, *Hitler and the Final Solution,* with an introduction by Saul Friedländer (Berkeley and Los Angeles: University of California Press, 1984; rpt., paperback ed., 1987). The fundamental challenge of coming to terms with the inconceivable is brilliantly analyzed in a concise monograph by Walter Laqueur, *The Terrible Secret: Suppression of the Truth about Hitler's "Final Solution"* (London: Weidenfeld and Nicolson, 1980; Boston: Little, Brown, 1981; paperback rpt., New York: Penguin Books, 1982). One of the most widely read works related to the Holocaust has been *Eichmann in Jerusalem: A Report on the Banality of Evil* (rev. ed., New York: Viking, 1964; paperback rpt., Viking Penguin), by Hannah Arendt, author of the previously cited standard work *The Origins of Totalitarianism.* She initially wrote her report on the SS genocide administrator's trial in Jerusalem as a series of articles for the *New Yorker.* At his trial, Eichmann touched on what proved to be a very sensitive point. In *The Destruction of the European Jews* (cited above), the Jewish historian Raul Hilberg had already reported on widespread Jewish acquiescence in the Holocaust. At the Jerusalem trial in 1961, however, Eichmann stressed that it had not merely been acquiescence, but active collaboration, immeasurably facilitating his work. A German Jewess by birth, Arendt wrote of this collaboration being to a Jew "undoubtedly the darkest chapter of the whole dark story" (p. 117). *They Fought Back: The Story of Jewish Resistance in Nazi Europe,* edited and translated by Yuri Suhl (New York: Crown, 1967; paperback rpt., New York: Schocken, 1975) documents the untenability of any allegation of universal acquiescence or collaboration, but also makes it clear that resistance was limited (Goebbels, for example, dismissed the Warsaw Ghetto uprising as an impressively grim joke). The central issue as restated by Eichmann (it was not new, but rather rekindled by him) and elaborated into a widely publicized indictment by Hannah Arendt, has been directly addressed in a meticulously researched seven-hundred-page study by Isaiah Trunk, *Judenrat: The Jewish Councils in Eastern Europe under Nazi Occupation,* with an introduction by Jacob Robinson (New York: Macmillan, 1972). Trunk makes it possible for his reader to begin to understand a situation in which for all but a few Jewish leaders the question whether to collaborate or to resist did not even arise. For most, including the great Berlin rabbi Leo Baeck (who was finally sent to Theresienstadt but lived to be liberated), the only meaningful question was what might be done to ease the tragic fate of the people looking to them for guidance and wisdom in the shadow of death. For a first-person account of Rabbi Leo Baeck, see Eric H. Boehm, *We Survived: Fourteen Histories of the Hidden and Hunted of Nazi Germany* (New Haven, Conn.: Yale University Press, 1949; rpt., Santa Barbara, Calif.: ABC-Clio Information Services, 1985).

The German Church Struggle and the Holocaust, edited by Franklin H. Littell and Hubert G. Locke (Detroit, Mich.: Wayne State University Press, 1974), grew out of an international and interdisciplinary conference of specialists on the National Socialist onslaught against both Jews and Christians, whether Catholic or Protestant. A comprehensive history of the Christian churches, including sects and free churches, under Hitler, was written by Ernst Christian Helmreich, *The German Churches under Hitler: Background, Struggle, and Epilogue* (Detroit, Mich.: Wayne State University Press, 1979), which begins with a hundred-page "Background" segment reviewing the churches' status and role in Germany from the Reformation to 1933. Peter Matheson, ed., *The Third Reich and the Christian Churches* (Edinburgh: T. & T. Clark, 1981), is a hundred-page volume with translated selections (many with explanatory headnotes) documenting church-state relations. On the Jewish community, see, in addition to the volume by Yehuda Bauer and related titles cited above, Leonard Baker, *Days of Sorrow and Pain: Leo Baeck and the Berlin Jews* (New York: Macmillan; London: Collier Macmillan, 1978), and, for general background, Heinz Moshe Graupe, *The Rise of Modern Judaism: An Intellectual History of German Jewry 1650–1942,* translated by John Robinson (Huntington, N.Y.: Krieger, 1979).

The means by which Hitler gained control of the German armed forces at the price of provoking clandestine opposition is traced by Harold C. Deutsch in *Hitler and His Generals: The Hidden Crisis, January–June 1938* (Minneapolis: University of Minnesota Press, 1974); see also Deutsch's study of the opposition to Hitler early in the war among leading military figures, *The Conspiracy against Hitler in the Twilight War* (Minneapolis: University of Minnesota Press, 1968). For comprehensive treatment, see Peter Hoffmann's large volume, *The History of the German Resistance, 1933–1945*, 3rd ed., translated by Richard Barry (London: MacDonald & Jane's; Cambridge: MIT Press, 1977). A concise early interpretation that has been borne out by research since its initial publication in 1948 is the essay by Hans Rothfels, *The German Opposition to Hitler: An Appraisal*, translated by Lawrence Wilson (London: Wolff, 1961; Chicago: Regnery, 1962; paperback rpt., 1970). See also Eberhard Zeller's prize-winning *The Flame of Freedom: The German Struggle against Hitler,* translated from the fourth German edition by R. P. Heller and D. R. Masters (Coral Gables, Fla.: University of Miami Press, 1969), a well-balanced, readable survey of the opposition in all walks of life, emphasizing the background and aftermath of the assassination attempt of 20 July 1944; Gerhard Ritter's *The German Resistance: Carl Goerdeler's Struggle against Tyranny*, abridged translation by R. T. Clark (New York: Praeger, 1958; rpt., Freeport, N.J.: Books for Libraries, 1970); Inge Scholl, *Students against Tyranny: The Resistance of the White Rose, Munich, 1942–1943*, translated by Arthur R. Schultz (Middletown, Conn.: Wesleyan University Press, 1970), a personal account of an idealistic student group, and the more recent study by Richard Hanser, *A Noble Treason: The Revolt of the Munich Students against Hitler* (New York: Putnam's, 1979); and the memoir by Sabine Leibholz-Bonhoeffer, twin sister of the theologian Dietrich Bonhoeffer, niece of General Paul von Hase, and sister-in-law of the jurist Hans von Dohnanyi (all three important resistance figures who were murdered in April 1945), *The Bonhoeffers: Portrait of a Family* (New York: St. Martin's, 1972), with a preface by Eberhard Bethge, author of her brother's biography, *Dietrich Bonhoeffer: Man of Vision, Man of Courage*, translated by Eric Mosbacher et al. (New York: Harper & Row, 1970). For an introduction to the opposition abroad, see *Exile Literature 1933–1945* (Bad Godesberg: Inter Nationes, 1968), with addresses by Golo Mann and Hans Mayer, and a listing of works written in exile; and the brilliant synopsis, with partially annotated bibliography, by Egbert Krispyn, *Anti-Nazi Writers in Exile* (Athens: University of Georgia Press, 1978).

A Selected Bibliography

One reason there was not more resistance to the National Socialist regime was that the climate of opinion in the Third Reich was controlled and cultivated with sophistication by Hitler's minister of propaganda, the subject of Ernest K. Bramsted's *Goebbels and National Socialist Propaganda, 1925–1945* (East Lansing: Michigan State University Press, 1965). See also Helmut Heiber, *Goebbels*, translated by John K. Dickinson (New York: Hawthorn, 1972); Oron J. Hale, *The Captive Press in the Third Reich* (Princeton, N.J.: Princeton University Press, 1964); Z. A. B. Zeman, *Nazi Propaganda* (2d ed., New York: Oxford University Press, 1973); Jay W. Baird, *The Mythical World of Nazi War Propaganda, 1939–1945* (Minneapolis: University of Minnesota Press, 1974); and Ian Kershaw, *Popular Opinion and Political Dissent in the Third Reich: Bavaria, 1933–1945* (New York: Oxford University Press, 1983). On art and film during the period, see Berthold Hinz, *Art in the Third Reich*, translated by Robert and Rita Kimber (New York: Pantheon, 1979); David Welch, *Propaganda and the German Cinema, 1933–1945* (New York: Oxford University Press, 1983); and Richard Meran Barsam, *Filmguide to "Triumph of the Will"*, Indiana University Press Filmguide Series, no. 10 (Bloomington: Indiana University Press, 1975), a guide to Leni Riefenstahl's remarkable film of the 1934 National Socialist Party Congress, which provides the most effective cinematographical projection of Hitler extant.

For a concise introduction to the German economy under Hitler, see the fourth chapter, "The Economy of the Third Reich 1933–1945," in Karl Hardach, *The Political Economy of Germany in the Twentieth Century* (Berkeley and Los Angeles: University of California Press, 1980). See also Jurgen Kuczynski, *Germany: Economic and Labour Conditions under Fascism* (New York: International Publishers, 1945); J. E. Farquharson's *The Plough and the Swastika: The NSDAP and Agriculture in Germany 1928–45* (London: Sage, 1976); and Arthur Schweitzer's *Big Business in the Third Reich* (Bloomington: Indiana University Press, 1964). William Manchester's *The Arms of Krupp, 1587–1968* (Boston: Little, Brown, 1968) is a journalistic account of the leading German steel and munitions concern and the family that owned it. It gives considerable emphasis to the role of the Krupp family and firm during the Third Reich and to the postwar period, when Alfried Krupp, who had managed the firm during World War II, using slave labor, was sentenced to imprisonment as a war criminal in 1948, only to be pardoned three years later. Manchester's book is not fully documented, but has an extensive bibliography with relevant works in English. See also Joseph Borkin, *The Crime and Punishment of I.G. Farben* (New York: The Free Press, 1978), on the German industrial cartel that during World War II operated a large production complex at Auschwitz; and Benjamin B. Ferencz, *Less than Slaves: Jewish Forced Labor and the Quest for Compensation*, foreword by Telford Taylor (Cambridge: Harvard University Press, 1979), on the postwar legal effort on behalf of forced laborers to secure belated financial reimbursement (postwar German indemnification law provided about a dollar a day for false imprisonment, but no compensation for their slave labor).

Standard works on economic mobilization and rearmament are Burton H. Klein, *Germany's Economic Preparations for War* (Cambridge: Harvard University Press, 1959); Berenice A. Carroll, *Design for Total War: Arms and Economics in the Third Reich* (The Hague: Mouton, 1968); Wilhelm Deist, *The Wehrmacht and German Rearmament* (Toronto: University of Toronto Press, 1981); Edward L. Homze, *Arming the Luftwaffe: The Reich Air Ministry and the German Aircraft Industry, 1919–39* (Lincoln: University of Nebraska Press, 1976); and Alan S. Milward, *The German Economy at War* (London: University of London, Athlone Press, 1965). On Albert Speer's best-selling, carefully crafted autobiography, *Inside the Third Reich: Memoirs,* translated by Richard and Clara Winston, introduction by Eugene Davidson (New York: Macmillan, 1970), see Matthias Schmidt, *Albert Speer: The End of a Myth,* translated by Joachim Neugroschel (New York: St. Martin's, 1984), a book-length critique, documenting inaccuracies and misrepresentations. An account of Speer that can be recommended will be found in *The Face of the Third Reich: Portraits of the Nazi Leadership,* translated by Michael Bullock (London: Weidenfeld and Nicolson; New York: Pantheon, 1970), by Joachim Fest. The volume includes a sixty-five-page study of Hitler and biographical essays on Hermann Göring, Joseph Goebbels, Reinhard Heydrich, Heinrich Himmler, Martin Bormann, Rudolf Hess, and others.

Gerhard Weinberg, *The Foreign Policy of Hitler's Germany,* vol. 1: *Diplomatic Revolution in Europe, 1933–36,* and vol. 2: *Starting World War II, 1937–1939* (Chicago: University of Chicago Press, 1970 & 1980, respectively) provides thoroughly documented, objective treatment of German foreign relations from Hitler's accession to power to his attack on Poland; it is complemented, for the war years, by Weinberg's *World in the Balance: Behind the Scenes of World War*

A Selected Bibliography

II (Hanover, N.H.: University Press of New England, 1981). See also Norman Rich, *Hitler's War Aims*, vol. 1: *Ideology, the Nazi State, and the Course of Expansion*, and vol. 2: *The Establishment of the New Order* (New York: Norton, 1973 and 1974, respectively), a scholarly but readable narrative of Hitler's aggression in the context of German history and National Socialist ideology; Rich's extensive backnotes (explanatory as well as documentary), indices, glossaries of abbreviations, biographical sketches, and together over fifty pages of critical bibliography make the work useful also for reference. A study of how the German Foreign Office was systematically undermined by the National Socialists (in a process analogous to that described by Harold Deutsch with reference to the military in *Hitler and His Generals*, cited above) is Paul Seabury's *The Wilhelmstrasse: A Study of German Diplomats under the Nazi Regime* (Berkeley and Los Angeles: University of California Press, 1954), which may be supplemented by the memoirs of a Foreign Office insider, Paul Schmidt, *Hitler's Interpreter*, abridged translation by R. H. C. Steed (New York: Macmillan, 1951). *German Foreign Policy, 1918–1945: A Guide to Research and Research Materials,* compiled and edited by Christoph M. Kimmich (Wilmington, Del.: Scholarly Resources, 1981), provides basic bibliography and information about reference resources on Germany from the end of the First World War to the end of the Second, including three major publications in English: *Documents on German Foreign Policy, 1918–1945,* Series C (1933–1937), 6 vols., and Series D (1937–1941), 13 vols. (Washington, D.C.: U.S. Government Printing Office; London: H.M. Stationery Office, 1949–1983); *The Trial of the Major War Criminals before the International Military Tribunal, Nuremberg, 14 November 1945–1 October 1946,* 42 vols. (Nuremberg, 1947–1949), with companion documentation issued by the Office of the U.S. Chief of Counsel as *Nazi Conspiracy and Aggression,* 10 vols. (Washington, D.C.: U.S. Government Printing Office, 1946–48); and records of the twelve U.S. Military Tribunal Trials, issued by the Department of the Army, *Trials of War Criminals before the Nuernberg Military Tribunals under Control Council Law No. 10, October 1946–April 1940,* 15 vols. (Washington, D.C.: U.S. Government Printing Office, 1949–1953).

Useful compilations of material on the background and origins of the Second World War, each with a bibliography, are Francis L. Loewenheim's *Peace or Appeasement? Hitler, Chamberlain, and the Munich Crisis* (Boston: Houghton Mifflin, 1965); Keith Eubank's *World War II: Roots and Causes* (Lexington, Mass.: Heath, 1975);

and Gordon Martel's *The Origins of the Second World War Reconsidered: The A. J. P. Taylor Debate after Twenty-five Years* (Boston and London: Allen & Unwin, 1986). On the course of the war, see, in addition to previously cited works such as the full-length biographies by Bullock and by Fest, the well-structured, extensively documented account by Hans-Adolf Jacobsen and Arthur L. Smith, Jr., *World War II Policy and Strategy: Selected Documents with Commentary* (Santa Barbara, Calif.: Clio Books, 1979), and Gordon Wright's classic synthesis, in the Rise of Modern Europe series, *The Ordeal of Total War, 1939–1945* (New York: Harper & Row, 1968; rpt., Harper Torchbooks), which has a thirty-five-page bibliographical essay. Williamson Murray, *Luftwaffe* (rev. ed., Baltimore, Md.: Nautical & Aviation, 1985), is a history of the German air force from its establishment as an independent service branch in the 1930s to its destruction at the end of World War II. On an area in which there has been a good deal of ill-informed, popular writing, German espionage and intelligence during the war, see David Kahn, *Hitler's Spies: German Military Intelligence in World War II* (New York: Macmillan, 1978), a readable history of the organization, operations, and rivalries of the military and party agencies in the "shadow war." Kahn's meticulously documented account, which grew out of his Oxford doctoral dissertation under H. R. Trevor-Roper, provides insight not only on German wartime intelligence, but on the structure and character of the Hitler regime and its conduct of the war.

The German perspective is reflected in Hans-Adolf Jacobsen and Jürgen Rohwer, eds., *Decisive Battles of World War II: The German View,* translated by Edward Fitzgerald, with an introduction by Cyril Falls (New York: Putnam, 1965), and Vice Admiral Friedrich Ruge, *Der Seekrieg: The German Navy's Story,* translated by M. G. Saunders (Annapolis, Md.: U.S. Naval Institute, 1957). On the ideological character of Hitler's military leadership and wartime strategy, see Andreas Dorpalen, "Hitler, the Nazi Party, and the Wehrmacht in World War II," pp. 66–90 in Harry L. Coles, ed., *Total War and Cold War: Problems in Civilian Control of the Military* (Columbus: Ohio State University Press, 1962). In Dorpalen's view, summarized in a letter to the writer on 9 January 1975, "Hitler's military strategy after 1941 should not be judged in military terms. Hitler knew by then that he could no longer win the war militarily; all he could do and did do was to play for time in the hope that he might find some non-military solution. From this perspective, I believe his was the best possible strategy he could pursue."

A Selected Bibliography

Whereas Dorpalen, in his illuminating article, makes a major contribution to our objective understanding of Hitler's war, the British historian David Irving, in his 926-page *Hitler's War* (New York: Viking, 1977), has attempted to go a step further, presenting the war from what he considers to have been the dictator's point of view. In a personal conversation at a symposium at the U.S. Naval Academy (Annapolis, Md., October 1977), he said quite seriously that his purpose had been to write the book Hitler would have written if he could have. Whether or not Irving's work would have been acceptable to Hitler, something approximating the dictator's cast of mind is provocatively reflected in much of what Irving has skillfully written, generating a debate that, in the end, may contribute to a deeper understanding of the Third Reich and the Second World War.

Another work presenting an historically significant but rarely appreciated perspective is *Rebel Patriot: A Biography of Franz von Papen* by Henry M. and Robin K. Adams (Santa Barbara, Calif.: McNally & Loftin, 1987), a full-length account of the life and times of a conservative, Catholic aristocrat who was one of the last chancellors of the Weimar Republic. Considering Hitler's accession to power inevitable, he supported him at the beginning of his regime as vice-chancellor and subsequently as ambassador to Austria on the eve of its annexation and as ambassador to Turkey during the war. Acquitted of major war crimes by the International Military Tribunal at Nuremberg but shunned in postwar Germany as an accomplice if not partner of Hitler, Papen found, in the last decade of his long life (1879–1969), a biographer to write this candidly sympathetic, copiously documented work. It is not a critical, definitive study of Papen, but it should be invaluable to anyone who may attempt such a work and it will be useful to anyone seeking insight into one of the more important and, in many ways, one of the most representative Germans of his time.

The human dimensions of the war and its immediate aftermath are reflected in *Last Letters from Stalingrad,* translated by Franz Schneider and Charles Gullans, introduction by S. L. A. Marshall (New York: Morrow; 1962; rpt., New York: Signet Books, 1965); Friedrich Percyval Reck-Malleczewen, *Diary of a Man in Despair,* translated by Paul Rubens (New York: Macmillan, 1970); and Count Hans von Lehndorff's *Token of a Covenant: Diary of an East Prussian Surgeon, 1945–1947,* translated by Elizabeth Mayer, introduction by Paul Tillich (Chicago: Regnery, 1964). Radically different in character is Ernst von Salomon's *Fragebogen: The Questionnaire,* translated by Constantine FitzGibbon, preface by Goronwy Rees (Garden City, N.Y.: Doubleday, 1955), a 525-page answer to the 131-item questionnaire to be filled out for the occupation authorities.

POSTWAR GERMANY

A concise, lucid introduction to postwar Germany is Henry Ashby Turner, Jr., *The Two Germanies since 1945* (New Haven, Conn.: Yale University Press, 1987). Other general works are Alfred Grosser, *Germany in Our Time: A Political History of the Postwar Years*, translated by Paul Stephenson (New York: Praeger, 1971), Arnold J. Heidenheimer, *The Governments of Germany* (rev. ed., New York: Crowell, 1966), and Rudolf Walter Leonhardt, *This Germany: The Story since the Third Reich*, translated by Catherine Hutter (New York: New York Graphic Society, 1964; rpt., Baltimore: Penguin, 1964). For a systematic analysis of the society of the Federal Republic comparable in intent to Alexis de Tocqueville's *Democracy in America*, see *Society and Democracy in Germany* (Garden City, N.Y.: Doubleday, 1967; paperback rpt., Doubleday Anchor, 1969) by Ralf Dahrendorf, a German sociologist and former liberal member of the Bonn parliament who became director of the London School of Economics. A number of key issues of historical, political, and cultural interest are dealt with in a symposium edited by Louis F. Helbig and Eberhard Reichmann, *Teaching Postwar Germany in America: Papers and Discussions — German Studies Conference, 1972* (Bloomington: Indiana University Institute of German Studies, 1972). The standard surveys in the Nations of the World series, *West Germany* by Michael Balfour and *East Germany* by David Childs (New York: Praeger, 1968 and 1969, respectively), have been superseded by Balfour, *West Germany: A Contemporary History* (London & Canberra: Croom Helm, 1982) and by Childs, *The GDR: Moscow's German Ally* and Childs, ed., *Honecker's Germany* (London: Allen & Unwin, 1983 and 1985, respectively).

The occupation of Germany as a whole is covered in *Documents on Germany under Occupation, 1945–1954*, selected and edited by Beate Ruhm von Oppen, with a preface by Alan Bullock (London: Oxford University Press, 1955). On the early Soviet occupation and establishment of the East German satellite regime, see John P. Nettl, *The Eastern Zone and Soviet Policy in Germany, 1945–1950* (London: Oxford University Press, 1951; rpt., Ann Arbor, Mich.: University Microfilms International, on demand). The crisis that shook the Ulbricht regime is the subject of Arnulf Baring's *Uprising in East Germany: June 17, 1953,* translated by Gerald Onn, with an introduction by David Schoenbaum and a foreword by Richard Lowenthal (Ithaca, N.Y.: Cornell University Press, 1972). On the first postwar East German dictator, see Carola Stern, *Ulbricht: A Political Biography,* translated by Abe Farbstein (New York: Praeger, 1965). On his successor, there is a study by Heinz Lippmann, *Honecker and the New Politics of Europe,* translated by Helen Sebba (New York: Macmillan, 1972), and, in the Leaders of the World series, the translation of Erich Honecker's autobiography, *From My Life,* preface by Robert Maxwell (Oxford: Pergamon, 1981). See also Jean Edward Smith, *Germany beyond the Wall: People, Politics . . . and Prosperity* (Boston: Little, Brown, 1969); John Dornberg, *The Other Germany* (Garden City, N.Y.: Doubleday, 1968), and his later work that deals with both West and East Germany, *The New Germans: Thirty Years After* (New York: Macmillan, 1975); Hans Axel Holm, *The Other Germans: Report from an East German Town,* translated from the Swedish by Thomas Teal (New York: Pantheon, 1970); Peter Christian Ludz, *The Changing Party Elite in East Germany,* translated by the Israel Program for Scientific Translations (Cambridge: MIT Press, 1972), as well as Ludz' *The German Democratic Republic from the Sixties to the Seventies* (Cambridge: Harvard University Center for International Affairs, 1970), with a bibliographical appendix; C. Bradley Scharf, *Politics and Change in East Germany: An Evaluation of Socialist Democracy* (Boulder, Colo.: Westview; London: Frances Pinter, 1984); *GDR Foreign Policy,* edited by Eberhard Schulz et al., translated by Michael Vale (Armonk, N.Y.: M. E. Sharpe, 1982); and two collections of nine papers each, edited by Ian Wallace and published in the GDR Monitor Series, *The GDR under Honecker 1971–1981* and *The GDR in the 1980s* (Dundee, Scotland: GDR Monitor, 1981 and 1984, respectively). Martin McCauley, *The German Democratic Republic since 1945* (London: Macmillan, 1983) includes an extensive chronological table of events.

Adolph Schalk, *The Germans* (Englewood Cliffs, N.J.: Prentice-Hall, 1971), with a detailed index, is a chatty, heavily detailed introduction to the Federal Republic by an American journalist with years of experience in writing on West Germany for Americans stationed there after World War II. Another American whose background is reflected in an authoritative work is the former chief of the Historical

Division of the U.S. High Commission for Germany, Harold Zink, author of *The United States in Germany, 1944–1955* (Princeton, N.J.: Van Nostrand, 1957). See also Eugene Davidson, *The Death and Life of Germany: An Account of the American Occupation* (New York: Alfred Knopf, 1959), and the 1421-page volume of documents on German-American relations from the war to the mid-1980s issued by the United States Department of State, *Documents on Germany 1944–1985* (Washington, D.C.: U.S. Government Printing Office, 1985).

The decisive role of the key figure in American policy in Germany in the late 1940s is brought out by John H. Backer, a former U.S. military government official in Germany, in his study *Winds of History: The German Years of Lucius DuBignon Clay,* foreword by John J. McCloy (New York: Van Nostrand Reinhold, 1983). As U.S. commander in chief in Europe and military governor of Germany, Clay played a crucial part reversing American policy toward Germany and laying the foundations for the establishment of a democratic West German republic. What emerges more clearly from Backer's account than from Clay's politic memoirs published after his retirement, *Decision in Germany* (Garden City, N.Y.: Doubleday, 1950), or from J. E. Smith, ed., *The Papers of General Lucius D. Clay: Germany, 1945–1949,* 2 vols. (Bloomington: Indiana University Press, 1974), is that however difficult Clay's relations may have been with the Russians and the French, the greatest challenge he faced in Germany was the combination of opposition, inertia, and lack of understanding with which he was confronted in Washington — where his views prevailed less because of his will to impose them than because it was no secret that he would insist on his well-deserved and long-deferred retirement if called upon to implement a policy that he could not in good faith support. See also two other studies by John H. Backer, *Priming the German Economy: American Occupational Policies, 1945–1948* and *The Decision to Divide Germany: American Foreign Policy in Transition* (Durham, N.C.: Duke University Press, 1971 and 1978, respectively), Edward N. Peterson, *The American Occupation of Germany: Retreat to Victory* (Detroit: Wayne State University Press, 1978), and Robert Wolfe, ed., *Americans as Proconsuls: United States Military Government in Germany and Japan, 1944–1952* (Carbondale and Edwardsville: Southern Illinois University Press, 1984), with reflections on the occupation of Germany by General Clay and by former U.S. high commissioner in Germany John J. McCloy, several illuminating papers on the occupation, and a listing of relevant archival holdings at the U.S. National Archives in Washington and the Public Record Office in London.

A local study of the U.S. occupation is John Gimbel, *A German Community under American Occupation: Marburg, 1945–52* (Stanford, Calif.: Stanford University Press, 1961), dealing with the town where Milton Mayer conducted the in-depth interviews on which he based his previously cited *They Thought They Were Free.* Books dealing with the British and French in postwar Germany are: Arthur Hearnden, ed., *The British in Germany* (London: Hamilton, 1978), and F. Roy Willis, *The French in Germany, 1945–1949* and *France, Germany, and the New Europe, 1945–1967,* rev. & exp. ed. (Stanford, Calif.: Stanford University Press, 1962 and 1968, respectively).

On the basis of his administrative role (as the former American secretary and secretary-general of the Allied High Commission in Bonn) in the complex process of drawing up the West German constitution and establishing the Bonn government, John Ford Golay wrote *The Founding of the Federal Republic of Germany* (Chicago: University of Chicago Press, 1958; rpt., University of Chicago Press Midway Reprints). Golay's detailed monograph, with its painstaking elucidation of the often technical considerations behind individual constitutional provisions, is complemented by the broader study of Peter H. Merkl, *The Origin of the West German Republic* (New York: Oxford University Press, 1963). On the postwar trials of German war criminals, see Bradley F. Smith, *The Road to Nuremberg* (New York: Basic Books, 1981), an account on the background of the trials; B. F. Smith, ed., *The American Road to Nuremberg: The Documentary Record, 1944–1945* (Stanford, Calif.: Hoover Institution Press, 1982), with American documentation on this background; and Smith's *Reaching Judgment at Nuremberg* (New York: Basic Books, 1977), an account of the trial of the major war criminals before the International Military Tribunal in Nuremberg. Adalbert Rückerl, *The Investigation of Nazi Crimes, 1945–1978: A Documentation,* translated by Derek Rutter (Hamden, Conn.: Archon Books, 1980), is a 145-page monograph, with documentary extracts, providing concise coverage not only of the International Military Tribunal, but also the prosecution of war criminals in Allied, West German, East German, and Austrian courts. See also the perceptive first-person account of a member of the British War Crimes Executive Team, Airey Neave, *On Trial at Nuremberg,* with a foreword by Rebecca West (Boston and Toronto: Little, Brown, 1978); Eugene Davidson, *The Trial of the Germans* (New York: Macmillan, 1966); the relevant selections in Jay

W. Baird, ed., *From Nuremberg to My Lai* (Lexington, Mass.: Heath, 1972), which has a useful bibliography; and Hannah Arendt's previously cited *Eichmann in Jerusalem.*

A readable study of West Germany's postwar recovery is Aidan Crawley's *The Rise of Western Germany, 1945–1972* (London: Collins, 1973, which was issued the same year in the United States by Bobbs-Merrill, Indianapolis, under the less appropriate title, *The Spoils of War: The Rise of Western Germany since 1945*). A veteran newscaster and television executive who served one term in Parliament as a Labourite and another as a Conservative, Crawley includes an account of the cooperative role of government and finance in the postwar economic recovery of West Germany, and also a concise explanation of the closely related system of compulsory industrial codetermination in heavy industry, a legally mandated program assuring employee representatives an important role in management — with the result that many of the conflicts that elsewhere would lead to strikes are frequently resolved in the relatively productive West German economy without a single person losing a single day of work (or a single order being delayed). For more recent, detailed treatment of this aspect of labor-management relations, see James C. Furlong, *Labor in the Boardroom: The Peaceful Revolution* (Princeton, N.J.: Dow Jones Books, 1977), which takes into account the extension, under the terms of the West German Codetermination Act of 1976, of what is called industrial democracy to joint-stock companies with more than two thousand employees.

A politically oriented introduction to the first Bonn administration is *The Adenauer Era* by Richard Hiscocks (Philadelphia: Lippincott, 1966). Arnold J. Heidenheimer's *Adenauer and the CDU: The Rise of the Leader and the Integration of the Party* (The Hague: Nijhoff, 1960) may be supplemented by the first volume of Adenauer's *Memoirs, 1945–53*, translated by Beate Ruhm von Oppen (Chicago: Regnery, 1966); the subsequent three volumes (covering 1953–55, 1955–59, and 1959–63, respectively), published in Stuttgart, 1966–68, have not yet been published in English translation. See also *Konrad Adenauer: 1876–1967* (Chicago: Cowles, 1971) by Terence Prittie, the German correspondent and bureau chief of the *Manchester Guardian* from 1949 to 1963, the year Adenauer stepped down from the chancellorship. Prittie also wrote a biography of Adenauer's first Social Democratic successor, *Willy Brandt: Portrait of a Statesman* (New York: Schocken, 1974); his survey of the postwar period, *The Velvet Chancellors: A History of Post-War Ger-*

many (London: Frederick Muller, 1979), covers Konrad Adenauer (1949–1963), Ludwig Erhard (1963–66), Kurt Georg Kiesinger (1966–69), Willy Brandt (1969–1974), and the first years of Helmut Schmidt (1974–1982). On Brandt, see also the volume in which selections from his earlier writings are interwoven with a biographical essay, an extensive interview, and editorial commentary by Klaus Harpprecht, *Willy Brandt: Portrait and Self-Portrait,* translated by Hank Keller (Los Angeles: Nash, 1971). Brandt's volume of memoirs, *People and Politics: The Years 1960–1975,* translated by J. Maxwell Brownjohn (Boston and Toronto: Little, Brown, 1976), opens with the period when he was mayor of beleaguered Berlin and closes with his assessment of the situation of Germany and the world in the mid-seventies, following his resignation from the chancellorship after having set the course of Germany's *Ostpolitik,* a conciliatory policy toward the East. For an early account of Brandt's successor, see Jonathan Carr, *Helmut Schmidt: Helmsman of Germany* (New York: St. Martin's, 1985). On the most important of Brandt's predecessors as head of the postwar Social Democratic party, Lewis J. Edinger wrote *Kurt Schumacher: A Study in Personality and Political Behavior* (Stanford, Calif.: Stanford University Press, 1965). See also Edinger's *Politics in Germany* (Boston: Little, Brown, 1968); the concise introduction by Geoffrey K. Roberts, *West German Politics* (New York: Taplinger, 1972); the collection of studies edited by Klaus von Beyme and Manfred G. Schmidt, *Policy and Politics in the Federal Republic of Germany,* translated by Eileen Martin (Aldershot, Hants, England: Gower Publishing Co. for the German Political Science Association, 1985); Kendall L. Baker, Russell J. Dalton, and Kai Hildebrandt, *Germany Transformed: Political Culture and the New Politics* (Cambridge: Harvard University Press, 1981); and the well-annotated collection of translated documentation, *Politics and Government in the Federal Republic of Germany: Basic Documents,* edited by Carl-Christoph Schweitzer et al. (Leamington Spa: Berg Publishers, 1984). On the functioning of the East German political system, see John M. Starrels and Anita M. Mallinckrodt, *Politics in the German Democratic Republic* (New York: Praeger, 1975).

The legislative branch in the Federal Republic is the subject of a standard work by Gerhard Loewenberg, *Parliament in the German Political System* (Ithaca, N.Y.: Cornell University Press, 1967). For the English translation of a periodically reissued handbook, see *Kürschner's Popular Guide to the German Bundestag — 10th Parliament 1983* (Rheinbreitbach: NDV Neue Darmstädter Verlagsanstalt,

1984). On the supreme court of the Federal Republic, see Donald P. Kommers, *Judicial Politics in West Germany: A Study of the Federal Constitutional Court* (Beverly Hills, Calif.: Sage, 1976) and, for a collection of essays addressed to the English reader by one of the more influential West German supreme court justices, Gerhard Leibholz, *Politics and Law* (Leyden: Sythoff, 1965). An East German booklet provides information on *Law and Justice in a Socialist Society: The Legal System of the German Democratic Republic* (Berlin [East]: Panorama DDR, 1976).

Eric Owen Smith, *The West German Economy* (London: Croom Helm, 1983), with numerous charts, graphs, and figures, is a systematic presentation of the economy of the Federal Republic during its first three decades. See also the more popular account of Germany's postwar economic recovery by Ludwig Erhard, who served as minister of economics under Adenauer and succeeded him as chancellor, *Prosperity through Competition*, translated by Edith Temple Roberts and John B. Wood (London: Thames and Hudson, 1958). Articles and speeches by Erhard, who advocated a "social market economy," i.e., a market-driven economy with a minimum of state regulation, were published in a collection entitled *The Economics of Success*, translated by J. A. Arengo-Jones and D. J. S. Thomson (London: Thames and Hudson, 1963).

Two useful collections of articles, commissioned by Atlantik-Brücke, Hamburg, an organization for German-American understanding, were edited by Walter Stahl, with introduction by Norbert Muhlen, *Education for Democracy in West Germany* and *The Politics of Postwar Germany* (New York: Praeger, 1961 and 1963, respectively). Frederic Spotts, *The Churches and Politics in Germany* (Middletown, Conn.: Wesleyan University Press, 1973) is a well-informed, readable account, in historical context, of the churches (both Protestant and Catholic) in Germany (particularly the Federal Republic) since 1945, accounting for their organization and their position in state and society.

Peter H. Merkl, *German Foreign Policies, West and East: On the Threshold of a New European Era* (Santa Barbara, Calif.: ABC-Clio, 1974), is a good introduction to postwar German foreign relations. In Hans W. Gatzke's already cited volume in the American Foreign Policy Library, *Germany and the United States: A "Special Relationship"?*, German-American relations are examined in historical context, with particularly close attention to ties since 1945 between America and West Germany, and with a chapter on the German

Democratic Republic since 1961. The question of German unity and the problem of relations between the parts of Germany is addressed by David Calleo in *The German Problem Reconsidered: Germany and the World Order, 1870 to the Present* (Cambridge: Cambridge University Press, 1978). William E. Griffith, *The Ostpolitik of the Federal Republic of Germany* (Cambridge: MIT Press, 1978) is a study of Bonn's conciliatory policy toward the East that began with the establishment in the mid-sixties of the Grand Coalition and reached its culmination under Chancellor Brandt.

On intra-German relations, see Peter Christian Ludz, *Two Germanys in One World* (Westmead, England: Saxon House for the Atlantic Institute for International Affairs, 1973), and Lawrence L. Whetten, *Germany East and West: Conflicts, Collaboration, and Confrontation* (New York: New York University Press, 1980). English translations of the "Treaty on the Basis of Relations between the Federal Republic of Germany and the German Democratic Republic" of 1972, more commonly referred to as the Basic Treaty, and of the West German constitutional court decision on that controversial treaty are included in *German Unity: Documentation and Commentaries on the Basic Treaty*, ed., Frederick W. Hess, East Europe Monographs, 4 (Kansas City, Mo. 64152: Governmental Research Bureau, Park College, 1974). The 296-page paperback *Documentation Relating to the Federal Government's Policy of Détente* (Bonn: Press and Information Office of the Federal Republic of Germany, 1978) includes, in addition to the Basic Treaty, English texts of the West German treaties with the Soviet Union (1970), Poland (1970), and Czechoslovakia (1973), together with the Quadripartite Berlin Agreement (1971) between the four powers continuing to exercise sovereignty over the fallen capital.

Mark Arnold-Foster, *The Siege of Berlin* (London: Collins, 1979), is a concise, readable survey by the author of the BBC television series "The World at War" of the ordeal of Berlin from the end of World War II until the stabilization of its status under the four-power agreement a quarter of a century later. Jean Edward Smith, *The Defense of Berlin* (Baltimore, Md.: Johns Hopkins Press, 1963), provides a more detailed, annotated account from the wartime agreements regarding the occupation of the enemy capital to the aftermath of the building of the Berlin Wall in August 1961. On the 1961 Berlin crisis, see also the 54-page essay by Howard Trivers, the senior U.S. diplomat in Berlin when the Wall was built, in *Three Crises in American Foreign Affairs and a Continuing Revolution* (Carbondale and Edwardsville: Southern Illinois University Press, 1972). Honoré M. Catudal, Jr., *A Balance Sheet of the Quadripartite Agreement on Berlin: Evaluation and Documentation*, with a foreword by Ambassador Kenneth Rush (Berlin: Berlin Verlag, 1978) analyzes the political and economic situation of the city after the conclusion of the four-power agreement. Insight into the legal status of the occupied city and the sovereign authority exercised until unification in the U.S. Sector of West Berlin by American officials is provided by the striking memoir of a U.S. federal judge's unique assignment to Berlin, *Judgment in Berlin*, by Herbert J. Stern (New York: Universe Books, 1984). In 1978, an East German couple had highjacked a Polish airliner, forcing it to land in West rather than East Berlin. To exercise criminal jurisdiction, the United States Court for Berlin, which had previously existed only on paper, was constituted in January 1979, with the author, on loan from the U.S. District Court for New Jersey, presiding. Flagrant violations of the constitutional rights of one defendant by U.S. military authorities led the court (with the prosecution's mortified consent) to dismiss her case. Despite strenuous objections by the occupation authorities, the other defendant was granted a trial before a jury of Berliners. Found guilty on only one of several charges, he was, in the end, sentenced to serve only the time he had already spent in detention—with the result that he left the court a free man. In addition to this criminal case, a civil case that could not be tried in a German court was brought to the United States Court for Berlin: a suit by a group of Berliners contesting the construction of a U.S. Army housing project in a public park. The State Department directed the judge not to exercise jurisdiction. When he refused to accept such direction, his Berlin appointment was immediately terminated—and with it the brief but memorable existence of the court.

Martin J. Hillenbrand, ed., *The Future of Berlin* (Montclair, N.J.: Allanheld, Osmun Publ., 1980), a collaborative volume edited by a former U.S. ambassador to the Federal Republic, with Peter C. Ludz as principal consultant, analyzes the city's situation in historical context and weighs its prospects for the future. On Germany as a whole, see Karl Jaspers, *The Future of Germany*, translated by E. B. Ashton, with a foreword by Hannah Arendt (Chicago: University of Chicago Press, 1967), with selections from two thoughtful books by the influential philosopher, published in the mid-1960s, just as Bonn's conciliatory new eastern policy was beginning to take shape.

CONTEMPORARY GERMANY

A concise account of the bloodless revolution of 1989 and the accession of the eastern German states to the Federal Republic concludes a lucid survey of German history since World War II by Henry Ashby Turner, Jr., in *Germany from Partition to Reunification* (New Haven, Conn.: Yale University Press, 1992), a revised edition of *The Two Germanies since 1945* cited in the foregoing section of this bibliography. Dennis L. Bark and David R. Gress provide a detailed account of the history and politics of the Federal Republic during the same period in *A History of West Germany*, vol. 1, *From Shadow to Substance, 1945–1963*; vol. 2, *Democracy and Its Discontents, 1963–1991*, 2d ed. (Oxford and Cambridge, Mass.: Blackwell, 1993), with a critical bibliographical essay, a listing of documents and sources, and an analyzed index for both volumes conveniently printed at the end of each. Mary Fulbrook, *Anatomy of a Dictatorship: Inside the GDR, 1949–1989* (Oxford: Oxford University Press, 1995), is an analysis of the East German regime; the story of its last year is told by David M. Keithly in *The Collapse of East German Communism: The Year the Wall Came Down, 1989* (Westport, Conn.: Praeger, 1992). *In Europe's Name: Germany and the Divided Continent* by Timothy Garton Ash (New York: Random House, 1993; paperback rpt., Vintage Books, 1994) is a readable, extensively annotated interpretive synthesis of the postwar era, focusing on divided Germany and explaining how its unification was brought about in conjunction with the end of the Cold War, with thoughtful, carefully documented coverage of West Germany's *Ostpolitik* during the two decades before unification. A. James McAdams, *Germany Divided: From the Wall to Reunification* (Princeton, N.J.: Princeton University Press, 1993), presents intra-German relations from the building of the Berlin Wall to unification; Ernest D. Plock, *East German–West German Relations and the Fall of the GDR* (Boulder: Westview Press, 1993), focuses on the 1980s.

Konrad H. Jarausch, *The Rush to German Unity* (New York and Oxford: Oxford University Press, 1994), is complemented by *Uniting Germany: Documents and Debates, 1944–1993*, edited by Konrad H. Jarausch and Volker Gransow, translated by Allison Brown and Belinda Cooper (Providence and Oxford: Berghahn, 1994). Manfred Görtemaker opens *Unifying Germany, 1989–1990* (New York: St. Martin's Press, 1994) with a chapter on "The German Question in Historical Perspective" and aug-ments his concise presentation of the course of unification with copious explanatory as well as documentary endnotes. Renata Fritsch-Bournazel's *Europe and German Unification* (New York and Oxford: Berg, 1992) provides a briefer account interspersed with excerpts of key documents. Elizabeth Pond, author of a hundred-page essay, *After the Wall: American Policy Toward Germany* (New York: Priority Press, 1990), followed by a full-length study, *Beyond the Wall: Germany's Road to Unification* (Washington, D.C.: Brookings Institution, 1993), joined David Schoenbaum as co-author of *The German Question and Other German Questions* (New York: St. Martin's Press in association with St. Antony's College, Oxford, 1996), a keen evaluation of German unification and its consequences (with critical commentary on publications about it in extensive notes).

Stephen F. Szabo in *The Diplomacy of German Unification* (New York: St. Martin's Press, 1992) gives a compact survey of the international negotiations leading to the Treaty on the Final Settlement with Respect to Germany, the "Two-Plus-Four Treaty." Those negotiations are explained, in connection with the redefinition of the mission of NATO and the integration of Europe, by Philip Zelikow and Condoleezza Rice, who served in Washington on the staff of the National Security Council at the time of German unification, in *Germany Unified and Europe Transformed: A Study in Statecraft* (Cambridge: Harvard University Press, 1995; paperback rpt., 1997); the "Preface, 1997" (pp. vi–xv) includes reflections on the "causal variables in the unification of Germany" and annotated references to the memoirs of James A. Baker, III, Hans-Dietrich Genscher, Mikhail Gorbachev, and Helmut Kohl. Peter H. Merkl's *German Unification in the European Context* (University Park: Pennsylvania State University Press, 1993), which includes on pp. 77–117 a chapter on the rise and decline of "Realistic Socialism" in the German Democratic Republic by Gert-Joachim Glaessner, analyzes the impact of German unification on the North Atlantic alliance, the Western European Union, and the Conference on Security and Cooperation in Europe (CSCE, renamed the Organization for Security and Cooperation in Europe, or OSCE, in 1995). See also Glaessner's article, "German Unification and the West," pp. 207–226 in *The German Revolution of 1989: Causes and Consequences*, which he edited with Ian Wallace (Oxford and Providence: Berg, 1992), which also includes on pp. 163–183 an article by Martin McCauley on "Gorbachev, the GDR and Germany." On the Soviet president's role, see Mikhail Gorbachev, *Memoirs* (Garden City, N.Y.: Doubleday, 1996); Jeffrey Gedmin, *The Hidden Hand: Gorbachev and the Collapse of East Germany* (Washington, D.C.: AEI Press, 1992); David H. Shumaker, *Gorbachev and the German Question: Soviet-West German Relations, 1985–1990* (Westport, Conn.: Praeger, 1995); and *At the Highest Levels: The Inside Story of the End of the Cold War* (Boston: Little, Brown, 1993), by Michael R. Beschloss and Strobe Talbott, which, like the work by Zelikow and Rice, is based in part on extensive interviews with responsible participants, but lacks their meticulous documentation.

In a book comparable in quality to Garton Ash's study of Europe and to the diplomatic history of Zelikow and Rice, Charles S. Maier in *Dissolution: The Crisis of Communism and the End of East Germany* (Princeton, N.J.: Princeton University Press, 1997) explains in historical context the failure of the German Democratic Republic. The unraveling of the Honecker regime is further illuminated by the sensitive, sophisticated account by G. Jonathan Greenwald, who served at the U.S. Embassy in East Berlin, in *Berlin Witness: An American Diplomat's Chronicle of East Germany's Revolution* (University Park: Pennsylvania State University Press, 1993). Informative accounts by two other Americans are *Behind the Wall: An American in East Germany, 1988–89* (Carbondale and Edwardsville: Southern Illinois University Press, 1991), by Paul Gleye, an urban planner who spent an academic year as a Fulbright lecturer in Weimar, and *Berlin Journal: 1989–1990* (New York: W. W. Norton, 1991), by Robert Darnton, an historian whose book is based in part on essays published at the time in *The New Republic*, one of which is included in a convenient volume of reprints or abstracts of three dozen well-chosen articles selected by Robert Emmet Long, *The Reunification of Germany* (New York: H. W. Wilson, 1992), vol. 64, no. 1 of *The Reference Shelf*. Another American historian, Dirk Philipsen, interviewed in spring 1990 roughly a score of participants in the East German revolution and wove the transcripts of his conversations with them into a valuable contribution to recent German historiography, *We Were the People: Voices from East Germany's Revolutionary Autumn of 1989* (Durham, N.C.: Duke University Press, 1993). Christian Joppke also interviewed participants in the East German revolution before writing *East German Dissidents and the Revolution of 1989: Social Movement in a Leninist Régime* (New York: New York University Press, 1995), with extensive, often explanatory endnotes. Philipsen and Joppke interviewed Protestant pastors. On the part churchmen played, see Richard Schröder, "The Role of the Protestant Church in German Unification," pp. 251–261 in a special issue of *Daedalus: Journal of the American Academy of Arts and Sciences*, vol. 123, no. 1 (Winter 1994), reprinted as *In Search of Germany*, edited by Michael Mertes et al. (New Brunswick, N.J.: Transaction, 1996), and John P. Burgess, *The East German Church and the End of Communism* (New York: Oxford University Press, 1997). Uwe Siemon-Netto shows in *The Fabricated Luther: The Rise and Fall of the Shirer Myth*, with a foreword by Peter L. Berger (St. Louis: Concordia Publishing House, 1993), that, contrary to William L. Shirer's cliché regarding Lutheran submission to government authority, the Lutheran tradition of resistance against tyranny was not only a source of spiritual strength to many who resisted National Socialism and the East German communist regime, but was instrumental in preparing German Protestant churchmen to play leading roles in the peaceful revolution of 1989.

When the Wall Came Down: Reactions to German Unification, edited by Harold James and Marla Stone (New York: Routledge, 1992), with articles and speeches from the two German republics, Czechoslovakia, France, Israel, Italy, Poland, the Soviet Union, the United Kingdom, and the United States, includes on pp. 117–18 New Forum's founding manifesto of 10 September 1989, on pp. 130–33 a Ministry of State Security analysis of the East German public's alienation in fall 1989, on pp. 233–39 a controversial memorandum by a member of Prime Minister Thatcher's staff synopsizing "What the PM Learnt about the Germans" from a private conference with six historians (together with an essay on the Chequers Affair, pp. 242–46, by Timothy Garton Ash, who was there), and on pp. 266–272 a *Le Monde* interview with Jacques Delors, the president of the European Commission, on German unification and European integration.

German Unification and Its Discontents: Documents from the Peaceful Revolution, edited and translated by Richard T. Gray and Sabine Wilke (Seattle and London: University of Washington Press, 1996), is a chronologically structured, well-annotated selection of speeches, political programs, and diplomatic documents, with an introductory essay, a chronology, a glossary, a bibliography, and an index of persons. The volume includes on pp. 186–205 an article from spring 1990 by Jürgen Habermas on "D-Mark Nationalism" and on pp. 265–277 a speech by Günter Grass, "A 'Steal' Called the GDR," given on the eve of unification. Related pieces by Grass, translated by Krishna Winston with A. S. Wensinger, appeared in the volume entitled *Two States—One Nation?* (San Diego and New York: Harcourt Brace Jovanovich, 1990). For a no less polemical rejoinder, see "Günter Grass & a Hollow Tin Drum" on pp. 81–98 of *Voices in a Revolution: The Collapse of East German Communism* (New Brunswick, N.J.: Transaction, 1992), a collection of essays that its author, Melvin J. Lasky, founder of the postwar German journal *Der Monat* and longtime editor of *Encounter*, calls a "notebook of 1989–90." *Culture in the Federal Republic of Germany, 1945–1995*, edited by Reiner Pommerin (Oxford and Washington, D.C.: Berg, 1996), includes on pp. 1–17 an introductory essay by the editor on German cultural history and on pp. 133–143 a contribution by one of the founders of New Forum, Jens Reich, on East German mentality five years after unification. On Germany after unification, see also Peter Schneider's perceptive essays in *The German Comedy: Scenes of Life after the Wall*, translated by Philip Boehm and Leigh Hafrey (New York: Farrar Straus Giroux, 1991; paperback rpt., Noonday Press, 1992), and the wide-ranging but sharply focused and well-documented overview by Alan Watson, *The Germans: Who Are They Now?*, 3d ed. (London: Mandarin Paperbacks, 1995; Carol Stream, Ill.: edition q, 1995). On the bitter heritage of the East German secret police and the way in which the records of surveillance accumulated in the course of four decades by the Ministry for State Security (Stasi) are being handled in unified Germany, see the article by the Federal Commissioner for Documents of the State Security Service of the former German Democratic Republic, Joachim Gauck, "Dealing with a Stasi Past," pp. 277-284 in the previously cited special issue of *Daedalus: Journal of the American Academy of Arts and Sciences*, reprinted as *In Search of Germany*, cited above. Timothy Garton Ash, *The File: A Personal History* (New York: Random House, 1997), is a remarkable memoir based on the secret police file, turned over to him by Gauck's agency, and on subsequent conversations with several of those who had informed on him.

On German relations with Europe and America, see, in addition to the landmark studies by Garton Ash and by Zelikow and Rice cited above, Klaus von Beyme, "The New German National State and Its Role in International Relations," on pp. 173–186 in *Shepherd of Democracy? America and Germany in the Twentieth Century*, edited by Carl C. Hodge and Cathal J. Nolan (Westport, Conn.: Greenwood Press, 1992); the updated edition of *Germany and the United States: The Transformation of the German Question since 1945* (New York: Twayne, 1995) by Frank A.

Ninkovich; W. R. Smyser, *Germany and America: New Identities, Fateful Rift?*, with a foreword by Paul Nitze (Boulder: Westview, 1993); and *Germany and Europe: The Crisis of Unity* (London: Heinemann, 1994) by David Marsh of the London *Financial Times*. The background of Germany's role in the European Union is concisely explained by the Brussels correspondent of the *Frankfurter Allgemeine Zeitung*, Peter Hort, in "Germany and the European Community," on pp. 267–276 of *Meet United Germany: Perspectives 1992/93*, edited by Susan Stern (Frankfurt am Main: Frankfurter Allgemeine Zeitung Information Services and Atlantik-Brücke, 1992), a volume of well-informed essays on German business and politics published as an introduction to post-unification Germany. On the German economy see Eric Owen Smith, *The German Economy* (London and New York: Routledge, 1994), which has an extensive bibliography (pp. 543–579, double-columned), and W. R. Smyser, *The German Economy: Colossus at the Crossroads*, 2d ed. (New York: St. Martin's, 1993), with chapters on the European Community (pp. 237–262) and European Monetary Integration (pp. 263–293).

The internal transformation of Germany since unification is placed in historical context by Alan Watson in *The Germans*, cited above, by Peter Pulzer in *German Politics, 1945–1995* (Oxford: Oxford University Press, 1995), and by Anthony Glees in *Reinventing Germany: German Political Development since 1945* (Oxford and Washington, D.C.: Berg, 1996). On the political scene in the early nineties, see David P. Conradt et al., eds., *Germany's New Politics* (Providence and Oxford: Berghahn, 1995), as well as Conradt's *The German Polity*, 5th ed. (New York and London: Longman, 1993). The process of unification and the attendant institutional challenges are analyzed in the twelve contributions in *The Domestic Politics of German Unification*, edited by Christopher Anderson et al. (Boulder and London: Lynne Rienner, 1993), which includes on pp. 135–154 "The Basic Law under Strain: Constitutional Dilemmas and Challenges" by Donald P. Kommers, who provides a brief introduction to the German supreme court in *The Federal Constitutional Court*, German Issues, no. 14 (Washington, D.C.: American Institute for Contemporary German Studies, 1994) and explains in *The Constitutional Jurisprudence of the Federal Republic of Germany*, 2d ed. (Durham, N.C., and London: Duke University Press, 1997) landmark supreme court decisions, such as the rejection in 1973 of the Bavarian challenge of the constitutionality of the Treaty on the Basis of Relations between the two German republics on pp. 153–54 and the approval in 1993 of the transfer of certain sovereign powers to the European Union under the Treaty of Maastricht, with excerpts, on pp. 107–114 (and endnotes on p. 551).

Economic and environmental problems are clearly dealt with by Alun Jones in *The New Germany: A Human Geography* (Chichester and New York: John Wiley, 1994), which is illustrated with numerous tables, maps, and photographs. Karl Kaltenthaler reports on the challenge of "Coping with the Legacy of East German Environmental Policy" on pp. 187–204 in Christopher Anderson et al., eds., *The Domestic Politics of German Unification*, cited above. For a concise introduction to the Trust Agency charged with the privatization of the East German economy, see "Making Your (D-)Marks in Eastern Germany," pp. 124–148 in *Meet United Germany: Handbook 1992/93*, edited by Susan Stern (Frankfurt am Main: Frankfurter Allgemeine Zeitung Information Services and Atlantik-Brücke, 1992), a readable companion volume to *Meet United Germany: Perspectives 1992/93* cited above (in a set addressed by no means only to potential investors in post-unification Germany). Helmut Haussmann and Hermann Horstkotte, *Europe Acquires New Dimensions: From Economic Community to European Union* (Bonn: Inter Nationes, 1997), a clarification of the dauntingly complex process of transforming the EC into the EU (with a social charter and monetary union), is one of a series of papers (Basis-Info 14-1997/European Affairs) issued by an information agency at Kennedyallee 91–103, D-53175 Bonn (http://www.inter-nationes.de).

On the inextricably related issues of foreigner workers, ethnic minorities, and manifestations of right-wing radicalism in Germany, see Jürgen Fijalkowski, "Aggressive Nationalism and Immigration in Germany," pp. 138–150 in *Europe's New Nationalism: States and Minorities in Conflict*, edited by Richard Caplan and John Feffer (New York: Oxford University Press, 1996); Meredith W. Watts, *Xenophobia in United Germany: Generations, Modernization, and Ideology* (New York: St. Martin's, 1997); Rand C. Lewis, *The Neo-Nazis and German Unification* (Westport, Conn.: Praeger, 1996); and Ulrich Wank, ed., *The Resurgence of Right-Wing Radicalism in Germany: New Forms of an Old Phenomenon?*, translated by James Knowlton (Atlantic Highlands, N.J.: Humanities Press, 1996). On Germany's native ethnic minority, a Slavic people living in Lusatia, see "German Unification and the Sorb Minority," by Horst Freyhofer, pp. 237–245 in *Changing Identities in East Germany*, edited by Margy Gerber and Roger Woods, Studies in GDR Culture and Society

14/15 (Lanham, Md.: University Press of America, 1996).

English translations of the text of the Treaty on Economic, Monetary, and Social Union of 18 May 1990, the Treaty on the Establishment of German Unity of 31 August 1990, and the Treaty on the Final Settlement with Respect to Germany (the "Two-Plus-Four Settlement") of 12 September 1990 are published (without annexes) in *The Unification of Germany in 1990: A Documentation*, with a foreword by Klaus Hildebrand (Bonn: Press and Information Office of the Federal Government, 1991). Further documentation on German unification, together with related NATO and European Community declarations, are in *Germany and Europe in Transition*, edited by Adam Daniel Rotfeld and Walther Stützle, Stockholm International Peace Research Institute (Oxford: Oxford University Press, 1991). The Basic Law of the Federal Republic, with the constitutional amendments that followed unification, is in *Documents on Democracy in the Federal Republic of Germany*, 2d ed. (Bonn: Press and Information Office of the Federal Government, 1994). Extensive excerpts from the constitution, laws, treaties, and the like are presented in translation, with explanatory headnotes and annotations, in *Politics and Government in Germany, 1944–1994: Basic Documents*, edited by Carl-Christoph Schweitzer et al. (Providence and Oxford: Berghahn, 1995).

A comprehensive, general introduction to contemporary Germany, superseding the area handbooks on the Federal Republic published in 1982 and on East Germany published in 1988 in the U.S. Department of the Army Country Studies Program, and including several maps, a glossary, over two dozen tables, an extensive bibliography, and an analyzed index, is Eric Solsten, ed., *Germany: A Country Study*, 3d ed. (Washington, D.C.: U.S. Government Printing Office for the Federal Research Division, Library of Congress, 1996). General statistics on population and the economy as well as educational data are provided in *Basic and Structural Data 1995/96* (Bonn: Federal Ministry of Education, Science, Research and Technology, 1995). Horst Thomsen and Frauke Siefkes in their 3,387-title *Bibliography on German Unification: Economic and Social Developments in Eastern Germany, November 1989 to June 1992* (Munich: K. G. Saur, 1993) include hundreds of listings, many in English, on unified Germany as a whole and on the European Community.

Index

Aachen: Treaty of, 12; coronation at, of Otto I, 19; coronation at, of Frederick II, 43

Adenauer, Konrad: career before 1949, 216; chancellorship, 216–17; compared with Bismarck, 252; mentioned, 218, 245

Agri Decumates, 4

Albert of Brandenburg, Archbishop-elector of Mainz, 69–71

Albert of Brandenburg-Ansbach: secularized Prussia, 85

Albert II (of Habsburg), Emperor, 56

Aliso: Roman base, 4, 7

"Alliance for Germany," 238–39

allodial lands: diminished during Investiture Contest, 33–34; retained by Henry the Lion, 37; granted by Great Elector, 88

Alsace-Lorraine: French by 1789, 96; German after 1871, 131, 132, 142; contested in World War I, 156; provisions for, in Wilson's Fourteen Points, 162, and in Versailles Treaty, 172, 174

Alvensleben Convention, 121–22

America. *See* United States of America

Amsterdam (Maastricht II), Treaty of (1997). *See* European Union

Anglo-German Naval Agreement, 191

anti-Semitism: of Hitler, 180, 184; Third Reich persecution and 1938 pogrom, 197; "Final Solution" (Holocaust), 197

Arminius: victory of, in Teutoburg Forest, 6; defeat of, in A.D. 16, 8; mentioned, 10

Arnulf (of Carinthia), Emperor, 16

Auerstedt. *See* Jena and Auerstedt

Augsburg: Imperial Diets of, in 1500, 58, and 1530, 75; Religious Peace of, 76–77, 79; War of League of, 91

Augsburg Confession, 75

Augustus, Emperor: German policy of, 4–10 passim; mentioned, 24

Austria: once known as Bavarian Eastern March, 19; acquired by Rudolf of Habsburg, 46; in German Confederation, 104–6; in Revolution of 1848, 111–12; as rival of Prussia, 114–15, 120–25; defeat of, in 1866, 126; post-1918 Republic of, 173; Hitler's annexation of, 195, 198; accession to European Union, 248; mentioned, 6, 54, 143, 192, 203, 209, 222. *See also* Austria-Hungary

Austria-Hungary (1867–1918): its strength compared to Germany's, 142; diplomacy of, during Bismarck era, 145–47, during reign of William II, 148; in World War I, 153–56

Baker, James A., III, 231, 236

Barmen Declaration of 1934, 200

Barth, Karl, 200

Basic Treaty. *See* Treaty on the Basis of Relations

Bavaria: early duchy in Carolingian pe-